D0758685

DISCARDED

UNIVERSITY OF WINNIPEG
PORTAGE & BALMORAL
WINNIPEG, MAN.   R3B 2E9
CANADA

THE SYSTEM OF THE INTERNATIONAL
ORGANIZATIONS OF THE COMMUNIST COUNTRIES

JX
1995
.S9

The System of the International Organizations of the Communist Countries

RICHARD SZAWLOWSKI

Professor of Political Science
University of Calgary
Alberta, Canada

A. W. SIJTHOFF LEYDEN 1976

ISBN 90 286 0335 2

© Copyright 1976 A. W. Sijthoff International Publishing
Company B. V.

All rights reserved, No part of this publication may be reproduced,
stored in a retrieval system, or transmitted, in any form or by
any means, electronic, mechanical, photocopying, recording, or
otherwise, without the prior permission of the copyright owner

Printed in the Netherlands

TABLE OF CONTENTS

Preface by Manlio Brosio ix

Foreword by the author xv

Introduction xxi

Chapter I   *The Warsaw Treaty Organization (WTO)*   1
1. Background   1
2. Membership, Casus Foederis and its Consequences, the
   Treaty's Duration   6
3. Structure of the WTO 15
4. Main Political and Military Activities........... 26
5. The WTO 1955–1975: General Appraisal 39

Chapter II   *The Council for Mutual Economic Assistance
             (Comecon)* 46
1. Background 46
2. Membership and Charter's Duration 51
3. Structure of Comecon 59
4. Main Activities................................. 71
5. Comecon 1949–1975: General Appraisal 93

Chapter III   *The Minor Organizations of the "Comecon Family"* 103
1. The Organization of the Joint Power Grid 106
2. The International Bank for Economic Cooperation .. 107
3. The Organization of the Common Waggon Pool 111
4. The Organization for the Cooperation of the Ball-bearing
   Industry 113
5. "Intermetall" 114
6. The International Centre for Scientific and Technical
   Information 115
7. "Interkhim" 117
8. The International Investment Bank............... 120
9. "Interatominstrument" 123

10. International Centre for the Training of Civil Aviation Personnel.   126
11. "Interelectro," "Interatomenergo" and "Intertextil-mash"   127
12. "Interkhimvolokno," "Interetalonpribor," "Inter-gasoochistka" and "Intervodoochistka"   129

Chapter IV   The Remaining Organizations of the System   131
1. The Joint Institute for Nuclear Research   131
2. "Intercosmos" and "Intersputnik"   135
3. The Organization for Cooperation of Railways and the Telecommunications and Postal Communications "Organi-zation".   141
4. The International Laboratory of Strong Magnetic Fields and Low Temperatures, the International Mathematical Centre and the International Centre for Electron Micros-copy.   143

Chapter V   The System of the International Organizations of the Communist Countries: Past, Present, and Prospects   147

Selected Bibliography   165

Annexes   171

   I Warsaw Treaty, 1955.   173
  II Convention concerning the Juridical Personality, Privi-leges and Immunities of the Staff and other Administra-tive Organs of the Joint Armed Forces of the States Parties to the Warsaw Treaty, 1973.   177
 III Charter of the Council for Mutual Economic Assistance, 1959 (with the 1962 and 1974 amendments).   181
  IV Convention concerning the Juridical Personality, Privi-leges and Immunities of Comecon, 1959 (with the 1962 and 1974 amendments).   190
   V Statute of the Secretariat of Comecon (with Rules con-cerning the conditions of work of the staff of the Secretariat of Comecon), 1962.   194
  VI Basic Provisions governing the financial activities of the Secretariat of Comecon, 1961/2.   206

VII Statute of the Audit Commission for the audit of the financial activities of the Secretariat of Comecon, 1962. 208

VIII Provisional Statute of the Standardization Institute of Comecon, 1962. 210

IX Agreement on Cooperation between Comecon and the Finnish Republic (with the Statute of the Commission on Cooperation of Comecon and the Finnish Republic), 1973. 214

X Protocol concerning the character and forms of cooperation between Comecon and the International Bank for Economic Cooperation, 1970. 220

XI Agreement concerning the creation and joint exploitation of the Common Waggon Pool, 1963........... 222

XII Agreement concerning the establishment of an Organization for Cooperation of the Ball-bearing Industry, 1964. 228

XIII Agreement concerning the establishment of an international Centre for Scientific and Technical Information, 1969. 233

XIV Agreement concerning the establishment of an International Branch Organization for cooperation in the field of small tonnage chemical production, "Interkhim", 1969. 239

XV Agreement concerning the establishment of an International Investment Bank (with the Charter of the Bank), 1970. 246

XVI Agreement concerning the establishment of an international economic association for the construction of nuclear instruments "Interatominstrument", 1972. ... 263

XVII Agreement concerning the organization of a Joint Institute for Nuclear Research (with the Charter of the Institute), 1956. 271

XVIII Agreement concerning the establishment of an International System and an Organization for Cosmic Communications "Intersputnik", 1971. 285

XIX Statute of the Organization for Cooperation of Railways, 1962. 294

XX Agreement concerning the establishment of an Organization for Cooperation of the Socialist countries in the field of Telecommunications and Postal Communications, 1957. 298

XXI Agreement concerning the establishment of an International Laboratory of Strong Magnetic Fields and Low Temperatures, 1968. 302

XXII Treaty concerning the establishment of the International Mathematical Centre "Stefan Banach" in Warsaw for the raising of the qualifications of scholarly cadres, 1972. 308

Subject Index 313

Name Index 320

PREFACE

I am glad to present this book on the System of the International Organizations of the Communist Countries, the result of prolonged work by Richard Szawlowski, a young professor of the University of Calgary who has studied the communist world for a long time, with particular emphasis on the Soviet Union and the countries of Eastern Europe.

This book deals only with the International *governmental* Organizations of the communist countries, and does not treat all the other organizations of a predominantly political nature which do not have an official governmental character, even if they are inspired and directed by the Soviet Union and even if they are also of great importance for propaganda and the diffusion of communist ideology on a world-wide scale (for example, the World Council of Peace, the World Federation of Trade Unions and the International Students' Union).

Consequently the work of Szawlowski does not have the political character it inevitably would have if it dealt with those organizations which are world-wide political instruments of influence and struggle of the Soviet Union.

It is, instead, an objective work, scientific in character, which strives to gather the greatest possible number of elements of the official multilateral organizations of the communist world, and the greatest possible amount of information on them, on their legal base, their structure and organization, and their tasks and actual activities.

We are dealing, then, with an objective work in the sense that the author does not assume excessively polemical or critical attitudes regarding the organizations he describes, among which the Warsaw Pact Organization and Comecon stand out for their notoriety and importance.

Objectivity, though, does not mean indifference nor the absence of an implicit but clear critical evaluation of the differences between the international communist organizations and the more or less corresponding organizations of the Western world. Professor Szawlowski is obviously a Westerner, influenced by the culture and fundamental political ideas of the free world: his book is, therefore, neither eulogistic nor propagandistic in its treatment of the communist world and its institutions. On the contrary, whoever reads this book and makes a comparison between the organizations analyzed in it and the equivalent organizations in the Western world, will easily arrive at a positive judgement of the superiority of the latter from the point of view of the equality and independence that are accorded to their member states.

In essence, it will be obvious to anyone examining the book for study purposes or merely for information that the Warsaw Pact Organization, Comecon and the other numerous dependent organizations are structured in a way that makes evident the predominant power of the Soviet Union in every phase and aspect of their activities. It could, of course, be said that, politically, in all international organizations the weight of the more powerful states will always prevail regardless of the juridical equality guaranteed by their statutes. But the juridical and organizational structure is also of considerable importance in ensuring effective parity of status and participation to all member states; and Professor Szawlowski's analysis points out that in the structure of the communist organizations the Soviet Union has reserved for itself all the commanding positions in a way not at all comparable to that of NATO and the OECD.

This book attempts to resolve a very difficult task, namely that of gathering information from reliable sources not only about legal texts, but also about their application in the development of the actual activities of the organizations studied. In this field there are still a great number of difficulties in gathering information, but the author has in great measure overcome them and gives a harmonic and complete picture of all the existing institutions in the field that he has examined. His work will certainly constitute a valuable working instrument for those who want to improve their knowledge of the universe of international communist organizations and, perhaps, to further deepen analysis and evaluation.

The book suggests, as I have said, many reflections and comparisons between the Western organizations and the analogous communist ones. To elaborate on these reflections and comparisons would make my presentation too lengthy. I shall limit myself to a few remarks and, for reasons of propriety, I shall not pick the most critical ones concerning the Warsaw Pact and Comecon. That would be too facile and artless on my part, as for seven years I presided over the Atlantic Council and directed the Organization of the Western Alliance. I am deeply convinced of the necessity for it, of its merits and its spirit of liberty, though it would not be fitting for me to elaborate on my convictions on this occasion. Instead, I shall limit myself to two observations, pointing out some weaknesses in the Western international organizations, with the aim of encouraging that they be overcome, so that their solidity and prestige may be strengthened.

From Professor Szawlowski's analysis it is evident that in the Warsaw Pact, by virtue of article 4, paragraph 1, the "casus foederis" is clearly limited to Europe. In point of fact, however, all the regions in the world where the Soviet Union has vital political and military interests are also considered to be of concern to all the members of the Treaty. This does not refer to consultation alone. Consultation is provided for in article 3, paragraph 1 in very broad terms and it concerns all the important international matters involving the common interests of the contracting parties. But in practice, the Warsaw Treaty has been applied in the sense of extending not only consultations but real co-operation, above all military co-operation, in non-European countries such as Vietnam, Laos, Cambodia and the Middle East countries.

The legal situation and procedure in the Atlantic Alliance are quite different. According to the North Atlantic Treaty (article 4), "The Parties will consult together whenever, in the opinion of any of them, the territorial integrity, political independence, or security of any of the Parties is threatened." Article 5 limits the direct responsibility of the partners to the case of an armed attack against one or more of them. In practice, consultation in the Atlantic Council has also been extended to situations occurring outside the territories of the alliance, but it has been, as a rule, mild and limited consultation, more informative than operative. Military actions in external areas have never even been considered, and the consultation itself has essentially been centred on political and military affairs directly concerning the allied countries.

This profound difference in norms and, above all, in their application, can be explained by the different nature of the two communities: one rigidly dominated by the Soviet power, the other far less rigid and one in which the unquestionable supremacy of the United States does not result in obedience and subservience to the directives and interests of Washington. Neither the European countries nor Canada will blindly share the same views regarding all the problems and conflicts of the United States: Korea, Vietnam, Israel and even Cuba, within certain limits, are striking examples.

This undoubted superiority of the free countries exacts, however, its price, as well as excessive consequences. This is noticeable above all in the field of consultation. Only the Atlantic Alliance has, unlike the Warsaw Pact, a permanent political council able to take care of all affairs of common interest and therefore able to apply extensively article 4 of the Treaty in a way corresponding to article 3 of the Warsaw Pact. This, however, has been done reluctantly and rarely, and without positive results. Common problems of vital interest such as those in the Middle East or North Africa have not been the object of any serious effort to achieve a common line of action or, at least, mutual co-ordination in order to avoid disruptive conflicts among the allies. We can find comfort in the consideration that some disagreement is a fair price to pay in order to maintain one's independence: but between a forced solidarity, according to the principles of "socialist internationalism," and the formula "each for himself," there should be room, even in an alliance of free countries, for a wider application of the necessity for consultation and co-operation.

As for Comecon, my observation derives from the very origin and nature of the organization. Comecon, as Professor Szawlowski reminds us, was created in 1949 in answer and as a counterbalance to the Marshall Plan and to the OEEC (now OECD); that is to say, a few months before the creation of the Atlantic Alliance and six years before the Warsaw Pact, created in 1955 and constituting the antithesis of NATO. Actually, the Warsaw Treaty and Comecon are two organizations that integrate perfectly, one in the military and political field, the other in the economic field. It is evident that Comecon works essentially as an economic instrument, if not an economic weapon in the communist world, in close connection with the Soviet Union and under its dominant direction. The OECD, on the other hand, is totally different, in its composition and functions, from the Atlantic Alliance. This organization includes many European and non-European countries which do not have and do not want to have any connection with it. We could legitimately add that the predominant feeling in the OECD is one of complete detachment from whatever is related to the military and political interests of NATO: whoever has been in contact, as I have been, with the Atlantic Alliance, vividly felt this detachment, which does not signify hostility, but a very rigid will to maintain distances.

All this should neither lead us to a critical attitude towards the OECD nor to the wish for a closer connection with the Atlantic Alliance. That would be neither possible nor desirable. Rather, comparison of the latter organization with Comecon could be very useful in underlining once more a great deficiency in the alliance, namely the non-application of article 2 of the Treaty concerning economic co-operation among allies.

So many questions have been raised about article 2 that this is certainly not the place to reopen that debate. But the above-mentioned article was evidently dictated by a very just concern that political and military power must be sustained by economic power, without which the very foundations would cease to exist. To further emphasize what has been said, we should realize that in the allied countries there are specific economic needs that should be satisfied in a concerted effort within the alliance itself and not from outside, in order to sustain their common political and defensive effort. This simple truth does not lead to any contradiction between the economic tasks of the alliance and the tasks of the OECD: the alliance is a nucleus of states within the OECD, which has several interests in common with it, but has, in addition, specific needs which, in order to be fulfilled, require special economic co-operation. This twofold order of needs does not exist, or exists in a very limited way, among the communist countries (there is, for example, an agreement on co-operation between Comecon and Finland, a non-communist country, but this is an exception); they have been able to solve their problem in the simplest way, through two institutions closely related and integrated under Soviet direction. The Western world is far wealthier and far more complex, but it could have saved its wealth and variety without sacrificing too much, as it has, the unitarian approach to the specific economic problems of the Atlantic Alliance.

I shall conclude my reflections by pointing out that the book by Professor Szawlowski is not only valuable because it gives a broad outline of the international communist organizations which constitute the structure of a world-wide policy, but also because it is a mean of comparison with the structure of the free world. I believe Professor Szawlowski's study is equally valuable and useful in those parts where it enumerates and describes the many minor organizations which exist under the Warsaw Pact Organization and Comecon. The history of their development, the clear distinction between the three important phases into which his work is divided (from the time of Stalin through that of Khrushchev to the time of Brezhnev), and the description of the tasks and the nature of each of the minor organizations constitute parts that are equally important and, in some points, even more original, of the patient and intelligent effort of the Author.

I believe that his work will deservingly take its place among the political-juridical studies on the institutions of the communist world under Soviet control, and I predict that it will draw the attention that it undoubtedly deserves.

Manlio Brosio

[Secretary-General of NATO 1964–1971, former Italian Ambassador to Moscow, at present Senator and leader of the Liberal group in the Italian Senate]

FOREWORD

1. This book on the System of the International Organizations of the Communist countries is based on close following of relevant developments on the spot (Poland) for some ten years, and from the outside (Western Europe and North America) for another fifteen. The latter period was coupled with research in many countries, the publication of some minor pertinent contributions (articles and reviews) in French, German and English, and with lectures in Western Europe, North and Latin America, Japan and Australia.

In preparing the present book, the idea was to keep it within reasonable limits, so that it would stand a chance of being *read* by as many interested people as possible, including University students. This is why the main body is kept within some 200 pages, though the topic could easily have been presented in double the size—or more.

On the other hand, it seemed desirable and useful to offer, in the form of Annexes, the English texts of twenty-two basic legal documents relating to the Organizations dealt with in the book. The guiding principle here was to refrain from reproducing those texts already published in the *United Nations Treaty Series*, with the exception of four treaties too important to be omitted: the Warsaw Treaty, the Charter of Comecon and the Convention concerning the Juridical Personality, Privileges and Immunities of Comecon (both requiring updating anyway, to include the 1962 and 1974 amendments) and the Agreement creating the Joint Institute for Nuclear Research (with the text of its Charter requiring translation in any case). Most of the rest, sixteen documents in all, are original translations by the author, most of them, to our knowledge, published for the first time in a pertinent English study.

2. Professor Jan Tinbergen (Nobel Prize in Economics 1969) already suggested, almost twenty years ago,[1] that in view of the over-produc-

---

1. See J. Tinbergen *Economic Policy. Principles and Design*, North-Holland Publishing Company, Amsterdam, 1956, Foreword, p. viii.

tion of scientific literature it would be desirable that each writer indicate himself, in the foreword or summary to any publication, what he considers to be new in his particular work. This, Tinbergen felt, would facilitate reading to quite some extent.

In accordance with this idea, a very useful one in our opinion, we would like to indicate a few points concerning this work which seem new to us.

First, one should note that there is no comprehensive monograph at all—let alone an updated one—embracing, in one book, the entirety of the international organizations of the Communist countries, plus the relevant legal documents, available in Anglo-Saxon literature. What is more, there does not seem to be any such work in the other Western literatures either.[2]

Secondly, one should draw the attention of the readers to the last chapter of the work, with its hypothetical projection of the final results of the integration processes realized through the international organizations of the Communist countries that might come about some two decades from now—or even earlier. Whether one agrees with such a projection or not, its possibility—under certain conditions—may not easily be dismissed. Again, it seems that this is the first time such a hypothesis has been formulated, in a fairly developed version, in print.

Thirdly, referring to the situation as it stands in the mid-seventies, the book conveys, in our opinion, the following general conclusions.

In the case of the international organizations of the Communist countries, one has to do with an extremely big, unique and steadily developing group of international bodies which may well surpass,

2. This assertion seems to hold true even if one refers to certain books, mostly older ones, covering the entirety of the then existing international Organizations of the Communist countries. Thus, e.g., K. Grzybowski's *The Socialist Commonwealth of Nations*, Yale University Press, New Haven and London, 1964 (see our critical review of that book in *Soviet Studies*, vol. XVI, No. 4, April, 1965), is a monograph on broader topics, and the relevant Organizations take up only slightly over half of the book; and no texts of the relevant legal documents are given. J. Hacker and A. Uschakow's *Die Integration Osteuropas 1961 bis 1965*, Verlag Wissenschaft und Politik, Cologne, 1965, deals exclusively with the relevant bodies and reproduces the German texts of the pertinent documents, but it is, as the title indicates, limited to the period between 1961 and 1965 (see our review of that book in *Soviet Studies*, vol. XIX, No. 2, October, 1967). The booklet by W. Gumpel and J. Hacker, *Comecon und Warschauer Pakt*, Schriftenreihe der Bundeszentrale für politische Bildung, Heft 73, Bonn, 1966, on the other hand, does not cover some of the Organizations of the System (e.g. the Joint Institute for Nuclear Research) and does not offer the texts of any documents.

around 1976, the total of thirty. All these organizations are tightly-knit together, representing a formidable combination of military and economic power. In spite of all the difficulties and short-comings, they represent a dynamically growing potential. In the economic field this is well reflected in the fact that while Western industrial production in the post-World War II period increased about four times, that of the Comecon group increased twelve times. This discrepancy in economic growth is especially dramatized during the present period of economic recession in the West.[3]

The whole gigantic economic and military complex is completely dominated by the USSR, conditioned, as it is, by the overwhelming disproportion of forces between the "senior" partner and all the remaining ones combined: over 3:1 in the military field (plus the Soviet monopoly of nuclear weapons) and over 2:1 in the economic field. This is also reflected in the absolute dominance of the Russians in the top positions in the WTO and Comecon, and in the fact that Russian is, in almost all the organizations, the only working language.

The growing force of what could be referred to as the WTO-Comecon complex is clearly helpful in expansionist designs on a global as well as on a local scale.

Penetration into all oceans and important seas, recently emphasized by naval manoeuvres on a world-wide scale, the largest in Soviet history; and the final military takeover of South Vietnam, an outrageous mockery of the January 1973 Paris Peace Agreement, impossible without Soviet tanks and rockets, and other East European equipment, are excellent cases in point.[4] This does not prevent someone

3. *Pravda*, February 21, 1975 produced, with an evident feeling of satisfaction, a graph on the 1974 percentage growth of the industrial output of the two economic blocs and the two "super-powers" as compared with 1973: Comecon 8.5, USSR 8, EEC 1, USA —0.6. The comparison further deteriorates during 1974: according to certain projections, the estimated real GNP for 1975 will increase by only 1 per cent in France and 0.5 in Britain, and decrease by 2, 2.8 and 3.3 per cent in W. Germany, Italy and the USA respectively—see *Time* (New York), September 15, 1975, p. 43.
On the other hand a certain damaging effect of the economic crisis on the Communist economies is admitted. Thus Brezhnev, addressing the XI Congress of the Hungarian Socialist Workers' Party, remarked: "The situation in the world market cannot, of course, fail to exert a certain influence on our economic affairs, as the socialist countries keep up fairly broad economic relations with the non-socialist world." See *Pravda*, March 19, 1975.
4. For the "global" naval exercises see, e.g., *The Christian Science Monitor*, April 25, 1975. Concerning "local" moves, apart from Vietnam, these may be

like Brezhnev from talking, as if nothing had happened, about the "peace is indivisible" principle,[5] and, what is more, from claiming that "the extinguishing of the conflagration of war in Indochina" would give a new impetus to détente with the United States and lead to a major improvement in the international climate.[6] Let us suggest, as further milestones in this direction, the "liberation" of West Berlin and of South Korea!

Unfortunately, the strength of the other side is increased, indirectly or even directly (see Anthony Sutton's works), by some Western actions, such as the massive pumping, for short-term profit, of credits, licences, know-how, etc., especially into the Soviet Union. This is sometimes coupled with politically irresponsible and totally unnecessary acts, such as the 1974 *de jure* recognition by the Australian Labour government of the Soviet annexations of Estonia, Latvia and Lithuania. Some astonishingly naive and confusing pertinent statements made by certain Western politicians should also be noted.[7] And the "Finnish carnival"[8] also, at least to a certain extent, played into the hands of the other side.

3. The material collected in the book also amply justifies, it would seem, the necessity of a close, systematic watch being kept, in the West,

---

illustrated by the cases of Yugoslavia and Albania. Regarding Yugoslavia, we refer to the anti-Tito plot, clearly inspired by Moscow, uncovered in 1974. Concerning Albania, we have in mind the 1974 plot by Gen. Beqir Balluku, Albanian Deputy Prime Minister and Minister of Defence, who was clearly working for Moscow. It resulted in big purges when it was discovered.

5. "It is impossible...to imagine a lasting, guaranteed peace only for Europe alone and thunderclouds hanging over other continents. Peace is indivisible—we communists do not cease to repeat this truth and act according to it"—see *Pravda*, March 19, 1975. The limit was reached by Hanoi, expressing hope, at the last stage of its offensive in South Vietnam, for American investments on the basis of...the 1973 Paris Peace Agreement! See *The New Yorker*, April 28, 1975, p. 115.

6. See *Pravda*, May 9, 1975.

7. Out of a variety of such statements, let us quote two. Edgar Faure, President of the French National Assembly, spoke, after a visit to Moscow in 1973 during which he was received by Brezhnev, etc., of "the climate of very great confidence" between France and the USSR, saying that "the danger of seeing Russian tanks deployed seems to me as non-existent as the presence of American troops in Europe seems, to me, to be outmoded"—see *L'Express* (Paris), August 6–12, 1973. And in June 1974, Averell Harriman, who should know better, voiced, after a meeting with Brezhnev, his "great confidence in [Brezhnev's] dedication to the principle of détente"—see, e.g., *The Christian Science Monitor*, June 6, 1974.

8. Expression used by Raymond Aron in *Le Figaro*, August 2–3, 1975.

on further developments in the field of the international organizations of the Communist countries, and on the integration phenomena going on through them that may well lead, if the worst comes to the worst, to attempts at the incorporation of the minor partners into the USSR.

Western knowledge of these organizations is, with laudable exceptions, generally poor.[9]

Yet another conclusion that comes to mind is the necessity of constant strengthening and further development of the international organizations of the Western countries, especially NATO, the European Community, the Council of Europe and the OECD. The same also strongly applies to the Organization of American States, which is going through a deep crisis.

4. Finally, we should like to thank all those who were helpful, in one way or another, during the preparation of the present book. Its final version was prepared under a Canada Council grant. Our special

---

9. Just a few examples out of dozens available, limited to some English-language publications. Thus Donald C. Blaisdell *International Organization*, The Ronald Press Company, New York, 1966, informs students that Comecon was founded in 1958. P. E. Jacob, A. L. Atherton, A. M. Wallenstein *The Dynamics of International Organization*, revised edition, The Dorsey Press, Homewood, Ill., 1972 (the biggest textbook in the field at present on the North American market), listing, on pp. 136–137, the "Principal Regional Organizations with Mutual Security Commitments as of January 1, 1971," quote China under the category "associate member or observer" within the WTO (just like the US within CENTO!). The few things that all these authors do say on these Organizations are, when they are not mistakes or half-truths, simple generalities and banalities. Even the renowned *Yearbook of International Organizations*, published by the Union of International Associations, 15th edition, Brussels, 1974, may be so misleading as to inform the reader (p. 618) that the Permanent Commission and the Secretariat of the WTO are located in the Ministry of Defence in Warsaw, though at the end of the entry it is Moscow that is named.
Finally, in the "standard" *International Governmental Organizations. Constitutional Documents*, by Amos J. Peaslee, revised third edition in five parts, prepared by Dorothy Peaslee Xydis, part one, Martinus Nijhoff, The Hague, 1974, in the pertinent "summaries," one reads, for instance, apropos Comecon, about the Session of the Council meeting twice yearly or the headquarters located in Moscow at Petrovka; regarding the WTO, one is informed that Albania is still a member and that the *casus foederis* is geographically unlimited. Concerning the International Bank for Economic Cooperation, it was "regrettably impossible" to include its Agreement in the collection, as the Bank itself and the Soviet Embassy in Athens did not reply to letters (p. 879). The fact that this text is published in the *UNTS* seems to be completely unknown to Mrs. Peaslee Xydis.

thanks go to Senator Manlio Brosio for his preface. Certainly one of the most outstanding political personalities of the Western world,[10] he indicates, against the background of the system of the international organizations of the Soviet bloc discussed in the book, "some weaknesses in the Western international organizations, with the aim of encouraging that they be overcome, so that their solidity and prestige may be strengthened." These suggestions require prompt attention.

University of Calgary,
Alberta, Canada.
November, 1975.   Richard Szawlowski

10. Perhaps the most striking homage to Manlio Brosio (and also the present Secretary-General of NATO) may be found in a booklet recently published by a former Polish press correspondent in Belgium—see Jerzy Kasprzycki *Widziane w Brukseli* ("Seen in Brussels"), Iskry, Warsaw, 1974, p. 135:
"I became acquainted with two people of this rank [i.e. Secretary-General of NATO]: the Italian Manlio Brosio and his successor, the Dutchman Joseph Luns. From the point of view of "cadre" they were both the right people at the right place—in the full meaning of the words. Both had in common not only an anecdotically tall height (over 1.85 m), but above all a brilliant intelligence, an enormous sense of humour (although, in my opinion, Manlio Brosio's is more subtle) and unusual diligence. Both of them also belonged—despite a big age difference—to the generation, now dying out, of artist politicians, who still pay attention to form, and not only to substance, who, in their activities, live through moments of inspiration and doubt, ecstasy and bitterness, and who are capable not only of living, but also of taking things to heart."
"Manlio Brosio's press conferences were usually of a one-sided character. The journalists posed stupid, boring and shallow questions, which the secretary general answered wisely, wittily, and comprehensively. There were not many correspondents in NATO who could perform as equal partners of Brosio on this arena."
Polish journalism of this kind is worth comparing to a Soviet effort entitled "Second Profession of Mr. Luns," in which he is simply referred to as a "rogue" *(zhulik)*—see *Pravda*, December 13, 1973.

XX

INTRODUCTION

This study on the System of the International Organizations of the Communist countries deals with the entirety of the international governmental bodies of that part of the world which we usually refer to, in the West, as the Soviet bloc. By the same token, it is also a study of multilateral "institutionalized" relations, in a variety of fields, between the members of that group *inter se* and also, to a certain extent, with the outside world, particularly the West.

By way of introduction, it may be useful to develop briefly the following points.

1. Modern international governmental relations are conducted both on a "non-institutionalized" and an "institutionalized" basis.

Concerning the latter, this institutionalization embraces both bilateral governmental relations, where its main manifestation is a network of thousands of diplomatic missions and consular posts (bilateral international organizations are a rare phenomenon), and multilateral relations, manifested by—at present—some 300 international governmental organizations.

The existence of international governmental organizations goes back to the nineteenth century. Until the end of the Second World War it was characteristic of these bodies that the vast majority of them were conceived to be universal institutions. Sectional as their respective fields of activity might have been: Telegraph, Postal Traffic, Weights and Measures, Publication of Customs Tariffs, Agriculture, Public Health, etc. (the League of Nations, established in 1919/1920, being an obvious exception), the bulk of them were world-wide open organizations. The Pan American Union, the Central Commission for Navigation on the Rhine, and the Danube Commission were exceptions to the general rule.

Regionalism in the field of international organizations (and our study is one in the field of Communist regionalism) is basically a post-World War II phenomenon. It is characterized by the emergence of dozens of regional intergovernmental organizations in the political, military, economic, technical, scientific, and other fields.

2. The lead in the field of institutionalized regionalism was taken by the Western countries, which created such international organizations as the Organization for European Economic Cooperation (now the Organization for Economic Cooperation and Development), the Western Union Defence Organization (now West European Union), NATO, SEATO, the European Organization for Nuclear Research ("CERN"), etc. The "Socialist Commonwealth" (*Sotsialisticheskoe Sodruzhestvo*), as they like to call themselves, only hesitantly followed suit.

This may be well illustrated by just comparing the respective dates: the OEEC was created in 1948, and the Council for Mutual Economic Assistance (Comecon) followed in 1949; the Western Union Defence Organization, NATO, SEATO, and the WEU were created in 1948, 1949, and 1954 respectively, and the Warsaw Treaty Organization followed in 1955; the European Organization for Nuclear Research ("CERN") was created in 1953, and the Communist Joint Institute for Nuclear Research followed in 1956; the European Investment Bank and the Inter-American Development Bank were created in 1957 and 1959 respectively (several similar non-Communist regional intergovernmental banks may also be mentioned)—and the International Investment Bank of Comecon followed in 1970; finally, the European Launcher Development Organization (ELDO), the European Space Research Organization (ESRO), and the International Telecommunications Satellite Consortium (INTELSAT), were created during the early sixties—and were followed by "Intercosmos" (not a fully-fledged international organization) at the end of the sixties and "Intersputnik" in 1971.

Communist commentators like to lay great stress on the fact that it was the West that first created the military and political regional organizations (especially NATO), which had to be countered by the peace-loving Soviet Union and her allies by the creation of the Warsaw Treaty Organization. They would never admit that it was, in fact, the "socialist camp" that actually copied the West, during a period of over twenty-six years, in respect of literally *all* kinds of regional international organizations.

3. The history of the twenty-six years of the existence of Communist international governmental organizations may be divided into three stages: (a) the "embryo" stage, 1949–53/54; (b) the "take-off" stage, 1954/55–68; and (c) the "maturity" (or pronounced integration stage), started after 1968 and still continuing.

Under Stalin, who was exceptionally suspicious of international governmental organizations, both universal and regional, only Comecon was created (1949), but even this body did not manifest any tangible activities, and was conceived rather as a propagandistic counter-maneouvre against the Marshall Plan and the OEEC. This period, which continued for a year or so after Stalin died in 1953, should therefore be treated as the embryonic stage in the development of the organizations which interest us in this study.

It was only some time after Stalin's death that the USSR, and, following her (and even more so), the rest of the "camp," very much changed their attitude vis-à-vis international multilateral cooperation. Communist activities in the United Nations were intensified; energetic demands were voiced for more jobs for citizens of the Communist countries on the staff of the United Nations Secretariat; several specialised agencies of the United Nations, such as UNESCO or the WHO, were joined or rejoined; and the same was true of the Expanded Programme for Technical Assistance and the Special Fund, later amalgamated into the United Nations Development Programme (UNDP), and UNICEF.[1]

Within the framework of the Communist camp, Comecon was revived, and during the period of fourteen years or so between 1955 and 1968, nine new "full-scale" Communist international governmental organizations were created, including the top-rank Warsaw Treaty Organization. To this should be added the two semi-

---

1. This, of course, does not mean that the USSR, after Stalin's death, *fully* joined international cooperation within universal governmental organizations. Even today she is not a member of FAO or GATT (in which some smaller Communist countries participate) or of the International Monetary Fund and the International Bank for Reconstruction and Development, which Rumania joined in 1972. It was only in the autumn of 1970 that she joined the International Civil Aviation Organization. She has never demonstrated any confidence in the idea of international adjudication (although a Soviet judge has sat on the International Court of Justice since 1946).
She did not contribute anything to the UN peace-keeping operations, even in the case of the UN Forces in Cyprus, although she voted for their creation in 1964 in the UN Security Council, and for the numerous extensions which followed (it is only starting with 1973/74 that the USSR, and with her the other countries of the bloc, have contributed to the newly created UN Emergency Force in the Middle East, established in October 1973, and the UN Disengagement Observer Force between Israel and Syria, established in May 1974). She also contributes embarrassingly little to the UNDP; her 1975 pledges (including the Byelorussian and the Ukrainian SSRs) amounted to some 4.2 million dollars out of the total of 401 million expected—whereas, e.g., Sweden pledged almost 41 million and Denmark almost 38 million—see *UNDP Business Bulletin* (New York), December 1974.

autonomous organizations which were created within Comecon, with a position comparable to that of the United Nations Industrial Development Organization (UNIDO) and the United Nations Conference for Trade and Development (UNCTAD) vis-à-vis the United Nations. All this fully warrants the classification of this period as that of a very energetic take-off in the history of these bodies.

Finally, under the impact of the shock of the Czechoslovakian affair, starting with the turn of 1968 and 1969, the newest era in the history of Communist international governmental organizations began. Not only were fifteen new organizations (and one semi-autonomous body) created during the period of seven years between 1969 and 1975, but, more important, far-reaching integration processes took place within the two main organizations of the system. This applies to military cooperation within the Warsaw Treaty Organization (an evident phenomenon in spite of purposeful veiling) and, especially, to Comecon, where it was particularly dramatized by the "Comprehensive Programme for the Further Deepening and Perfecting of Cooperation and Development of Socialist Economic Integration of the Member Countries of Comecon" adopted in July, 1971 (see below). And new organizations of the system will be created in the years to come.[2] The advent of a new era in the field under discussion is thus obvious.

4. The chronological list of the Communist international governmental organizations, in mid-1975, embraces the following[3] (the

2. The "Comprehensive Programme for the Further Deepening and Perfecting of Cooperation and Development of Socialist Economic Integration of Member Countries of Comecon" adopted in 1971 (see below) mentions several times the creation in the future of new international organizations, especially economic ones (see, e.g., the introduction to its chapter VII). Thus, for instance, mention was made in the summer of 1972 about the consideration of proposals for the creation of an international organization of the Comecon countries, specializing in the fields of the oil and gas industries—see *Pravda*, June 30, 1972. And in the late summer of 1973 came news of the recommendation voted by Comecon's Council for Environmental Protection that "countries of the socialist commonwealth" should create international bodies in the field of research and production to coordinate their cooperation in this realm—see *Życie Warszawy*, September 23–24, 1973. The latter initiative will probably materialize at the turn of 1975/76, when "Intergasoochistka" and "Intervodoochistka" (see below) will, in all likelihood, be established.
3. With the proviso that the tiny research (information) coordination (cooperation) centres of the Comecon countries, which are mostly not truly international organizations (especially because of the lack of international staff) are missed

three semi-autonomous bodies within Comecon are listed in brackets):[4]

1.	Comecon	1949
2.	Warsaw Treaty Organization	1955
3.	Joint Institute for Nuclear Research	1956
4.	Organization for Cooperation of Railways	1956
5.	Telecommunications and Postal "Organization"	1957
6.	Organization of the Joint Power Grid	1962
7.	(Institute for Standardization)	1962
8.	(Bureau for the Coordination of Ship Freighting)	1962
9.	International Bank for Economic Cooperation	1963
10.	Organization of the Common Waggon Pool	1963
11.	Organization for Cooperation of the Ball-bearing Industry	1964
12.	Intermetall	1964
13.	International Laboratory of Low Temperatures and Strong Magnetic Fields	1968
14.	International Scientific and Technical Information Centre	1969
15.	Interkhim	1969
16.	International Investment Bank	1970

---

out. These are, for instance: the Coordination Centre for Synthetic Leather (see *Pravda*, February 12, 1972); the Coordination Centre for Sea and Ocean Research (see *Pravda*, February 24, 1972); the Centre for Research on New Methods of the Use of Coal, created in 1972 by six countries in Katowice, Poland, and located in the (national) Main Institute for Mining in that city (see *Neues Deutschland*, September 19, 1972). Comecon's Secretary Faddeev, at the beginning of 1974, mentioned already thirty six of them—see, e.g., *Zycie Warszawy*, January 4, 1974. This number continues to increase. Thus, for instance, a Viticultural Centre was created at Yalta, USSR (see *Soviet News*, London, April 9, 1974) and an International Organization for Scientific and Technical Information in the Field of Black Metallurgy was established in Moscow (see *Rynki Zagraniczne*, Warsaw, May 11, 1974). *Neues Deutschland*, November 20, 1974, mentioned the existence of already forty of these Centres.

4. Apart from the above-listed "hundred per cent" Communist international governmental organizations, there are two other international bodies which, although not exclusively Communist, are clearly Communist-dominated. One is the Danube Commission, created in 1948 and replacing the previous one, going back historically to 1856; the headquarters of the new Danube Commission are in Budapest, and the USSR, Bulgaria, Czechoslovakia, Hungary, Rumania, Yugoslavia, and Austria are members (and West Germany an observer). The second organization to be mentioned here is the International Radio and Television Organization, created in 1946, in which Finland, Algeria, Iraq, Mali, the Sudan, Egypt and Syria also participate, apart from the Communist countries. "Intervision" (Intervidenye), embracing most of the European Communist countries and Finland, functions within the framework of this organization; it is a counterpart of the West European "Eurovision."

17. (International Institute for the Economic Problems of the World Socialist System)   1971
18. Intersputnik   1971
19. International Mathematical Centre   1972
20. Interatominstrument   1972
21. International Centre for the Training of Civil Aviation Personnel   1973
22. Interelectro   1973
23. Interatomenergo   1973
24. Intertextilmash   1973
25. Interetalonpribor   1974
26. Interkhimvolokno   1974
27. International Centre for Electron Microscopy   1975
28. Intergasoochistka   (probably)   1976
29. Intervodoochistka   (probably)   1976
30. International Scientific Research Institute for Management Problems   (probably)   1976

These Communist *intergovernmental* organizations should not be confused with another group—that of the Communist or Communist-dominated non-governmental international organizations.[5]

Some of these bodies are "universal" ones (e.g., the World Council of

5. What is striking in the field of the Communist non-governmental "ideological front organizations" is the fact that since the Comintern, created in 1919, was officially liquidated in 1943, and the Cominform, founded in 1947, was disbanded in 1956, there have been no clearly Moscow-controlled general "political revolutionary" Communist international organizations. A relic of the Cominform is the periodical *Problemy Mira i Sotsializma* (*Problems of Peace and Socialism, World Marxist Review* in its English version), a continuation of the former *For Lasting Peace, For People's Democracy*, published from 1958 in Prague by the Moscow-oriented Communist Parties. A meeting of the Editorial Council of that periodical, which took place in Prague between October 30 and November 3, 1969 (the first one since 1960), brought together representatives of 58 Communist parties (for the final communiqué see *Pravda*, November 4, 1969). The next such meeting, which took place in December 1971, was allegedly attended by representatives of 63 Communist parties (see *Pravda*, December 17, 1971), and the latest one, in January 1974, by representatives of 67 parties (see *Pravda*, January 10, 1974). The periodical is issued in 26 languages and claims to circulate in 145 countries. Its Editor-in-Chief is the Russian Konstantin Zarodov.
In 1972 the periodical organized an international "Marxist Discussion Seminar" on Environmental Protection, in which "Marxist scientists" and representatives of Communist parties from 36 countries participated (see *World Marxist Review*, June, 1972). In October 1973 there took place in Prague a meeting of representatives of 38 Communist parties "devoted to the problems of

Peace, the World Federation of Trade Unions or the International Union of Students) and some "regional" (e.g., the Organization for the Solidarity of the Nations of Asia and Africa, the Afro-Asian Lawyers' Conference or the Latin American Solidarity Organization).[6] They mainly specialize in the "ideological export business" to Western

---

publishing and dissemination" of the periodical; on that occasion 39 national editions of the periodical were already mentioned, as was the fact that it has a circulation of about 500,000 copies—see *Pravda*, October 19, 1973. In December 1973 there took place in Prague an "exchange of opinions," organized by the periodical, between representatives of 13 European Communist parties on "Visual agitation under present conditions—an important means of political activity of communists"—see *Pravda*, December 22, 1973. In November 1974 the periodical organized a conference in Sofia on "Contemporary problems of socialist democracy and the prospects of its development" with the participation of nine communist parties—see *Pravda*, November 13, 1974. In April 1975, on the occasion of the 40th anniversary of the VII (last) Congress of the Comintern, the periodical organized an international symposium on "Communists in the fight for the unity of democratic and anti-imperialist forces"—see *Trybuna Ludu*, April 12–13, 1975. Gradually, it seems, the activities centred around the periodical are developing into a sort of small "Cominform."

6. The Latin American Solidarity Organization (LASO), created by the "tricontinental" conference of Havana in 1966, held its first session in July-August 1967, also in Havana (for its origins, see Hermann P. Gebhardt, "Castro und die OLAS-Konferenz von Havana" in *Aussenpolitik* (Freiburg) No. 12/1967, pp. 743–750 and *90th Congress, 1st Session. The First Conference of the Latin American Solidarity Organization July 28-August 5, 1967. A Staff Study Prepared for the Subcommittee to Investigate the Administration of the Internal Security Act and other Internal Security Laws of the Committee on the Judiciary, United States Senate.* U.S. Government Printing Office, Washington, 1967). As to the reaction of the Organization of American States to the creation of LASO, see *The OAS Chronicle* (Washington, D.C.), Vol. III, No. 2, October, 1967, p. 20. The pertinent resolution of the OAS was transmitted for information to the UN Security Council (see *Report of the Security Council July 16, 1967-July 15, 1968, General Assembly, Official Records:* Twenty-Third Session, Supplement No. 2 (A/7202), p. 117). Though LASO does not seem to have been particularly active during its eight years of existence, Havana still has ambitions of "multilaterally" indoctrinating Latin America. See, e.g., the first meeting of the activists in the field of the plastic arts of Latin America in Havana in May, 1972, which issued an address to the creative intelligentsia of the continent. In that address there was "decisive condemnation of the penetration of bourgeois ideas into the cultural life of Latin America, leading to decline and decay," and an appeal was made for "genuine national art"—see *Pravda*, May 30, 1972. And in February 1975 Fidel Castro declared that Cuba is prepared to "give help" to the trade union movement in Latin America in the training of their activists. The Cuban trade unions will soon open a school, which will train not only local activists, but also those from "the remaining countries of the Latin American continent." The school will have 500 places—see *Polityka* (Warsaw), February 15, 1975.

and/or underdeveloped countries. These organizations, the total number of which at present is over fifteen, will not be discussed in this study.[7]

5. The international governmental organizations of the Communist countries which were listed above are not by any means equal to one another in importance.

If one attempts to establish a hierarchy among these different bodies, one may safely say that the most important position is occupied by two "key" organizations: the Warsaw Treaty Organization and Comecon (including its semi-autonomous international bodies). The leading role of these two bodies is also emphasized by Communist sources. Thus, in connection with the 25th anniversary of Comecon, it was stated:[8]

> Together with the Warsaw Treaty Organization, which coordinates cooperation of the socialist countries in the political and defence spheres, the Council for Mutual Economic Assistance, which has laid down the basis for an extensive process of economic integration, contributes to that constant change in the correlation of forces in favour of socialism and democracy which is determined by the entire course of contemporary development.

These two organizations are followed—at a certain distance—by the Joint Institute for Nuclear Research. And the latter, in turn, is followed by almost twenty organizations, most of them representing a roughly similar "calibre," though both Banks should perhaps be given first place in this group; they form our "class III."

The smallest body in "class IV" is perhaps the International Laboratory of Strong Magnetic Fields and Low Temperatures.

Finally, regarding "class V," the Telecommunications and Postal "Organization," because of the lack of an *international* secretariat (see below), must be put at the very bottom of our list. The same applies to the International Mathematical Centre.

The overall picture could be presented as follows:

---

7. Most of these bodies and their recent activities are discussed in the *Yearbook on International Communist Affairs*, published by the Hoover Institution on War, Revolution, and Peace, Stanford, California (LASO is not covered by the yearbook—see, e.g., *Yearbook 1973*; this is perhaps due to the lack of tangible activities). See also Robert Orth, *Hilfsorganisationen des Weltkommunismus*, Ilmgau Verlag, Pfaffenhofen/Ilm, 7th edition, 1971.
8. See *Pravda*, January 23, 1974.

Class I

WARSAW PACT ORGANIZATION

COMECON (including the Institute for Standardization, the Bureau for the Coordination of Ship Freighting and the International Institute for Economic Problems of the World Socialist System)

Class II

Joint Institute for Nuclear Research

Class III

International Bank for Economic Cooperation

International Investment Bank

Organization for Cooperation of Railways

Organization of the Joint Power Grid

Organization of the Common Waggon Pool

Organization for Cooperation of the Ball-bearing Industry

Intermetall

International Scientific and Technical Information Centre

Interkhim

Intersputnik

Interatominstrument

Interelectro

Interatomenergo

Intertextilmash

Interetalonpribor

Interkhimvolokno

Intergasoochistka

Intervodoochistka

International Scientific Research Institute for Management Problems[9]

Class IV

International Laboratory of Strong Magnetic Fields and Low Temperatures

International Centre for the Training of Civil Aviation Personnel

Class V

Telecommunications and Postal "Organization"

International Mathematical Centre

International Centre for Electron Microscopy[10]

9. The decision to create the Institute was taken at the XXIX Session of Comecon—see *Pravda*, June 27, 1975. The final allotment of the Institute to one of our "classes" will only be possible after the respective treaty is signed and published.
10. At the moment of this writing we do not yet have at our disposal the text of the March 1975 agreement, creating the International Centre for Electron Microscopy. We placed it under "Class V" though it may turn out that its proper place would be under "Class IV."

Chapter I

THE WARSAW TREATY ORGANIZATION (WTO)

1. *Background*

The official "direct" reason given for the creation of the WTO was the inclusion of the Federal Republic of Germany into the Western defence system. Thus the preamble to the Warsaw Treaty[1] reads:

> The Contracting Parties...taking into consideration...the situation that has come about in Europe as a result of the ratification of the Paris Agreements, which provide for the constitution of a new military group in the form of a 'West European Union,' with the participation of a remilitarized West Germany and its inclusion in the North Atlantic bloc, thereby increasing the danger of a new war and creating a threat to the national security of peace-loving states...

The same argument has been dutifully repeated by the Eastern "interpreters." At the same time, they placed the genesis and the *raison d'être* of the WTO in the broader context of alleged "Western aggressiveness" in general.

Thus one Soviet author insisted that the Warsaw Treaty was a necessary countermeasure of the "peace-loving countries" against aggressive Western military blocs, created by the United States, England and other "imperialist countries" and directed against the socialist countries, and the danger of a war against these countries resulting from this.[2]

The same author, in his 1971 booklet,[3] offers an even broader background as far as the alleged reasons for the creation of the WTO

---

1. English text of the Warsaw Treaty in *United Nations Treaty Series* (*UNTS*), Vol. 219 (1955), No. 2962. Text reproduced in our Annexes (No. I).
2. See A. S. Bakhov, "Legal Aspects of the Warsaw Treaty" in *Sovetskij Yezhegodnik Mezhdunarodnovo Prava* 1964–1965, Moscow, 1966, p. 134.
3. See A. S. Bakhov, *Organizatsya Varshavskovo Dogovora (pravovye aspekty)*, ("The Organization of the Warsaw Treaty—Legal Aspects"), Izdatel'stvo "Nauka," Moscow, 1971.

are concerned, and elaborates on the ones given previously. World War II did not, it is argued, bring about the results that were expected by the United States and their "imperialist allies." The USSR was not "hopelessly weakened" and, what is more, in Europe and Asia there emerged a group of people's democracies, representing, together with the Soviet Union, the world socialist system (no clarification is given, of course, as to the *methods* used by the USSR to create these "people's democracies").

Reference is made to the 1947 Truman doctrine and the creation, starting with 1948, of the "imperialist aggressive blocs." Lenin is quoted in this connection as saying that all imperialist coalitions are, of necessity, just "peredyshki" (respites) between wars. Again, no word is said, of course, of the *reasons* for the creation and development of the Western defence organizations, such as the Communist coup d'état in Czechoslovakia, the blockade of West Berlin and the invasion of South Korea.

In this connection Spaak's remark comes to mind:[4]

> Plusieurs hommes d'Etat d'Occident ont été, au cours de ces vingt dernières années, appelés pères de l'Europe ou pères de l'Alliance atlantique. Aucun ne mérite ce titre. Il appartient à Staline. Sans Staline, sans sa politique agressive, sans la menace qu'il a fait planer sur le monde libre, l'Alliance atlantique n'aurait jamais vu le jour et le mouvement pour une Europe unie, englobant l'Allemagne, n'aurait jamais connu son étonnant succès. Dans l'un et l'autre cas, c'est un réflexe défensif qui est à la base de ces deux grandes réalisations.

Finally, very recently, Marshal Yakubovsky gave the simplest, most down-to-earth explanation when he qualified the creation of the Warsaw Treaty as a "retaliatory and temporary measure, by which the socialist countries liquidated the monopoly of imperialism in military alliances."[5] In other words, "you formed multilateral alliances, we followed by creating our own."

In any case, when the Paris 1954 Agreements finally came into force on May 5, 1955, the USSR unilaterally terminated her alliance treaties with Britain and France. And two days after Western Germany (on May 9, 1955) was admitted to NATO, the Warsaw Conference (May 11–14, 1955) led to the conclusion of the "Treaty of Friendship,

---

4. Paul-Henri Spaak, *Les combats inachevés, De l'Indépendance à l'Alliance*, Fayard, Paris, 1969, pp. 249–250.
5. See *Krasnaya Zvezda*, February 23, 1975.

2

Cooperation and Mutual Assistance" between the USSR and the seven European "people's democracies."

Reflecting on the true reasons for the creation of the WTO, one cannot, perhaps, reject the official version totally. It is true that the USSR (especially until the conclusion of the 1970 treaties between Bonn and Moscow and Warsaw) was deliberately trying to magnify the "West German threat," her military potential and other things, in order, for instance, to alarm public opinion in Poland and elsewhere. On the other hand, as the situation stood 19–20 years ago, around 1954/55, when the USSR and the "people's democracies" were—economically and militarily—very considerably weaker than they are today, with the shock of the German invasion in World War II still fresh in their minds, and when they were, moreover, stupefied by the West German *Wirtschaftswunder*, while the Ulbricht regime in Eastern Germany was extremely weak, with riots in 1953 and massive defections from Eastern to Western Germany (the Berlin Wall came only in 1961), there could have been quite genuine fear in Moscow (and also in Warsaw and Prague) of a militarily strong Germany, playing a major role in NATO.[6] A situation which, in the final analysis, they brought about themselves.

But the *main* reasons were certainly different.

One of these was undoubtedly the wish to have an even closer, uniform, and internationally institutionalized control over the military and political life of the "people's democracies." If we assume that there were political and military strategists with foresight at that time in Moscow, it is obvious that around 1954/55 they must have realized that with Stalin's death in March, 1953, something had started to change in the cohesion of the Eastern bloc.

6. This Soviet fear, certainly consciously exaggerated, in the early fifties, of a remilitarized West Germany, was recently recalled by Jules Moch, who relates a tête-à-tête conversation with the then Soviet Deputy Foreign Minister Gromyko, in which the latter said: "Quand je pense que, lorsque les Américains étaient nos alliés et nous fournissaient autant d'armes qu'ils pouvaient, par Mourmansk au nord et par l'Iran au sud, nous n'avons pu arrêter les Allemands que sur la Volga et dans le Caucase, que serait-ce maintenant qu'ils sont les alliés des Allemands contre nous et qu'ils les réarment?" Moch believes that this apprehension was real—see *La Nouvelle Revue des deux Mondes* (Paris), March 1975, pp. 583–584.
After the 1970 treaty between Bonn and Moscow, Marshal Grechko in his article in *Kommunist*, October 1972, when dealing with the alleged reasons for the creation of the WTO, did not refer to the "(West) German danger" at all. The same was true of the article by Yakubovsky in *Krasnaya Zvezda*, May 13, 1973. Shtemenko's article in *Krasnaya Zvezda*, May 14, 1975, though, specifically mentions the "inclusion of West Germany into NATO in October 1954."

3

Let us mention such things as the already noted East German riots; serious discredit and a certain disruption of control by the Soviet secret police over at least some "satellites" after the shooting of Beria and the defection of a Polish secret police dignitary to the West and his revelations;[7] the strike in Pilzno;[8] and symptoms of intellectual ferment in Poland and Hungary.[9] All this should have indicated to them that more serious trouble might be ahead. Bilateral treaties on "friendship, cooperation and mutual assistance" which the USSR had with the "people's democracies" (with the exception of Albania and, at that time, of East Germany) were apparently not considered to be sufficient. The WTO offered the possibility of a more "elegant" (and sometimes more convenient) multilateral institutionalized control.

7. After October, 1956, in the short period when the Polish press was able to publish almost without any censorship, *Nowa Kultura*, (Warsaw), No. 52–53 (23–30 December, 1956) mentioned that Swiatło defected after Beria's fall in Moscow. "It is no secret that Beria not only attempted to subordinate the CPSU substantially to the security services, but also attempted to supervise and to shadow, through his own residents and subordinate units, the activities of other Communist parties."

8. For a firsthand account of that strike by a man who was then an assistant judge there, see Otto Ulc "Pilzen: The Unknown Revolt" in *Problems of Communism*, May-June, 1965, pp. 46–49.

9. Concerning Poland see, e.g., the account of Jerzy Putrament in his memoirs *Pół Wieku* (Half a Century), Vol. IV, *Literaci* (The Writers), Czytelnik, Warsaw, 1970. Putrament, member of the Central Committee of the Polish Communist Party (PZPR), former ambassador to Berne and later to Paris, and Secretary-General or vice-president of the Polish Writers Association for over twenty years, referring to the 1954–1955 period in the writers' milieu in Poland, gives abundant testimony to this ferment, coupled with what he calls "lack of ideas and conceptions" in the party leadership. He mentions that "in the spring of 1954 the role of criticizing cultural policy was seized by those who a few years later would be called revisionists" (p. 225); and the fact that at the Writers' Congress in June, 1954, during the elections to the governing body, "for the first time the phenomenon, so frequent later, occurred, of a united front of the non-party and party right, which frenziedly castigated candidates of the party." Other similar interesting events are also mentioned. Regarding Hungary, many intellectuals, especially numerous writers and journalists, gave strong support to the reformist Imre Nagy, appointed prime minister in July 1953, a man hated by powerful Hungarian Stalinists such as Rakosi or Gerö. Although formally removed from his post (and the party) only in April 1955, Nagy was already made powerless during the second half of 1954. Stalinists strongly attacked and later settled accounts with intellectuals supporting Nagy, which, in turn, caused a further escalation of ferment. For some details see, e.g., Miklós Molnár *Budapest 1956. A History of the Hungarian Revolution*, George Allen and Unwin, London, 1971, pp. 58–80. Molnar, who was managing editor of the Hungarian writers' journal Literary Gazette, is especially well-informed about the pertinent situation.

4

Another important reason for the creation of the WTO seems to have been the idea of using it as a "pawn" in the attempt to achieve the dismantling of NATO and the withdrawal of American troops from Europe. These proposals were already made by the USSR during the February 1954 Foreign Ministers Conference in Berlin, and were connected with the "European Security System." The creation of the WTO in May, 1955, could have been considered as the creation of a useful *quid pro quo* in the advancing, only a few weeks later, during the June, 1955 Geneva Summit Conference, of similar initiatives, coupled this time with a proposal of simultaneous liquidation of *both* organizations (a proposal later repeated many times, though it was always evident that the West is not inclined to commit political suicide by liquidating NATO).

Two other reasons for the creation of the WTO could also be mentioned.

On May 15, 1955, one day after the Warsaw Treaty was signed, the State Treaty with Austria was concluded. This treaty provided (Article 20, para. 3) that "the forces of the Allied and Associated Powers... shall be withdrawn from Austria within ninety days from the coming into force of the present Treaty [this took place on July 27, 1955], and insofar as possible not later than December 31, 1955." This clearly affected the further stationing of Soviet troops in Hungary and Rumania. The peace treaties with these countries, signed in Paris on February 10, 1947,[10] both provide (Article 22, para. 1 of the Treaty with Hungary, and Article 21, para. 1 of that with Rumania) that "Upon the coming into force of the present Treaty, all Allied forces shall, within a period of ninety days, be withdrawn from Hungary, or Rumania, respectively, subject to the right of the Soviet Union to keep on [Hungarian, or Rumanian, respectively] territory such armed forces as it may need for the maintenance of the lines of communication of the Soviet Army with the Soviet zone of occupation in Austria." The post-1955 stay of Soviet troops on Hungarian soil until today, and in Rumania until 1958, could be explained by references to military cooperation within the WTO. The presence of Soviet troops in Rumania and Hungary was, in fact, justified by the Soviets by the Warsaw Treaty (and some obscure "governmental agreements").[11]

10. For the text of the State Treaty with Austria see *UNTS*, vol. 217 (1955), No. 2949; for the texts of the Peace Treaties with Hungary and Rumania see *UNTS*, vols. 41 and 42 (1949), Nos. 644 and 645.
11. See, e.g., "The Declaration of the Soviet Government on the Principles of the Development and Further Strengthening of Friendship and Cooperation Between the Soviet Union and Other Socialist States," *Pravda*, October 31, 1956.

This was supplemented by bilateral agreements on troop stationing concluded in 1957.

The Warsaw Treaty could also have been seen as a sort of counter-action against the so-called Balkan Pact, signed in August, 1954 between Yugoslavia, Greece, and Turkey. Through the WTO, Albania, totally encircled by Yugoslavia and Greece, and with only one bilateral treaty on "friendship, cooperation and mutual assistance" (with Bulgaria), was linked more closely with Moscow. All this, of course, is history today.

2. *Membership, Casus Foederis and its Consequences, the Treaty's Duration*

The Warsaw Treaty was signed and ratified in 1955 by eight countries: the USSR, Poland, East Germany, Czechoslovakia, Hungary, Rumania, Bulgaria, and Albania.

During the autumn 1956 Hungarian Revolution, the government of Imre Nagy issued a declaration about Hungary's withdrawal from the Warsaw Treaty.[12] And although the uprising was quickly put down by Soviet intervention, and the denunciation therefore had no practical consequences, it is worth remembering.

On September 13, 1968, a few weeks after the invasion of Czechoslovakia, Albania formally withdrew from the Warsaw Treaty. In his speech to the Albanian People's Assembly, the country's premier, after denouncing practically everybody: the Soviet "clique of renegades," the "Novotny revisionist group and the Dubcek revisionist group," the malpractices of the WTO, including its "fascist-type aggression," etc., stated *inter alia*[13]

> By withdrawing from the Warsaw Treaty, the People's Republic of Albania is taking a revolutionary step. The Warsaw Treaty no

12. On 31 October 1956 the Hungarian government sent a message to UN Secretary-General Hammarskjöld, announcing Hungary's withdrawal from the Warsaw Treaty and appealing to the UN and the great powers to guarantee Hungary's permanent neutrality. The same was announced by Budapest radio the same day. See *United Nations. Report of the Special Committee on the Problem of Hungary*. General Assembly. Official Records: Eleventh Session, Supplement No. 18 (A/3592), New York, 1957.
13. See "Warsaw Treaty Has Become Instrument for Soviet Revisionists' Aggression and Enslavement of the People of Member States—Speech by Comrade Shetu at Session of Albanian People's Assembly," *Peking Review*, September 20, 1968, p. 13.

longer serves socialism and peace, it no longer serves the cause of the working class and proletarian internationalism, it has lost the ideological and class basis on which it was created. It now serves the revisionist bourgeoisie, it serves the big-power chauvinistic narrow interests of the Soviet revisionist leadership as well as the U.S.-Soviet counter-revolutionary alliance for the domination of the world.

Although, under the Treaty itself, withdrawal was possible only by giving notice one year before the Treaty had been in force twenty years (see below), withdrawal was, in our opinion, warranted under international law in this case as a consequence of the flagrant breach of the Treaty, especially of its Article 1.

It is true that the Vienna 1969 Convention on the Law of Treaties (not yet in force) provides in Article 60, para. 2 that in the case of a material breach of a *multilateral* treaty, a party in the situation of Albania—or Hungary in 1956—can only suspend the application of the treaty. However, in the case of an exceptionally grave violation of international law like the invasion of Czechoslovakia—or previously Hungary—this evidently does not go far enough. If, under the same Convention (Article 53), a treaty in conflict with the peremptory norms of international law *(ius cogens)*—and to these norms now firmly belongs the prohibition of the threat or use of force in international relations—is null and void *ex tunc*, it is hard to understand why, if these norms were violated in the most brutal way by one or more partners under the rule of a treaty which was concluded precisely to eliminate or repeal such violations, the innocent partners could not terminate such a treaty immediately. One could even go as far as to argue that an invasion of this sort, a grave breach of international trust, coupled with disturbance of the international balance and the creation of new international tensions and suspicions, means a fundamental change of circumstances *(rebus sic stantibus* clause) which may, with certain provisos not applying in our cases, be invoked for the termination of a treaty even under the provisions of the 1969 Vienna Convention (Article 62).[14]

14. This is why one cannot agree with what Krzysztof Skubiszewski said in his otherwise excellent and bold article entitled "L'Organisation du Traité de Varsovie" in *Revue belge de droit international*, 1967, p. 82. Without even mentioning the possibility of suspension, he just asserted (p. 82)—keeping to the solution also adopted in the earlier drafts of the Law of Treaties— that Hungary, in 1956, could not unilaterally denounce the Warsaw Treaty. The absurd conclusions to which adherence to such a legal position might lead may be illustrated by the following hypothetical case.

An Eastern commentator,[15] adhering to the provisions of the Treaty itself, and noting that the Albanian decision may not be classified as an annulment because no fact of an essential violation of the Warsaw Treaty by its parties vis-à-vis Albania is known (the locking out of Albania from any cooperation within the framework of the treaty is completely ignored), considers that act as illegal and not bearing, *per se*, legal consequences. He nevertheless concludes that "taking into consideration the lack of protest on the part of the remaining Warsaw Treaty countries, one may come to the conclusion that these countries tacitly accepted Albania's withdrawal from the Warsaw Treaty." He does not say that, keeping to the reasoning used by him in the Albanian case, Hungary's withdrawal from the Warsaw Treaty in 1956 was legal under international law.

The total membership in the Organizations was thus reduced from eight to seven. And if one takes into consideration the Rumanian stand and her persistent opposition to many aspects of military cooperation in particular, within the WTO, one may—with some licence—consider the actual total membership of the Organization as six and a half. It should be noted, though, that in spite of Rumania's successful opposition, tremendous pressure is, in many cases, evidently

---

Suppose the U.S.S.R. and her four "aides" issued, before undertaking the invasion in August 1968, an ultimatum, clearly threatening such an invasion if concrete conditions were not fulfilled by Prague. Or had the five countries started the invasion and Czechoslovakia put up, as she should have done, armed resistance—if for no other reason than to demonstrate, at least once in its relatively short but troublesome history, her will for independence. The Czechoslovak government then decides to withdraw from the Warsaw Treaty. But it could not do so, because Rumania had not signed the ultimatum and had not attacked her, though, afraid as she was, she was not prepared to terminate the Treaty herself. Thus, from the point of view of Czechoslovakia's being able to react properly to a flagrant violation of the Treaty (and a basic norm of contemporary *ius cogens*), and to leave, definitely, the arrangement that proved to be a disaster for the smaller partners, it would be essential that there be no exceptions in the behaviour of all the remaining parties—and, looking at it from this angle, it would have been better had Rumania also threatened or attacked her. For this reason should Czechoslovakia have even perhaps asked Rumania to do so? And would Hungary, in 1956, have been better served, from the same legal standpoint, had she been attacked by all the other parties and not only by the USSR?

15. See Jerzy Tyranowski *Traktaty sojusznicze Polski Ludowej* ("Alliance Treaties of People's Poland"), Książka i Wiedza, Warsaw, 1972, pp. 166–167. The Soviet textbook *Kurs mezhdunarodnovo prava* ("Course in International Law"), in its volume VI dealing with "international law in relations between the socialist states," Izdatel'stvo Nauka, Moscow, 1973, just mentions the decision of Albania in a footnote on p. 113, without any comment whatsoever on the legal or other aspects of that act.

put on that country, aiming especially at her consent to the holding of "joint manoeuvres," with the participation of Soviet troops, on her soil (Rumania has permitted no such manoeuvres on her territory since 1962) and, more recently, allegedly also at Soviet *droit de passage* to and from Bulgaria, coupled with the construction of a railway.[16]

During the early stage of the WTO's existence, until the beginning of the sixties, China was present, as an observer, at the consecutive meetings of the Political Consultative Committee (1956, 1958, 1960, and 1961); and in 1959 she took part, as "full" participant, in the Conference of the Foreign Ministers of the Warsaw Treaty countries. Mongolia and North Korea were represented by observers at the 1960 and 1961 meetings of the Political Consultative Committee. In recent years the two latter countries—and Cuba—were mentioned as sending observers to the big multilateral manoeuvres of the WTO forces (see p. 32). But starting with 1962 no Communist "outsider" was represented at the meetings of the Political Consultative Committee.

By virtue of Article 4, paragraph 1 of the Treaty, the *casus foederis* is clearly limited to Europe. The relevant passage reads as follows:

> In the event of an armed attack in Europe on one or more of the States Parties to the Treaty by any State or group of States, each State Party to the Treaty shall, in the exercise of the right of individual or collective self-defence, in accordance with Article 51 of the United Nations Charter, afford the State or States so attacked immediate assistance, individually and in agreement with the other States Parties to the Treaty, by all the means it considers necessary, including the use of armed force. The States Parties to

16. Thus, for instance, between February 12 and 21, 1973, joint staff exercises —on maps—took place in Rumania, with the participation of the Joint Staff of the WTO and the national army, air defence and navy staffs of Bulgaria, Rumania and the USSR; the exercises were led by Yakubovsky—see *Życie Warszawy*, February 22, 1973. In June 1974 there were reports that strong pressure was being put on Rumania that she allow the construction of a Soviet military railway through the province of Dobrudja to Bulgaria, perhaps even coupled with the demand that extraterritorial status be granted to such a railway—see *The Financial Times* (London), June 12, 1974; and *Frankfurter Allgemeine Zeitung*, June 20, 1974.

In August 1974, the Western press mentioned that Rumania had granted permission for the passage of a convoy of Soviet military lorries to Bulgaria, on the condition that this be done during the night—see *The Times*, August 26, 1974. And in September 1974, news from Bucharest read that: "Both British and American diplomats were told here of concern that Russia may seek an excuse to send troops through Rumania because of tensions between Greece and Turkey and the Cyprus crisis"—see *The Christian Science Monitor*, September 5, 1974.

the Treaty shall consult together immediately concerning the joint measures necessary to restore and maintain international peace and security.

But, in fact, regions all over the world where Soviet political and military interests are involved—and these are increasingly conceived to be "global"—are also considered to be of common concern to all Warsaw Treaty members. "Consultations" are provided for by Article 3, para. 1 of the Treaty, reading:

The Contracting Parties shall consult together on all important international questions involving their common interests, with a view to strengthening international peace and security.

These "consultations," coupled with the taking of a "common position," may cover, as was the case, for instance, with the April, 1974 meeting of the Political Consultative Committee, Indochina, the Middle East, Chile, and Korea.[17] But apart from "consultations," this cooperation, in practice, also included *par excellence* military steps in connection with conflicts very much outside Europe and, what is more, not connected with an attack on the member countries of the WTO.

Thus, for instance, in his report to the Central Committee of the CPSU in February, 1964, Suslov, criticizing China, said that she had done nothing to support the "defence measures" undertaken by the Warsaw Treaty states against possible imperialist aggression against Cuba.[18] The WTO's Political Consultative Committee declared in 1966 and 1968[19] that they had already been giving and would continue to give even more help, including weapons, to North Vietnam, and stated their readiness to make it possible for so-called volunteers from their countries to go to fight in Vietnam if asked to do so by the North Vietnamese government.

In December, 1970 the same body, referring to what were classified as "insolent actions of American imperialism," declared solidarity with the nations of Vietnam, Laos and Cambodia, and stated that "acting in the spirit of the principle of proletarian internationalism, defending the cause of peace and progress, the socialist countries will continue to grant the nations of Indochina all-round support in order to oppose

17. See the communiqué and the four separate declarations in *Pravda*, April 19, 1974.
18. See *Pravda*, April 3, 1964.
19. For the final communiqués of these meetings, see *Pravda*, July 8, 1966 and March 9, 1968.

armed imperialist intervention."[20] The same was repeated in January, 1972.[21] Thus the Organization's activities were, officially, extended from Vietnam to the whole of Indochina.

In December, 1971, addressing the VI Congress of the Polish United Workers' Party, Brezhnev, referring to the Warsaw Treaty, mentioned aid given to Vietnam: "On all levels of the struggle—military, political and diplomatic—the Vietnamese nation may always rely on the aid of its friends." He then continued in one and the same breath:

> Fulfilling their international duty, the socialist countries are doing everything to cancel out the plans of the Israeli aggressors and their principals, to help the Arab nations in the defence of their just rights, to contribute to the assurance of a just peace in the Middle East.[22]

Thus, though not in an official document, the activities of the Warsaw Treaty Organization in the Middle East also were admitted to.

In 1969, allegedly, the USSR tried to extend the WTO's activities to participation in her conflict with China. There were, in this connection, Western reports on the failure of her attempts to obtain a common declaration condemning Peking for the Ussuri fighting,[23] quite apart from her proposal to bring Mongolia into the Organization to strengthen the Soviet position in her conflict with China.[24] (Mongolia was, on Soviet initiative, brought into Comecon in 1962.)

However limited the text of the 1955 Warsaw Treaty itself may be geographically concerning the *casus foederis*, the bilateral treaties on "friendship, cooperation and mutual assistance" of the new series, concluded between the USSR and its Warsaw treaty partners (starting with that concluded with Bulgaria in May, 1967),[25] provide for an absolutely unlimited *casus foederis* geographically. Thus, for instance, the Soviet-Czechoslovak treaty of May, 1970 stipulates in Article 10:

> Should any of the contracting Parties be subjected to an armed

20. See *Pravda*, December 4, 1970.
21. The "Declaration in connection with the U.S.A. aggression in Indochina," issued by the January, 1972 meeting of the Consultative Political Committee of the WTO. See *Pravda*, January 27, 1972.
22. See *Trybuna Ludu*, December 8, 1971.
23. See, e.g., *Frankfurter Allgemeine Zeitung*, March 24, 1969.
24. See, e.g., *The Guardian* (London), April 16, 1969.
25. See the USSR-Bulgarian treaty of May 1967 (*UNTS*, vol. 631 (1971), pp. 239–255); the USSR-Hungarian treaty of September 1967 (*UNTS*, vol. 632 (1971), pp. 89–103); the USSR-Czechoslovak treaty of May 1970 (*Pravda*, May 7, 1970); the USSR-Rumanian treaty of July 1970 (*Pravda*, July 8, 1970); and the USSR-East German treaty of October 1975 (*Pravda*, October 8, 1975).

attack by any country or group of countries whatsoever, the other party...will immediately give it all help, including military....

More recent Communist literature on the Warsaw Treaty also does not leave any doubt as to that fact. As two Polish authors remarked in 1971:[26]

...the Warsaw Treaty embraces the European part of the Soviet Union exclusively. Thus, in the case of a threat to the Far Eastern territories of the USSR, collective defence, provided for in Article 4 of the Warsaw Treaty, cannot be started. The Soviet Union may, from the formally legal point of view, demand help, but on the basis of bilateral treaties or because of its membership in the U.N. It is obvious that in such a case feelings of class and ideological solidarity may become the decisively important factor. For there is no doubt that even simple political common sense requires paying attention to phenomena taking place in distant regions of the world, because given the present technical possibilities they may exert direct influence also on problems of vital and direct interest to us.

There is also the problem of *what* help should be furnished by the contracting parties to each other in the case of *casus foederis*: whether this should be automatic full-scale involvement, including military forces, or whether the kind of help to be given should be up to the individual allies in each concrete situation.

One recalls that in the case of the negotiations on the text of the North Atlantic Treaty in 1948–1949 this problem was, from the point of view of the United States, a very delicate one.[27] It was precisely because automatic military involvement was unacceptable to the US Senate that Article V, para. 1 of the North Atlantic Treaty was drafted as it still stands.[28]

26. See M. Jurek and E. Skrzypkowski, *Układ Warszawski* ("The Warsaw Treaty"), Publishing House of the Ministry of National Defence, second edition, Warsaw, 1971, pp. 73–74.
27. See, e.g., the memoirs of Dean Acheson, *Present at the Creation, My Years in the State Department*, Norton and Company, New York, 1969, pp. 280–281. See also the memoirs of Harry Truman, Vol. II, *1946–1952. Years of Trial and Hope*, Signet Books, New York, 1965, pp. 286–287.
28. "The Parties agree that an armed attack against one or more of them in Europe or North America shall be considered an attack against them all and consequently they agree that, if such an armed attack occurs, each of them, in exercise of the right of individual or collective self-defence recognized by Article 51 of the Charter of the United Nations, will assist the Party or Parties so attacked by taking forthwith, individually and in concert with the other parties, *such*

As the text of the Warsaw Treaty was so drafted, for obvious reasons, as not to go beyond the relevant stipulations of its Western counterpart (strongly attacked!), the provision of its Article 4, para. 1 stipulates:

> In the event of an armed attack...each State Party...shall ...afford the State or States so attacked immediate assistance... by *all the means it considers necessary*, including the use of armed force (our italics).

But in this case also, as with the limitation of the Warsaw Treaty to Europe, the "limiting" provisions are, in reality, of no importance. Again one should refer here to the bilateral treaties of the new series on "friendship, cooperation and mutual assistance" (the same, incidentally, applied in this case to the analogous treaties of the old series), which provide for the obligation of each of the parties to "immediately afford it (i.e. the attacked party) all possible assistance, including military assistance, and support *with all the means at its disposal* (our italics)," and to the principle of "socialist (proletarian) internationalism."

What is more, a zealous Communist writer goes so far as to assert that even under Article 4 of the Warsaw Treaty, in view of the fact that military help would certainly be of decisive importance, the formulation "which it considers necessary" does not mean leaving freedom as far as the means are concerned to the country granting assistance (sic). "A state party to the Warsaw Treaty—the author preaches—should render all help necessary to repel an armed attack on an ally."[29]

---

action as it deems necessary, including the use of armed force, to restore and maintain the security of the North Atlantic area" (our italics). This is a much more cautious provision than that contained in Article IV of the Brussels 1948 Treaty.

29. See Tyranowski, *op. cit.*, pp. 185–186. The same allegation is repeated by Tyranowski's article "The Warsaw Treaty" in the *Polish Yearbook of International Law*, vol. IV (1971), Ossolineum, Wrocław-Warsaw-Cracow-Gdansk, 1973, p. 113. This is a strange overzealousness on the part of a "junior man," which one does not find in relevant Soviet works, e.g. in Bakhov, *op. cit.*, or in the already mentioned vol. VI of the *Kurs mezhdunarodnovo Prava*. Instead of trying to outdo his Soviet colleagues, Tyranowski would be well advised to improve the factual quality of his work. In his article, for instance, he misses out Rumania as one of the signatories of the Warsaw Treaty (p. 102), misses out the 1961 and 1963 meetings of the Political Consultative Committee and the 1966 meeting of the Ministers of Foreign Affairs, quotes the English text of Art. 4 of the Treaty twice, but in different wordings (pp. 112 and 117), avoids "delicate" issues, evidently has not read the proofs carefully, and demonstrates poor English.

Finally, as far as the *duration* of the Warsaw Treaty is concerned, its Article 11, para. 1 stipulates that the agreement would remain in force for twenty years. And, for the contracting parties which do not, one year before the expiry of that term, give notice of termination, it would remain in force for a further ten years. Thus, the Treaty was, initially, to be in force until May 1975, and for the countries which did not serve notice of termination before May 14, 1974, for a further period of ten years, i.e., until May 1985.

But, here again, one realizes that the stipulation about giving notice was, to a large extent, a paper provision. With the exception of Albania, which, separated from Moscow's direct grip, could risk withdrawal from the Treaty even earlier than the possibility provided for by it, these chances must have been considered almost non-existent for the other states-parties.

Should, for instance, Rumania have given notice of termination in 1974, she would have been taking a great risk because of the Soviet theory of "proletarian (socialist) internationalism"[30] or, more recently, "the class interpretation of sovereignty," amounting to what has been labelled in the West as the "limited sovereignty theory" or the "Brezhnev doctrine." The fear of this "doctrine" is still alive.[31]

30. See, in this connection, especially the speech by Gromyko to the Supreme Soviet in June, 1968 (*Pravda*, June 28, 1968); the now "famous" article entitled "Sovereignty and the International Duties of the Socialist Countries," by S. Kovalev in *Pravda*, September 26, 1968; Brezhnev in his speech at the Fifth Congress of the Polish Communist Party in Warsaw in November, 1968 (*Pravda*, November 13, 1968); the article entitled "Proletarian Internationalism and the Defence of the Conquests of Socialism" by E. Chekharin (*Pravda*, April 30, 1969).
In his speech in June, 1969 at the International Communist Conference in Moscow (*Pravda*, June 8, 1969), Brezhnev "indignantly" remarked: "Bourgeois propaganda goes out of its way to malign the principles of the independence, sovereignty and equality of the national contingents of the working class and communist movement. That is the purpose for which imperialist propagandists have fabricated and put into circulation the notorious theory of 'limited sovereignty.' " The Joint Soviet-Czechoslovakian communiqué of October, 1969 (*Pravda*, October 29, 1969), in which Czechoslovakia was obliged, barely one year after August, 1968, to "agree" that the invasion of her territory was an act of international solidarity, launched the term "class interpretation of sovereignty." Ample documentation on the "Brezhnev doctrine" is collected in Boris Meissner *Die "Brezhnev-Doktrin." Dokumentation*, Verlag Wissenschaft und Politik, Cologne, 1969.
31. See, e.g., Brezhnev's rather naive attempt to dispel Yugoslavia's fear of the potential application of the doctrine to her during his trip to that country in September 1971 (*Pravda*, September 23, 1971):
"We well know that there are in the world various forces that would have nothing

14

After the invasion of Czechoslovakia, a high-ranking Communist general remarked: "In the modern world the defence of a country in isolation, in a sort of autarchic way, independently of defence alliances, is not possible."[32]

And, in 1973, another high-ranking general repeated the same thesis, referring specifically to the Polish case:[33]

> ...we realize that within the configuration of forces in coalitions characteristic of the present era, a country like Poland cannot safeguard its security and permanent independence if it acts individually. It is only possible for us to achieve this in a close alliance with other states, in an alliance based on uniform political aims, a common socialist ideology, a homogeneous political and economic system and common state interests—in other words in the Warsaw Treaty.

The practical corollary to this kind of reasoning would be that any member country, in serving notice of termination to the Warsaw Treaty, would "multilaterally" disarm itself (though the bilateral treaties on "friendship, cooperation and mutual assistance," especially those with the USSR, would, of course, still exist) and thus also weaken the bloc as a whole. This, in turn, could hardly be tolerated by the rest of the "socialist camp," with the Soviet Union at the top.

3. Structure of the WTO

At the top of the Organization's structure is the Political Consultative Committee, in which the members are represented by the First (General) Secretaries of their respective Parties' Central Committees, the Prime Ministers, the Ministers for Foreign Affairs, and, in most

---

against hindering such a good development of our relations, that would try to exaggerate any divergencies, and endeavour by one means or another to drive a wedge between us. It was they that spread the tale about the so-called 'doctrine of limited sovereignty,' spread rumours about the Soviet armies being allegedly ready to move towards the Balkans, and many other fables (...) I think that it is not worth wasting time to refute all these slanderous fabrications."

32. Józef Urbanowicz "Basic Problems of the Defence Policy and Defence of the Polish People's Republic" in *Nowe Drogi* (Polish counterpart of the Soviet *Kommunist*), No. 10, October, 1968, p. 11. The author is Deputy Minister of National Defence and was Chief of the "Main Political Administration" of the Polish Armed Forces.

33. General Florian Sawicki, Chief of the General Staff and Deputy Polish Minister of National Defence, see *Życie Warszawy*, October 9, 1973.

cases, the Ministers of Defence (though they were, according to the published communiqués, absent during the 1972 and 1974 meetings). Other personalities may also participate (e.g., in 1974, the Chairmen of the State Councils from East Germany and Poland, and some high-ranking party "apparatchiki"—secretaries of the respective Central Committees, heads of the international departments of these committees, etc.). There have been, until now, fourteen meetings of this body (1956, 1958, 1960, 1961, 1962, 1963, 1965, 1966, 1968, 1969, 1970 (twice), 1972, and 1974).[34]

Twice in the Organization's history (August, 1961 and December, 1969), top-level extra-constitutional meetings took place. These were the Conference of the First Secretaries of the Communist Parties of the WTO's Member States which met in Moscow to reach a decision on the Berlin Wall;[35] and what was officially labelled as a "meeting of the leaders of the fraternal countries," which, apart from passing a new declaration on Vietnam, was mainly concerned with the old "European security" topic.[36]

Voting in the Political Consultative Committee of the WTO, in order that a resolution may be passed by that body, must be unanimous. Thus, in the kind of situation when, as in 1968, unanimity was not achieved on one item, due to Rumanian opposition, the following resulted: the final communiqué of the Committee's meeting, dated March 7, 1968,[37] voiced, concerning Vietnam, unanimous condemnation of the "criminal acts of American imperialists," and a suitable declaration was adopted and published in the name of all the seven participating States-parties to the Warsaw Treaty. Concerning the

34. Though there was no formal meeting of the Political Consultative Committee in 1971, there was, in the summer of that year, what was referred to as a "friendly meeting of the top-level leaders of the fraternal countries," which took place in the Crimea without the participation of Rumania, but with the participation of Mongolia—see *Pravda*, August 3, 1971. Similar "friendly meetings," this time with Rumania represented, also took place in 1972—see *Pravda*, August 1, 1972, and in 1973—see *Pravda*, August 1, 1973. There were no such meetings in the summer of 1974 and 1975.

35. See communiqué published in *Pravda*, August 6, 1961. A report on the discussions during those closed meetings was carried by *Der Spiegel*, August 15, 1966—"Konjev liess aufmarschieren."

36. Although, in contrast to the August 1961 meeting, the term "Warsaw Treaty" was not used in the relevant documents published in *Pravda*, December 5, 1969, the participants were identical with the top-level political figures from the Members of the WTO, and, for instance, *Polityka* (Warsaw) of December 6, 1969, spoke of the "party and governmental leaders *of the countries of the Warsaw Treaty*" (our italics).

37. See *Pravda*, March 9, 1968.

16

problem of the non-proliferation of atomic weapons and the pertinent draft treaty, on the other hand, the States Parties, according to the communiqué, "stated their respective attitudes." This was followed by a separate statement issued on behalf of six countries (without Rumania), not referred to as States-parties of the Warsaw Treaty.

Generally speaking, Moscow has always found, by one means or another, a "practical solution" to legally hopeless situations. When, in late 1961, she did not wish Albania, Peking's ally, to continue participation in the WTO, she simply "locked her out" from all cooperation, claiming that it was Albania that did not want to continue to participate. Albanian sources indicate that the contrary was true.[38]

And in the case of the invasion of Czechoslovakia in August, 1968, clearly illegal even from the point of view of Article 1 of the Warsaw Treaty (let alone the UN Charter), and in which Rumania would certainly not participate, they simply referred to it as an action by five countries (the USSR, Poland, East Germany, Hungary, and Bulgaria), with the WTO officially "forgotten."

Further down the scale, below the Political Consultative Committee, the Organization's structure splits into the "political" and the "military" parts.

The first is represented—on paper at least—by a Joint Secretariat and by a Standing Committee for the Elaboration of Recommendations in the Field of Foreign Policy Problems. While even the existence of the latter is rather doubtful, the Joint Secretariat is a very mysterious body. The Eastern press does not report any of its activities; formerly it was allegedly headed by the Chief of Staff of the Warsaw Treaty Organization's Joint Command, but early in 1969 Firyubin, one of the Soviet Deputy Foreign Ministers, was appointed to this post.[39] What is interesting to note is the fact that the appointee is not, as one might have expected, the Soviet Deputy Foreign Minister in charge of European affairs, but the one basically in charge of Asian affairs, a phenomenon of some significance in the context of the WTO.[40]

38. The texts of the pertinent Albanian notes of protest and declarations are given, in German translation, in Jens Hacker and Alexander Uschakow, *op. cit.* For an earlier collection of relevant documents see W. E. Griffith *Albania and the Sino-Soviet Rift*, The MIT Press, Cambridge, Mass., 1963.
39. This information, apparently not given by the Eastern press, was allegedly disseminated through the Bulgarian News Agency early in 1969. Firyubin's appointment was mentioned in M. MacIntosh "The Evolution of the Warsaw Pact," *Adelphi Papers*, No. 58 (London: The Institute for Strategic Studies), June, 1969, p. 19.
40. The fact that in his capacity as one of the Soviet Deputy Foreign Ministers Firyubin specializes in Asian affairs is confirmed, e.g., by his visit to Hanoi "on

The first time that Firyubin was officially mentioned in his capacity within the WTO was in January, 1972, when, in connection with a meeting of the Political Consultative Committee, he was twice referred to as "the Secretary-General of the Political Consultative Committee of States Parties to the Warsaw Treaty."[41] Identical references were made to him in connection with the 1974 Committee's meeting.[42] This title, one may note, is not "Secretary-General of the Warsaw Treaty Organization" (like Secretary-General of NATO, etc.), but Secretary-General of the Organization's top policy-making organ. And, as in the military part of the WTO (see below), the appointment of a non-Russian to this responsible post was apparently considered out of the question. Observing the WTO for years, one gains the impression that its Joint Secretariat—if it existed at all until recently—was only a tiny and extremely well "conspired" body.[43] The complete contrast to NATO's Secretariat is striking.

The conferences of the Ministers of Foreign Affairs (1959, 1966, 1967, 1969, 1970, 1971 (twice), and January 1973)[44] are an extra-constitutional body within the Organization's "political part." If more frequently repeated in the future, these conferences could be "insti-

---

the invitation of the Ministry of Foreign Affairs of the Democratic Republic of Vietnam" in February, 1970 (*Pravda*, February 17 and 25, 1970) or his presiding over the Soviet delegation at a "bilateral consultative meeting with representatives of the Ministry of Foreign Affairs of India" in May, 1970 (*Pravda*, June 2, 1970), etc. In June, 1972 the same Firyubin, already officially presented in January in his WTO capacity, was, without any reference whatsoever to the latter position, mentioned as Deputy Minister of Foreign Affairs of the USSR, accompanying Podgorny during his visit to North Vietnam (see *Pravda*, June 20, 1972). In October, 1973 he was the only one of the numerous Soviet Deputy Ministers of Foreign Affairs to attend to the Japanese Prime Minister and his group during their visit to Moscow (see *Pravda*, October 8–11, 1973). And in December, 1974, the same applied to his role in connection with the visit to Moscow of the Indonesian Minister of Foreign Affairs (see *Pravda*, December 24, 25 and 27, 1974).

41. See *Pravda*, January 26 and 27, 1972.

42. See *Pravda*, April 18 and 19, 1974.

43. A Western diplomat, later with NATO, who spent several years in Moscow and was very much interested in the WTO, told the present writer in the summer of 1969 in Brussels that he was never able to come across information about any kind of activities of the WTO's Joint Secretariat.

44. The January, 1973 Moscow meeting of the Foreign Ministers of all Warsaw Treaty countries was just labelled as a conference of these ministers from the seven countries, without any reference to the WTO (see *Pravda*, January 17, 1973). This was probably connected with the decision to go to the Vienna multilateral balanced disarmament talks as individual countries rather than as the WTO.

tutionalized" and thus become a *pendant* to what has been, since 1969, the Committee of the Ministers of Defence of the Organization.

Some meetings of Deputy Foreign Ministers also took place—in 1969, 1970 and 1973 (with the participation of Mongolia)—the latest two being held in January and March, 1975 in Moscow and Warsaw respectively.[45] The January 1975 meeting was attended, according to the communiqué, by "Secretary-General" Firyubin.

The "military part" comprised, until 1969, only two bodies: the Joint Command and the Staff of the Joint Armed Forces.

The Joint Command had always been headed by a Russian, at the same time Soviet First Deputy Minister of Defence: Marshals Koniev, 1955–1960; Grechko, 1960–1967; since then Yakubovsky. Thus, Soviet Deputy Ministers of Defence and of Foreign Affairs—without giving up their national positions!—head both the military and the political parts of the WTO. According to Western sources, Rumania's Ceaucescu has campaigned, to no avail, for the Commander-in-Chief to be rotated among generals of all member states.[46]

What is more, the Deputy Commander-in-Chief is also a Soviet military man—one should mention here I. Stepaniuk, Lt. General of Engineering and Technical Services, referred to in this capacity several times by the "central organ" of the Soviet Ministry of Defence, the newspaper *Krasnaya Zvezda*.[47] It seems that his responsibilities have been mostly in the field of infrastructure. Absolute Russian domination in the Joint Command is thus obvious.[48]

---

45. See *Pravda*, February 1, 1975, and March 22, 1975.
46. See Reuter from Bucharest in, e.g., *The Christian Science Monitor*, June 28, 1974. Similar Rumanian demands were, allegedly, presented already in 1966—see, e.g., *Frankfurter Allgemeine Zeitung*, May 21, 1966.
47. See, e.g., his WTO "anniversary" articles in *Krasnaya Zvezda* of May 14, 1970, May 14, 1971, and May 14, 1972. Characteristically, Communist literature never refers to the existence of a (Soviet) Deputy Commander-in-Chief of the WTO's forces.
48. The extent to which the Soviets just ignore the alleged "international character" of the WTO is well illustrated not only by the fact that their top military men, sent to head the "Joint Command," retain their functions as Soviet First Deputy Ministers of Defence (the same also applies, as was mentioned, to the Secretary-General of the Political Consultative Committee, who retains his position as one of the Soviet Deputy Ministers of Foreign Affairs), but also by the fact that very frequently the Soviet press does not even bother to refer to their "international" function. When, for instance, after the death of Marshal Malinovsky in 1967, Marshal Grechko, at that time Commander-in-Chief of the WTO forces, was appointed Minister of Defence, his biography in *Pravda* (April 14, 1967) did not even mention his WTO position held between 1960 and 1967. When Yakubovsky published his "anniversary" articles on the

The staff of the Joint Forces has also always been headed by Russian generals: Antonov, 1955–1962; Batov, 1962–1965; Kozakov, 1965–1968; Shtemenko since the summer of 1968. Absolute Russian domination in the Staff was obvious at least until 1969.[49] It is only starting with the second half of 1969 that more participation of high-ranking officers from the other members may be observed,[50] without

WTO in May for many years in *Pravda*, he was referred to in the heading as "Marshal of the Soviet Union" exclusively (see e.g., *Pravda*, May 14, 1972). The same applies to a reference to Yakubovsky's participation in a meeting in Moscow to celebrate the 30th anniversary of the Bulgarian People's Army — see *Pravda*, September 20, 1974, and to references to his participation during the visit to Moscow of the East German Minister of National Defence — see, e.g., *Pravda*, September 30; and October 3, 1975. Concerning the "Secretary-General" see footnote 40.

49. The situation, as it looked in 1959 (and, with possible minor changes, probably up to 1969) was reported by the defected former Polish Colonel Monat: "It [the WTO] does have its headquarters in Moscow. And all seven satellite countries are represented there. But the representation is ludicrous. Each satellite keeps only one officer stationed regularly at pact headquarters. In the case of Poland, it is a colonel. Hungary sends a lieutenant colonel. Only Bulgaria seems to have enough generals on hand to waste one in Moscow. These officers have the softest jobs I have ever heard of. They are nothing but glorified liaison officers and office boys. Their duties consist mainly of sending unimportant papers back and forth between Moscow and their own general staffs back home. The real military orders go through the same channels they have always taken — direct from Moscow to the general staffs of the subordinate satellite armies." See Pawel Monat with John Dille *Spy in the U.S.*, Harper and Row, New York, Evanston, 1961, p. 189.

50. The final communiqué of the Budapest March, 1969 meeting of the Political Consultive Committee (published in *Pravda*, March 18, 1969) mentions, *inter alia*, the adoption of a new Statute of the Joint Armed Forces and the Joint Command, and of other documents. These texts were not published, but one outcome may be greater participation of "allied" officers in the Joint Command, a thing much demanded by Rumania and also by Czechoslovakia (in 1968). In the autumn of 1969 Polish newspapers (see, e.g., *Życie Warszawy*, November 20, 1969) reported the departure of Polish Vice-Admiral Studziński for a "responsible post" on the staff of the Joint Armed Forces of the WTO. This was the first mention of this kind in the Eastern press that the present writer ever came across. In the summer of 1971 the Polish press, reporting on the arrival of the new Polish Ambassador to Moscow, mentioned, among the people who greeted him, the same vice-admiral, referred to as "Deputy Chief of Staff of the Joint Armed Forces of the Warsaw Treaty," — see, e.g., *Życie Warszawy*, June 29, 1971. He was mentioned, once again in the same capacity, in October 1973 in connection with a solemn meeting at the Staff of the Joint Armed Forces in Moscow, devoted to the 30th anniversary of the Polish People's Army. During that meeting, opened by Yakubovsky, Studziński read a paper, and the floor was also taken by one of the Polish Deputy Prime Ministers visiting Moscow — see *Życie Warszawy*, October 10, 1973.

changing the situation in principle.[51] This is not only characterized by a situation in which the Chief of Staff "must" always be a Soviet military man, but the same, evidently, is also a "must" concerning the First Deputy Chief of Staff (at present Lt. General K. K. Pashuk).[52]

According to the April 1973 Convention concerning the Juridical Personality, Privileges and Immunities of the Staff and other Administrative Organs of the Joint Armed Forces of the States-Parties to the Warsaw Treaty,[53] "The Staff of the Joint Armed Forces consists of generals, admirals and officers of the states-parties to the Warsaw Treaty..." (Article 1, para. 1). There are working in the Staff "employees detached by the state in which the Staff is located" (Article 1, second sentence). As the Headquarters of the Staff are in Moscow (Article 1, para. 3), all these employees are Russians. The preamble to the Convention refers, *inter alia*, to the fact that "the general tasks and the role of the Staff and other administrative organs of the Joint Armed Forces are determined by documents accepted by the States-Parties to the Warsaw Treaty." These mysterious documents were never published.

The address of the Joint Command and the Staff, apart from the fact that they are located in Moscow, has never been disclosed; they are probably located in the Soviet Ministry of Defence.[54] The Joint Command and the Staff of the Joint Armed Forces have their permanent representatives in the WTO's member countries; they are always

---

51. Generally speaking, the situation seems to be well characterized by an alleged gibe of the Soviet Defence Minister Marshal Grechko, in conversation with a group of East European generals assigned to Warsaw Treaty headquarters: "You can have a voice in the policy-making process—but not a vote"—See *Newsweek*, May 19, 1969.

52. It was mentioned, for example, that he delivered a report during a meeting organized in Moscow to celebrate the 19th anniversary of the signing of the Warsaw Treaty—see *Krasnaya Zvezda*, May 14, 1974. Here again, as is also the case with the (Soviet) Deputy Commander-in Chief, pertinent Communist literature never mentions the existence of a (Soviet) First Deputy Chief of Staff of the WTO's forces.

53. The full text of the Convention was carried by *Krasnaya Zvezda*, April 27, 1973. An English translation is given in our Annexes (No II.) This convention, in our opinion, could mean a step towards the building-up of an international façade to what *de facto* still basically remains an appendix to the Soviet Ministry of Defence.

54. According to the Moscow correspondent of the *International Herald Tribune* (October 4, 1972), there were rumours that new military headquarters of the WTO were to be established outside the city of Lvov (Lwów). But after the clear statement in the April 1973 Convention that the staff (and other administrative organs of the WTO) are located in Moscow, these rumours should be dismissed.

Russian generals, e.g., in Poland Col. General Kosmin and in East Germany Col. General Rudakov.[55]

In 1969 two new military bodies of the Organization were created: the Committee of the Defence Ministers and the Military Council. This was coupled with a fairly far-reaching reorganization of the whole "military part" of the WTO.

The turning point was the March, 1969 meeting in Budapest of the Political Consultative Committee. Its final communiqué stated in this connection:[56]

> The Political Consultative Committee heard the report of the Commander-in-Chief of the Joint Armed Forces on the measures worked out by the Ministers of Defence with the approval of the respective governments. The states-participants of the Conference considered in detail and unanimously accepted the statute concerning the Committee of the Defence Ministers of the States-parties to the Warsaw Treaty, the new statute of the Joint Armed Forces and the Joint Command and other documents aimed at the further perfecting of the structure and of the administrative organs of the defence organization of the Warsaw Treaty.
>
> The Commander-in-Chief of the Joint Armed Forces was instructed to ensure, in accordance with established procedure, that the adopted decisions are put into practice.

Concerning the background of the Committee of Defence Ministers, one should recall the five conferences of the Organization's Defence Ministers, which were already held in 1961, 1962, 1963, 1966, and 1968. Starting with its institutionalization in 1969 (the statute mentioned in the March 1969 communiqué was never published), it should be considered, on paper at least, the Organization's top military body. Its first announced meeting took place in December 1969,[57] and was followed by one meeting every year.

In May 1970 Marshal Yakubovsky, referring to the Committee, mentioned that it occupied itself with the "elaboration of agreed upon recommendations and proposals in the field of the strengthening of the defence capabilities of the allied countries."[58] The formulation, in

55. See, e.g., *Życie Warszawy*, December 23–26, 1973; and *Neues Deutschland*, September 29, 1973.
56. See *Pravda*, March 18, 1969.
57. See *Pravda*, December 24, 1969.
58. See *Pravda*, May 14, 1970. An identical formulation regarding the Committee of Defence Ministers of the WTO is used in the *Yezhegodnik Bol'shoi Sovetskoi Entsiklopedii* ("Yearbook of the Great Soviet Encyclopaedia"), 1972, p. 471.

22

the context of the article, would indicate that these recommendations and proposals may be prepared for presentation to and final approval by the Political Consultative Committee or the governments of the individual member countries.

The communiqué on the Committee's 1971 meeting stated, *inter alia*:[59]

> During the meeting, problems of perfecting the structures of the armies of the Warsaw Treaty were considered. The participants in the meeting consider it fit to take appropriate steps for the future development of the system of communications and the means of command.
>
> The Comittee of Ministers of Defence subsequently heard a report on the prospective development of the armies and navies of the member states of the Warsaw Treaty.
>
> Taking into consideration the steady strengthening of the aggressive NATO bloc, the participants in the meeting decided to continue to strengthen the armies of the Warsaw Treaty and equip them with modern arms and military equipment.
>
> Decisions agreed upon on the questions discussed were passed.

According to the above fomulation—and those used in the communiqués of the 1973, 1974 and 1975 meetings—the Committee itself took the pertinent decisions. There might well be two categories of matters to be dealt with, some of an "ad referendum" character, and some being conclusively decided by the Ministers of Defence themselves.

The communiqué of the two-day meeting in February, 1972 refers to the Committee's deliberations as follows:[60]

> During the deliberations the military and political situation in Europe and the problems of further perfecting the means of communication and transportation, as well as other problems of the functioning of the Joint Armed Forces, were examined.

Finally, the communiqués of the meetings of the Committee of Defence Ministers of February 1973, February 1974 and January 1975 were quite general.[61] They just stated that "during the meeting questions connected with the current activities of the military organs ("command organs" in 1975) of the Warsaw Treaty Organization were dealt with." The passing of agreed upon decisions on the questions discussed was also mentioned.

59. See *Pravda*, March 4, 1971.
60. See *Pravda*, February 10, 1972.
61. See *Pravda*, February 9, 1973; February 8, 1974; and January 9, 1975.

To the Commander-in-Chief of the Joint Armed Forces was added, also in 1969, apart from the Staff, a Military Council formed of himself, the Deputy Ministers of National Defence of the member countries (thus holding the same national position as that of Yakubovsky and his other Soviet predecessors), and the Chief of Staff of the Joint Armed Forces. Any statute or other legal document concerning this new body was also never published.

The first news of the Council's existence came in January 1970, when General Shtemenko mentioned it in his article in *Krasnaya Zvezda*.[62] He referred to a meeting of that body which took place in December, 1969, two weeks before the already mentioned December, 1969 meeting of the Committee of Defence Ministers. Since then the Eastern press reports successive meetings of the Military Council, taking place twice a year.

We reproduce here the main parts of the short communiqués issued after the March 1974 (Budapest) and November 1974 (East Berlin) meetings of the WTO's Military Council (the second coupled with a conference of the "leading cadres" of the armies of the Warsaw Treaty countries):[63]

> In the Military Council current problems concerning the activities of the Joint Armed Forces were discussed and agreed upon recommendations were adopted.

And:

> The results of the land, air and sea training of the Joint Armed Forces and of the operative preparedness of the staffs were summed up and the tasks for 1975 set. Problems of the future activities of the Joint Armed Forces, of mutual interest to the armies of the member states of the Warsaw Treaty, were considered.
> The Ministry of National Defence of the GDR shared with the participants of the meeting and of the conference the experience gained in conducting a series of training measures in the units of the National People's Army.

Also in 1969 yet another, though rarely mentioned body, the Technical Committee of the Joint Armed Forces, was created.[64] It is in charge of

62. See *Krasnaya Zvezda*, January 24, 1970.
63. See *Pravda*, March 29, 1974, and November 22, 1974.
64. See, e.g., the collective work *Wybrane Problemy Międzynarodowe* ("Selected International Problems"), Książka i Wiedza, Warsaw, 1972, p. 503; and Gen. Shtemenko in *Krasnaya Zvezda*, May 14, 1975.

24

the coordination of armament and technical problems. It is probably here that most of the co-operation between the WTO and Comecon takes place.[65]

Finally, in February 1973, according to information unconfirmed officially,[66] the already mentioned February 6–8, 1973 meeting of the Committee of Defence Ministers passed a resolution on the establishment of a central organ for the coordination and "standardization" of the activities of the Security Forces of the WTO's member countries.[67] This new organ was planned to be a "sub-committee" attached to the Joint Command of the armies of the WTO. That secret resolution was subject to ratification by the governments of the member countries, and was, in fact, ratified with the exception of Rumania.

By the end of February 1973, still according to Radio Free Europe information, the first meeting of the ministers of internal affairs of the WTO countries, or their delegates (with the exception of Rumania), took place in Warsaw. It was after that meeting that the Polish and Czechoslovak Ministers of the Interior, together with a group of high-ranking collaborators, went by helicopter to Szczecin and were killed in an air crash.[68]

Later news from the same source,[69] while confirming the creation of the

65. Concerning the link existing between the work of the WTO and Comecon, the Polish *Rocznik Polityczny i Gospodarczy 1973* ("Political and Economic Yearbook 1973"), Państwowe Wydawnictwo Ekonomiczne, Warsaw 1974, p. 19, in an article by Gen. Sawczuk (one of the Polish Deputy Ministers of National Defence) states the following: "The production of some kinds of armaments would be too expensive and too complicated under our conditions. That is why only Soviet deliveries can fully satisfy our needs in this field. Of course, the developing process of socialist integration and the rational division of labour between the countries of Comecon and the Warsaw Treaty allow much more effective use of common resources."
66. See *Na Antenie*, April, 1973, pp. 30–31. This monthly is published in London by the Polish section of Radio Free Europe.
67. One may note in this connection that the "Security Forces" in the Communist countries include whole military-type units, used in cases of big-scale riots, etc. (e.g. in December 1970-January 1971 in Poland). In October 1974 these units were given the name, in Poland, of "Military Units of the Ministry of the Interior"—see *Dziennik Polski* (London), December 17, 1974.
68. This air crash was officially reported—see, e.g., *Trybuna Ludu*, March 2, 1973.
69. See *Na Antenie*, June-July, 1973, p. 44.

new body, whose provisional name allegedly runs "Committee on Internal Security of the Warsaw Treaty States," stated that, contrary to initial plans, the Committee would not function within the military part of the WTO but would be directly subordinated to the leadership of the Communist parties of these countries.

During 1974 there was news of further "integration" of the security forces of the Warsaw Treaty countries. According to this information,[70] an international centre specializing in the combatting of defections to the Western countries has been established, on the initiative of East Germany, with headquarters in Świdnica (Poland). And Czechoslovak legislation on the tasks of the security forces, passed in April 1974, stipulates that these forces are co-responsible for the security of the whole "camp" and obliges Czechoslovak forces to co-operate with the security forces of the other countries of the "camp." The August 1974 Bulgarian decree on "The Security of the State" makes it mandatory for Bulgarian citizens to report to the authorities facts, acts and "intentions" aimed against the security not only of Bulgaria, but also of the other countries of the "bloc."

4. *Main Political and Military Activities*

Reflecting on the main activities of the WTO, one can try to distinguish between the political and military fields—although both aspects are closely related, interdependent and overlapping.

Regarding the political side, it should be noted that at the 24th Congress of the CPSU in 1971 Brezhnev stated that the Organization was continuing to serve "as the main centre for coordinating the external political activity of the fraternal countries."[71]

In this field one witnesses various "coordinated" moves reflected in declarations of the Organization's Political Consultative Committee. An analysis of these reveals certain "type declarations," varying from the rather insignificant to the very consequential.

On the one hand, we observe some declarations which one would initially have qualified as mainly propaganda, though they were partially coupled with a "useful" plan (of internationally upgrading

70. See *Der Kurier* (Vienna), August 4 and 8; and September 21, 1974.
71. See *Pravda*, March 31, 1971.

the Ulbricht régime). This was the case with the ideas put forward many times of liquidating simultaneously both the WTO and NATO or, as a compromise (1968, repeated in 1974), their military parts only, and/or (and here the practical aim of upgrading East Germany came into play until this was achieved in the early seventies) of signing a non-aggression pact between the member states of the two organizations or even an all-European security treaty. The latter idea, brought forward by the WTO's Political Consultative Committee in 1966, was very energetically re-launched in 1969, and strong pressure started to be exerted on the West to hold what was initially labelled an "All-European" Conference and later the "Conference on Security and Cooperation in Europe."

All these proposals were initially given the cold shoulder by the West.

The acceptance of the first proposal (i.e. the simultaneous liquidation of the WTO and NATO) would mean a dismantling of Western North Atlantic military and political institutionalized multilateral cooperation, leaving Eastern cooperation still in existence on the basis of the complete network of bilateral treaties on "friendship, cooperation, and mutual assistance," and the absolutely dominating position of the CPSU and the Soviet armed forces in the "camp." The conclusion of a non-aggression pact, on the other hand, was unnecessary in the light of the relevant provisions of international law (the UN Charter and the Briand-Kellogg Pact), and, secondly, its political aim (international recognition of East Germany) was obvious.

But the propagandistic use of these Communist proposals was clear—to create the impression that they are looking for peace, offering the liquidation of hostile military organizations, and the signing of non-aggression pacts, whereas the Western powers are rejecting the friendly hand stretched out towards them.

Later, the constant pressure from Moscow and its mobilized allies (especially the Poles), coupled with playing on the Berlin situation and with actions well organized by Communists and fellow-travellers from inside,[72] finally brought evident success to what was once referred to

72. For instance, "The European Conference of Communist and Workers' Parties" which took place in Moscow in 1970, dealing with "Collective Security and Peace" in Europe (see *Pravda*, January 16, 1970) or the so-called "Conference of the Representatives of the Social Forces of European Countries for Security and Cooperation," which took place in Brussels in June, 1972 with the alleged participation of around a thousand people. On the activities of the so-called "International Committee of the Representatives of Social Forces acting in favour of security and cooperation in Europe," which created three standing Commissions—political, economic, and cultural—and a "permanent secretariat" —see, e.g., *Życie Warszawy*, December 5, 1972. Sessions of the "International

as a "coordinated diplomatic offensive of the member countries of the Warsaw Treaty."[73,74] This success is reflected by the fact that in 1973 a *de jure* recognition of East Germany by the Western powers was achieved, she was admitted to the UN specialized agencies and, in September, was admitted to the UN itself. Thus a long-standing political aim of the WTO has definitely been achieved.

Another success was the holding of the Helsinki preparatory talks between November 1972 and June 1973,[75] the July 1973 meeting at ministerial level, the second stage of the Conference being held in Geneva between September, 1973 and July, 1975.

Committee" were also arranged during the period when the CSCE was taking place, to put additional pressure on the Western governments and accelerate its conclusion according to Moscow's wishes—see, e.g., the communiqué of the April 1974 Brussels session—*Pravda*, April 9, 1974. The timing and the "identity of views" of that session with those of the Political Consultative Committee of the WTO, which met nine days later, are striking. A new meeting of the Committee took place in early 1975 (see *Pravda*, February 2, 1975), and the second conference took place at the end of April 1975 in Belgium (see *Pravda*, April 30, 1975). One may also mention in this context such ventures as the October 1973 "World Congress of the Forces of Peace" in Moscow, with its "International Committee for Continuation of Activities and Liaison," whose chairman is the notorious Ramesh Chandra, Secretary-General of the World Council of Peace—concerning its autumn 1974 meeting, see, e.g., *Życie Warszawy*, October 29, 1974.

73. Formulation used in an article entitled "Our Place in the Alliance," published in *Życie Warszawy*, January 26, 1971.

74. As an ambassador to NATO pointed out to the present writer in the summer of 1972, "NATO people" know that the West does not need that Conference and that it is in the interests of the other side. But strong pressure was exerted for years, pressure that was energetically supported by certain elements from within NATO countries. What is worse, it was added, some politicians at home (his own Foreign Minister was quoted) just do not fully believe and understand what is known by the inner circles of NATO about the "other side."

75. The disappointing developments concerning European security that took place precisely during the period when the Helsinki preparatory talks were being held, and the rather pessimistic outlook for the future were excellently characterized (with sound conclusions) by *The Economist*, June 9–16, 1973—"European conference. It's not won yet.": "The only change in the security situation in those six months is that Russia has reportedly put another 1,200 tanks into central Europe. (. .) Six months' preliminary hard labour at Dipoli (. . .) has not in fact opened up any real crack in the monolith that is the biggest obstacle to European cooperation and security. Further months of second-stage work, in commissions that may meet in the milder setting of Geneva, lie ahead. During these months it will be essential for the western delegates not to lose sight of the crucial importance of shifting the barriers that now divide Europe, nor to lose hope of shifting them. If they cannot be budged, it would be better to let the whole conference peter out than to fake a final declaration that gave

28

Now that the other side has achieved, on August 1st, 1975, the signing of the Final Act of the Conference on Security and Cooperation in Europe, the whole idea, of course, has attained new dimensions. It was clearly intended, apart from gaining a "final" multilateral confirmation of the *status quo* in Europe, to tap Western resources to the utmost—and finally precipitate what is considered to be unavoidable victory in the intensifying international class struggle.[76] Some Western "concessions" in this respect are, incidentally, quite inexplicable.[77]

Concerning the psychological impact of the relevant Communist offensive on many Westerners, one well-known Polish journalist mentioned at the end of 1972:[78]

> ...the conscious activity of the Socialist states, which are persistently working for détente. They have an ally in West European public opinion, or at least a considerable part of it. The process of détente has already produced its own dynamics and "infected" public opinion. Détente—and this is not at all of such small importance at a time of various snobisms—has become fashionable; he who declares for it is not subject to ostracism.

Europeans a perilously misleading impression that something had really been done to increase the security of their continent."

76. See, e.g., Erich Honecker: "...the ideological struggle is increasing in scope and intensity—and this is not in spite of the policy of peaceful coexistence, but precisely as a consequence of it"—*Schlusswort des Ersten Sekretärs des ZK der SED...auf der 8. Tagung des ZK*" in the weekly *Volksarmee* (East Berlin), no. 51/1972.

77. A striking case in point was the construction, by Fiat, of the 800 million dollar Togliatti auto plant in the USSR. Its general wisdom apart, according, e.g., to *Time*, March 5, 1973 ("Ordeal on the Volga"), the venture has been, for Fiat, a "virtually profitless ordeal"—unexpected costs ate up 100 million in fees that it received from Moscow (sic). How it came about that such a gigantic contract did not contain sufficient built-in guarantees assuring a profit independently of any rising costs remains a mystery. Another example was the American-Soviet wheat deal of 1972, which, according to John Melcher, member of the US House of Representatives' Agriculture Committee, "unnecessarily cost the U.S. taxpayers about 300 million dollars in subsidies and gave the Russians a bargain buy, instead of making them pay the full market price"—see *New York Times*, April 9, 1973. The fact that the 1972 deal was "subsidized excessively by the U.S. government" was later confirmed by a report of the US General Accounting Office—see, e.g., *The Christian Science Monitor*, July 19, 1973.

78. See Zygmunt Broniarek in *Polityka*, December 23, 1972.

Some other declarations of the Political Consultative Committee involved mixed propagandistic and intimidation aims. This may be said of the 1966 and 1968 declarations on the readiness to make it possible for "volunteers" from the Warsaw Treaty countries to go to Vietnam if asked to do so by the North Vietnamese government.

Still another of these declarations, clearly intended to intimidate, turned out to be a large-scale political bluff. This was especially the case with the threat of the signing of a separate peace treaty with East Germany, including the so-called "guarantees of the sovereign rights of the German Democratic Republic" and the so-called "regulation of the situation in West Berlin." The declaration of August 5, 1961 voiced the "unshakable determination" of the Warsaw Treaty States to achieve this before the end of 1961. Fortunately enough for world peace, nothing of this sort ever happened.

But there were also important decisions of immediate consequence, to mention only three: the construction of the Berlin Wall in 1961; the official announcement of massive help, including what are called "defensive weapons," sent to North Vietnam, made by the Consultative Political Committee starting with the second half of the sixties; and the official announcement of all-round help to Communist forces throughout the whole of Indochina, made in 1970 and repeated in 1972.

Turning to the military side of the Warsaw Treaty Organization's activities, an analysis of this aspect must be made against the background of a situation when the proportion between the armed forces of the USSR and the armed forces of all the other six members is over three to one; and the USSR has a monopoly of nuclear weapons. Small wonder, then, that—apart from dependence on Soviet arms supplies—the Soviets can make the decisions in the fields of organizational structure, standardization of arms and methods of training, and that Soviet military doctrine prevails.[79] This disproportion of powers within the alliance also leads to a situation where the USSR can, as it did in 1972, speak quite unceremoniously on behalf of the Organization without bothering to have an appropriate multilateral resolution passed.[80]

79. Thus, for instance, in his article in *Pravda*, May 14, 1972, devoted to the 17th anniversary of the signing of the Warsaw Treaty, Marshal Yakubovsky referred to the "socialist armies" as "developing on the Leninist principles of military construction, having generally a one-type organizational structure, combat technique and armament."

80. In February, 1972, upon instructions from their government, the Soviet

30

Starting with the early sixties, scores of officially announced joint military manoeuvres of the Warsaw Treaty Organization countries' forces and joint staff exercises have taken place. Their scope has gradually been broadened and their frequency increased, especially in 1969.[81]

Special attention should be paid to the big multilateral WTO manoeuvres. Here one should mention: "Oder" in 1962 on the territory of East Germany, with the participation of Soviet, East German, Polish, and Czechoslovak troops; "Quartet" in 1963, same territory and participants; "October Storm" in 1965, same territory and

Ambassadors to Athens and Washington handed in declarations in connection with the plans to establish naval bases in Greece for the American VI Fleet. In the note to Greece, couched in fairly threatening terms, there was, among other things, a passage stating that in this connection "the Member Countries of the Warsaw Treaty must draw appropriate conclusions, important from the point of view of their security"—see *Pravda*, February 16, 1972.

81. During 1969 alone the following WTO manoeuvres and exercises were reported: (1) joint Soviet-East German exercises at the beginning of March (*Życie Warszawy*, March 5, 1969); (2) joint Soviet, Bulgarian and Rumanian exercises between March 25 and April 1, 1969 (*Pravda*, April 2, 1969); (3) joint Soviet, Polish, East German, and Czechoslovak exercises between March 30 and April 4, 1969 (*Pravda*, April 6, 1969); (4) joint air defence exercises on the territories of Poland, Czechoslovakia, Hungary, and the western parts of the Soviet Union and "those of other countries" between April 14–16, 1969 (*Pravda*, April 15, 1969); (5) joint army exercises, on the territory of the USSR, of Soviet, Rumanian, Bulgarian and Hungarian troops between May 14–19, 1969 (*Yezhegodnik Bol'shoi Sovetskoi Entsiklopedii*, 1970, p. 446); (6) joint Soviet-Hungarian exercises at the beginning of June, 1969 (*Życie Warszawy*, June 8–9, 1969); (7) joint Soviet-Czechoslovak exercises at the end of June 1969 (*Pravda*, June 27, 1969); (8) joint Soviet-Polish and East German exercises between July 4–11, 1969 (*Pravda*, July 12, 1969); (9) joint air force exercises in Czechoslovakia and other member countries between July 23 and August 2 (announced by the spokesman of the Czechoslovak Defence Ministry, here quoted after *Le Monde* (Paris), August 5, 1969); (10) joint Soviet-Czechoslovak exercises between August 10–15, 1969 (*Pravda*, August 16, 1969); (11) the big-scale "Oder-Neisse 69" manoeuvres of September, 1969; (12) joint Soviet, Polish, East German and Czechoslovak exercises in October, 1969 (*Pravda*, October 10, 1969).

These joint military exercises, individually reported by the press, embrace only a small part of the total number of joint, especially bilateral, exercises. Thus in October, 1967 the East German Defence Minister, in an interview with *Neues Deutschland* (East Berlin)—here quoted after *Neue Zürcher Zeitung*, October 29, 1967—disclosed that, since 1964, Soviet and East German armed forces held ten joint command exercises of higher staffs, ten joint command exercises of higher staffs with the participation of one Soviet and one East German division, sixteen joint land manoeuvres, four joint air defence exercises, and five joint naval exercises.

participants; "Rodhopi" in 1967 on the territory of Bulgaria, with Soviet, Bulgarian and Rumanian troops. In 1968 the "big manoeuvre" was the invasion of Czechoslovakia; during the same year the first big joint exercises of the Soviet, Polish, and East German Navies, known under the cryptonym "North," and extending to the Baltic, and, for the first time, to the Atlantic and the Barents Sea, also took place; the "Oder-Neisse" in 1969 on the territory of Poland, with the participation of Soviet, Polish, East German, and Czechoslovak troops; present at these manoeuvres were the Ministers of National Defence of Mongolia and North Korea and a representative of the "Revolutionary Armed Forces" of Cuba.[82] [In 1972 military manoeuvres of the Cuban Army were watched by "high-ranking representatives of the Soviet Union."][83] The manoeuvres "Brother-hood in Arms" were organized in 1970 on the territory of East Germany, with the participation of Soviet, East German, Polish, Czechoslovak, Hungarian, Bulgarian, and Rumanian troops (the last, according to Western sources, only represented by a group of officers). And, in 1972, "Shield-72" on the territory of Czechoslovakia, with the participation of Soviet, Czechoslovak, Polish, East German, and Hungarian troops. Also present during these last manoeuvres, apart from the Ministers of National Defence of the Warsaw Treaty members, were the same Ministers of "other socialist countries" (unspecified).[84] No such large-scale manoeuvres were organized in 1973 and 1974, evidently because Moscow did not want them to coincide with the first two stages of the "Conference on Security and Cooperation in Europe."

The question of the degree of the integration of the national armed forces under WTO command requires clarification. There was considerable confusion in this respect in the West.

In October 1968, in connection with the twenty-fifth anniversary of the "Polish People's Army," the following was stated:

Poland, according to the stipulations of the [Warsaw] Treaty, pledged to detach *in the case of war* and place at the disposal of the Joint Command a part of its armed forces, which we conventionally call *operative troops*. The operative troops are... destined to carry out operations within the framework of the Joint Command of the Warsaw Treaty; to realize, within allied cooperation, operational and strategic tasks in the case of an attack on the

82. See, e.g., *Życie Warszawy*, September 24, 1969.
83. See *Polityka*, December 23, 1972.
84. See, e.g., *Życie Warszawy*, September 13, 1972.

countries of the Warsaw Treaty, on the potential *external front* of the struggle against the imperialistic states of the military NATO bloc (our italics).[85]

Thus, according to the above-quoted, there was no integration of national troops of the WTO countries under an international (or rather Russian) command in "normal" peace time until the second half of 1968. Only the situation of the East German "National People's Army" was probably different.[86]

But when a crisis situation emerged, part or perhaps all of the operative troops *were* put under the Joint Command already in the early sixties. This apparently happened in the summer of 1961 in connection with the Berlin crisis (construction of the Wall) when, apart from Soviet and East German, also Polish and Czechoslovak troops were put on the alert and deployed;[87] and it also took place in the autumn of 1962, in connection with the Cuban crisis. In the latter case it was, probably in order to give more weight to the Communist "we mean business" posture, officially announced. In October 1962 a short communiqué was issued, reading as follows:[88]

In the Staff of the Joint Armed Forces of the Countries of the Warsaw Treaty.

85. Urbanowicz, *op. cit.*, (footnote 32), pp. 18 and 20. In spite of what Urbanowicz stated, one should keep in mind the *de facto* situation, characterized by Monat (*op. cit.*, p. 189) as follows: "The Soviet general staff still decides where each division is stationed, where the anti-aircraft guns are placed, how many tanks the Czechs will produce, how many guns and planes the Poles will build, how many trucks the Hungarians must provide and which army gets them. The pact is only a front. And its commander is the same Soviet marshal who in reality is the real boss of the satellite armies."
86. In the speech by Gen. Heinz Kessler, member of the C.C. of the SED and Deputy Minister of National Defence of East Germany, delivered in connection with the 54th anniversary of the Soviet Army (*Neues Deutschland*, February 23, 1972), it was stated: "Security and military policy have always been considered by our party and government as a collective problem of the States of the Warsaw Treaty, and the National People's Army was conceived, built up, educated and trained as solid part and parcel of the Joint Armed Forces."
87. The proviso, though, should be made that the man who took over the joint command in August, 1961 in East Germany was not Grechko, who was, starting with 1960, Commander-in-Chief of the WTO forces, but Marshal Konev, who held this function between 1955 and 1960, and, in the summer of 1961, was "reactivated" by Khrushchev, after Marshal Zhukov, also retired, declined the same proposal. At that juncture Konev temporarily replaced the then Army General Yakubovsky (now Commander-in-Chief of the WTO forces), who was, in 1961, Commander-in-Chief of the Soviet Forces in East Germany.
88. See *Pravda*, October 24, 1962.

As has become known, in connection with the provocateur activities of the American government and the aggressive intentions of the American militarists, the Commander-in-Chief of the Joint Armed Forces of the Warsaw Treaty countries, Marshal of the Soviet Union Grechko, A. A., called together officers representing the armies of the Warsaw Treaty countries on October 23, 1962 and issued directives pertaining to the bringing into force of a number of measures relating to a heightening of the war readiness of the armies and navies included in the Joint Armed Forces.

In November 1962 another communiqué under an identical title followed suit:[89]

In connection with the weakening of tension in the region of the Caribbean Sea and, linked to this, the weakening of tension in Europe, the Commander-in-Chief of the Joint Armed Forces of the Warsaw Treaty countries, Marshal of the Soviet Union Grechko A. A., issued a directive on November 21, 1962 concerning the revocation of a number of measures, decided upon on October 23, 1962, aimed at a heightening of the war readiness of the armies and navies included in the Joint Armed Forces.

Formal integration of some troops, also in normal peace time, occurred in 1969. Already in November 1968 Brezhnev mentioned "the work [then] carried out... on the strengthening and perfecting of the military mechanism of our union of brother countries..."[90] The final communiqué of the March 1969 Political Consultative Committee's meeting referred, as already quoted, to the *new* statute of the Joint Armed Forces and the Joint Command (which, of course, was never published).

The "permanent" integration of some elements, probably the best ones, of the members' operative armed forces under the Joint Command seems now to be beyond any doubt. It was first clearly admitted by General Shtemenko in January 1970.[91]

He stated *inter alia:*

For the collective defence of the socialist cause they [the Warsaw Treaty member states] have created mighty Joint Armed Forces. Allocated to them from the national armies by the decisions of

89. See *Pravda*, November 22, 1962.
90. Speech at the Fifth Congress of the Polish United Workers' Party—see *Pravda*, November 13, 1968.
91. See *Krasnaya Zvezda*, January 24, 1970.

34

their governments are formations and units, and also administrative units and rear headquarters. The Joint Armed Forces now include ground forces, air and naval forces, and also air defence forces.

Incidentally, the Joint Command, still according to Shtemenko, does not engage in day-to-day routine training of troops (which is still done at the national level), reserving for itself final decisions on important questions:

> The troop contingents allocated by the Warsaw Treaty member states for the Joint Armed Forces engage in daily combat and political training according to the plans of the national commands. However, the final decisions on the various issues concerning joint operations of the allocated troops, mutual assistance, and the exchange of experience are effected according to the plans of the joint command. A particularly important role is played here by troop and command-staff exercises.

And in 1972, Marshal Yakubovsky remarked:

> A clear manifestation of the close cooperation of the fraternal countries and armies is the creation of the Joint Command, the military council, the staff and other organs, exercising *direct* command over the Joint Armed Forces, *detached* according to the treaty by the allied socialist countries.[92] (our italics)

How this may look in a concrete case can be illustrated by the Polish situation. Poland, apart from its airforce, allegedly has four divisions of her elitarian land forces integrated under the WTO "Joint Command."[93] These are two mechanized divisions (the 1st Warsaw Mechanized Division "Tadeusz Kościuszko" and the 12th Mechanized Division "People's Army"), one armoured division (the 10th Sudetan Armoured Division "Heroes of the Soviet Army") and one airborne (the 6th Pomeranian Airborne Division).[94,95]

92. See *Pravda*, May 14, 1972.
93. See *Dziennik Polski*, September 2, 1974. The elitarian character of the 10th Armoured Sudetan Division "Soviet Army's Heroes" was referred to in connection with the sending of elements of that division to serve as the Polish contingent of the UN Emergency Force in the Middle East. This division—it was stated—belongs to the leading ones in the Silesian Military District—see *Życie Warszawy*, November 16, 1974. It may be added that the first Polish detachment to the UNEF was composed of soldiers of the 6th Pomeranian Airborne Division—see, e.g., *Życie Warszawy*, November 13, 1974.
94. According to other information, the number of the integrated Polish divisions may be higher than the four listed above.
95. In the book by R. A. Remington *The Warsaw Pact. Case Studies in*

One should also keep in mind the existence of the integrated air defence system within the WTO. There also probably exists an integrated command for the navies of the WTO member countries in the Baltic Sea.

The only problem which slightly complicates this otherwise clear picture regarding military integration within the WTO is the answer to the question of how Rumania and her armed forces fit into the general picture. Is this a case of a certain exception to the general rule, still grudgingly tolerated by Moscow? Or is the tolerance probably limited to respect for just one, most sensitive aspect—opposition to allowing foreign troops to hold manoeuvres on Rumanian soil?

Finally, one should mention that the whole attitude of the WTO is clearly militant, if not aggressive. In spite of all the declarations about its defensive character as an alliance of peace-loving countries, and about not interfering in the internal affairs of other countries,[96] and despite the constant accusations of NATO harbouring the most aggressive ideas, seriously threatening the outbreak of a new world war, etc.,[97] the real spirit of the WTO corresponds rather to what it accuses the other side of.

Soviet (and thus the Warsaw Treaty Organization's) military doctrine has always been "offensive," to an unbelievable extent in the past.[98] This military orientation still very much prevails, and military

---

Communist Conflict Resolution, The MIT Press, Cambridge, Mass, and London, 1971, the author voices the opinion on p. 184 that (in the early seventies!) "the East European troops allotted to the Warsaw Pact joint command would be under the military command of the pact commander-in-chief only in case of a generalized war." Remington seems to have relied completely on Radio Liberty Research No. CRD 374/70, which drew much too far-reaching conclusions from a Soviet book published just then (*Sovremennye problemy razoruzhenya*, Izdatel'stvo Mysl', Moscow, 1970). Later she goes so far as to predict that even in the future "political considerations make it most unlikely that this situation will change. The rule of unanimity and the extent of Rumanian objections would seem to preclude the establishment of an actually integrated command."
96. See, e.g., Marshal Yakubovsky in connection with the WTO's fifteenth anniversary, in *Pravda*, May 14, 1970.
97. See, e.g., Yakubovsky in connection with the WTO's seventeenth anniversary, in *Pravda*, May 14, 1972.
98. A good illustration of this may be found in the memoirs of the Soviet Marshal Ivan Bagramian *Tak nachinalas' vojna* ("Thus Began the War"), Vojenizdat, Moscow, 1970 (quoted here after the Polish translation, Warsaw, 1972, p. 226): "There is no point in hiding that before the war we mostly learned to attack, and did not pay enough attention to such an important manoeuvre as retreat. Now we have paid for this. It turned out that the commanders and the staff were not sufficiently prepared to prepare and execute the retreat manoeuvre. Now, in

plans are prepared accordingly, as was revealed, for instance, by the Czechoslovak General Sejna some time after he defected to the West (1971 and 1974).[99]

Nor should one dismiss too easily certain recent fairly alarming rumours.[100] What is more, the spirit just indicated is often coupled with attempts to incite hatred against the West. This seems to apply, for instance, to the indoctrination of the East German armed forces: "Our love for socialism includes our hatred for its enemies...love for socialism demands hatred for imperialism. This is our morality...."[101]

In *official* declarations, the top Communist military men are mostly very cautious. But from time to time some of them, especially the "younger brothers," offer us quite clear-cut ideas. To quote only a few: In 1967, Poland's Marshal Spychalski (now in disgrace) stated:[102]

> The countries of the Warsaw Treaty and the whole socialist system are developing their defences, whose aim is not only the defence of the present steadily increasing material and spiritual

the second week of war, we had in fact to learn from the beginning the most difficult art—the art of the execution of retreat."

99. See *Paris-Match* (here quoted after *Le Monde*, August 11, 1971). According to Sejna, secret military plans of the WTO envisaged that in the case of war its armies should reach the Rhine three days from the start of hostilities, and conquer France (which the Soviet Union hopes would not fight), the Benelux countries and Britain. New revelations followed in early 1974, when Sejna gave an interview for the Austrian TV and a report was published in the Viennese periodical *Profil*. According to that information the Eastern military plans provide for an immediate attack and occupation of (neutral!) Austria in the case of a "global" conflict and also in the case of a potential intervention in Yugoslavia. Whereas the ruling socialist party and Chancellor Kreisky tried to play down these allegations, the Austrian Defence Minister Gen. Lütgendorff admitted that these things are taken very seriously by his ministry—see, e.g., *Frankfurter Allgemeine Zeitung*, February 25, 1974, and *Neue Zürcher Zeitung*, March 3, 1974.

100. We are referring here to news carried by a serious Danish newspaper, *Berlingske Tidende* (here quoted after *Le Monde*, March 13, 1974), according to which four thousand soldiers of the 6th Polish airborne division are taking an extensive course in the Danish language, preparing them for potential commando action in Denmark in case of a conflict. This news was allegedly communicated to the Danish Ministry of Defence by West German intelligence. According to *Na Antenie* (published, since 1974, as an appendix to *Orzeł Biały*, London), April 1974, Danish military regulations are also being studied, in addition to the language, and exercises are taking place in full Danish and West German uniforms. Similar exercises were allegedly also embarked upon by the 5th East German parachute batallion stationed on the island of Rugen.

101. See *Armeerundschau* (a periodical for soldiers published in East Berlin), No. 1/1974.

102. See *Nowe Drogi*, November 11, 1967.

achievements of the socialist nations, but also a fight to *limit* imperialistic influence, expansion and intervention, a struggle with the prospect of the *elimination* of exploiters and the old regime from the life of nations. It is not a passive, wait-and-see posture, but active defence of eminent international importance; a defence involved in a permanent, multi-levelled offensive of the forces of progress and peace (our italics).

In 1972 the East German Minister of National Defence, General Heinz Hoffmann, said:

> Strongly united with our class brothers, the glorious Red Army, and with all the allies of our community in arms, we are in a position from which the peace offensive of socialism may, at any time, be protected militarily with confidence.[103]

And Peter Florin, who became, starting with September 1973, Permanent Representative of East Germany to the United Nations, had this to say on the WTO members' foreign policy:

> The common foreign policy of the socialist community of states is aimed at the securing of favourable international conditions for the construction of socialism in our countries and for the further advance of all revolutionary forces in the world.[104]

What is more, all these recent formulations should be seen against the general background of Marxist-Leninist teaching in this field, well illustrated, for instance, by the following formulation of Lenin going back to 1918:

> If war is waged by the proletariat after it has conquered the bourgeoisie in its own country, and is waged with the object of strengthening and developing socialism, such a war is legitimate and 'holy.'[105]

Similar statements have been repeated again and again.[106] And in 1974 a Soviet military writer had, among other things, this to say:

103. See *Junge Welt* (East Berlin), September 29, 1972.
104. See *Horizont* (East Berlin weekly), No. 41/1972.
105. See V. I. Lenin, *Collected Works*, Lawrence & Wishart, London—Progress Publishers, Moscow, 1965, vol. 27, p. 332.
106. See, in this connection, e.g., *Istoria Vsesojuznoi Kommunisticheskoi Partii (bol'shevikov), kratkij kurs* ("History of the All-Union Communist Party [Bolsheviks], Short Course"), Moscow 1952—the Communist "ideological bible" between 1938, when it appeared, and the condemnation of Stalin in 1956—p. 161. The "History" refers to bolsheviks distinguishing between just

38

THE
UNIVERSITY OF WINNIPEG
PORTAGE AVE
WINNIPEG
CANADA
DISCARDED
2E9

The Marxist-Leninist thesis about two kinds of wars—just and unjust—makes it possible to assess each concrete war correctly, to determine the role which it will be able to play or has already been playing in the development of society, in the liberation of the peoples and classes from oppression of various kinds. While dealing with the question it would be a grave mistake to rely upon the statements of the belligerents, as well as to judge the war only by the formal symptoms: who attacked first and where the troops stand...(...)...the social character of each war in our time must be determined proceeding from the interests of the socialist revolution of the proletariat and the national-liberation revolutions of the oppressed peoples, it must be assessed from the positions of the major motive forces of social progress—the world socialist system, the international working-class movement and the national-liberation movement of the peoples.[107]

The potential consequences of such a militant philosophy for the West should be constantly kept in mind.

5. *The WTO 1955–1975: General Appraisal*

The decision to create the Warsaw Treaty Organization, which gradually matured in Moscow in 1954 and finally materialized in May 1955, was based on a variety of considerations. To quote, in this connection, just one reason, as is done by the "other side," is hardly acceptable.

During its existence of twenty years' duration, the Organization has undergone considerable development.

Its publicized activities between 1955/56 and 1960 were mostly

---

and unjust wars, defining the first as "just war, not a war of conquest, but a war of liberation, having as its aim either the defence of a nation from external attack... or *the liberation of a nation from capitalist slavery*, or, finally, the liberation of colonies and dependent countries from the yoke of imperialism" (our italics). In a 1973 article by Z. J. Pietraś entitled "An Attempt at Classification of Wars" in the quarterly *Studia Nauk Politycznych* ("Studies in Political Science"), published in Warsaw (No. 4/1973, p. 93), we read: "In Marxist teaching a distinction is made between two types of war, according to their historical content: 1. a just war, not of conquest, having as its aim the defence of a nation from external attack, or the *liberation of a people from capitalist suppression*, or the liberation of colonies or dependent countries, 2. an unjust war of conquest, ..." (our italics).
107. See Colonel Ye. Rybkin, D.Sc. (Philosophy) "Just and Unjust Wars"— *Soviet Military Review* (Moscow), No. 4 (April) 1974, p. 10.

limited to the political field, to certain declarations of the Political Consultative Committee. These may be considered as first exercises in "institutionalized" political multilateralism.

Here belong, for instance, appeals for a summit meeting, under the condition, however, that the problem of the reunification of Germany will not be dealt with by it (as this, allegedly, could be done only by the two German states between themselves); an East-West non-aggression pact (unnecessary in view of the UN Charter and the Briand-Kellogg Pact); disarmament (though, let us add, without agreeing on on-the-spot inspection); the "Rapacki Plan," etc. Already then (1958) the "expansion of commercial ties" was also referred to. On the other hand, the decisions formally endorsed by the Political Consultative Committee meeting of 1958 to withdraw Soviet troops from Rumania—a decision now certainly very much regretted by Moscow—and about troop reduction (because of a changed strategic concept) should also be mentioned.

It is worth noting that already in those earliest years the WTO was beginning to demonstrate, to a certain degree, some "global" ambitions. This is well reflected in the communiqué of the 1958 meeting of the Political Consultative Committee,[108] in which "serious concern" was voiced about the alleged attempts of the governments of the United States, England, France, and "other colonial powers" to interfere in the internal affairs of countries of Asia and Africa; Indonesia, Algeria, Lebanon, the Yemen and Oman were specifically referred to in this connection.

Bigger developments connected directly or indirectly with the WTO started to take place in the sixties.

Initially these were perhaps most spectacular in the military field, with the great "take-off" of the early sixties, the joint manoeuvres, especially the big multilateral ones, and the starting of the meetings of Defence Ministers. Later, after the invasion of Czechoslovakia, a big institutional build-up, partially obscured by lack of publicity but nevertheless pretty evident, took place, including integration of part of the troops of the member countries also in peaceful times. Tiny Albania, it is true, was lost, Rumania started causing—and still continues to do so—certain inconvenience during the last ten years or so (also, occasionally, embarrassing politically), but, generally speaking, the situation seems to be satisfactory for the time being from Moscow's point of view.

In the political field, apart from some misfired attempts at bluff

108. See *Pravda*, May 25, 1958.

(especially regarding West Berlin) and the painful decision to invade Czechoslovakia,[109] obvious achievements may be noted. One should mention the decision, successfully realized, on the construction of the Berlin Wall; the treaties between Moscow, Warsaw, East Berlin and Prague on the one hand and Bonn on the other; and the four-power treaty on Berlin—connected with the acceptance of "the realities of post World War II Europe," and the *de jure* recognition of East Germany by the Western countries.

The results achieved, an arrogant East German commentator stated, "clearly reflect that as the *power and influence* of the Soviet Union and of the socialist states fraternally allied with her grow, positive changes in the political climate in Europe are also gradually achieved"[110] (our italics).

The pathetic January 1973 Paris "Peace Agreement," followed by the offensive leading to the total taking over of South Vietnam in April, 1975, should also be mentioned. Gromyko stated in this connection in May 1975[111]: "The help given by the socialist countries to heroic Vietnam will never leave the memories of the nations. The many years of the struggle of that nation... were crowned with success to a tremendous degree precisely because of the acts of solidarity of the countries of the socialist Commonwealth..."

Lastly, whatever one may think of the Final Act of the CSCE,[112] it was clearly a considerable success for Moscow, if for no other reason then because it was Brezhnev who wished to have this Conference take place, its conclusion being his main political objective for many years. The rest will much depend on how persistently the West will

109. The invasion of Czechoslovakia is still scarcely mentioned in Communist literature on the WTO. On the contrary, as if such a thing had never happened, the *Kurs mezhdunarodnovo prava*, vol. VI, 1973 *(op. cit.)*, p. 116, e.g., states that "in the mutual relations of the socialist countries such pressure as threat of force or its application cannot be exerted on one another." The existence of these facts in the case of the foreign policy of the "Mao group" in China is explained by classifying them as "excesses," conditioned by the departure of that group, in international relations, from the principles of Marxism-Leninism and proletarian internationalism.

110. See Anton Latzo *Der Warschauer Vertrag—sozialistische Bündnisorganisation des Friedens* ("The Warsaw Treaty—Socialist Alliance Organization of Peace")—*Staat und Recht* (East Berlin), No. 5 (May) 1973, pp. 759–760.

111. See *Pravda*, May 15, 1975.

112. See, e.g., the very far-reaching criticism of Helsinki by Alexander Solzhenitsyn: "Soon, at the conference of the "35", the countries of Western Europe will of their free will ratify the enslavement of the brother countries of the East ... in the belief they are reinforcing peace." See *The New York Times, Week in Review*, June 22, 1975.

demand the observation of its content, especially the part on cooperation in humanitarian and other questions.

What also strikes one as regards the more recent political activities of the WTO is its attempt to extend its "global approach" to world politics. As was just mentioned, such attempts were already demonstrated, it is true, as early as in 1958. But they were, in principle, just short passages in the respective communiqués, expressing only "serious concern." What has changed in the meantime is the content, length and tone of similar declarations.

Characteristic in this respect is, for instance, the separate declaration entitled "An End to Imperialist Provocations Against the Independent African States!" adopted by the Political Consultative Committee of the WTO in December 1972.[113] Here, already in the title, the party agitation style was simply taken over for an intergovernmental document. Another illustration is the separate declaration adopted by the same organ in April 1974, entitled "Stop the Outrages and Persecution of Democrats in Chile!", containing, among other things, the passage that "In their struggle the people of Chile can continue to rely on the consistent support of the socialist nations." Such a declaration, of course, does not cost much *per se*, though it certainly increases international sabre-rattling.

In connection with her intention to have the CSCE successfully terminated, Moscow tried, during 1973–4, to tone down the military presence of the WTO: we already mentioned that there were no big multilateral manoeuvres organized, or at least announced, in 1973 and 1974. The same applies to 1975.

Also, in connection with the 19th anniversary, in May 1974, of the signing of the Warsaw Treaty, *Pravda* did not, in spite of a practice in existence for years, carry any pertinent article at all. The 1974 "anniversary" article in *Izvestia*,[114] written, this time, by a civilian (and not, as was usually the case, by Gen. Shtemenko), was strictly limited to political problems, and though it mentioned the Vienna talks it did not touch in any way on the military aspects of the WTO. But in *Krasnaya Zvezda* there was a relevant article by Marshal Yakubovsky,[115] referring, among other things, to NATO, "which was and remains an aggressive imperialist grouping" (in the communiqué of the April 1974 meeting of the Political Consultative Committee

113. See *Pravda*, December 4, 1971.
114. See W. Aleksandrov "The Mighty Factor of Peace and Socialism"— *Izvestia*, May 14, 1974.
115. See Yakubovsky "Reliable Guard of Peace"—*Krasnaya Zvezda*, May 14, 1974.

of the WTO, addressed to the broad public, NATO was classified as a "closed imperialist military bloc," but "aggressive" was not added).

The press coverage in connection with the 20th anniversary in May 1975, though, was more extensive and explicit. *Pravda* carried an unsigned article,[116] and in *Izvestia* Yakubovsky preached that "as before, a big danger to peace is presented by the aggressive North Atlantic bloc."[117] And in *Krasnaya Zvezda* Shtemenko published an article in the same vein.[118]

The very important position of the WTO in intra-bloc relations is now firmly established. One manifestation of this is the *expressis verbis* inclusion of references to the Warsaw Treaty in the texts of all the bilateral treaties on "friendship, cooperation and mutual assistance" now in force between the USSR and her six minor Warsaw Treaty partners (and also in the texts of the analogous treaties in force between the six *inter se*). In one particular case (the treaty of 1964 between the USSR and East Germany),[119] the Warsaw Treaty was even mentioned three times (!). In most cases it is mentioned twice (in the preamble and in one of the "operative" articles), and in one case—the treaty of 1965 between the USSR and Poland[120]—only once.

The importance of the WTO and its necessity for the "socialist camp," especially in the military field, is very strongly emphasized in the latest Communist literature. In this respect the East Germans try, as in many other fields, to outdo their Soviet masters. One of them states, for instance:[121]

> The alliance of the socialist states around the Soviet Union in a socialist military coalition offers the most advantageous possibilities for transposing the experience of the USSR, in the shortest time and in the most effective form, in the interest of the defence

116. "The Treaty of Peace and Socialism" in *Pravda*, May 14, 1975.
117. "On Guard for Peace and Socialism" in *Izvestia*, May 14, 1975.
118. "In Joint Battle Order" in *Krasnaya Zvezda*, May 14, 1975.
119. See *UNTS*, vol. 553 (1967), pp. 249–269.
120. See *UNTS*, vol. 540 (1965), pp. 97–100.
121. See Anton Latzo *Die Bedeutung des Warschauer Vertrages und der bilateralen Freundschafts—und Beistandsverträge für die Festigung der Einheit und Geschlossenheit der sozialistischen Staatengemeinschaft in Europa*. ("The significance of the Warsaw Treaty and the Bilateral Treaties of Friendship and Mutual Assistance for the Strengthening of the Unity and Cohesion of the Socialist Community of States in Europe"), in Siegmar Quilitzsch and Joachim Krüger (eds.) *Sozialistische Staatengemeinschaft. Die Entwicklung der Zusammenarbeit und der Friedenspolitik der sozialistischen Staaten* ("The Socialist Community of States. The Development of the Cooperation and Policy of

of socialism and peace. The necessity of the military coalition of the socialist countries and of their alliance around the Soviet Union is strengthened by the scientific and technical revolution which is also taking place in the military field. (. . .) The national defence of each European socialist country is most effective when it is firmly embedded in the coalition system of the Warsaw Treaty states and acts as an inseparable, stable part of the global defence of socialism . . .

Incidentally, the military capabilities which the other side generates "for the global defence of socialism" are characterized by our side, in the May 1975 NATO summit communiqué, as continuing "to grow in strength beyond any apparent defensive needs."[122]

Also strongly emphasized is the absolutely necessary coordination of the foreign policy of the communist countries, which, as was stated in the report of the Central Committee of the CPSU to the XXIV Party Congress (see p. 26), is centred within the WTO. Thus one Soviet writer states:[123]

The coordination of the foreign policy of the socialist countries is, in our days, one of the decisive factors in advancing the process of the normalization of international relations, creating favourable internal conditions for the construction of a socialist and communist society, furthering *the gradual march forward of the world revolutionary process* . . . (our italics).

In conclusion, the WTO has grown considerably, in every respect, during its existence of twenty years. The great role it is given, and is

Peace of the Socialist States"), Staatsverlag der DDR, Berlin, 1972, pp. 197 and 200. Concerning a certain difference in "militancy" between the East German *Scharfmacher* and their Soviet comrades, one may compare, for instance, the product of Latzo with the chapter on the WTO in the collective work *Mezhdunarodnye organizatsii sotsialisticheskikh stran (pravovye voprosy organizatsii i diejatel'nosti)* ("The International Organizations of the Socialist Countries (legal aspects of organization and activities"), Izdatel'stvo Mezhdunarodnye Otnoshenia, Moscow 1971, pp. 57–79.

122. See, e.g., *The Times* (London), May 31, 1975. And in an interview for *Der Spiegel*, September 15, 1975, the West German Defence Minister Georg Leber remarked: " . . . the fact should give everybody food for thought that we can prove objectively that the arms of the Warsaw Pact are of a pronouncedly offensive nature and far exceed what would be required for the defence of these countries. They are producing military superiority with the aim of capability for a military offensive."

123. See P. Tolmachev "The Coordination of the Foreign Policy of the Socialist Countries" in *Politicheskoe Obrazovanie*, No. 10 (October) 1973. Article reprinted in *Kommunist Estonii*, No. 11 (November) 1973.

supposed to play in the forseeable future, is beyond doubt. Thus, for the time being, the Organization will not only very much continue to exist, but will also, if Moscow has her way, grow even more—in law and in fact—and be continually used as an integration device in the military and political fields.[124]

124. Regarding the potential new provisions which may be imposed by Moscow into the text of the Warsaw Treaty No. II, probably to be concluded during the second half of the seventies, see p. 159.

Chapter II

THE COUNCIL FOR MUTUAL ECONOMIC ASSISTANCE (COMECON)[1]

1. *Background*

Comecon was created in January 1949 as what may strongly be suspected to have been Stalin's propagandistic countermove to the Marshall Plan and the creation of the OEEC in April 1948.[2] Stalin compelled the East European countries to reject Marshall aid,[3] and apparently wanted to create an "ersatz" Communist façade counterpart of the OEEC.

Eastern writers, of course, dutifully deny such an interpretation. They try to convince their readers that Comecon just had to emerge "as the manifestation of an objective necessity, resulting from the

1. The topic "Comecon" (and the organizations belonging to the "Comecon family") until 1968 has been extensively treated by the present writer in "The International Economic Organizations of the Communist Countries," two parts, *Canadian Slavonic Papers*, Vol. X, No. 3, 1968, pp. 254–277 and Vol. XI, No. 1, 1969, pp. 82–107.
2. Charles Alexandrowicz commented on this at the end of 1949 in "Comecon. The Soviet Retort to the Marshall Plan"—*World Affairs* (London), January 1950, pp. 35–36: "The answer of the East to the Marshall plan, though violent, did not at first take the form of coordinated action. Violence, however, did not prove to be its strength which was finally sought in organizational forms also (. . .) the East finally decided to supplement this negative attitude by taking positive steps. In January 1949, the press all over the world reported on a meeting of East European countries in Moscow, at which an economic agency was called into life, the Council of Mutual Economic Aid (Comecon)." On the other hand, future developments did not corroborate Alexandrowicz's fears of Comecon's "chief aim . . . in all probability, to attempt the disorganization of the international markets and to sow the seeds of unrest in the world" (p. 46). It is only much later, when the Comecon group is considerably stronger, that it may embark on certain practices damaging to the Western economy—see, e.g., "EEC Shipowners Complain about 'Unfair' Comecon Competition" in *Die Zeit* (Hamburg), February 14, 1975.
3. See in this respect Milovan Djilas: *Conversations with Stalin*, Harcourt, Brace and World Inc., 1962, pp. 127–128: "Yugoslavia and the Soviet Union were the only two East European countries that were decisively against the

development of the world socialist system."[4] The "declaration of cold war" (!), the "tricky" Marshall Plan, the "political and economic blockade," in other words "imperialist policy," "has only precipitated the objective process of the rapproachement of the socialist countries," and thus also the creation of Comecon.[5] Only exceptionally is something more "refreshing" suggested.[6]

The attempt to explain almost everything (including timing) by the "laws of historic materialism" would have been bearable, at least in this case, had Comecon, starting with its creation, embarked on

Marshall Plan—the former largely out of revolutionary dogmatism, and the latter from fear that American economic aid might shake up the empire it had so recently acquired militarily. Regarding the Marshall Plan, Molotov wondered whether a conference should not be called in which the Eastern countries would also participate, but only for propaganda reasons, with the aim of exploiting the publicity and then walking out of the conference at a convenient moment.... However, Molotov received a message from the Politburo in Moscow that he should not agree even to this. Immediately upon my return to Belgrade I learned that a conference of East European countries was to be held in Moscow to take a stand with respect to the Marshall Plan. I was designated to represent Yugoslavia. The real aim of the conference was to bring collective pressure to bear on Czechoslovakia, whose government was not against participating in the Marshall Plan. The Soviet plane was already waiting in the Belgrade airfield, but I did not fly the next day, for a telegram arrived from Moscow stating that there was no need for the conference—the Czechoslovak Government had abandoned its original stand."

4. See, e.g., as a typical example, Henryk de Fiumel *Rada Wzajemnej Pomocy Gospodarczej. Studium prawnomiedzynarodowe* ("Comecon. Study in International Law"), Państwowe Wydawnictwo Naukowe, Warsaw, 1967, p. 11. De Fiumel refers several times in his book to the present writer's article quoted in footnote 16, a few times with approval, but several times somewhat patronizingly, as a "bourgeois writer" who (like Agoston, Uschakow, and others) has a poor understanding of the realities of socialism (!). The fact that we were both junior scholars at the University of Warsaw until the end of the fifties seems to have been forgotten. As far as my opinion of his book is concerned, I consider it to be fairly superficial and clearly overcautious, the latter reflecting the posture of so many scared members of the "licenced" Democratic Party *(Stronnictwo Demokratyczne)* in Poland, one of whose top activists is de Fiumel.
5. See Nikolai Faddeev (Secretary of Comecon) "Internationale Wirtschafts-organisation sozialistischer Länder" in *Einheit* (East German counterpart of *Kommunist*), No. 1 (January), 1974. See also p. 34 of his book quoted in footnote 9.
6. See Tibor Kiss, *Hol áll a KGST—integratio?* ("How Far has the Comecon Integration Gone?"), Kossúth Könyvkiadó, Budapest, 1972, p. 15. He refers to "the opinion of some economists" in Hungary and in other socialist countries that the creation of Comecon meant a step back to the original idea of a customs union, proposed in 1947 by Dimitrov and Tito. Denying this, Kiss only admits that Stalin rejected the idea for political reasons. The thought easily comes to the reader's mind that the decision to create Comecon was perhaps conceived by Stalin to demonstrate an ersatz façade initiative.

tangible and gradually increasing activities. As, in fact, the Organization remained almost dormant during the first five years of its existence, and, as is also mentioned by the same author, its Secretariat was actually created only in 1954, the Western version of a "façade organization" during this first period is much more plausible.

The communiqué published by the Communist press under the title "About the Outcome of the Economic Conference in Moscow (regarding the creation of the Council for Mutual Economic Assistance)" appeared on January 25, 1949. That day was, until recently, considered to be Comecon's "birthday." In a press interview given by Faddeev, the Organization's Secretary, in early January 1974, he mentioned that the conference took place between the 5th and 8th of January 1949 and that Comecon was thus born on January 8th twenty-five years ago.[7] The question arises, of course, why, for two weeks or so, the conference and its outcome were kept secret—something that Faddeev does not mention.

The January 1949 communiqué had the following content:[8]

> In January of this year an economic conference was held in Moscow of representatives from Bulgaria, Czechoslovakia, Poland, Rumania, Hungary, and the Soviet Union, at which it was decided to create a Council for Mutual Economic Assistance. The conference ascertained considerable success in the development of economic relations between the countries named, reflected above all in a big increase in turnover of goods. Owing to the stabilization of economic relations and the realizing of a policy of economic cooperation, the countries of the people's democracies and the Soviet Union acquired the possibility of speeding up the reconstruction and development of their national economies.
>
> The conference then stated that the governments of the United States, England, and certain other countries of Western Europe are, as a matter of fact, boycotting trade relations with the countries of the people's democracies and with the Soviet Union, because these countries do not consider it possible to subordinate themselves to the dictates of the Marshall plan, as this plan infringes on the sovereignty of countries and the interests of their national economies.
>
> Taking this factor into consideration, the conference discussed the question of the possibility of organizing broader economic

7. See, e.g., *Życie Warszawy*, January 4, 1974.
8. See, e.g., *Pravda*, January 25, 1949.

cooperation between the countries of the people's democracies and the Soviet Union.

In order to realize broader economic cooperation between the countries of the people's democracies and the Soviet Union, the conference judged it indispensable to create a Council for Mutual Economic Assistance, consisting of representatives from countries participating in the conference on the basis of equal representation, whose task it would be to exchange economic experience and to lend mutual technical aid and mutual aid in raw materials, foodstuffs, machines and industrial equipment, etc.

The conference decided that the Council for Mutual Economic Assistance be an open organization which can be joined by other countries of Europe adhering to the principles of Comecon and wishing to participate in broad economic cooperation with the countries named.

The Council for Mutual Economic Assistance will adopt resolutions only with the consent of the country whose interests are involved.

The Council will periodically hold sessions in turn in the capitals of participating countries, under the chairmanship of the representative of that country in whose capital the session takes place.

Thus, as conceived in 1949, Comecon was to be a "clearing house" for the exchange of economic experience, granting of technical aid and for foreign trade. As a matter of fact there is not trace in the communiqué of what Faddeev tries to sell to his readers as the alleged first task given to the newly-established Organization: "the necessary coordination of plans for economic development on the basis of specialization and cooperation of production."[9]

Curiously enough, apart from the 1949 communiqué, no other—more normal—constitutional document of Comecon is known. Probably there did exist an unpublished agreement. But it was not until almost eleven years later, in December 1959, that the Charter of the Organization (and its Convention) were signed in Sofia, ratified

9. See N. W. Faddeev *Sovet Ekonomicheskoi Vzaimopomoshchi* ("The Council for Mutual Economic Assistance"), Izdatel'stvo Ekonomika, Moscow 1974, p. 35. Putting forward the standard arguments for the creation of Comecon that were already briefly discussed above, Faddeev (or his "ghost writer") commits a humoristic error in his zeal when he claims that Czechoslovakia received only one third of the reparations which had to be paid to her by the Federal Republic of Germany in . . . 1947! (*op. cit.*, p. 32).

and published in the Members' Official Gazettes, and later registered with the United Nations.[10]

The 1959 text was first amended by the XVI (Extraordinary) Session of Comecon of June 1962 and the XVII Session of December 1962.[11] These amendments, agreed upon without the participation of Albania, still formally a member, in a situation when Article XVI of Comecon's Statute requires, for the coming into force of amendments, their ratification by *all* Member States, must be considered illegal. Characteristically enough, these amendments were not registered with the United Nations and are not published in the UN Treaty Series.

The situation, legally speaking, is crystal clear. A most recent East European publication admits: "Formally the amendements did not enter into force, because the statutory requirement of ratification by all member states was not fulfilled (Albania being the only member that did not ratify the amendments). In practice Comecon functions on the basis of the new version..."[12]

10. English text in *United Nations Treaty Series*, Vol. 368 (1960), No. 5245.
11. The updated text was published, e.g., in *Rada Wzajemnej Pomocy Gospodarczej, Wybór materiałów i dokumentów* ("Comecon, Selection of Material and Documents"), Książka i Wiedza, Warsaw, 1964. The text reproduced in our Annexes (No. III) gives the original version and also indicates the 1962 and 1974 changes.
12. See Zbigniew M. Klepacki (ed.), *Encyklopedia Organizacji Międzynarodowych* ("Encyclopedia of International Organizations"), Książka i Wiedza, Warsaw, 1975, p. 446. Michael Kaser who, otherwise, seems to have taken into consideration, in the second (1967) edition, most of the critical remarks and additions which we made on the first edition of his *Comecon. Integration Problems of the Planned Economies*, Oxford University Press, 1965, in our review in *Soviet Studies*, Vol. XVII, No. 2 (October 1965)—see, e.g., pp. 4, 11, 82, 154 of his second edition, on pp. 245–246, though in principle admitting the illegality of the 1962 "amendments", nevertheless embarks on the strange and unnecessary argument that perhaps the admission of Mongolia was not illegal. His argument: "The excision of 'of Europe' by the Sixteenth Session has not been ratified, but it might be argued that the original Charter did not specify 'only to countries of Europe.'" Such an interpretation, from the legal viewpoint, and even from the point of view of common sense, is below criticism. Incidentally, the Comecon Charter reads "open to other countries of Europe" and not, as Kaser wrongly quotes it on p. 246—"open to all countries of Europe." It is also not clear why the second sentence of para. 2 of Article II of Comecon's Charter is missed out by Kaser on p. 236. The references by Kaser to the Rules of Procedure of the Session of the Council have the same value, but polemics with them are unnecessary in view of the things said above. Finally, when the present writer criticized Kaser for not knowing, in 1965, the texts of the 1962 "amendments", he referred to Kaser's formulation that the Bureau for integrated planning problems is "extra-statutory," which resulted from the fact that Kaser did not know at that time that in July 1962 this organ was brought—albeit illegally—into the text of

And the communiqué of the XXVIII Session of Comecon, which took place in June 1974,[13] stated that the Session had "approved amendments to the Charter of the Council for Mutual Economic Assistance and to the Convention concerning the Juridical Personality, Privileges and Immunities of Comecon, resulting from the [1971] Comprehensive Programme and the decisions adopted earlier by the Sessions of the Council." These amendments, which, legally speaking, should be classified identically with the 1962 ones, became available only in 1975.[14]

Comecon was, as already mentioned, almost completely dormant prior to 1954. Thus, certain things asserted by the Communists in connection with the Organization's anniversaries in 1959, 1969 and 1974 are not much more than propagandistic legends.[15]

2. Membership and Charter's Duration

The original members of Comecon in 1949 were the USSR, Poland, Czechoslovakia, Rumania, Hungary, and Bulgaria. Albania was admitted in February 1949, but has not participated since 1961,[16] although she never withdrew formally (she also never joined any of

---

the Charter. As we referred to the illegality of the 1962 changes in previous and later publications—e.g., in our French paper (see footnote 16), our review article in *Soviet Studies*, Vol. XVI, No. 4, April 1965 (quoted by Kaser), and in *Osteuropa-Recht* (see footnote 3 to Chapter III), we are obviously beyond suspicion of recognizing these amendments as legal. One cannot, of course, repeat it all in a review.

13. See *Pravda*, June 22, 1974.

14. The fully updated text of Comecon's Charter was published in the newly-established Comecon bulletin *Ekonomicheskoe Sotrudnichestvo Stran Chlenov SEV*, No. 1/1975, pp. 109–112. I am grateful to my friend Dr. Alexander Uschakow of the University of Cologne for furnishing me with a copy of this text. He was also the first to publish a Western translation (into German) of the 1974 texts of the Charter and the Convention—see *Europa-Archiv*, June 10, 1975.

15. See, e.g., Alexei Kosygin (then Deputy Chairman of the Council of Ministers of the USSR) in "Great Community of the Socialist Countries" (*Pravda*, April 28, 1959): "The creation, in 1949, of the Council for Mutual Economic Assistance, was an important occurrence in the life of the nations of the socialist countries."

16. For some details, see Richard Szawlowski, "Evolution du Comecon 1949–1963" in *Annuaire français de droit international*, 1963 (Paris, 1964), pp. 684–5 The texts of some Albanian declarations and notes of protest are reproduced in Hacker-Uschakow, *op. cit.*, pp. 201–202 and 242–244.

Comecon's "specialized agencies"); East Germany was admitted in September 1950, Mongolia in 1962 and Cuba in 1972.

The admission of Mongolia, and, ten years later, also Cuba, was illegal. Comecon's 1959 Charter, registered with the Secretariat of the United Nations and published in the UN Treaty Series (see footnote 10), stipulates in Article II, para. 2 that "Membership in the Council shall be open to other European countries..." This, *a contrario*, excludes non-European members. Changing this, in order to accept Mongolia (and later Cuba), would require an amendment to the Charter, which, according to Article XVI of that treaty, "...when approved by the Session of the Council, shall come into force immediately after the ratifications of those amendments have been deposited with the depositary by *all* member countries of the Council" (our italics). As Albania, a member then—and today—did not ratify, the amendment could not come into force (see above).

Yugoslavia was admitted as a sort of associate member (with participation in some organs only) in 1964. Article 1 of the 1964 agreement reads:[17]

> The Socialist Federal Republic of Yugoslavia will cooperate within the framework of Comecon regarding problems which are the object of mutual interest for the member countries of Comecon and the SFRY in the fields of foreign trade, monetary and financial relations, iron and colour metallurgy, the machine and chemical industries and the coordination of scientific and technical research. By way of agreement between the Executive Board of Comecon and the SFRY other fields may also be determined in which cooperation will be realized regarding problems which are the object of common interest to member countries and the SFRY.

As the situation looked until December 1973, Yugoslavia was participating in 12 out of 24 permanent organs of Comecon, and since then—in thirteen.[18] She has a permanent mission to Comecon in

17. Russian text of the agreement in P. A. Tokareva (ed.) *Mnogostoronnieje ekonomicheskoe sotrudnichestvo sotsialisticheskikh gosudarstv, sbornik dokumentov* ("Multilateral Economic Cooperation of the Socialist Countries, Collection of documents"), second edition, Juridicheskaya Literatura, Moscow, 1972, pp. 213–217. The Polish translation of this agreement is given in Bogusław W. Reutt (ed.) *Podstawowe dokumenty RWPG i organizacji wyspecjalizowanych* ("Basic Documents of Comecon and the Specialized Organizations"), Książka i Wiedza, Warsaw, 1972.
18. See, e.g., J. F. Charnicki "Yugoslavia and Comecon" in *Życie Warszawy*, February 7, 1973. During the 65th meeting of Comecon's Executive Board in December 1973, the Board agreed to extend Yugoslavia's cooperation within

Moscow. The XXVI Session of Comecon in July 1972 was, for the first time, attended by the Prime Minister (Chairman of the Federal Executive Council) of Yugoslavia. In connection with the tenth anniversary of cooperation with Yugoslavia, the 69th meeting of Comecon's Executive Board underlined in its communiqué that during that period the number of fields in which Yugoslavia had participated in the work of Comecon organs had increased over twofold.[19]

Trade exchange between that country and "full" Comecon members, which increased by 40 per cent during the period 1966–1970, was planned to increase, by 1975, by 85 per cent. During recent years, including 1974, it has been about 30 per cent of the total foreign trade of Yugoslavia. At the same time she also has fairly close links with Western international economic organizations.[20]

Some other Communist countries frequently send observers to the meetings of the Session of the Council, and especially to the meetings of certain Standing Commissions: North Korea, North Vietnam, and Cuba (and Mongolia) before joining the Organization. It is interesting to note that China was represented at the meetings of some Standing Commissions of Comecon up to the mid-sixties.[21]

The Comecon Charter provides in Article II, para. 2, that "Membership in the Council shall be open to other countries[22] which subscribe to the purposes and principles of the Council and declare that they

the organization to the field of construction problems—see *Pravda*, December 14, 1973; this entails her participation in the respective Standing Commission.

19. See *Pravda*, October 19, 1974.

20. Thus Yugoslavia has a sort of associate status with the OECD, cooperating fully in certain of the bodies and sending observers to some others. Concerning the EEC, she established (as the only Communist country before China followed her in May 1975) a permanent mission to that body in 1968, and three consecutive Presidents of the Commission of the Community, Malfatti, Mansholt and Ortoli, visited Yugoslavia in 1971, 1972 and 1975, respectively. A new trade agreement with the EEC was signed in June 1973. It provides, among other things, for the maintenance of the most-favoured nation clause, adds a "development clause," etc.—see, e.g., *Neue Zürcher Zeitung*, June 28, 1973. In November 1974 Miloš Minič, Vice-President of the Federal Council and foreign minister of Yugoslavia, had talks in Brussels with Ortoli and Soames, Vice-President of the Commission.

21. As late as February 1965 the participation of observers from China at the Session of Comecon's Standing Commission on Geology was reported—see *Życie Warszawy*, February 17, 1965. It may be noted in passing that the April 1964 declaration of the Rumanian Workers' Party (see footnote 91) suggested that ways should be found for all socialist countries (thus mainly implying China) to participate in Comecon.

22. The word "European" was missed out from the text of the Charter in the

agree to accept the obligations contained in the present Charter." As one of the purposes reflected in the preamble is stated as being "to continue the development of comprehensive economic cooperation based on consistent implementation of the international socialist division of labour in the interests of the building of socialism and communism in their countries...," the membership of non-communist countries is out of the question.

But the Charter itself provides in its Article X that the Council "may invite countries which are not members of the Council to take part in the work of the organs of the Council."

And the 1971 "Comprehensive Programme" (see below) also shows flexibility in this respect. In its Chapter XVII, para. 6 it stipulates *inter alia*:

> Any country which is not a member of Comecon may participate, in full or partially, in the realization of the Comprehensive Programme. A country which is not a member of Comecon may participate fully, if it shares the aims and principles of the Programme.

Thus, under these provisions, non-Communist countries may participate "partially" in the work of Comecon, and two of them in particular are envisaged by Moscow to be prevailed upon, under certain pressure if necessary, to establish fairly close relations with Comecon: first of all Finland, and also Austria. But whereas the latter will perhaps avoid these advances,[23] Finland has already been linked with Comecon.

Between March 12th and 13th, 1973, negotiations took place in Moscow between delegations of Comecon and Finland.[24] The first delegation was composed of Comecon's Secretary Faddeev (chief

---

summer of 1962 to make it possible for Mongolia to become a member. About the illegality of this amendment see footnote 16.

23. Concerning Austria and Comecon, it may be mentioned that when Chancellor Kreisky was asked by a Polish journalist, during his visit to Brussels in 1972, whether Austria intended to participate in some agreements with Comecon, his answer was noncommittal: "There is no one answer to this question. Any question concerning ourselves will be considered by us"— see *Życie Warszawy*, February 29, 1972. Over one year later Kreisky, during his visit to Budapest, appealed, at a meeting of the Hungarian Academy of Science, for direct cooperation between the EEC (to which Austria does not belong!) and Comecon—see, e.g., *Dziennik Polski*, March 31, 1973.

24. See *Pravda*, March 14, 1973. Already in July 1971 the Finnish government announced its intention to find out about the possibilities of closer relations with Comecon; the Foreign Ministry—it was announced—had already carried out detailed studies on this; and the Minister for Foreign Trade announced

delegate) and the deputy permanent representatives of all nine member countries to Comecon; the Finnish delegation was headed by that country's Minister of Foreign Trade. A draft agreement was agreed upon, providing for mutual cooperation in various fields of economy, science and technology. The creation of a cooperation committee composed of representatives of the Comecon members and Finland was also provided for. The delegations agreed that they would present the draft agreement to their respective (national) organs for consideration.

During Podgorny's April 1973 visit to Finland, speeches were exchanged with Kekkonen.[25] The latter, president since 1956, just confirmed, unconstitutionally, in his post for another four years (1974–1978), extolled the results of the Finnish-Soviet Treaty of 1948 as an example for everybody, and stressed Finland's pioneer role in the field of economic, scientific and technical cooperation with the USSR, followed only later by other countries. "In the light of this development"—he continued—"we are 'guilty' only because we were first. Now we are also preparing ourselves to take the first step, by concluding an agreement on cooperation between Finland and the Council for Mutual Economic Assistance."

The next day, *Pravda* announced that President Kekkonen had authorized the Minister for Foreign Trade to sign on behalf of Finland an agreement on cooperation of that country with Comecon.[26] The agreement was finally signed in May 1973,[27] ratified by the Finnish parliament at the end of the same month,[28] and "ratified" by the XXVII Session of Comecon in June.[29] The agreement between Finland and the European Community, on the other hand, though initialled already in the summer of 1972, was signed only in October 1973 and ratified in November 1973. But at the same time a characteristic declaration was passed by the Finnish parliament. It says that the agreement with the

---

that first contacts at the level of civil servants would be taken up with Comecon during 1971—see, e.g., *Neue Zürcher Zeitung*, July 31, 1971.

25. See *Pravda*, April 5, 1973.

26. See *Pravda*, April 6, 1973.

27. See *Pravda*, May 17, 1973. English text of the agreement reproduced in our Annexes (No. IX).

28. See, e.g., *Frankfurter Allgemeine Zeitung*, June 2, 1973.

29. See communiqué of the XXVII Session in *Pravda*, June 9, 1973. At the end of June Faddeev received a delegation of the Foreign Affairs Committee of the Finnish parliament, on the latter's request, and a discussion was held on the prospects of cooperation on the basis of the May agreement—see *Życie Warszawy*, June 26, 1973.

European Community has no influence on treaties previously concluded by Finland and does not imply any political connection; the foreign policy of Finland continues to be based on the Friendship and Assistance Treaty with the USSR. Finland will increase her cooperation with the USSR and the other Comecon countries. And if the agreement with the European Community were to damage closer relations with the USSR. Finland would give notice of withdrawal.[30]

The agreement with Comecon was evidently the price the country had to pay for Moscow's "fiat" to the treaty with Brussels.

The first meeting of the Finland-Comecon Commission took place at the turn of November and December 1973 in Moscow. It was agreed to start cooperation in selected fields of mechanical engineering, chemistry, transport, standardization and statistics, and in the scientific and technical fields.[31]

In March 1974, there were reports of a Conference of experts in the field of the chemical industry from Finland and from the member countries of Comecon, at which "concrete directions of future co-operation" were established. The results were to be presented for consideration to a working group composed of representatives of Finland and the Comecon countries.[32] And in May 1974, the first meeting of the working group in the field of mechanical engineering took place in Moscow.[33]

The second meeting of the Finland-Comecon Commission took place in October 1974 in Helsinki.[34] In this connection it was stated that after considering the proposals prepared by the working groups in the fields of foreign trade, mechanical engineering and the chemical industries, and in the fields of transport and scientific-technical co-operation, the Commission approved their activities and passed pertinent recommendations and decisions. It was decided that the next meeting of the Commission would take place in December 1975 in Budapest.

In the 1973 foreign trade of Finland, as compared with 1972, exports to Comecon countries decreased from 15.2 to 14.1 per cent, while imports increased from 15.1 to 15.3 per cent. Both figures increased considerably in 1974: to some 16.8 per cent of the total exports

30. See, e.g., *Frankfurter Allgemeine Zeitung*, November 20, 1973.
31. See *Neues Deutschland*, December 4, 1973.
32. See *Rynki Zagraniczne* (Warsaw), May 9, 1974.
33. See *Ekonomicheskaya Gazeta* (Moscow), No. 20, May 1974.
34. See *Życie Warszawy*, October 26, 1974.

and 22.1 per cent of total imports.[35] They will increase further in 1975.

Certain developing countries were also reported as being interested in establishing some ties with Comecon. In this context Iraq, India, Mexico, South Yemen, Iran and Argentina were already mentioned, in that chronological order, by the press.

Thus, in the autumn of 1972, there was news about the initiative taken by the leftist government of Iraq to obtain associate status with Comecon.[36] New negotiations were held in May 1973.[37] Finally, an agreement, the first of its kind concluded between Comecon and a developing country, was signed in July 1975.[38]

During October 1972, the Indian press reported from Moscow that Comecon "will welcome Indian participation in it as a full member (?—R. S.), or even as an observer...For its part the Soviet Union... would back India in any form of association it would like to develop with the community. Indian interest was indicated during the planning minister, Mr. D. P. Dhar's discussion with Soviet leaders last month."[39] But a few days later Mrs. Indira Gandhi clarified that India would not joint Comecon.[40] In April 1975 the Indian Ambassador to Moscow had a two and a half hour meeting with Faddeev.[41] It was mentioned on this occasion that one of the Ambassador's tasks in Moscow "is also to explore possibilities of mutually beneficial association with this body."

During the visit of the President of Mexico Echeverria Alvarez to Moscow in April 1973, there was news about a meeting of his deputy

35. For the 1973 figures, as compared with the 1972 ones, see *Rynki Zagraniczne*, March 9, 1974; for the 1974 ones, as compared with 1973, we rely on information kindly sent to us by the Pohjoismaiden Yhdyspankki in Helsinki. There are certain differences regarding the 1973 percentages as indicated by the two sources.
36. See, e.g., *The Financial Times* (London), October 10, 1972; and *Le Commerce du Levant* (Beirut), October 18, 1972.
37. See *Pravda*, May 17, 1973. The short piece of information reads: "Between May 10th and 15th meetings took place in Moscow between delegations of Comecon, headed by the Council's Secretary Faddeev, and of Iraq, headed by the ambassador of the Iraqi Republic in the USSR Salikh Mahdi Amash. The problem of the establishment of cooperation between Comecon and the Iraqi Republic was discussed. The talks took place in a spirit of mutual understanding and friendship."
38. See *Pravda*, July 5, 1975.
39. See *The Times of India* (Bombay), October 11, 1972—"Comecon Ready to Admit India."
40. See *The Times of India*, October 14, 1972—"India Not to Join Comecon."
41. See *The Hindu* (Madras), April 6, 1975.

minister of industry and trade with Soviet Deputy Prime Minister Lesechko and the Organization's Secretary Faddeev.[42] During that meeting a discussion took place on the activities of Comecon and possible future contacts between Mexico and the Organization. In October 1973 it was reported that Faddeev had received the Mexican Ambassador to the USSR and had had a conversation with him on problems of possible cooperation between Mexico and Comecon.[43] In October, 1974 there came news of new Mexican-Comecon negotiations.[44] In this connection the chief of the Mexican delegation, deputy minister of trade and industry E. Mendoza, declared that certain directions of concrete cooperation between Mexico and the Comecon countries were agreed upon with representatives of the Comecon Secretariat. He further stated that Mexico was interested in cooperating with Comecon in foreign trade, in the common development of industry, the working out of new technological processes, and exchange of experience in the field of transportation, agriculture and energy. Finally, in August 1975, an agreement between Comecon and Mexico, apparently similar to that with Iraq, was signed.[45]

In September 1973 the Soviet press[46] printed a short note with the information that Faddeev had received the deputy prime minister of the People's Democratic Republic of Yemen M.A. Ysheish, and had had a conversation with him concerning possible cooperation between the PDRY and Comecon.

In 1974 Columbia and Iran were also mentioned, rather casually, as countries showing interest in cooperation with Comecon.[47]

Finally, in May 1974, the joint Soviet-Argentinian communiqué, issued after the visit of the Argentinian Minister of Economy to Moscow, contained the following passage:[48]

42. See *Pravda*, April 14, 1973.
43. See *Pravda*, October 10, 1973.
44. See *Rudé Právo* (Prague), October 29, 1974.
45. See *Pravda*, August 14, 1975.
46. See *Pravda*, September 21, 1973. According to *Le Commerce du Levant*, September 1, 1973, the PDRY (traditionally referred to by the paper as Aden) was asking only for the status of an observer. The question was first raised, according to the same paper, in August 1973 by Abdul Fattah Ismail, Secretary-General of the political organization of the National Front of the Democratic Yemen, during a meeting with Brezhnev in the Crimea, and later discussed by him with Faddeev in Moscow.
47. Concerning Columbia, see N. W. Faddeev's book, *op. cit.*, p. 59; regarding Iran, see Faddeev, *op. cit.*, in *Einheit*, No. 1 (January) 1974.
48. See *Pravda*, May 11, 1974.

The Argentinian side expressed interest on the part of its government in establishing contacts with the Council for Mutual Economic Assistance, with the aim of organizing direct links with that organization and carrying out common operations with member countries of Comecon.

The Soviet side expressed its positive attitude towards such a possibility and noted that it would give its support in this matter. The Argentinian side received this declaration with satisfaction and announced that it would take appropriate steps in that direction in the near future.

Comecon's Charter—in contrast to that of the Warsaw Treaty—was signed for an unlimited period of time. It provides in Article II, para. 3 for giving of notice by Members and withdrawal from the Organization. But concerning the *real* possibilities of such a decision, which Moscow would consider to be dangerous "defection" and a clear weakening of the "Socialist Commonwealth," the situation is, *mutatis mutandis*, similar to that regarding the Warsaw Treaty Organization (see pp. 14–15).

Concerning Comecon specifically, one may draw attention to the formulation used in Chapter I, para. 2 of the 1971 "Comprehensive Programme." When elaborating on the further deepening and perfecting of economic and scientific and technical cooperation between the member countries of Comecon and the development of socialist economic integration, it is said that these are made "vitally indispensable" by, among other things, the "exigences of the class struggle with imperialism." The conclusion to be drawn is that any attempted "defection" from Comecon would be, "objectively speaking," a weakening of the fight against imperialism, and could not be tolerated.

And it would certainly be denounced by Moscow as a breach of the bilateral treaties of "Friendship, Cooperation and Mutual Assistance," all of them now providing for cooperation within Comecon.

3. *Structure of Comecon*

At the top of Comecon's structure, starting with the end of the fifties, were the Conferences of the Party and Government Leaders, meetings of which took place in 1958, 1960, 1962, 1963, and 1966. Although extra-statutory, they played, in fact, the most important role. Such a conference in June 1962, for instance, approved the "Basic Principles of International Socialist Division of Labour" and admitted Mongolia to Comecon; this only had to be rubber-stamped by the Session of the

Council. But after 1966 these Conferences were abandoned and the leading role of the Session of the Council was reestablished.

De jure, by virtue of the Charter, the highest organ of Comecon is the Session of the Council. Until the present, twenty-nine Sessions of the Council have taken place.[49] National delegations to the meetings of the Sessions of the Council were previously led by Deputy Prime Ministers of the member countries in charge of economic affairs; probably in order to upgrade that organ's importance, delegations were recently led by the Prime Ministers themselves, as was the case in May 1970, June 1971, July 1972 and June 1973, 1974 and 1975.[50]

In April 1969 the especially important XXIII "Special" Session of Comecon was attended by the First (General) Secretaries of the Communist parties and the prime ministers. Therefore that meeting did not differ, from the point of view of its participants, from the 1958, 1960, 1962, 1963, and 1966 conferences of the Party and Government Leaders mentioned above. But for some reason it was decided to hold the meeting withing the formal framework of a Special Session of the Council.

Since 1965, representatives of the Yugoslav government have also been participating in the meetings of the Sessions of the Council; in 1972 and 1974, Yugoslav delegations were headed by the Chairman of the Federal Executive Council (Prime Minister). And the Ambassadors of North Korea and North Vietnam have been participating in the capacity of observers (e.g., in 1973, the Ambassadors of the two states to Czechoslovakia, and, in 1974, the ones to Bulgaria). But as regards the 1972 Session, only the Ambassador of North Korea was mentioned in the communiqué, and in 1975, only that of North Vietnam. Observers from these countries (and China) were already present at the meetings of the Session of the Council in the late fifties and early sixties, though in the late sixties this participation almost petered out.

The competences of the Session of the Council are provided for in Article VI, paras. 1, 5 and 6 of the Charter of Comecon (see Annex No. III).

Immediately below the Session of the Council is the Executive Board,

49. Apart from twenty-seven ordinary sessions there was one (the XVI Session) called "extraordinary" in Moscow in June 1962 and one (the XXIII Session) called "special" in Moscow in April 1969.
50. At the June 1973 Session two members (Cuba and East Germany) were represented by their Deputy Prime Ministers; at the June 1974 and June 1975 Sessions Cuba was again represented by a Deputy Prime Minister.

created in 1962 to replace the so-called "Conference of the Representatives of the Countries in the Council." The Executive Board is composed of representatives of all Member States, and now meets "as a rule, once in a quarter" (every two months before July 1971); seventy-two meetings of that body took place up to June 1975. Deputy Prime Ministers head the national delegations.

The competences of the Executive Board are provided for in Article VII, paras. 1 (second sentence), 3, 4, and 5 of the Charter of Comecon (see Annex No. III).

The communiqué of the XXIII Session of Comecon's Council in April 1969[51] mentioned that "agreement was reached concerning the commencement of work for the preparation of proposals on the further streamlining of the functioning of the organs of Comecon and increasing of their role in the organization of cooperation."

This reform finally took place in the summer of 1971,[52] when two new bodies were created: the Committee for Cooperation in the Field of Planning, under which a Bureau works as the Committee's standing working organ (the former "Bureau for Integrated Problems of the Economic Plans," subordinated to the Executive Board), and the Committee for Scientific and Technical Cooperation (in connection with which the Standing Commission for Coordination of Scientific and Technical Research was liquidated). Both Committees are located in Moscow. The first of these bodies first met in January 1972,[53] whereas the first meeting of the second one took place slightly earlier — in December 1971.[54] The national delegations to these meetings are headed by the Chairmen of the State Planning Committees and the ministers or the chairmen of state organs for science and technology, respectively. And in June 1974 the XXVIII Session of Comecon decided upon the creation of a third committee — the Committee for Cooperation in the Field of Material and Technical Supplies.[55] Its first meeting took place in September 1974.[56] Article VIII, newly added to Comecon's Charter in June 1974, deals with the competeness of the Committees in its paragraphs 1, 3 and 4 (see Annex No. III).

---

51. See *Pravda*, April 21, 1969.
52. See communiqué of the XXV Session of the Council of Comecon in *Pravda*, July 30, 1971.
53. See *Pravda*, January 28, 1972.
54. See *Pravda*, December 3, 1971.
55. See communiqué of the XXVIII Session of Comecon in *Pravda*, June 22, 1974.
56. See *Pravda*, September 6, 1974.

In addition to these new bodies, the "Comprehensive Programme" (Chapter XV, para. 3) provides for the study of proposals concerning the creation of an international arbitration organ of Comecon. Nothing has materialized so far in this respect.

Following the Seventh Session of the Council (1956), Comecon started to set up its Standing Commissions. Until June 1975 there were twenty of them,[57] with headquarters in the capitals of different member states: 7 in Moscow, 3 in East Berlin, 2 in Budapest, 2 in Prague, 2 in Sofia, 2 in Warsaw, 1 in Bucharest, and 1 in Ulan Bator. In June 1975 the Standing Commissions for Civil Aviation and Medical Problems were created.[58] There are normally two or at least one meeting of each of the Standing Commissions in one year. The chairmen of these bodies are the respective ministers of the governments of the states in whose capital cities the individual Standing Commissions are located (e.g., the Polish minister of transport in the case of Comecon's Standing Commission for Transport, etc.). In those Standing Commissions in which cooperation is being developed in different fields, sections or standing groups are created.

In 1963 the Eastern press disclosed plans to concentrate all the Standing Commissions in Moscow,[59] once the construction of the new building for Comecon was terminated. This construction dragged on until 1969, but finally the above-mentioned plans, whose realization would mean an almost complete concentration of all Comecon business in Moscow, did not fully materialize, at least in the sense that most of them are still located in other capitals and their meetings take place there. One should mention, though, that the provision of the old Article VIII (now IX), para. 5 of Comecon's Charter in its pre-June 1974 version, reading "The meetings of the Standing Commissions shall, as a rule, be held at their permanent headquarters,

---

57. In existence were the Standing Commissions for: Electrical Energy, Mechanical Engineering, Agriculture, Black Metallurgy, Colour Metallurgy, the Petrol and Gas Industry, Chemical Industry, Coal Industry, Foreign Trade, Transport Problems, Construction Problems, Peaceful Uses of Nuclear Energy, Standardization, Statistics, Monetary and Financial Problems, Light Industry, Food Industry, Radio and Electronic Industry, Geology, and Communications. See, e.g., *Ekonomicheskoe sotrudnichestvo stran-chlenov SEV*, No. 1/1975, p. 105.
58. See *Pravda*, June 27, 1975.
59. See *Zycie Warszawy*, August 15, 1963.

which shall be designated by the Session of the Councils," was missed out from the text of the Charter in June 1974. Most of the preparatory work, on the other hand, is done in the respective divisions of Comecon's Secretariat in Moscow.

Apart from the Session of the Council, the Executive Board, the three Committees and the Standing Commissions, yet another type of organ (not provided for in Comecon's Charter) has developed: the so called Conferences (Russian: *Soveshchania*). There were, in early 1974, six of them: the Conference of the Member Countries of Comecon for Legal Problems, the Conference of Ministers of Internal Trade, the Conference of the Chiefs of the Water Resources Authorities, the Conference of the Chiefs of the Patent Authorities, the Conference of the Chiefs of the Pricing Authorities and the Conference of Representatives of the Freight and Shipping Organizations. Later in 1974 yet another Conference, that of the Chiefs of the Labour Authorities, was established.[60]

There are two basic types of resolutions adopted by the above-mentioned organs of Comecon: recommendations (Russian: *rekomendatsii*) and decisions (Russian: *reshenia*).[61] Comecon's Charter provides, in this respect (Article IV, paras. 1 and 2), that recommendations be adopted on questions of economic and scientific and technical cooperation, whereas decisions be passed on organizational and procedural matters.[62]

---

60. See *Pravda*, October 19, 1974.
61. Recommendations and decisions being the *basic* types of resolutions in the case of Comecon, one has to bear in mind that there are also other forms of legal activity of the various organs of the Organization. Thus, the Executive Board may present proposals (*predlozhenia* in Russian) to the Session of the Council and the Committees and Standing Commissions to the Session of the Council and to the Executive Board—see Article VII, para. 3; Article VIII, para. 3(b); and Article IX, para. 3(b) of the Charter. "Proposals" are just one example. If one turns to the lower-ranking legal documents of Comecon and to actual practice, one also finds other forms of legal activity.
62. The topic of the two basic forms of resolutions in Comecon (and also that of resolutions in the other economic and scientific and technical Communist international organizations) was developed by the present writer in his paper *Die Resolutionen der internationalen Wirtschaftsorganisationen der sozialistischen Länder als Quelle des Rechts der Integration*, delivered at the International Conference at Bergisch-Gladbach in June 1974. Papers presented at that Conference are going to be published in West Germany in 1975.

Recommendations do not have immediately binding legal force. They are adopted, so to say, *ad referendum*, because after being passed in the respective Comecon organ they have to be presented to the member countries for final acceptance or rejection. This category of recommendation could therefore be referred to as "qualified," and is coupled with the possibility of "opting out." The pertinent national decisions, according to the Rules of Procedure of the Session of the Council, the Rules of Procedure of the Executive Board and the Standard Rules of Procedure of the Standing Commissions (Rules 25, 23 and 33 respectively), must be communicated, within sixty days from the date on which the minutes of the pertinent meeting of the respective Comecon organ are signed, to the Secretary of the Council or—in the case of the recommendations of the Standing Commissions—to the director of the respective division of the Council's Secretariat.

Decisions, on the other hand, enter into force, unless it is provided otherwise in the decisions themselves, or follows from the nature of the decisions, starting with the date on which the minutes of the meeting of the respective organ of Comecon are signed.

Closely connected with the problem of resolutions, their types and legal effects, is the problem of voting and the number of votes required to have a resolution passed. This may vary in different international Organizations from the requirements of consensus (or quasi-consensus) to qualified or simple majorities.

In the case of Comecon the relevant provisions (Article IV, para. 3 of the Charter) stipulate that all recommendations and decisions be adopted only with the agreement of the member countries interested, each country being authorized to declare interest in any question dealt with by the Organization. Recommendations and decisions do not apply to countries which declare their lack of interest in a given question.[63] However, each of these countries may later accede to recommendations and decisions adopted by the remaining member countries.

If one agrees "genuine" consensus requires, for the adoption of a

---

63. It seems obvious that the arrangements connected with the "interested" versus the "non-interested" positions must be limited mostly to the types of resolutions called recommendations. Concerning the other main type of resolution—the decisions—limited, as they are, to organizational and procedural matters, it is difficult to imagine a member country being, say, "uninterested" in the question of the Organization's budget or the appointment of the Organization's Secretary, with the absurd consequences of such a decision not applying to that member.

resolution, that *all* member countries vote in its favour (and such a solution does exist, for example, in the case of the Organization of the Common Waggon Pool—see below), then the basic idea reflected in Comecon's Charter is the attempt to limit this to what could be called "quasi-consensus," i.e. the positive vote of *all interested* countries, the non-interested ones keeping out of the whole procedure, with the guarantee that the resolution does not apply to them, but that they may, should they so wish, accede to it later.

The situation becomes more complicated, of course, in the case of a country declaring its interest in a question, but in a negative way, that is to say with the intention of "vetoeing" a resolution altogether. In such a case a situation of consensus starts to prevail. The question arises, though, how far such action, e.g. by Rumania, would be tolerated, especially by the "big brother."

In 1969 one Eastern interpreter referred to the situation as having been "controversial for many years," mentioning the "imperfection of Article IV of the Charter," but concluded that the accepted correct interpretation is that a member state may "effectively" block the adoption of a resolution "in principle" only if such a resolution directly touches, because of its subject, upon the interests of that state.[64] This is obviously a *contra legem* interpretation. The situation is obscured by the fact that Comecon, and the Communist press, do not release information on the actual voting, nor, in the case of recommendations, on the "acceptance and rejection" behaviour of the individual member countries.

Generally speaking, one may note that in the case of the more recent international organizations of the Communist countries, the trend is to abandon the institution of recommendations altogether and to introduce, in certain fields (or under certain circumstances), apart from unanimity, majority decisions as well (International Investment Bank, Interatominstrument, Intersputnik, International Mathematical Centre).

The non-existence of the institution of recommendations in the constitutional documents of the younger organizations of the group is a development that should be confronted with the over-zealous formulations of a Soviet interpreter[65] who asserted, in 1965, that

64. See Andrzej Wasilkowski *Zalecenia Rady Wzajemnej Pomocy Gospodarczej* ("The Recommendations of Comecon"), Państwowe Wydawnictwo Naukowe, Warsaw 1969, pp. 238–239, 246.
65. See E. Usenko, *Formy regulirovania sotsialisticheskovo mezhdunarodnovo razdelenia truda* ("Forms of the Regulation of the International Socialist

recommendations are "a more democratic" means of cooperation between socialist countries than decisions. This was followed by an attack on the EEC: there, it was asserted, the weaker are coerced by the stronger—and this was followed by a statement on the superiority of the socialist countries in this field also.

It would be interesting to know if Usenko[66] would still, in view of the clear trend in recent years outlined above, advocate recommendations, as "being more democratic," thus having to concede that developments in the relevant organizations are, alas, going in a "less democratic direction?" Or would a *volte face* be demonstrated, as has so often been the case, the previous assertion being conveniently forgotten, or "dialectically" replaced by a completely different statement?

Finally, the Secretariat, headed by a Secretary, always a Russian—first Pavlov, and, starting with 1958 until the present, Nikolai Faddeev (a situation identical to that in the WTO)—with a total staff, at present, of probably some 1,000, should be mentioned.[67] What is striking is that the chief administrative officer of Comecon is just called "Secretary," and not Secretary-General (or Director-General), as is usual in the universal and Western regional international organizations, sometimes even much smaller in size than Comecon. Until 1965 there were three Assistant Secretaries. In the late sixties this number was increased so that each member state (except the USSR, a national of which always occupies the post of Secretary) had a citizen in the rank of Assistant Secretary. But in the early seventies this number was evidently reduced to four.[68] The Secretary is appointed

---

Division of Labour"), Izdatel'stvo "Mezhdunarodnye Otnoshenia," Moscow 1965, pp. 398–399.

66. The chance of putting this question to Usenko in person was missed during the June 1974 Bergisch-Gladbach Conference, at which the Soviet delegation—which was supposed to include Usenko—evidently under orders from a "high authority," simply did not show up. Other Eastern countries, especially Poland and East Germany, were represented.

67. No announcement was made on the appointment of Faddeev by the IX Session of Comecon in June 1958, and no official biography was published. For the text of an English translation of the Statute of the Secretariat of Comecon, with the Rules concerning the conditions of work of the staff of the Secretariat, see our Annexes (No. V).

68. For a graph of the organizational structure of Comecon's Secretariat, see Faddeev's book, *op. cit.*, pp. 80–81. It is striking that among the few dozen

by the Session of the Council, the Assistant Secretaries by the Executive Board.

They are all appointed for initial four-year terms, and re-appointment is allowable. The case of Secretary Faddeev, who is now serving his fifth (!) term of office, is unique in the history of international governmental organizations, beating the records previously set by Messrs. Candau in the WHO and Morse in the ILO—in all cases, of course, a highly undesirable situation.

It should be noted that there is no such thing as a professional "tenured" international civil service in the case of Comecon (and in the case of Communist international organizations generally). Appointments are granted for four years only (which may be extended), but an appointee may be recalled at any time by his national government. In the case of dismissal, there is no "due process of law" in the form of special appeal bodies, let alone tribunals. And there is no such thing as the Organization's retirement pensions' fund. In short, there is a complete difference here between Communist international organizations on the one hand, and the universal (UN family) and Western regional organizations (e.g., OECD or the European Community) on the other.

Whereas the official languages of all organs, including the Secretariat, are the languages of all the member countries, the working language is exclusively Russian.

A few words may be said about the financial problems of Comecon. One aspect here is the procedure of the drafting, execution and audit of the Organization's budget which is provided for in the two documents reproduced in our Annexes Nos. VI and VII. We already elaborated on them elsewhere.[69] The annual budget is approved by the Executive Board, which is also in charge of dealing with the report on its execution. The role of the Session of the Council in the budgetary field is limited to the fixing of the scale of assessments.

Another aspect is the *concrete* amount of the budget and the scale of assessments.

The budget of Comecon for 1969 reached a total of 8.4 million roubles, out of which 0.4 million roubles were in freely convertible

---

different units the Secretariat is composed of, including, e.g., a "protocol group," there is no trace of any information or press unit, considered elementary in any of the bigger Western (and universal) international organizations.

69. See Richard Szawlowski, "Das Finanzrecht des Comecon" in *Internationales Recht und Diplomatie*, Jahrgang 1965, pp. 100–108.

Western currencies.[70] The scale of assessments, again in 1969, looked as follows:

USSR	64.3 per cent
Poland	8.3 per cent
East Germany	8.2 per cent
Czechoslovakia	8.0 per cent
Rumania	4.1 per cent
Hungary	4.0 per cent
Bulgaria	2.1 per cent
Mongolia	1.0 per cent

Supposing the budget of Comecon increases by some ten per cent per annum, its total amount may reach up to a total of 15 million roubles in 1975. The scale of assessments, on the other hand, after the admission of Cuba in 1972 (probably assessed, like Mongolia, at one per cent), must have been slightly modified by (minimal) reductions for all, or some, of the eight member countries listed above.

It should be repeated that within Comecon there are three semi-autonomous bodies: Comecon's Institute for Standardization, the Bureau for the Coordination of Ship Freighting, and the "International Institute for the Economic Problems of the World Socialist System."

A brief review of these bodies follows.

a. The Institute for Standardization was created in 1962 in accordance with a decision of the XVI (Extraordinary) Session of Comecon, and is located in Moscow.[71] Its main task is theoretical and experimental research concerning the solution of scientific and technical problems

---

70. See Gunnar Amundsen *Le Conseil d'Entraide économique. Structure, réalisations, perspectives,* Université des Sciences Humaines Strasbourg II, 1971, p. 174 (see my review of this book in *Soviet Studies,* Vol. XXVI, No. 2 (October) 1974). Amundsen was the first author—including Eastern writers!— who was able to publish, on the basis of an internal Comecon document, the amount of the Organization's 1969 budget and its scale of assessments. The present writer feels a certain satisfaction, as, in 1965, without having any access to the relevant Comecon documents, he was able to estimate, fairly exactly, the scale of assessments of Comecon's budget—see paper quoted in footnote 69, p. 67. Only the contribution of the poorest member—Mongolia (and now apparently also Cuba), amounting to 1 per cent, turned out to be much higher than it should be according to its relative capacity to pay.
71. The Provisional Statute of the Standardization Institute is given in an English translation in our Annexes (No. VIII). See also Z. Kamiński and A. Ruszkowski *Prace Normalizacyjne w RWPG* ("Standardization work in

in the field of standardization and unification important to member countries of Comecon, and the preparation of drafts of relevant recommendations and presentation of them to the competent organs of the Organization (especially the Standing Commission for Standardization).

The approval, in June 1974, by the XXVIII Session of Comecon, of two international agreements—"On the Standard of Comecon" and the "Convention on the Application of Comecon Standards"—will certainly mean considerable development of the work of the Institute in the near future.

Work has been intensified, during the second half of 1974, in the field of standardization. At the 35th meeting of the Standing Commission on Standardization held in Moscow in September 1974, a protocol was signed on Comecon standards to be worked out during 1975, and on measures to put them into effect. As an Eastern paper noted in this connection, "this starts a qualitatively new stage of work in this field in the Comecon countries."[72] Already three months later the 36th meeting of the same Standing Commission was held in East Berlin, dealing, among other things, with the working plan of the Standardization Organs of Comecon for 1976–1980 and for 1975, and with a number of concrete Comecon norms.[73] Finally, in January 1975, it was stated that between 1962 and 1974 the volume of work on standardization within Comecon increased tenfold.[74] Until the beginning of 1975 Comecon adopted 4,871 recommendations on standardization. During 1975 the preparation of another 2,280 Comecon standards and recommendations is planned.

The Institute has its Director and his deputies, is staffed by experts and technical and auxiliary personnel, and has an advisory Council. The Director and his deputies are appointed by the Executive Board of Comecon upon presentation by the Secretary of Comecon, agreed upon with the Standing Commission on Standardization. Its merely semi-autonomous position is confirmed by, among other things, the fact that the financing of the Institute is done out of the budget of the Secretariat of Comecon, and that it does not have its own policy-making body, the Council being purely advisory.

Comecon"), Wydawnictwa Normalizacyjne, Warsaw, 1965; and S. I. Stepanenko *Sotrudnichestvo stran-chlenov SEW v oblasti standardizatsii* ("Cooperation of the Member Countries of Comecon in the Field of Standardization"), second edition, Izdatel'stvo Standartov, 1972.

72. See *Zycie Warszawy*, September 13, 1974.
73. See *Zycie Warszawy*, December 12, 1974.
74. See *Pravda*, January 21, 1975.

Though no pertinent provision is included in the text of the 1962 Provisional Statute of the Standardization Institute, it is fairly obvious that—as is the case in the two other semi-autonomous bodies (see below) and in Comecon itself—Russian is the only working language.

b.   The Bureau for the Coordination of Ship Freighting was created in December, 1962 by the decision *(postanovlenie)* of the Executive Board of Comecon, and is located in Moscow. The Bureau is the permanent executive organ of the Conference of Representatives of the Freight and Shipping Organizations of the member countries of Comecon, which meets within the framework of its Standing Commission on Transport.[75]

The aim of the Bureau is the improvement of the organization of cooperation between the Comecon countries in the field of shipping, with a view to a more rational use of the members' respective capabilities and the coordination of the activities of these countries in the use of the freight services of the capitalist countries.

The conclusion between seven Comecon countries, in 1971, of an agreement on cooperation in the field of maritime commercial navigation, which entered into force in 1973, and yet another document— the "General conditions of mutual assignment of maritime tonnage for the transportation of the foreign trade cargo of the member countries of Comecon"[76]—probably means an intensification of the work of the Bureau.

The Bureau consists of specialists and of technical personnel. The 1963 Statute provides (Article 13) that the Director (*Zavedujushchyj* in Russian) of the Bureau should be a specialist of the country where the Bureau is located, thus always a Soviet citizen. The only working language is Russian. The financing of the Bureau is done out of the budget of the Secretariat of Comecon.

c.   Finally, the International Institute for the Economic Problems of the World Socialist System was created in 1970 in accordance with the

75. For the text of the Statue of the Bureau for the Coodination of Ship Freighting, approved by the Standing Commission of Comecon on Transport on July 3, 1963, see *Mnogostoronnieje ekonomicheskoe sotrudnichestvo . . .*, 1972, *op. cit.*, pp. 198–201. See also Ignacy Tarski (ed.) *Współpraca krajów RWPG w zakresie transportu* ("Cooperation of the Comecon Countries in the Field of Transport"), Państwowe Wydawnictwo Ekonomiczne, Warsaw 1970, p. 123. In April 1973 the 24th Conference of Representatives of the Freight and Shipping Organizations introduced amendments to the Statute of the Bureau—see the Polish Almanach *Świat w przekroju 1974*, Wiedza Powszechna 1974, p. 418.
76. See, e.g., Faddeev's book, *op. cit.*, pp. 329–330.

decision of the XXIV Session of Comecon, and is located in Moscow.[77] Its main task is the preparation of theoretical, methodological and applied problems of the development of the "world socialist system," economic cooperation between socialist countries, and the problems of socialist economic integration.

The Institute, which is directly subordinated to the Executive Board of Comecon, has a Scientific Council which is supposed to meet as often as necessary but not less frequently than twice a year, and is presided over by the Director of the Institute. The Director and his deputies are appointed by the Executive Board of Comecon, upon presentation by the Secretary of Comecon on the basis of proposals of the member countries. In appointing the Director and his deputies, the executive Board has to go by the criteria of scholarly competence and take into consideration potential proposals concerning the order of priority in the filling of these positions and also the ensuring of the representation of the individual countries. The first Director appointed is the Russian professor Sienin. The organization of the Institute must have taken several years, as it was not until as late as the beginning of 1974 that it was reported that "at present the organizational take-off of the Institute is basically finished."[78]

Financing of the Institute is done out of the budget of the Secretariat of Comecon. Russian is the only working language.

4. *Main Activities*

Comecon, according to its Charter, is intended to promote the economic development of the Member States, basing itself on the "international socialist division of labour," and to improve the living standard of the population. The political aspect is "to strengthen the unity and solidarity" of the Members, and develop cooperation "in the interest of the building of socialism and communism."

The 1959 Charter was further developed by two fundamental documents: the 1962 "Basic Principles of International Socialist Division of Labour" and the 1971 "Comprehensive Programme for the Further Deepening and Perfecting of Cooperation and Development of Socialist Economic Integration of Member Countries of Comecon."

Space permits only a short review of the main practical activities of

77. For the text of the Statute of the International Institute for the Economic Problems of the World Socialist System see *Mnogostoronnieje ekonomicheskoe sotrudnichestvo . . .*, 1972, *op. cit.*, pp. 194–198.
78. See Faddeev in *Einheit*, *op. cit.*, No. 1 (January) 1974.

Comecon as they stood in the late sixties, and then attention will be concentrated on the basic provisions of the "Comprehensive Programme" and the main activities of Comecon under that Programme until the mid-seventies. Considerable overlapping does, of course, exist between those two periods, as the new stage started in 1971 is, in many respects, just an attempt at an improved, "deepened," continuation of activities already fairly well on their way in the sixties. But apart from that, there are also interesting new features.

The main method applied by Comecon—according to the "Basic Principles of International Socialist Division of Labour" adopted in 1962[79]—was the coordination of national economic plans. The first effective attempts at such coordination were started in 1958 in connection with the drafting of the members' economic plans for the period 1961–1965.[80] In 1966, after a considerable delay, a very limited coordination of these plans was accomplished for the period 1966–1970.

But the coordination of the five-year economic plans was, in principle, arranged on a bilateral basis and mostly limited to trade agreements. It did not, for instance, embrace coordination of investment plans on a proper scale.[81] It was only after the April, 1969 XXIII "Special" Comecon Session that the coordination of economic plans was supposed to be organized on a continuous basis, and attempts were to be made to develop comprehensive coordination, embracing scientific research, draughting and construction works, production, exchange and investments.[82] Long-term economic prognostication (for 15–20 years) was also provided for. This was already an announcement of what was elaborated on two years later in the "Comprehensive Programme."

Specialization and cooperation in production were also being

79. For an English translation of the "Basic Principles" see the text published by Comecon's Secretariat in Moscow in 1962 (brochure of 31 pages).
80. This was clearly admitted by P. Jaroszewicz, then Polish deputy prime minister in charge of Comecon affairs, in his introduction to the collection of documents quoted in footnote 11. As Jaroszewicz states (p. 9), "In the initial period the activity of Comecon was limited to the planning of mutual exchange of goods. Although resolutions on coordination of the development plans have been passed since the creation of Comecon, their realization in fact was started only in 1958."
81. See, e.g., M. Mazurski "After the Moscow Session," in *Polityka*, May 10, 1969.
82. See, e.g., M. Lesechko "New Stage of Cooperation," in *Pravda*, June 21, 1969. The author is Deputy Chairman of the Council of Ministers of the USSR and his country's representative to Comecon.

developed in the sixties, particularly in the field of engineering and the chemical industry. For the period 1966–1970, specialization embraced over 2,000 kinds of machines and equipment, and over 2,200 chemical products.[83] But for many years complaints were voiced about the serious difficulties encountered and the poor results achieved in this field. In April, 1969 Piotr Jaroszewicz (Prime Minister of Poland since December 1970) remarked in this connection that "in spite of the considerable efforts of the member countries of Comecon aiming at the development of an international division of labour, one has not, unfortunately, succeeded, until now, in attaining any kind of significant results in this field."[84]

In the mid-sixties multilateral specialization and cooperation was started within Comecon in the field of "more important" scientific and technical research.[85]

Other common activities of Comecon countries were joint investments in the field of mining (especially coal, sulphur, copper, potassium), and the pipeline "Druzhba." But all these investments were bilateral in nature—either in the sense of only two countries participating (e.g., Poland and Czechoslovakia in the joint venture in sulphur in Poland) or at least in the sense that though more than two countries participated, cooperation was based on a number of bilateral agreements between the "host country" and individual foreign partners (the case of potassium exploitation in the USSR).

A new chapter in the activities of Comecon was opened by the adoption of the already mentioned "Comprehensive Programme for the Further Deepening and Perfecting of Cooperation and Development of Socialist Economic Integration of Member Countries of Comecon," adopted in July 1971 by the XXV Session of Comecon.[86] It took over

83. See, e.g., *Pravda*, January 13, 1968.
84. See *Życie Warszawy*, April 10, 1969. One of the most outspoken critics of Comecon's achievements, Jaroszewicz, criticized the shortcomings of the attempts at larger-scale specialization of production many times during the sixties. See, e.g., *Życie Warszawy*, February 13–14, 1966, and May 17, 1966; *Trybuna Ludu*, December 30–31, 1967, and January 1, 1968.
85. For details see J. Metera *Współpraca naukowo-techniczna krajów RWPG* ("Scientific and Technical Cooperation of the Comecon Countries"), Państwowe Wydawnictwo Ekonomiczne, Warsaw, 1969; second revised edition, under the same title, by J. Metera and Z. Ziołkowski, Warsaw, 1972.
86. The full Russian text of the "Comprehensive Programme" was printed in *Pravda*, August 1, 1971; the Polish one in *Trybuna Ludu* of the same date. An English text was published in *Soviet and East European Foreign Trade*, Fall 1971-Winter 1972 issue, pp. 187–305. One cannot understand why S. Wasowski, in "Economic Integration in the Comecon" in *Orbis*, Vol. XVI, No. 3 (Fall

two years to prepare the final version of this document. Rumanian opposition towards any aspects of "supranationalism" was strong as usual. The final text was adopted unanimously, but according to the Hungarian Prime Minister Fock, the July 1971 meeting was "not without clashes," and there were "serious discussions."[87]

However that may be, a joint meeting of the Soviet Politbureau and the Council of Ministers of August, 1971, classified the "Comprehensive Programme" as a document of great political importance, and also mentioned its importance for the strengthening of the "defence capabilities" of the member countries,[88] a clear reference to the overlapping of the broad fields of responsibilities of Comecon with those of the Warsaw Treaty Organization.

The "Comprehensive Programme" being a very voluminous document,[89] only its basic provisions may be discussed here.

The document starts out with statements on the great successes already achieved in the construction of socialism and communism and in the development of the economy, science, and technology; on the quickly growing national income and the "considerable" rise in the material and cultural living standards of the populations of the Comecon countries; and with the statement that "the consolidating all-embracing cooperation of the member countries of Comecon has become an important factor in the rapid growth of the national economies of these countries, the guarantee of their independence, the strengthening of the might of the whole socialist commonwealth." The necessity of the "class struggle with imperialism" is also mentioned slightly later as one of the reasons why socialist economic integration is needed.

Claims are made regarding the "superiority" of the member countries of Comecon over the developed capitalist countries in the speed of economic growth, steadily consolidating the position of the former in the world economy. The further deepening and perfecting of cooperation and the development of socialist economic integration — the document goes on — contribute to the growth of the economic

---

1972), footnote 18 on p. 772, refers to the title "Comprehensive Programme" as "unfelicitous"; it is rather the automatic taking over by him of "Complex Programme" that is bad, as the meaning of "complex" in English may be misleading. This is why, quite correctly, the English equivalent of the title used in Eastern publications is "Comprehensive Programme" (see, e.g., *International Affairs*, Moscow).

87. Here quoted after *Le Monde*, July 31, 1971.

88. See *Pravda*, August 10, 1971.

89. It takes up over fifty columns in *Pravda* and some 130 pages in a Polish paperback edition (Książka i Wiedza, Warsaw, 1971).

might of the world socialist system, strengthen the national economy of each country, and are important factors in the strengthening of the unity of the socialist countries and their superiority over capitalism in all fields of social life, and the guaranteeing of victory in the competition between socialism and capitalism.

Here follow what are perhaps the crucial formulations of the "Comprehensive Programme:"[90]

> The deepening and perfecting of economic, scientific and technical cooperation, and the development of socialist economic integration of the member countries of Comecon, consist of a process regulated consciously and in a planned way by the communist and workers' parties as well as the governments of the member countries of Comecon, of international socialist division of labour, the approximation of their economies and the formation of a modern, highly effective structure of national economy, gradual approximation and equalization of the levels of their economic development, *the formation of deep and lasting links in the basic branches of the economy, science and technology*, the broadening and strengthening of the international market of these countries, and the perfecting of exchange of goods on a monetary basis.

> This process creates favourable conditions for a more effective use of the resources of the countries and the broad development of the scientific and technical revolution, which has become one of the more important sectors of the historic competition between capitalism and socialism, being an important condition of the development of a socialist society.

While announcing large-scale economic integration, the "Comprehensive Programme" at the same time hastens to assure that "socialist economic integration takes place on the basis of full free will and does not lead to the creation of supranational organs..." The experience made with the Khrushchev initiative of 1962 does not seem to have been forgotten yet.[91]

'I he Programme then declares the following seven points to be the

90. This passage is contained in Chapter I, para. 2 of the Programme. Italics were added.
91. Initial proposals for the creation of a "supranational" Comecon planning body were made by Khrushchev during the Plenum of the C.C. of the CPSU of November 1962. An editorial in *Pravda* (February 16, 1963) quoted him urging the creation of a unified planning body common to all the Comecon countries. And *Trybuna Ludu* of February 19, 1963 noted that "Comrade Khrushchev indicated that in the near future yet another step forward in the

basic ways and means towards a further deepening and perfecting of economic, scientific, and technical cooperation and the development of socialist economic integration.[92]

1. The conducting of multilateral and bilateral mutual consultations in the sphere of basic economic problems;

2. The deepening of multilateral and bilateral cooperation in the field of planned activities of countries, including cooperation in the field of prognostication, the coordination of five-year plans and coordination of plans for the more distant future in the more important branches of national industry and types of production, joint planning by interested countries of certain agreed upon branches of industry and individual fields of production, and the sharing of experiences in the field of the perfecting of the system of planning and directing of the national economy;

3. The planned development of international specialization and cooperation in the fields of production, science, and technology, the uniting of efforts on the part of interested countries with the aim of a common search for and exploitation of usable fossils, building of industrial constructions, and conducting of scientific research projects;

---

direction of developing economic cooperation will be taken. This step—comrade Khrushchev said—will be the creation of a unified planning organ common to all countries, embracing representatives of all countries belonging to Comecon."

As late as the end of 1963, G. Sorokin (see also p. 150 in Chapter V, in his identical, "well concerted" article of the end of 1968) in *Planovoe Khoziaistvo*, No. 12/1963, preached: "Just as capitalist concentration gives birth to monopolies, so socialist concentration leads to international planning, coordination of plans of individual countries, and, as a further consequence, to the construction of a unified plan for all countries" and "The socialist countries now coordinate their economic plans. This coordination may be treated as the first step in international planning. The next, higher step, will be the setting up of one plan for the world socialist economy."

Finally, in April, 1964 there came the bombshell of the declaration of the Rumanian Workers' Party (published in *Scinteia*, April 26, 1964) which, among other things, strongly objected against those forms of economic cooperation which provide for the possibility of supranational economic management. The declaration considered this to be a tendency to skip the present stage of economic development and a violation of "objective laws of the present stage of the development of the world economy, consisting of national organisms of sovereign and independent countries."

92. Chapter I, para. 6 of the Programme.

4. The planned development and raising of the effectiveness of mutual trade exchange, the perfecting of its organizational forms based upon state monopoly, the expansion of mutual exchange of trade, linked with the perfecting of currency and financial relations, and of the price system in foreign trade;

5. The developing of direct contacts between ministries, central agencies and other state organs, and economic, scientific and research, project and construction organizations of member countries of Comecon;

6. The development of existing international economic organizations and the calling into being by interested countries of new ones;

7. The perfecting of the legal bases for economic and scientific and technical cooperation, paying particular attention to the raising of financial responsibility of parties in cases of non-fulfilment or unsatisfactory fulfilment of mutual commitments.

The "Comprehensive Programme" is planned to be realized in 15–20 years, thus its targets should be achieved between 1986 and 1991.

In its Chapter II it also provides for the gradual approximation and evening out of the levels of the economic development of the member countries of Comecon. In this connection it declares that a "special place" is taken by the problem of securing accelerated development and the raising of the economic effectiveness of the People's Republic of Mongolia. This, it is continued, requires considerable investment and the giving of help by other countries of Comecon. Thus, after including Mongolia into Comecon in 1962, Moscow now wants to pump as much money as possible from its smaller partners into that country, making them pay for the strained Soviet-Chinese relations.

A similar "privileged" position is also gradually being given, it seems, to Cuba, after her admission into Comecon in July, 1972 (see below).

Let us now have a brief look at some practical activities in these fields over the few years after the adoption of the "Comprehensive Programme."

Concerning coordination of national economic plans, it is provided this time to take place on a much broader basis than used to be the case earlier. In this connection the "Comprehensive Programme" (Chapter IV, para. 2) stipulates:

The indispensable condition for the high effectiveness of cooperation in the field of planning is the comprehensive solution of coordinated problems, embracing problems of science and technology, investments, specialization and cooperation in production and the coordination in this way of mutual deliveries of goods and the basic conditions for these deliveries.

Coordination is now under way for the plans for the period 1976–1980 (apart from perspective planning for the period up to 1990). The coordination of the plans for 1976–1980, according to a recommendation of the XXVI Session of the Council, was to be carried out in the period between 1972 and 1974 in such a manner as to assure the conclusion, at the proper time, of long term economic agreements between member countries. The Communiqué of the 61st meeting of Comecon's Executive Board in January, 1973[93] mentions the acceptance of the relevant proposals presented by the Committee for Cooperation in the Field of Planning.

Discussing the situation in 1972, a Polish author remarked:

Coordination of economic development plans for the years 1971–1975 was limited, in principle, to determining the future mutual trade turnovers. It did, however, contribute to cooperation in the field of production.[94]

He also indicated that not very much was achieved in the field of coordination of investments. Coordination for 1971–1975 did not go much beyond that for 1966–70. What is more, he added:

Tendencies are making themselves felt to make work in this field basically boil down to determining the deliveries of individual elements and sub-aggregates. This would indicate that we are remaining once again on a basis of individual effort, and that cooperation in this immensely important field amounts, as before, only to coordination of mutual deliveries.

Thus the amount of work and effort necessary in the field of coordination of national economic plans in order to achieve even roughly satisfactory results for 1976–1980, is tremendous.[95] In the already

93. See *Pravda*, January 28, 1973.
94. See Jan Ptaszek, *Polska-ZSRR, Gospodarka, Współpraca* ("Poland-USSR, Economy, Cooperation"), Państwowe Wydawnictwo Ekonomiczne, Warsaw, 1972, p. 243. The other references to the author in the same paragraph of our text are on pp. 242 and 245 of his book. See the review of Ptaszek's book in *International Affairs* (Moscow), No. 11 (November) 1973, pp. 102–104.
95. For an account of the coordination of the national economic plans

quoted communiqué of the XXVIII Session of Comecon of June 1974, it was stated that the "first stage" of the relevant coordination work was terminated. At the same time it was also stated that, for the first time in the activities of the Organization, work had started on a coordinated five-year plan of multilateral integration measures—"a qualitatively new, higher form of cooperation in the field of joint planning activity." In March 1975 the respective parts of the draft plan were discussed at meetings of Comecon's Committee for Scientific and Technical Cooperation and the Committee for Cooperation in the Field of Planning, and, in April 1975, at the meeting of the Executive Board.[96] The Session of the Council accepted the plan in June 1975.

Regarding specialization and cooperation in production,[97] a fairly large number of bilateral and a much smaller number of multilateral agreements were signed in several fields. A good case in point is the field of car and truck production. Here, one should mention an agreement between seven Comecon countries and Yugoslavia on "multilateral international specialization and cooperation in the production of certain groups of trucks of high loading capacity."[98] The agreement embraces: three-axle trucks with an allowed load of six tons per axle—production by the USSR and Rumania; trucks with a loading capacity of twelve tons and more—production by Czechoslovakia; trucks with a loading capacity of twenty-seven tons and more—USSR. These three groups of trucks will, in 1975, make up 36 per cent of the total production of trucks of high loading capacity in the Comecon countries.

Some specialization and cooperation was also started fairly recently in the field of automobile production. Here a good example is coopera-

---

see, e.g., Maciej Deniszczuk in *Gospodarka Planowa* (Warsaw), No. 1 (January) 1974, pp. 7–14.

96. See *Życie Warszawy*, March 15, 1975, *Pravda*, March 29, 1975 and *Pravda*, April 25, 1975.

97. As far as specialization and cooperation of production within Comecon go, see three monographs: Ju. F. Kormnov *Spetsializatsia i kooperatsia proizvodstva stran SEV* ("Specialization and Cooperation in Production of the Countries of Comecon"), Izdatel'stvo "Ekonomika," Moscow, 1972; Tadeusz Madej *Ekonomiczne problemy specjalizacji i kooperacji w przemyśle krajów RWPG* ("Economic Problems of Specialization and Cooperation in Industry of the Countries of Comecon"), Państwowe Wydawnictwo Naukowe, Warsaw, 1972; and Stanisław Góra and Zygmunt Knyziak *Międzynarodowa specjalizacja produkcji krajów RWPG* ("International Specialization of Production in the Comecon Countries"), second edition, Państwowe Wydawnictwo Ekonomiczne, Warsaw, 1974.

98. See, e.g., *Życie Warszawy*, August 4, 1972.

tion between Czechoslovakia and East Germany, with the participation of Hungary.[99] According to Czechoslovak opinion, the production of cars in relatively short series is ineffective. Therefore one should produce more, but Czechoslovakia does not intend to become a big exporter in this field, and her internal market is already saturated 'to a great extent'. Hence the decision on cooperation with East Germany. The "Škoda" plant will produce engines with a capacity of 1100 and 1300 cc. for both countries, and East Germany chassis. Total production is planned at 600,000 cars in 1985.

Difficulties in the field of specialization and cooperation, especially as far as such "status symbol production" as that of cars goes, are great. Questions of prestige, national ambitions and similar imponderables must be taken into consideration. Here, even small and generally docile Bulgaria started car production already some nine years ago, on which a Polish newspaper commented:[100]

> From the general, if one may say so, Comecon point of view, the construction of a car factory in Bulgaria may seem irrational, but from the national, Bulgarian standpoint, it is otherwise.

In the meantime, it may be added, Bulgaria plans to reach the production target of 250,000 to 300,000 cars in a big new factory at Lavetsh.[101] What is more, there is information that Rumania, for example, is interested in producing her own aeroplanes on a licence given by Fokker, and that this was a point of interest for Ceaucescu during his April 1973 state visit to Holland.[102]

As was pointed out by the already quoted Polish author in 1972, "the work to-date on specialization was too dispersed and embraced too broad a range of problems." He also states that concerning co-operation in the field of production of parts of machines and equipment, no work had yet been commenced in Comecon, everything being limited to bilateral cooperation.[103]

A publication of the International Centre for Scientific and Technical Information (see below) of December 1973[104] gives, in its annex, a

99. See, e.g., *Życie Warszawy*, January 4, 1973.
100. See *Życie Warszawy*, August 6, 1966.
101. See *Życie Warszawy*, October 28, 1971.
102. See, e.g., *The Times*, April 12, 1973. Similar interest was demonstrated by Ceaucescu during his June 1973 visit to West Germany, when, according, e.g., to the *International Herald Tribune*, June 28, 1973, he "prepared to sign a contract that will give Rumania a share in producing West German jet aircraft."
103. See Jan Ptaszek, *op. cit.*, pp. 250–252.
104. See Ju. F. Kormnov and A. D. Leznik *Soglashenia o spetsializatsii i*

list of the basic documents then in existence on specialization and cooperation in production between the Comecon countries in the fields of mechanical engineering and the chemical and light industries. In the first field, most highly developed in this respect, are listed 9 multi-lateral and 61 bilateral agreements; in the second field only one multilateral and 7 bilateral; and in the third field not one multilateral and 7 bilateral ones.

In general, the impression arises that these are just modest beginnings. The already quoted communiqué of the XXVIII Session of Comecon of June 1974 mentioned that in the period of one year after the XXVII Session (June 1973) eleven multilateral agreements in the sphere of specialization and cooperation of production in the fields of mechanical engineering, the food industry, agriculture and the use of atomic energy for peaceful purposes were signed. And the communiqué of the XXIX Session of June 1975 mentions the signing of a number of new multilateral agreements in that field.

Specialization and cooperation in the field of scientific and technical research continue to be developed.

The detailed and supplemented summary plan for coordination of scientific and technical research for 1971–1975 contains 147 problems and 213 independent topics, out of which 25 problems and one in-dependent topic are of an interdisciplinary character, and 122 problems and 212 independent topics are unidisciplinary.[105]

On the multilateral level, basic scientific research is in the realm of co-operation between the Academies of Science of the member countries, whereas applied research and development studies are organized through Comecon. The mechanism of the functioning of pertinent Comecon cooperation, which has partially been, after 1971, intensified and broadened cooperation along previously established lines, may be illustrated by the example of research on the protection of metals against corrosion in the 1966–1970 plan.[106]

Seven member countries took it upon themselves to undertake

---

kooperatsii v proizvodstve mezhdu stranami-chlenami SEV (osnovnye elementy). *Obzor* ("Agreements on Specialization and Cooperation in Production between the Member Countries of Comecon (basic elements). A Review"), International Centre for Scientific and Technical Information, Moscow, 1973.

105. See S. I. Stepanenko *Sovershenstvovanie nauchno-tekhnicheskovo sotrud-nichestva stran SEV* ("The Perfecting of Scientific-Technical Cooperation of the Comecon Countries"), Izdatel'stvo Mysl', Moscow, 1974, p. 204.

106. See J. Metera and Z. Ziółkowski, *op. cit.*, pp. 100–106.

coordinated research in this field. Ten topics were specified and five countries took over the "leadership" in one or more topics. Their role was to supervise and coordinate national research on much more detailed sub-topics. A common scientific and technical council, composed of the Members' leading specialists, was formed to deal with the whole problem of corrosion, and it was also decided to publish an international journal devoted to problems of corrosion and metal protection.

A more recent form of specialization and cooperation in the field of scientific and technical research are the rapidly proliferating (international) coordination centres.[107] A Soviet author characterizes these centres as follows:[108]

> It should be noted that these coordination centres are not established through the formation of new international bodies, but through the assumption under agreement by specified national research establishments (institutes) of the functions of coordinators in the study and development of concrete scientific and technical problems. It is in fulfilling these functions that national establishments (institutes) act as international coordination centres. In this capacity they may establish direct ties with cooperating organizations, and request information from them about progress and results of scientific and technical research carried on under the agreements. The coordination centres have their own working staff consisting, as a rule, of citizens of the countries where these centres are located. To solve problems arising in the course of their activity, the agreements provide for the establishment of councils of representatives of all the participants in the agreements. These councils, like the coordination centres themselves, take into account CMEA agencies' recommendations concerning their research and development.

Yet another form of cooperation in the same field are the "temporary international scientific-research collectives," e.g. the 1969-created international collective of scholars attached to the Institute for Management Problems in Moscow.[109]

The Executive Board of Comecon also charged the Committee for

107. See footnote 3 to the Introduction, p. xxv.
108. See V. Morozov "CMEA Countries: Wide International Cooperation (The 25th Anniversary of CMEA)" in *International Affairs* (Moscow), No. 4 (April) 1974, pp. 10–11. More details in Stepanenko, *op. cit.*, pp. 109–116.
109. For more details see Stepanenko, *op. cit.*, pp. 119–122.

Scientific and Technical Cooperation, in January 1973, with the coordination of multilateral cooperation of the member countries in the field of environmental protection and improvement, and with the rational exploitation of natural resources connected with it.[110] Extensive work has been started in this field. Pertinent action is coordinated by the Council for the Protection and Improvement of the Environment, a body at the deputy ministers level established under the Committee for Scientific and Technical Cooperation.[111]

In October 1974 the 69th meeting of Comecon's Executive Board approved a general programme of cooperation of the member countries of the Organization and Yugoslavia for the period until 1980 for the protection and improvement of the environment, and the rational exploitation of natural resources.[112]

In this connection it was stated[113] that this programme

> is based primarily on the experience of multilateral cooperation...
> developed in this sphere in the past few years. There are about 360
> research and designing organizations in the CMEA countries and
> Yugoslavia taking part in its implementation. In carrying out
> joint research programmes in the past two years they have studied
> the state of health of the population and sanitary control at
> given levels of pollution of the atmosphere (Humboldt University's
> Institute of Hygiene, GDR); the effect ejections of metalworks
> have on people's health (State Institute of Hygiene, Poland);
> pollution of the atmosphere in modern cities by cancerogenic
> hydrocarbons and concomitant chemical agents, depending on
> the type of industry, and the effect of pollution on people's
> health (State Institute of Health, Hungary); and have hygienically
> assessed the pollution of the atmosphere in the cities by auto-
> mobile exhaust gases, elaborated sanitation measures and
> suggested the basic principles of methods of studying the effect
> of atmospheric pollution on the rate of illnesses (Sysin Institute
> of General and Communal Hygiene, USSR).

Big new common investments have been embarked on, according to agreements arrived at within Comecon. Just a few weeks after the "Comprehensive Programme" was adopted, one of the deputy chairmen of the *Gosplan* (Soviet Committee for Economic Planning), in an

110. See communiqué quoted in footnote 93.
111. See, e.g., "The Protection of the Environment—an Important Field of Cooperation of the Comecon Countries" in *Życie Warszawy*, January 23, 1974.
112. See *Pravda*, October 19, 1974.
113. See *International Affairs* (Moscow), No. 12 (December), 1974, p. 131.

interview given to TASS,[114] recalled that the USSR is the main supplier of combustibles and certain raw materials to Comecon countries. The rapid growth of their economies requires a continuous growth of supplies. But in order to increase the output of oil and natural gas, the Soviet state has to explore and start exploitation of new deposits which are often located in poorly accessible and uninhabited regions. It is therefore only natural, he continued, that interested countries decided to take upon themselves a part of the big capital investments connected with this. For that they obtained a guaranteed long-term source of deficitary combustibles. In this connection he mentioned agreements on cooperation between the USSR and Czechoslovakia and East Germany in the field of increased output of Soviet oil and natural gas. The energy crisis which erupted in the autumn of 1973 (and which also affects, to a certain degree, the smaller Comecon partners) is certainly a strong stimulus to intensified cooperation in this field within Comecon.

Whereas previous agreements of a similar nature were, as already mentioned, of a bilateral character, the new ones are partially large-scale multilateral agreements. The best example here is the joint construction by the USSR, Poland, East Germany, Rumania, Hungary, and Bulgaria of a gigantic cellulose plant in Ust'-Illim (close to the Baikal Lake in Siberia), with a production of 500,000 tons a year.[115] Production is supposed to start in 1978.

Future common ventures were mentioned, already in 1972, in the fields of asbestos, nickel, iron and oil.[116] Some of them are already under way. Thus over a thousand workers are employed on the construction of an asbestos mine at Kijembayevsk (southern region of the Urals), including the construction of a power line, canal, highway, and railway. Partial exploitation is planned to start in 1979. All the Comecon countries, except Mongolia and Cuba, are participating in this joint investment.[117]

During the 67th meeting of the Executive Board (April 1974)[118] multilateral "basic agreements" were signed concerning the development of the manufacture, in the USSR, of ferrous raw materials and

114. Here quoted after *Polityka*, September 4, 1971.
115. See communiqué of the XXVI Session of Comecon's Council in *Pravda*, July 13, 1972. The foundations were built for this investment in March 1975—see *Życie Warszawy*, March 15–16, 1975.
116. See speech of Jaroszewicz at the XXVI Session of Comecon's Council in *Życie Warszawy*, July 12, 1972.
117. See *Życie Warszawy*, August 25, 1973; and November 29, 1973.
118. See communiqué in *Pravda*, April 26, 1974.

some specific metal alloys. The agreement providing for cooperation in the development of the manufacture of ferrous raw materials was signed by the chairmen of the central planning organs of Bulgaria, Czechoslovakia, Poland, Hungary, East Germany, and the USSR, and the agreement concerning the development of some specific metal alloys was signed by "authorized representatives" of the same countries plus Rumania.

And during the XXVIII Session of Comecon in June 1974 all member countries (minus Mongolia and Cuba) signed a "general agreement" on cooperation in the exploitation of the Orenburg condensed gas deposits and the joint construction of a gas pipeline from there to Central Europe, with a length of 2,750 kilometres. Work on the pipeline started in the spring of 1975, and big national workers' teams are in charge of the construction of certain sectors. The construction is planned to be terminated by October 1978.

Another way is the common financing of some productive investments through the International Investment Bank (see Chapter III).

Massive aid has also started to be pumped into Mongolia by the Comecon countries.[119] In January 1975 it was announced that Comecon's Executive Board had considered the report of the Standing Commission for Geology on work done on the organization of an international geological expedition to Mongolia, and recommended that the interested countries sign an agreement on the organization of this expedition; it was signed in June 1975.[120]

The trend to involve Comecon more in Far Eastern problems was confirmed by the communiqué on the meeting of the Organization's Committee on Scientific and Technical Cooperation of December 1973, in which one reads that "the Committee determined ways of deepening cooperation in the study of processes taking place in the Pacific Ocean and the exploitation of its resources."[121]

Concerning Cuba, in December 1972 a top-level Comecon mission headed by the chairman of the Executive Board and Secretary Faddeev visited the island, was received by Fidel Castro, and held discussions

119. See, e.g., correspondence in *Pravda*, April 13, 1973, entitled "Smithy of Brotherhood," published within a series entitled "Steps of Integration." It reports on the construction of a whole new industrial town in Mongolia. With the help of the USSR the town itself was constructed, a railway station, a feeding plant complex, a feed complex; Bulgaria helped in the construction of a sheepskin coat factory, Czechoslovakia a cement works, and Poland a silicate brick works. Hungarian specialists participated in the building of a meat complex.
120. See *Pravda*, January 24, 1975; and June 27, 1975.
121. See *Pravda*, December 7, 1973.

with the seven Cuban deputy prime ministers responsible for the individual branches of the country's national economy.[122] In June 1974 it was announced that the "interested countries" would develop nickel production collectively in Cuba, and in December 1974 Cuban cobalt was also mentioned.[123] This would indicate the beginning of the pumping of multilateral aid also to the second badly underdeveloped member of Comecon—quite apart from the fact that these metals are, in fact, needed by all the Comecon countries.

A revolutionary experiment—by Communist standards—was embarked upon on a sub-regional basis between Poland and East Germany, starting with the beginning of 1972. It was based on decisions taken by the meeting of the top political leaders of the two countries of September 1971,[124] only four months after the "Comprehensive Programme" of Comecon was adopted.

The first step was the opening of the border between the two countries in January 1972, and during 1972 16.7 million people crossed the frontier in both directions.[125] During the two and a half year period between 1972 and mid-1974 this hit the 30 million mark.

Large-scale exchange facilities and customs duties exemptions were granted, though they were limited in the late fall of 1972 on the Polish side because of balance of payments repercussions. The *Berliner Zeitung* started the publication of a Polish edition, and *Życie Warszawy* the publication of a German one, which now, incidentally, also sells in some Western countries.

Movement of manpower, especially from Poland to East Germany, this time much beyond the commuter labour force already used for a fairly long time, has started to develop. In 1973 there were thousands of Polish workers in Magdeburg, Erfurt, Leipzig, and East Berlin.[126]

122. See, e.g., *Życie Warszawy*, December 1972.
123. See *Pravda*, June 22, 1974 and *Życie Warszawy*, December 11, 1974.
124. See, e.g., *Trybuna Ludu*, September 21, 1971.
125. See *Neues Deutschland*, January 10, 1973.
126. Honecker, in his interview with C. L. Sulzberger, published in *Neues Deutschland*, November 25, 1972 indicated that there were about 12,000 of these workers. The *Neue Zürcher Zeitung*, August 29, 1973, referring to the *Berliner Zeitung*, reported that, in 1972, there were 19,000 Hungarians, a few thousand Turks, over 500 Bulgarians and "a large number" of Poles in the G.D.R.; the USSR employs "thousands" of Bulgarians, etc. According to an article in *Pravda*, April 25, 1974, 9,000 Bulgarians are working on forestry enterprises in the Komi ASSR. And some 7,000 Polish construction workers alone were working in the GDR in 1974—see *Życie Warszawy*, December 12, 1974. Thus the exchange of manpower in Comecon is on the increase.

When they felt that they were being discriminated against, four thousand of them organized a two-day strike in Erfurt, something quite unusual in the "host country"; a commission quickly dispatched from East Berlin agreed to all their demands.[127] German engineers and workers are employed in Poland in Pruszków, Zawiercie, and Warsaw.

In June 1973, after a new bilateral summit meeting, a declaration on "the strengthening of friendship and the deepening of cooperation" was signed.[128]

A large bilateral Polish-East German investment—the construction of a new textile mill in Zawiercie—was started in 1972 and was planned to be terminated in 1974, employing some 2,000 people.[129] And in 1974 another joint investment, the construction of a factory of barrel bearings of the highest standard, located in Poland, to supply both countries, was decided upon.[130]

What is new here is not the common investment but the fact that it will be run as a joint Polish-East German enterprise. Other bilateral investments embrace a furniture factory, which may also be run as a joint enterprise.

In December 1973 a bilateral Polish-East German economic organization—"Interport"—was created.[131] This new body, which started its activities in January 1974, is intended to contribute to the rational use of the capacities of the Polish ports in Gdańsk, Gdynia and Szczecin, and the East German ports in Rostock, Stralsund and Wismar. Many "lower level" agreements between individual ministries and factories of both countries should also be mentioned.[132] *In toto*, 160 different economic agreements were concluded between the two countries up to June 1974, out of which 117 were in the field of specialization and cooperation of production.[133]

The rapprochement also embraces other fields. Thus all members of the Council of the county *(Kreis)* of Walgast, located opposite the Polish district of Świnoujście on the Baltic Sea, have started learning Polish to communicate better with their counterparts; heavy participation in these classes is also demonstrated by shop assistants,

127. See *Na Antenie*, January 1973, p. 39.
128. See, e.g., *Trybuna Ludu*, June 21, 1973.
129. See, e.g., *Życie Warszawy*, June 13, 1972. The official opening of the object finally took place in June 1975—see *Życie Warszawy*, June 17, 1975.
130. See *Życie Warszawy*, September 29–30, 1974.
131. See, e.g., *Życie Warszawy*, December 6, 1973.
132. See, e.g., *Życie Warszawy*, December 27, 1972.
133. Honecker during his speech in Warsaw in June 1974—see, e.g., *Życie Warszawy*, June 9–10, 1974.

teachers and medical workers.[134] And the decision was made that before 1980 high schools with Polish as the language of instruction would be established in all district (Bezirke) cities.[135]

This Polish-East German experiment, a revolutionary phenomenon in traditional Communist cooperation, is certainly a testing-ground for similar ventures between other countries of the Eastern bloc. Its "political function" is strongly emphasized, and it is referred to as "the historic process" of strengthening of friendship and of constant mutual rapproachement of neighbouring [Communist] nations.

Among the very weak spots in cooperation within Comecon are monetary problems, including the so-called transferable rouble and the settling of accounts (both briefly referred to in Chapter III under the International Bank for Economic Cooperation), the problem of "fair" pricing and, to a certain extent, also the problem of proper legal mechanisms in the field of mutual deliveries of goods and services.

As for pricing, this was always a sore point. Under Stalin, there was brutal exploitation of the minor partners by the USSR, subsequently even admitted by Communist sources.[136] Later the situation in this respect improved to a certain extent,[137] though there were, for instance,

134. See *Neues Deutschland*, January 14, 1973.
135. See *Życie Warszawy*, May 26–27, 1974.
136. The story of the Polish coal delivered to the Soviet Union in the period 1945–1953 is well known. In November 1956 the Soviet Union was compelled to annul Polish debts as compensation for those deliveries (see the text of the Polish-Soviet declaration of 18 November 1956 in *Trybuna Ludu*, November 19, 1956). What is perhaps less known is the character of "commercial relations" between the Soviet Union and Czechoslovakia even before the Communist coup d'état in the latter country in February 1948. In this respect there is an interesting passage in Trygve Lie's memoirs *In the Cause of Peace*, The Macmillan Company, New York 1954, pp. 224–225. He describes his talk in the summer of 1946 with Jan Masaryk, on the Soviet-Czechoslovakian trade agreement which had just been signed: 'Trygve,' he began, 'you've heard of this big trade agreement. Well, it's not what it seems to be. Everything looks fine on paper, but I'll tell you the Russians have the whole thing fixed.' He then gave me a short account of the Czech-Russian trade talks—brilliant and bitter—employing choice American slang and epithets.... 'the whole thing is humbug,' he continued, 'They control the rate of exchange: what they lose on one thing, they'll make on another, and with those prices they'll strip us clean.'... In the end he hunched his shoulders. 'But what can we do? We've got to play along with them. Gottwald looks to Molotov before he dares take a breath.' He clenched both fists against his vest, thumbs up, 'Molotov, "Da",' he mimicked, lifting his left fist, 'Gottwald, "Da, da",' lifting the right. 'Molotov, "Niet", Gottwald, "Niet, niet."''
137. Particularly dramatic proof of the fact that things are still not looking

88

consistent news that the price paid by the minor Comecon countries for oil imported by them from the USSR was up to a hundred per cent higher than that which they would pay importing it from elsewhere.[138]

The discussion on whether prices in foreign trade *inter se* should be oriented according to world (dollar) prices, or whether the Comecon countries should create their own price system, has a long history. Attempts to create a price basis of their own in the foreign trade of the Comecon countries *inter se* did not succeed.[139]

The solution adopted in the late fifties was the introduction of so-called "stop-prices," based on average world prices during a prolonged period of time, which were, in principle, "frozen" for the Comecon countries and mutually binding for the duration of their respective five-year trade agreements, coinciding with their national economic plans.[140]

The "in principle" proviso seems to be an elastic one. Faddeev mentioned, in his 1974 book (*op. cit.*, pp. 295–296), that during the periods when long-term (trade) agreements are in force, and contracts are concluded for the next year, changes are made in contractual prices for individual goods "in cases of necessity," on the proposal of one of the parties and upon agreement between them. He also mentioned that as a result of changing prices on world markets, the contractual prices in existence in the trade between Comecon member countries sometimes deviate substantially from the average world market

---

well in the field of prices, conditions, etc., prevailing between the USSR and her minor partners in Comecon was the suicide, in December 1965, of Dr. Erich Apel, Deputy Prime Minister and Chairman of the State Planning Commission of East Germany. As *Der Spiegel* later put it: instead of reaching for a pen (to sign the trade agreement with the USSR for 1966–1970), Apel chose to reach for a revolver. One may recall that 8 years earlier, in December 1957, the Secretary of the Central Committee of the SED Gerhart Ziller, in charge of economic problems, committed suicide "in a bout of depression."

138. Thus, e.g., Tad Szulc *Czechoslovakia Since World War* II, The Viking Press, New York, 1971, p. 210, referring to the 1960–1966 period, reports that Czechoslovakia had to provide Moscow with 877 million dollars in credits to cover deliveries of Czechoslovak petroleum industry equipment for the development of new Soviet oil fields. The Czechs then had to buy Soviet crude oil at twice the world price.

139. See, e.g., Ju. S. Shirjayev *Ekonomicheskij mekhanizm sotsialisticheskoi integratsii* ("The Economic Mechanism of Socialist Integration"), Izdatel'stvo Ekonomika, Moscow, 1973, pp. 109–111.

140. For some details see, e.g., Jaroszewicz "On the directions of Comecon work" in *Zycie Gospodarcze*, January 26, 1969. See also W. I. Zolotarev *Programma ekonomicheskovo sotrudnichestva sotsialisticheskikh stran* ("The Programme of Economic Cooperation of the Socialist Countries"), Izdatel'stvo Mezhdunarodnye Otnoshenia, Moscow, 1973, p. 47.

prices. In connection with this, an adjustment of prices is periodically undertaken, upon agreement between the member countries of Comecon.

At the 70th Session of Comecon's Executive Board in January 1975 recommendations were adopted (though not elaborated on in the final communiqué) to adjust prices between the member countries each year. The basis to be used, as it turned out later, are world prices for the last five years, hence the basis for the 1975 prices are those for 1970–1974, for 1976 it will be those for 1971–1975, etc.[141,142]

Previously, until the beginning of the seventies, intra-Comecon prices have, on the whole, always been substantially higher than world market prices.[143] On the basis of this, a Soviet author stated that "in fact one may already, with a certain justification, speak of the existence of regional prices in the mutual trade of the Comecon countries."[144]

The "Comprehensive Programme," very laconic on the problem of pricing, provides in its Chapter VI, paras. 28 and 29 that in the "nearest period" the member countries of Comecon will base themselves on the present principles of the determination of prices in their mutual trade. It was provided, on the other hand, that before the end of 1972 the member countries will realize, on the basis of an agreed upon programme, a comprehensive study of the problems of the perfecting

141. See *Życie Gospodarcze*, February 16, 1975—"Prices in Comecon."
142. According to *The New York Times*, January 28, 1975 ("Soviets Double Oil Price in East Europe"), the USSR increased the price of oil delivered to her Comecon partners, starting with January 1st, 1975, from under $3 to over $6 per barrel (the world market price being about $10). The news dispatched from Budapest also mentioned that "the Russians reportedly pressed to make the increase retroactive for the last year. Hungary, however, stood fast, it was reported, and the Russians finally agreed to begin the new charge effective Jan. 1 this year." The organ of the Hungarian Communist party, *Nepszabadsag* (here quoted after *Życie Gospodarcze*, March 16, 1975), after discussing the price increases both in Hungary's imports from the USSR and her exports to that country, admits that the increase in import prices in the scale of a year is greater than that in export prices. The attempt is made to minimize that fact by referring to Soviet readiness to grant loans to Hungary in 1975, and during the next five years, on "exceptionally advantageous conditions," etc.
143. See the conclusions of Paul Marer in *Postwar Pricing and Price Patterns in Socialist Foreign Trade (1946–1971)*, International Development Research Center, Indiana University, 1972. See also the relevant data offered regarding Polish foreign trade with the "socialist" and the "capitalist" countries in the sixties in Paweł Bożyk and Bronisław Wojciechowski *Handel Zagraniczny Polski 1945–1969* ("The Foreign Trade of Poland 1945–1969"), Państwowe Wydawnictwo Ekonomiczne, Warsaw, 1971, pp. 215–223.
144. See Ju. S. Shirjayev, *op. cit.*, p. 108.

of the system of foreign trade prices. This deadline was not met.[145] The reform of early 1975, referred to above, was evidently dictated by pressing circumstances. The complex problems of pricing within Comecon still seem to be very much open.

In 1972 opinions were voiced that prices for "elements and aggregates" supplied within Comecon's cooperation should be lower than the average world prices, in order to stimulate international (Comecon) specialization and cooperation.[146]

In 1973 another opinion emerged which, though against the idea of basing prices in trade between the Communist countries *totally* on current world prices, advocated the free formation of prices in a *limited* field of trade in the so-called non-contingental exchanges.[147] This liberalization, which, according to the author, should be introduced cautiously and gradually, could, in his opinion, embrace 20–40 per cent of the total intra-bloc trade turnover in the future.

As far as the legal problems are concerned, it should be mentioned that already in December 1969 a permanent organ labelled "The Conference of Member Countries of Comecon for Legal Problems" was created by Comecon's Executive Board.

Chapter XV of the "Comprehensive Programme," entitled "The Perfecting of the Legal Bases of Cooperation of the Member Countries of Comecon," provides, *inter alia*, for the perfecting of the legal bases of cooperation by means of the preparation and acceptance of legal acts, regulating the economic, scientific and technical cooperation of the member countries of Comecon and of their economic, scientific-research and other organizations, the perfecting of the means and procedures of settling disputed problems emerging out of cooperation, and through the approximation of relevant national legal norms and also their unification by interested countries. The study of proposals on the creation of an international arbitration organ of Comecon was already mentioned above (p. 62).[148]

145. A certain embarrassment about the fact that a fixed deadline for the "Comprehensive Programme" was not met is reflected in W. I. Zolotarev, *op. cit.*, p. 47. In referring to the comprehensive study provided for by the 1971 Programme he just misses out the 1972 deadline. Similar rather childish manipulations are, unfortunately, to be found fairly often with Soviet authors especially. Another typical example is, for instance, the frequent failure to mention Albania while discussing the WTO and Comecon.
146. See J. Ptaszek, *op. cit.*, p. 255.
147. See Stanisław Polaczek "The Principles of Trade Exchange between Socialist Countries" in *Sprawy Miedzynarodowe*, No. 10 (October), 1973.
148. For a discussion of the problems connected with the creation of a common

The above previously existing sectional international "codes of obligations" of the Comecon countries were replaced by "perfected texts"—"The General Conditions of Supply of Goods between the Organizations of Comecon Countries" of 1968, "The General Conditions of Assembling of Comecon Countries" of 1973 and "The General Conditions of Technical Servicing of Comecon Countries," also of 1973.[149] In October 1974 the 69th meeting of Comecon's Executive Board approved proposals by the Conference of the member countries for legal problems concerning the increase of the material responsibility of the economic organizations for the non-fulfilment or improper fulfilment of mutual obligations. The Executive Board instructed the Standing Commission for Foreign Trade to introduce relevant amendments and additions to the "General Conditions of Supply of Goods."[150]

Yet another document in the field of legal cooperation of the Comecon countries should be mentioned—the Convention on the Settlement by Arbitration of Civil Law Disputes Resulting from the Economic and Scientific and Technical Cooperation of 1972. A few other documents in the legal field are under preparation.[151]

In January 1973 the Executive Board of Comecon accepted the proposals of the Conference of Member Countries of Comecon for Legal Problems on exemplary regulations regarding the creation and activities of international economic organizations in member countries of Comecon.[152] And, in March 1974, the Executive Board accepted Standard Regulations for the arbitration courts connected with the Chambers of Commerce of the member countries, prepared by the same Conference.[153]

---

arbitration court of the Comecon countries see, e.g., Jerzy Jakubowski *Prawo jednolite w międzynarodowym obrocie gospodarczym, Problemy stosowania* ("Uniform Law in the Field of International Trade, Problems of Application"), Państwowe Wydawnictwo Naukowe, Warsaw, 1972, pp. 235–243.

149. "The General Conditions of Supply of Goods between the Organizations of Comecon Countries" of 1968, now in force, replaced the previous ones, adopted in December 1957 and put into force starting with January 1958. Concerning the two 1973 documents, they replaced two previous ones, adopted in 1962.

150. See *Pravda*, October 19, 1974.

151. See, e.g., the "Theses" on *Integration und Rechtsvereinheitlichung sowie das Verhältnis zum innerstaatlichen Recht im RGW* by Jerzy Jakubowski, presented to the already-mentioned international conference at Bergisch-Gladbach in June 1974.

152. See *Pravda*, January 28, 1973.

153. See *Pravda*, March 2, 1974.

Finally, the XXVII Session of Comecon in June 1973[154] decided upon the creation of the Organization's Scholarship Fund, with the aim of assisting the developing countries in the preparation of their national cadres in the academic schools of Comecon's member states. It was planned that the Fund would start its activities with the 1974/75 academic year.

This seems to be the first instance when Comecon ventured into the field of non-reimbursable developmental aid to "third world" countries. It may well be that a good number of scholarships, previously granted by individual Comecon countries, will be channelled through this new Fund in the years to come. It is worth remembering, in this connection, that in the 1972/73 academic year about 30,000 students from over a hundred developing countries were studying in the Communist countries.[155]

5. Comecon 1949–1975: General Appraisal

The idea of the creation of Comecon must have matured in Stalin's mind during 1948, especially after the Organization for European Economic Cooperation was established in April of that year. The founding meeting of Comecon took place under "conspiratorial" conditions in Moscow in early January 1949, and, for obscure reasons, was only announced a few weeks later.

Though formally over twenty-six years old, Comecon's active history starts only with 1954, as between 1949 and 1954 the Organization was not much more than a decoration. It was only during the second half of the fifties that the Secretariat was, for the first time, built up to any meaningful size. Over ten Standing Commissions were established, and at the end of 1959 the Organization was given its first formal constitutional document (the Charter). The first attempts at a very limited coordination of the national economic plans (mostly in the field of foreign trade) and specialization and cooperation of production (limited to certain branches of engineering and equipment) were started in the late fifties.

The adoption of the "Basic Principles of International Socialist Division of Labour" followed in 1962, but the fiasco, around 1962/63, of Khrushchev's plans for "supranational" economic planning, was a setback almost comparable to the fiasco—in another field and in

154. See *Pravda*, June 9, 1973.
155. See, e.g., V. Morozov, *op. cit., International Affairs*, No. 4 (April), 1974, p. 13.

another region—of the European Defence Community in 1954.

Developments until 1968 were characterized by attempts at the further build-up of processes already started earlier, among them the increase in the coordination of national economic plans and specialization and cooperation in production, the proliferation of the Standing Commissions, and the creation of a number of "specialized agencies." Some innovations, among them coordination and specialization in certain important fields of scientific and technical research, were also introduced.

The latest stage of Comecon's development began with the adoption of the 1971 "Comprehensive Programme," work on which started in 1969. Here again, as in the case of the creation of Comecon, "purely objective" reasons were indicated for the integration of the socialist economies.[156] For any independent observer it is evident, however, that, as with the 1969 reforms within the Warsaw Treaty Organization, it was very much the impact of the shock of the Czechoslovak events that prompted Moscow's decision on large-scale economic integration.

Attempts at improved and comprehensive coordination of the national economic plans; consultations in the basic fields of economic policy and long-term prognostication; intensified cooperation and specialization in production and scientific and technical research; large-scale multilateral investments; the creation of new international organizations, including international economic associations, and of dozens of research coordination centres; and far-reaching experiments on a subregional scale (Poland—East Germany) were already reviewed in this chapter or are briefly discussed in Chapter III.

Twenty-five years after Comecon's inception Communist publications proudly indicated that the member countries of the Organization, which embrace ten per cent of the world's population and 18 per cent of the world's surface, represent some 33 per cent of the world industrial production, whereas this was only 18 per cent in 1950.[157] This considerable increase in industrial production does indeed indicate success, and certain results were also achieved in various kinds of coordination, cooperation, etc.

But on the other hand one is struck, for instance, by the small share of the Comecon group in world trade. In 1973 it even dropped, as compared with that in 1966, from 11.4 to 9.5 per cent, and in 1974 to 8.5 per cent.[158]

156. See, e.g., Faddeev in *Einheit*, *op. cit.*, No. 1 (January), 1974, p. 16.
157. See, e.g., *ut supra*, p. 20.
158. Figures indicated to us by the *Wiener Institut für Internationale Wirtschaftsvergleiche.*

Furthermore, the Comecon group is faced with serious, extremely frustrating, and almost perpetual problems, such as the lack of realistic "uniform" exchange rates, of a convertible currency and of developed multilateral settlements of accounts, problems of pricing and economic modernization in general. Various kinds of other difficulties also have to be faced now or in the very near future—to mention only the deficit of certain raw materials or the general deficit, already signalized, in the labour force (with the exception, for the time being, of Poland and Rumania).[159]

Generally speaking, the area covered by Comecon, especially since the admission of Mongolia and Cuba, is very heterogeneous economically and geographically, and this makes things even worse. In this respect the priority of purely political considerations is obvious.

In the resolution adopted by the XXVIII Session of Comecon in June 1974 to celebrate the Organization's twenty-fifth anniversary,[160] considerable pride is evinced, and perhaps artificially boosted a bit, by formulations such as the reference to the "nine countries of Europe, Asia and Latin America," although precisely Mongolia, and especially Cuba, are heavy economic mortgages.

A certain "politization" of Comecon, evident in the same June 1974 resolution, a "Warsaw Treaty Organization style," should also be mentioned. Here one reads of the Comecon countries' fulfilling their international obligation by having supported with effect the fight of the Vietnamese nation against imperialist aggression and, at present, helping the D. R. V. in the reconstruction and development of her national economy. The "new possibilities" of cooperation between countries belonging to different social systems, which would result from "the successful conclusion of the Conference on Security and Cooperation in Europe," are referred to. A reference is also to be found to the general course in the direction of an alliance of socialism with the national-liberation movement, the further deepening of cooperation with the developing countries and the giving to them of "the necessary support in the fight against imperialism and neocolonialism."

On the other hand there has been, in recent times, a certain nervousness, an obvious over-sensitiveness regarding Western references

159. See J. Manevich "Ways of Better Management of the Labour Force" in *Voprosy Ekonomiki*, No. 12 (December), 1973 and the leading article "Problems of the Labour Force" in *Rynki Zagraniczne*, July 13, 1974. Gradually, difficulties in the supply of labour force were also noted in Poland—see, e.g., *Życie Warszawy*, November 24–25, 1974 and *Polityka*, February 15, 1975.
160. See *Pravda*, June 20, 1974.

to the obvious difficulties Comecon is having and to the deadlines of the 1971 "Comprehensive Programme" not being met. This is well reflected in the following statement:[161]

It is in vain that slanderers have been trying to belittle what are actually the early steps in implementing this programme. On January 4, for instance, the *Financial Times*...tried to prove that the main point for Comecon now was disappointment with the slow progress made in carrying out the Comprehensive Programme. The socialist countries are well aware of the cost in time even without the *Financial Times* telling them, but they also realize the entire complexity of carrying out integration (this is excellently illustrated, incidentally, by the really slow, zigzag road of Western European integration).

A similar nervousness (and aggressiveness) is also demonstrated by Secretary Faddeev in his book of 1974. He refers, for instance, to what he calls "ideological diversion against Comecon," which is, he says, an "unnecessary proof of its effectiveness" (*op. cit.*, p. 15). But at the same time he openly embarks, to use his own terms, on "ideological diversion" against the European Community, e.g. when he attacks the (imperialist) apologists of the Common Market, who compare their "successes" (Faddeev's quotes) with the achievements (no quotes this time) of the Comecon countries (p. 29). Is *this* not an "unnecessary proof" of the Common Market's effectiveness?[162]

In spite of all the constant boasts of success, a Polish writer frankly admitted already in December 1973 that "the ambitious presages of the development of the integration of the Comecon states, adopted in July 1971...are already now encountering difficulties..."[163]

Massive attacks on Comecon coming from China[164] must also be

161. See *Pravda*, January 23, 1974.
162. In this connection one may note a certain difference between senior apparatchik Faddeev and the Soviet professor Oleg Bogomolov, who admits, for instance, the fact that trade in the European Community increased, between 1958 and 1971, seven times; that "a certain level of pooling of means at the level of the Community" was achieved in the agricultural field and in some others, that certain common programmes do exist, etc. "We appraise these and other aspects of the development of the EEC realistically, as a fact of great importance"—see *Trybuna Ludu*, October 16, 1974.
163. See Józef Rutkowski "The Concept of the Monetary Union of the Socialist Countries" in *Sprawy Międzynarodowe*, No. 12 (December), 1973, p. 103.
164. See, e.g., "C.M.E.A.—Soviet Revisionism's Instrument for Neo-Colonialism" in *Peking Review*, July 5, 1974.

getting on Moscow's nerves. The very low "social awareness" of Comecon among the population ia admitted.[165]

The need for *spectacular* successes in Comecon cooperation is evidently being badly felt. Certain Eastern writers express the opinion that tangible results will be achieved in the eighties, and that, in consequence, "one may foresee the liquidation of the qualitative differences in production, scientific and technical progress, etc., between the Comecon countries and the economically developed capitalist ones."[166] Other authors, on the other hand, doubt that even such things as the introduction of an "exchangeable international currency" or uniform exchange rates for national currencies will be possible by the end of the seventies.[167]

Contacts, institutionalized and otherwise, with the outside world, are energetically looked for. Developing countries are flattered and encouraged in the direction of a rapprochement with Comecon, as is well illustrated by the following passage in the message sent by Brezhnev to the participants of the XXVIII Session of Comecon:[168]

> The activities of the Council for Mutual Economic Assistance, and the principles on the basis of which its work rests, meet with deserved recognition in the developing countries. Asserting their lawful rights to national resources, striving to overcome the dictate of imperialist monopolies and to consolidate economic independence, these countries are manifesting a growing interest in business-like cooperation with the Council for Mutual

165. The already quoted Polish journalist Jerzy Kasprzycki reports, in connection with the starting of the publication of an "open" Comecon bulletin, that society's lack of information re Comecon is such that one often hears the formulation that "Comecon is sort of our EEC" (!)—see *Życie Warszawy*, February 3, 1975. In this regard one has to state (also admitted by Kasprzycki) that the West European population is infinitely better informed about their Community. Though, when asked about Comecon, they may, as the present writer has witnessed even in Brussels, try to consider it as a Communist counterpart of the EEC, nobody would dream, when asked about "his" Community, of answering that it is "sort of our Comecon." The fact reported by Kasprzycki would indicate something extremely embarrassing for the Polish "rulers," namely that their own population knows more (or thinks it does) about the Western EEC and demonstrates more interest in it, than in their "own" Comecon.
166. See, e.g., Paweł Bożyk "The Economic Integration of the Socialist Countries. Present State, Perspectives" in *Gospodarka Planowa*, No. 1 (January), 1974, p. 7.
167. See, e.g., Maciej Deniszczuk, *op. cit.*, *Gospodarka Planowa*, No. 1 (January), 1974, p. 13, footnote 21.
168. See *Pravda*, June 19, 1974.

Economic Assistance and its participants, whose international policy they know well and value highly.

The closest possible contacts are also looked for with universal and non-communist international regional organizations, and are already partially well established.[169] The various UN bodies especially, but also the Centre for Industrial Development of the Arab States and the Nordic Council, were mentioned in this respect. In October 1974, Comecon was invited to participate in the sessions and work of the UN General Assembly in the capacity of observer.[170] And in early 1975 it was given consultative status with the UN Economic Commission for Europe.[171]

Only relations with the European Community are still unclear. Moscow vehemently attacked the EEC, especially in the early sixties. No contacts whatsoever were wanted, in spite of certain Western proposals.[172] When, for instance, the first UNCTAD meeting took place in Geneva in 1964, the delegation of the EEC, headed by Jean Rey, and that of Comecon were seated next to each other. Some polite, meaningless words were exchanged through interpreters, and that was it.[173] In the early seventies, for obvious reasons, a "dialectical change" occurred. In August 1973 Faddeev ventured an attempt at establishing a "dialogue" with Brussels. In September 1973 the Council of Ministers of the Community informed Comecon, in an informal way, that they would be prepared to establish contacts. Faddeev, for

169. A review of these contacts is given, for instance, in *Sovet Ekonomicheskoi Vzaimopomoshchi. Sekretariat. Obzor diejatel'nosti SEV za 1972 god* ("The Council for Mutual Economic Assistance. The Secretariat. Review of the Activities of Comecon for 1972"), Moscow, 1973, pp. 93–97. See also Faddeev's book, *op. cit.*, pp. 93–96.
170. UN General Assembly Resolution 3209 (XXIX of October 14, 1974. By Resolution 3208 (XXIX) of the same date an identical invitation was extended to the European Community.
171. See *Pravda*, April 25, 1975.
172. Thus, for instance, Jean Rey, then the EEC's Commissioner in Charge of Foreign Affairs, suggested, at a conference of the European Movement in January 1964, that the East European countries establish diplomatic relations with the Communities—see, e.g., *Nachrichten für Aussenhandel* (Frankfurt), January 15, 1964. In February 1965, during a press conference held in Prague, when Faddeev was asked if contacts between Comecon and the EEC were being considered, his answer was in the negative—see *Życie Warszawy*, February 3, 1965.
173. Related by Monsieur Rey when we delivered lectures during the international colloquium on *Les trois réalités économiques européennes* at Liège in the spring of 1965.

98

obscure reasons, complained at the beginning of 1974 that there was no reaction from Brussels. In May 1974 the West German Ambassador to Moscow called on Faddeev to present formally the September 1973 answer and "establish a dialogue."[174] In September 1974 Faddeev received the French chargé d'affaires a.i. in Moscow as representative of the country then holding the chairmanship in the Council of Ministers of the Community and held a conversation with him on the establishing of contacts between Comecon and the EC.[175]

Finally, in October 1974 Faddeev invited Ortoli to visit Moscow, and the invitation was accepted, but at a lower level.[176] These first direct contacts took place in February 1975, when a delegation of the Community, headed by the Director-General for External Relations, visited Moscow. After thirty hours of talks (half of which were used for interpretation, which was not simultaneous but consecutive), the two parties were not even able to agree on a final communiqué. Neither was the delegation received by Faddeev, who allegedly fell ill (!). Comecon was mostly interested in fixing a date for a visit by Ortoli. Instead, it was invited to send a delegation to Brussels.[177]

Secretary Faddeev also demonstrates something akin to ideological and political schizophrenia with regard to the appraisal of the European Community. In his 1974 book one first reads, in general terms, that "there are no crimes against humanity that monopolistic capital would not use for the preservation of its rule" (p. 7). As the Community is a domain of this "monopolistic capital," and, what is more, its achievements are referred to by Faddeev in quotation marks, a "principled" Communist (if there is such a thing) should fight it, or at least want nothing to do with it. But in actual fact, the same Faddeev went out of his way to establish mutual relations with Brussels, and later, in the very same book (p. 96), remarks: "Indeed, the question poses itself as to what contribution two such big economic organizations as the "Common Market" and the Council for Mutual Economic Assistance can make towards the task of strengthening peace and lessening tensions..." This "schizophrenia" of the other side should be constantly borne in mind by the Brussels negotiators.

Great hopes were placed on the successful outcome of the CSCE. In this context the "basket II" problems, and their follow-up, are of great importance for Comecon.

Indeed, though gradual progress will continue within the Comecon

174. See., e.g., *Frankfurter Allgemeine Zeitung*, May 16, 1974.
175. See, e.g., *Trybuna Ludu*, September 20, 1974.
176. See *Frankfurter Allgemeine Zeitung*, October 16, 1974.
177. See, e.g., *The Times*, February 8 and 10, 1975.

group regardless, its extent and speed will partially depend on the West.

The amount of capital, technology, etc., which has already been pumped by the West into the Soviet Union, especially in the short period starting with the late sixties, is, in fact, astonishing. Referring to what has mostly been connected with an inflow from the West, the already quoted Soviet author openly admits:[178]

> Thanks to such cooperation, the Soviet Union, for example, has been able to develop its sources of raw materials more rapidly, erect new production facilities, and raise the technical level of branches of its national economy. Exports of newly-developed resources will earn the USSR large amounts of convertible foreign currency to buy equipment and goods. All this will help to further stimulate the economy and raise the fraternal countries' living standards. Cooperation with the USA, Japan and other countries also helps the Soviet Union to solve more rapidly such an important national economic problem as the development of the North, Siberia and the Far East. This cooperation also helps to make Soviet agriculture more efficient.

Almost all these Western transfers, incidentally, strengthen, directly or indirectly—as they have for over fifty years now—the military power of the Soviet Union. Sceptics should refer to the recent revealing book by Antony Sutton, which should, by the way, become one of the primers for all Western politicians and administrators involved in relations with the "Soviet camp."[179]

Doubts about going too far in the export of "critical technology" to the USSR were also voiced, in the autumn of 1974, by Gen. George Brown, chairman of the US Joint Chiefs of Staff.[180, 181]

178. See V. Morozov, *op. cit.*, *International Affairs*, No. 4 (April), 1974, p. 15.
179. Anthony C. Sutton *National Suicide: Military Aid to the Soviet Union*, Arlington House, New Rochelle, N. Y., 1973. See the review of this book by Vice Adm. Harold D. Baker, USN (Ret.) in *Strategic Review* (Washington, D. C.), Winter 1974, pp. 76–77. In conclusion the reviewer states that the book "raises challenging questions of national policy that require urgent attention." An earlier three-volume work by Sutton, *Western Technology and Soviet Economic Development 1917–1930*, Hoover Institution, Stanford, California, 1968, is also worth studying.
180. See *The Christian Science Monitor*, October 11, 1974. The general mentioned specifically Soviet visits to American plants making wide-bodied commercial jets, produced by McDonnel-Douglas and Lockheed.
181. The warning by Alexander Solzhenitsyn should also be noted: "(. . .) The

A constant and thorough soul-searching analysis of the evident "cons" and potential "pros," if any, of such transfers, close pertinent consultation and rigorous coordination within NATO and COCOM (Consultative Group Coordinating Committee), the European Community and through other channels, are badly needed. The present situation, increasingly uncontrolled, can hardly be tolerated. What one now witnesses in this field is, indeed, starting to look—to extend Sutton's title—like Western suicide. A drastic clamp-down on certain greedy "business circles" and certain government circles corrupted by them should no longer be shied away from.

One should, in this connection, always bear in mind something that the other side readily admits:[182] "The strengthening of the economy of the socialist states leads to a change in the relation of forces on the world arena to the advantage of socialism and peace, and facilitates the realization of the foreign policy tasks of the countries of the Warsaw Treaty."

Apart from that one should also bear in mind the immediate and practical consequences of such behaviour in terms of certain dumping practices, on which the other side started to embark recently. Complaints in the field of freighting were already mentioned.[183] Perhaps the most spectacular thing are the exports of Fiat cars, produced since fairly recently in the USSR and Poland on Italian licences, to the West,[184] but other recent complaints may also be quoted.[185] These

---

whole existence of our slave owners from beginning to end relies on Western economic assistance.(...) ... if in the frenzied competition one country after another continues to rush in with loans and advanced technology [for the USSR], if they present earth-moving equipment to our gravediggers, then I'm afraid Lenin will turn out to have been right when he said, "The bourgeoisie will sell us rope, and then we shall let the bourgeoisie hang itself."—See *The New Leader* (New York), August 4, 1975, p. 11.

182. See *Pravda*, May 14, 1975.
183. See footnote 2 to this chapter.
184. In Britain, for instance, the Polish Fiat four-door, $1\frac{1}{2}$ litre family saloon sells at £1,159 including tax—compared with a standard 850 Mini which costs £1,184—see *The Daily Telegraph*, April 28, 1975. Concerning the Soviet Fiat ("Lada"), "Western automakers are agog at the whole turn of events, including Lada's low low price, and Fiat is beginning to suspect the Russian plant was a mistake. Umberto Agnelli, Fiat chairman, has been quoted several times recently as saying that the Lada is being offered at cutthroat prices in West Germany. It sells for roughly $ 1,200 less than the nearest-sized Fiat competitor."—See *The Christian Science Monitor*, September 8, 1975.
185. E.g. the British footwear industry complaining about cut-price shoe imports from Czechoslovakia, Poland and Rumania—see *The Times*, February

Eastern attempts will increase in the future and require energetic political and legal decisions on our side.

Comecon, for its part, is here to stay, and will develop as the centre of large-scale economic, scientific and technical integration, though the process may be much less rapid than originally planned in the 1971 "Comprehensive Programme." The Council's important position in intra-bloc relations, similar to that of the Warsaw Treaty Organization, is firmly entrenched in the bilateral treaties on "friendship, cooperation and mutual assistance."

Certain Western predictions, made as late as 1968, that Comecon will basically remain only a "clearing house" and an "advisory body," were shortsighted and rather incompetent.[186]

10, 1975; or the complaint about horticultural glass coming from the USSR, Czechoslovakia and Rumania "priced at a level well below reasonable manufacturing costs, even for Eastern Europe"—see *The Financial Times*, April 25, 1975.
186. See, for such false prophesies, Richard F. Staar (ed.) *Aspects of Modern Communism*, University of South Carolina Press, Columbia, S. C., 1968, p. 172.

Chapter III

THE MINOR ORGANIZATIONS OF THE "COMECON FAMILY"

The activities of Comecon itself are complemented by a growing group of smaller international organizations—Comecon's "specialized agencies."

The initiative to set up these organizations was taken, in the big majority of relevant cases, at various meetings of Comecon, and the respective international agreements were, again in most cases, signed in Moscow during such meetings. Comecon is *expressis verbis* referred to in most of these agreements. This already establishes a certain hierarchy.

There is also a legal argument. By Treaty Law, when an international agreement (thus also one providing for the creation of an international governmental organization) is entered upon, its original text is deposited with a State (or more than one) or an international organization (or the chief administrative officer of such a body).[1] Comecon's Charter, according to its Article XVIII, was to be deposited with the government of the USSR. But the constitutional documents of some of the other international economic organizations of the Communist countries have to be deposited not with the government of a member state, but with the Secretariat of Comecon (see Article XIII of the Agreement on the Central Control Office for the Combined Power Systems, Article XVI of the Agreement on Multilateral Clearing in Transferable Roubles and the International Bank for Economic Cooperation, and Article XXVII of the Agreement on the creation of the International Investment Bank).

Incidentally, a similar situation exists in the case of the International Bank for Reconstruction and Development ("World Bank") on the

1. The already-mentioned Vienna Convention on the Law of Treaties of 1969 stipulates in Article 76, para. 1:
"The designation of the depositary of a treaty may be made by the negotiating States, either in the treaty itself or in some other manner. The depositary may be one or more States, an international organization or the chief administrative officer of the organization."

one hand, and the International Development Association, the International Finance Corporation, and the International Centre for Settlement of Investment Disputes on the other: the original constitutional texts of the three latter organizations must be deposited with the IBRD.

This is an additional argument for permitting one to speak of a "family" of international organizations, with one "parent" and several "offspring" organizations.[2]

In short, an analogy with the United Nations "family" (the UN itself and its specialized agencies) easily comes to mind. This is why the present writer referred to this group already in 1965–1966 as the international organizations of the "Comecon family."[3]

The situation in this respect became even more pronounced with the adoption of the 1971 "Comprehensive Programme."

The Programme stipulates in its Chapter XVI (para. 5):

> The member countries of Comecon will adopt means in order that the activities of the international organizations based on the principles of Comecon, created already and also in the future by the interested countries, to which wide responsibilities in the field of economy, science and technology are given, by properly mutually coordinated with the activities of Comecon.
>
> Problems which are the object of mutual interest of Comecon and the above-mentioned organizations will be covered by that coordination; coordination will be realized on the basis of agreements and protocols concluded between Comecon and these organizations, providing in particular that these organizations will cooperate within Comecon as specialized organizations. (. . .)

2. This reasoning applies only to situations where the international organization used as a depositary has, in fact, a "seniority status" vis-à-vis another, younger organization. Quite obviously, the mere fact that the original constitutional document of an international body has been deposited with an international organization, and not with a state, does not give the depositary organization any "seniority." This is exemplified by the kind of situation where, according to Article 20 of the Convention for the Establishment of the European Organization for Nuclear Research of 1953, the convention's original text was deposited in the archives of UNESCO; or when, according to Article 63 of the Agreement establishing the Asian Development Bank of 1965, the original of the agreement was deposited with the Secretary-General of the UN. In these cases, of course, there is no reason for attempting to find any kind of "parent" and "offspring" relationship.
3. See, e.g., Richard Szawlowski "The International Organizations of the 'Comecon Family'" in *Osteuropa-Recht*, No. 2/1966, based on a lecture delivered during an international colloquium called "Les trois réalités économiques européennes" (EEC, EFTA, Comecon) in April, 1965 at Liège (Belgium).

While creating intergovernmental economic organizations the member countries of Comecon will introduce into the legal documents of these organizations provisions necessary for the establishment of their relations with Comecon.

As a matter of fact, already in the summer of 1970 and the winter of 1971, that is before the adoption of the "Comprehensive Programme," five such standard agreements between Comecon and the following organizations were concluded: "Intermetall," the International Bank for Economic Cooperation, the Organization for Cooperation of the Ball-Bearing Industry, the Central Control Office of the Combined Power Systems and the Common Waggon Pool. One of these standard agreements is reproduced in our Annexes (No. X).

And during 1972 and 1973 certain new actions followed to bring all these smaller organizations under more formal coordination, if not *de facto* supervision, by Comecon. Thus in May 1972, for instance, the Eastern press reported about the signing of documents on cooperation between Comecon and the International Investment Bank, the International Scientific and Technical Information Centre and (apparently new agreements) with the International Bank for Economic Cooperation and the Common Waggon Pool.[4] This was followed by the signing of a similar protocol on cooperation between Comecon and "Interkhim."[5]

The Communiqué of the XXVI Session of the Comecon Council of July 1972[6] mentioned that, among other people, the directors of the "international organizations of the Comecon countries" were also present as observers, and the same also applies to the communiqués of the consecutive sessions of 1973, 1974 and 1975.[7] And in January 1973 a conference took place in Moscow, attended by the chairmen of the Committees, Standing Commissions and other Comecon organs, with the participation of the directors of the "international organizations of the Comecon countries."[8] The aim of the conference was the exchange of work experience within the organs of Comecon.

What follows is a short chronological review of the individual "specialized agencies" of Comecon.

4. See, e.g., *Życie Warszawy*, May 7–8, 1972.
5. See *Pravda*, May 18, 1972.
6. See *Pravda*, July 13, 1972.
7. See *Pravda*, June 9, 1973, June 22, 1974 and June 27, 1975. One must add, though, that the 1973 and 1975 communiqués refer only to "the representatives of a number of international organizations of the member countries of Comecon."
8. See *Pravda*, January 10, 1973.

1. *The Organization of the Joint Power Grid*

The Agreement creating this organization, whose official name runs "Central Control Office for the Combined Power Systems,"[9] was signed in July 1962.[10]

The electric power systems of Poland, East Germany, Czechoslovakia, Hungary, and the Western Ukraine, already combined at the beginning of the sixties, were joined slightly later by Rumania and, in 1967, by Bulgaria.[11]

The Organization of the Joint Power Grid has as its task the coordination of the operations of these combined power systems, called "Mir" (Peace), especially the exchange of energy. Its headquarters are in Prague.

The highest organ of the Organization is the Council, composed of representatives of the competent organs of the member countries. The Agreement creating the Organization (Article IV, last two paragraphs) provides for only one form of resolution, namely decisions (*reshenia* in Russian). They must be taken unanimously by the representatives of all the interested contracting parties, each of which may declare its interest in any problem dealt with by the Council ("quasi-consensus"). Decisions of the Council do not apply to those parties whose representatives declare lack of interest in a given problem. Each party may, however, accede later to such decisions.

The role of the Secretariat is performed by a Board, composed of a director, his deputy, and "the necessary number" of specialists and auxiliary personnel. Russian is the only working language.

A 1973 report on the Joint Power Grid says, *inter alia*:[12]

> The unified Mir power networks save the countries concerned large sums. The overall installed capacity of the Mir power stations by the end of 1971 exceeded 58 million kilowatts, or more than doubled in the past ten years. The amount of electric power exchanged in 1971 totalled 15,500 million kWh (in 1960 it was 1,200 million kWh). It is estimated that the amount saved on

9. Other translations sometimes used are "Central Power Control Administration" or "Central Dispatcher Administration." The Russian term used is *Tsentral'noe Dispatcherskoe Upravlenie*.
10. English text of the Agreement published in the *United Nations Treaty Series*, Vol. 506 (1964), No. 7387.
11. See N. Afonin "Cooperation of the Comecon Countries in the Field of Electric Power," *Voprosy Ekonomiki*, No. 9/1967.
12. See L. Bauman "CMEA Countries' Cooperation in Power Industry," *International Affairs* (Moscow), No. 2 (February), 1973.

investments and operational expenses as a result of the amalgamation of the power networks is more than twice the sum expended on the connecting transmission lines. The Mir power networks thus received, as it were, an additional 1,200 megawatts of capacity.

In 1974 an agreement was signed by six countries (without Rumania and, of course, Cuba and Mongolia) on cooperation in the construction and exploitation of a relay line for electric energy from Vinnitsa in the Ukraine to Albertirsha in Hungary.[13] The communiqué emphasized the importance of this construction, which will, among other things, increase the reliability of the work of the Combined Power Systems.

2. The International Bank for Economic Cooperation

The Agreement on multilateral settlements in transferable roubles and the establishment of the International Bank for Economic Cooperation was signed in October 1963.[14] It was put into force provisionally between the eight Comecon countries starting with January 1, 1964, and formally came into effect in May of 1964. The agreement (and the Bank's Charter) were amended in December 1970.[15] Cuba was admitted to the Bank in January 1974.[16]

The essence of multilateral settlements in transferable roubles is given in Article I of the Agreement, as amended:

Settlements under bilateral and multilateral agreements, or special contracts, for reciprocal deliveries of goods, and under agreements concerning other payments between the Contracting Parties shall, as from 1 January 1964, be effected in transferable roubles.

. . .

Any member country of the Bank having funds in transferable-rouble accounts may freely draw on such funds.

When concluding trade agreements, each member country of the Bank shall make provision for the setting off of its total receipts

13. See communiqué of the 66th meeting of the Executive Board of Comecon— *Pravda*, March 2, 1974.
14. English text of the Agreement and the Bank's Charter in their 1963 version were published in the *United Nations Treaty Series*, Vol. 506 (1964), No. 7388.
15. See mention at the very beginning of the text of the amended Agreement reproduced in *Mnogostoronnieje ekonomicheskoe sotrudnichestvo...*, *op. cit.*, 1972, p. 237.
16. See, e.g., *Życie Warszawy*, January 23, 1974.

from, and total payments to, all the other member countries of the Bank in transferable roubles within the calender year or within another period agreed upon by the member countries of the Bank. This exercise may include the formation of favourable balances in transferable roubles, the utilization of such balances if any already exist, and also credit operations.

. . .

The main aims of the Bank, whose headquarters are in Moscow, are to administer the system of multilateral settlements in transferable roubles and to provide credits (mostly short term), mainly for foreign trade between the member countries.[17]

The highest organ of the Bank is its Council, composed of representatives of all member countries, each of them having one vote irrespective of his country's share in the Bank's capital (an unusual provision in the field of international governmental banks).

The Charter of the Bank, an annex to the Agreement (Article 27, first sentence), provides only for one category of resolutions of the Council—decisions. No distinction is made between the "interested" and "uninterested" parties. Thus, for any resolution to be passed, a genuine consensus must exist.

The executive of the Bank is its Board of Management, consisting of a Chairman (the Russian Nazarkin) and members appointed from nationals of all member countries "for a period of not more than five years." According to Article 33 of the Bank's Charter "the Bank shall have departments, sections, branches, agencies and missions..."[18] Though neither the Agreement nor the Bank's Charter refer to this problem, it is pretty obvious that the only working language is Russian.

During the eleven years of its activities, the Bank has had certain achievements. It was announced, for instance,[19] that the total volume

17. D. L. Williams (in Brzezinski, *The Soviet Bloc. Unity and Conflict*, Harvard University Press, Cambridge, Mass., 1967, second 1971 reprint, p. 462) mentions as the first task of the Bank "loans for reconstruction and industrial projects." This task, listed, in fact, as the very last potential field of the activities of the Bank under Article II of the 1963 Agreement, was not made use of in practice. And it was formally missed out of the Agreement in December 1970.
18. The structure of the Bank is given in A. Ja. Rotlejder *Mezhdunarodnye kreditnye organizatsii stran-chlenov SEV* ("The International Credit Organizations of the Member Countries of Comecon"), Izdatel'stvo Finansy, Moscow 1973, p. 75. There is no trace yet of the existence of "branches, agencies and missions."
19. See *IBEC*, 1974 [Annual Report], published probably in April 1975 (without page numbers!).

of the Bank's operations (including credit and deposit operations) in transferable roubles reached 74 billion in 1974, which means an increase of 77 per cent as compared with 1973. On the other hand, the amount of loans granted by the Bank in 1974 was 3.2 billion transferable roubles, whereas in 1973 it was 3.8 billion (3.0 in 1972 and 2.8 in 1971).

In January 1974 the Bank celebrated its tenth anniversary, an occasion attended by about 150 representatives of the biggest Eastern and Western banks. One of the speeches was delivered by the vice-president of *Credit Lyonnais*, Maurice Schlogel.[20]

But basically the situation is still far short of initial expectations. In brief, the Bank has developed a clearing mechanism, but it remains limited, in practice, to bilateral settlements between the member countries. Multilateral settlements, as a matter of fact, represented only 1.5 per cent (!) of the total settlements.[21]

The fully-fledged "transferable rouble," the Red dream of a "truly collective socialist currency," has not yet come true.[22]

It is instructive to follow how obstinately this demand has been repeated for all these years, without as yet bringing a decisive break-through.

Thus, already in 1966, Jaroszewicz stated:[23]

> The International Bank for Economic Cooperation has already been functioning for two years. Its work has a positive influence on financial relations between member countries of Comecon. However, we consider that this is only a modest beginning. At the last meeting of the Executive Board an agreement was adopted regarding the creation of the gold reserves.... We consider the agreed upon solution of this question to be a constructive step forward in the desired direction. But nevertheless this is not a step which would influence the perfecting of the system of multi-lateral settlements in a tangible way. It does not yet signify setting

---

20. See *Życie Warszawy*, January 25, 1974.
21. See Eugeniusz Drabowski *Rubel transferowy—międzynarodowa waluta krajów RWPG* ("The Transferable Rouble—the International Currency of the Comecon Countries"), Państwowe Wydawnictwo Naukowe, Warsaw, 1974, p. 26.
22. It should be emphasized that the transferable rouble, referred to as "socialist common currency," is used exclusively for external, international settlements. It is not issued in the form of banknotes, and functions only in the clearing of settlements in bank accounts.
23. See Jaroszewicz "Step by Step Forward" in *Ekonomicheskaya Gazeta*, No. 7/1966.

out on the path leading to the conversion of the rouble. We will work further on these problems in Comecon.

In the spring of 1969 the same Jaroszewicz that:[24]

the transferable rouble has not become an international socialist currency in relations between the Comecon countries, and it is only a conventional unit used in bilateral settlements between individual partners.

The Polish author already quoted several times remarked in 1972:[25]

But in spite of the introduction of that system [of multilateral settlements] it has not, as yet, played its intended role fully in practice.

One has not managed, as yet, to elaborate an effective method of multilateral balancing of transactions. Only the abandonment of the principle of bilateral balancing will enable the system of the transferable rouble to fulfil its basic task.

One systematically strives to make the International Bank for Economic Cooperation become a bank in the full sense of the word, having an attractive currency in the form of the transferable rouble.

The "Comprehensive Programme" contains fairly detailed provisions about the further development not only of the Bank itself (Chapter VII, paras. 26–29) but also regarding the strengthening and increasing of the role of the "socialist common currency—the transferable rouble" (Chapter VII, paras. 1–20). A timetable was established in this respect.
    Thus (para. 18, second part):

During 1973 the member countries of Comecon will mutually prepare the modalities and procedures for the realization of actions regarding the introduction of convertibility of the common currency (transferable rouble) into the national currencies of the member countries of Comecon and the mutual convertibility of national currencies.

And (para. 14):

In 1974 the member countries of Comecon will do a summing-up of work concerning the application and use of the common currency (the transferable rouble), and, taking into account the

24. See *Zycie Warszawy*, April 10, 1969.
25. See J. Ptaszek, *op. cit.*, p. 263.

accumulated experience, will outline further concrete actions in the field of its reinforcement and the increasing of its role.

One should thus have expected fairly far-reaching decisions in this particular field already during 1973 and 1974, but an obvious delay took place in this important sector.[26]

The communiqué of the 70th meeting of Comecon's Executive Board in January 1975[27] contained the following passage:

> At the meeting of the Executive Board problems connected with the further strengthening and intensifying of the role of the international socialist collective currency of the member countries of Comecon (transferable rouble) and the multilateral balancing of mutual trade exchanges were dealt with. The increased role of the collective currency in the development of the economic, scientific and technical and other forms of cooperation of the member countries of Comecon was noted. Concrete measures for its further strengthening and the increase of its role in the development of cooperation and of socialist economic integration were mapped out.

The above-quoted passage is, evidently, so general that it does not allow one to infer any break-through in the solution of the problems sketched in this sub-chapter.

3. *The Organization of the Common Waggon Pool*

The agreement on the Creation and the Joint Exploitation of the Common Waggon Pool was signed in December 1963[28] and came into force in August 1964. Members of the Pool are the USSR, Poland, East Germany, Czechoslovakia, Hungary, Rumania, and Bulgaria. Mongolia (and, of course, Cuba) are not members.

The railway administrations of the member countries want to reduce the circulation of empty freightcars, both at home and abroad, to accelerate the return of these cars, and thus increase the turnover and the economic efficiency of their exploitation.

The Common Waggon Pool is located in Prague. Its top organ is a

26. For a Western discussion of the monetary problems of the Comecon group see Gunnar L. Amundsen *Problèmes de Coordination monétaire dans la Région du CAEM (Comecon): Exigences fondamentales et implications théoriques*, mimeographed text published by the Norwegian Institute of Foreign Policy, Oslo, 1973.
27. See *Pravda*, January 24, 1975.
28. For the text in an English translation see our Annexes (No. XI).

Council, composed of representatives of each of the member countries. Decisions are the only type of resolution passed by the Council (Article II, para. 3 of the Agreement). They are adopted only with the agreement of all the contracting parties. Thus a genuine consensus, analogous to the respective situation in the case of the International Bank for Economic Cooperation, prevails here.

The functions of a secretariat are executed by the Bureau for the exploitation of the Common Waggon Pool, composed of a Director, his deputy (in practice there seem to be more than one), and the "necessary number" of specialists and technical and service personnel. Russian is the only working language. According to a recent report in *Pravda*, the Director is a Czech and his "first deputy" a Soviet railway specialist.[29]

The percentage of mutually returned empty cars was, in 1967, 35 per cent, and at the end of 1969 the Pool consisted of 108,600 waggons.[30] At the beginning of 1972 it was stated that the number of waggons had "doubled" when compared with the initial 92,000, which would amount to over 180,000 waggons.[31] And at the end of 1974 mention was made of 250,000 waggons, to which, in the nearest future, an additional 20,000 would be added.[32] And it was stated on the same occasion that although the share of rail transport in the total goods transportation of the member countries is decreasing (because of the development of pipelines, aviation, water and automobile transport), it still represents the "lion's share" of 64 per cent.

It is worth noting that the East European waggon pool was created after long observation of the (West) European Railway Waggon Pool, *Europ*, initiated in 1953, on the basis of a common French-West German Waggon Pool, created in 1951. This is a new example of Eastern imitation in the field of international organizations, to which we refer in discussing Comecon, the Warsaw Treaty Organization, the Joint Institute for Nuclear Research, the International Investment Bank and "Intersputnik." Beginning with the summer of 1964, a large number of waggons in Eastern Europe circulated with the inscription OPV *(Obshchij Park Vagonov)*—a counterpart of those freight cars in Western Europe bearing the well-known inscription *Europ*.

29. See *Pravda*, December 24, 1974.
30. See J. Tarski (ed.), *op. cit.*, p. 103.
31. See B. Griniuk "The Strategy of the Loading Stream," *Pravda*, January 25, 1972. *Neues Deutschland*, February 16, 1972 indicated the total number of "about 200,000 waggons."
32. See *Pravda*, December 24, 1974.

4. *The Organization for Cooperation of the Ball-bearing Industry*

The Agreement on the creation of this Organization was signed in April 1964,[33] initially by Poland, East Germany, Czechoslovakia, Hungary, and Bulgaria. Slightly later the USSR acceded to it. Rumania joined in 1972.[34] Mongolia and Cuba are not members. The membership of Yugoslavia was under consideration in the spring of 1974.[35]

The general aim of the Organization, as stated in the preamble to the Agreement, is to ensure a faster development of the ball-bearing industries, to improve their technical level and satisfy as fully as possible the needs of their countries in ball-bearings.

The headquarters of the Organization are in Warsaw. The top organ is the Directorate (*Upravlenie* in Russian), composed of one representative for each member country. The Directorate may, according to Articles IV (para. 4) and V of the Agreement, pass two types of resolutions: decisions and recommendations, depending on topics listed in Article III. They are taken only with the consent of all contracting parties (genuine consensus). Later, things go further than in any other organization of the Comecon family: here even decisions do not enter into force after the protocol of the pertinent meeting has been signed (which is, for instance, the situation in "Intermetall"), but only if there is no rejection of them in the 30 days following by the competent organs of the states-parties. Recommendations, on the other hand, have to be accepted or rejected within 60 days.

The executive is the Secretariat of the Directorate, composed of the Director of the Secretariat (*Zavedujushchij Sekretariatom* in Russian), his deputies and the "necessary number" of specialists and technical and administrative personnel. The only working language is Russian.

In 1972 it was stated that 98 per cent of the demand of the member countries was already covered by their own production.[36] Specialization embraces 93 per cent of the total amount of the ball-bearings used in the member countries; a breakdown reserve of ball-bearings was created; on the other hand, the quality of ball-bearings was criticized.[37]

Finally, in January 1975, the Executive Board of Comecon, discussing the activities of the Organization during its first ten years, stated "with satisfaction" that it had done big work in the development

---

33. For the text in an English translation see our Annexes (No. XII).
34. See, e.g., *Pravda*, May 9, 1974.
35. See V. Morozov, *op. cit.*, *International Affairs*, No. 4 (April), 1974.
36. See J. Ptaszek, *op. cit.*, p. 280.
37. *Ut supra*, pp. 281–282.

and specialization of ball-bearings.[38] Production increased almost twofold during this period.

5. *"Intermetall"*

Intermetall, an international organization of the Comecon countries for the purpose of coordinating production, development and cooperation in the iron and steel industry, was created by an Agreement signed in July, 1964[39] which came into force in November of the same year.

The original contracting parties were Poland, Czechoslovakia, and Hungary. They were promptly joined by the USSR, East Germany, and Bulgaria. Rumania (and Mongolia and Cuba) are not members. There are, though, links with Rumania through cooperation with her foreign trade corporation "Metalimport," starting with 1970,[40] and Yugoslavia, at the end of 1968, signed an agreement on cooperation with Intermetall.[41]

Intermetall is located in Budapest. The highest organ of the Organization is its Council. Member countries are represented by delegations composed of three representatives, each delegation having one vote. The Council, according to Article VI, paras. 3, 4, 5, and 8 of the Agreement, passes two types of resolutions: decisions and recommendations. They are taken only with the consent of the chiefs of the delegations of all States Parties (genuine consensus). There are no provisions as to the delimitation of topics covered by the two types of resolutions. Decisions, it says, "are taken on the merits of the problems discussed" (but *what* problems?) and in procedural matters. On what topics recommendations are passed it is not said. There are no precise provisions for the acceptance or rejection of voted recommendations by national authorities except the provision of Article VI, para. 5, stipulating that "Recommendations shall be carried out by the Contracting Parties in accordance with the decisions of the competent authorities of the various countries." Thus this category of resolutions could be called "unqualified." The chiefs of the delegations of the

38. See *Pravda*, January 23, 1975.
39. English text of the Agreement published in the *United Nations Treaty Series*, Vol. 610 (1967), No. 8840.
40. Texts of the Agreement and Protocol in *Mnogostoronnieje ekonomicheskoe sotrudnichestvo . . . , op. cit.*, 1972, pp. 296–298.
41. Text of the Agreement in *Mnogostoronnieje ekonomicheskoe sotrudnichestvo . . . , op. cit.*, 1972, pp. 294–296.

member countries have to inform the Council about the progress of the realization of the decisions and recommendations adopted by the Council.

Its executive organ is a Bureau, composed of a director, his deputies, experts, and administrative and technical staff. According to a recent report in *Pravda*, the Director is a Pole and his "first deputy" a Soviet specialist.[42] Russian is the only working language.

Intermetall is active, among other things, in promoting trade exchanges and specialization of production, dissemination of relevant information, and the furthering of technical progress in the iron and steel industry. Whereas during the first years the members of "Intermetall" basically exchanged steel and supplies, this has changed, so that at present it is increasingly becoming finished metallurgical products.[43]

Upon instructions from Intermetall, the technical and economic foundation was prepared for the construction of a big metallurgical plant, based on the ores of the Kursk "magnetic anomaly" and Polish coke. The Council of Intermetall accepted the plan and sent it to Comecon's Committee for Cooperation in the Field of Planning for further study and the preparation of an international agreement on the construction of the plant by interested countries.

6. *The International Centre for Scientific and Technical Information*

The Agreement on the creation of the International Centre was signed by eight countries in February 1969 during the second meeting of the Heads of Committees and Ministries of Science and Technology of the Comecon countries.[44] It came into force in April 1970.

The basic tasks of the Centre may be summarized as follows:

1. the working out of an international system of scientific and technical information,

2. the supplying of countries participating in the Centre with information, primarily in the field of problems of great importance for the national economy, to guarantee scientific and technical progress, taking advantage on a large scale of the new techniques of communication,

42. See *Pravda*, November 20, 1974.
43. For an account of Intermetall's activities in connection with its tenth anniversary see *Życie Gospodarcze,* July 28, 1974.
44. For the text in an English translation see our Annexes (No. XIII).

3. the running of informative publications,

4. the carrying out of research in the field of the theory and practice of scientific and technical information, in particular the working out of forms, methods, and organization of processes of information on a contemporary level,

5. the lending, upon demand, of organizational, methodical, and scientific and technical aid to members of the Centre,

6. cooperation in the formation and perfecting of cadres for organs of scientific and technical information.

The Organization is located in Moscow. It was given a new building in May 1974.[45]

The policy-making organ of the International Centre is the Committee of Plenipotentiaries. It is composed of representatives of each member country, each having one vote. The Committee (Article VI, paras. 5–7 of the Agreement) passes two categories of resolutions: decisions and recommendations. Decisions deal with "problems of the functioning of the Centre," and they enter into force on the date of the signing of the minutes of the respective meeting of the Committee. Recommendations deal with "problems connected with cooperation of the national systems of scientific and technical information of the contracting countries," and enter into force after their acceptance by the competent national organs. No deadlines are provided for the acceptance or rejection of recommendations.

Certain subjects listed in the Agreement (and repeated in the Centre's Statute) require unanimous decisions, with the proviso that "abstention from voting does not influence the adoption of a decision." To this category belong, for instance, the decision on the total amount of the yearly budget, the appointment of the Director and his deputies or the admission of new members.

The procedure for the adoption of decisions and recommendations which do not require unanimity, the Agreement adds, is determined by the Statute of the Centre. According to Article 14 of the Centre's Statute, "decisions on other problems of the work of the Centre and also recommendations...are adopted with the agreement *(s soglasia)* of the representatives of the interested member countries of the Centre." *A contrario*, these are majority decisions; but the formulation used does not determine *what* majority is required. The possibility of declaring lack of interest, with the option of joining the respective

45. See *Pravda*, May 14, 1974.

recommendations or decisions[46] later, is also provided for.

The executive of the International Centre is in the hands of a Director, who has an unspecified number of deputies. They are all appointed by the Committee of Plenipotentiaries, the Director for a five-year term and his deputies for three-year terms. The Director (Article VIII of the Agreement) is appointed "on the proposal of the host country" (i.e. the Soviet Union), a stipulation which may perhaps be explained by the fact that the USSR contributes 74 per cent of the Organization's budget.[47] The deputies are appointed from among the citizens of all the contracting countries in turn, according to the interest demonstrated by each of these members.

A Scientific Council of the International Centre, with advisory capacities, was also established, and the possibility of the creation of branch (field) offices of the Centre is also provided for.

Russian is the only working language of the International Centre.

7. *"Interkhim"*

The Agreement on the creation of the International Branch Organization for cooperation in the field of small tonnage chemical production, "Interkhim," was signed in July 1969.[48] The original members were six Comecon countries. Rumania acceded in 1971 and Yugoslavia in 1973.[49] Mongolia (and Cuba) are not members.

The aim of the Organization, as stated in the preamble to the Agreement, is to promote specialization, cooperation in production, and coordination of plans for development of production, more rational development and use of productive capacities, an increase in the technical and economic level of production, further development of mutual exchange, and the guaranteeing of full supply of the member countries in this particular field.

The Organization specializes in such products as synthetic dyestuffs, auxiliary materials for the textile, leather and paper industries, plant protecting chemicals, chemical admixtures for polymeric materials, etc.[50]

46. Regarding the absurdity of a member country declaring itself "uninterested" in certain resolutions, see p. 64, footnote 63.
47. See J. Metera and Z. Ziółkowski, *op. cit.*, p. 125.
48. For the text in an English translation see our Annexes (No. XIV).
49. See, e.g., V. Morozov, *op. cit.*, *International Affairs*, No. 4 (April), 1974.
50. See, e.g., A. Nagovitsin in "CMEA Countries' Cooperation in the Chemical Industry," *International Affairs*, No. 1 (January), 1973, p. 101.

Its headquarters are in Halle/Saale in East Germany, and it has, as its leading organ, a Council in which each member country is represented by a delegation composed of up to three members, each delegation having one vote. The only category of resolutions passed by the Council, according to Article VIII, paras. 3–5 of the Agreement, are decisions (exceptionally called, in Russian, *postanovlenia* and not, as is the case in the basic legal documents of the other Organizations of the group, *reshenia*).[51] The Agreement provides that decisions of the Council be taken only with the agreement of (all) contracting countries which declare their interest in the solving of a given problem ("quasi-consensus"). Decisions of the Council from which obligations may result for the contracting countries enter into force (automatically) 50 days from the signing of the minutes of the pertinent meeting of the Council, if during that period there is no objection on the part of a contracting country. This notwithstanding, such a decision enters into force in relation to the rest of the interested parties.

The executive organ is the Directorate, with a director, his deputies, specialists, and administrative-technical and service personnel. The working languages are Russian and German (concession to Ulbricht?).[52]

The acceptance by the Council of Interkhim of a plan of action for the elimination of DDT insecticides and the substitution of preparations inoffensive to human organisms was classified as an event of "exceptional social and economic importance."[53]

There is one important stipulation in the Agreement creating "Interkhim" which clearly distinguishes it from most of the other bodies belonging to Comecon's specialized agencies. We are referring here to Article XII of that Agreement, dealing with financial problems.

The standard situation concerning the financing of international governmental organizations is the paying of the expenses involved by

51. The term *postanovlenia* is also used in Rule 27 of the Rules of Procedure of the Session of Comecon, in Rule 25 of the Rules of Procedure of its Executive Board and in Rule 35 of the Standard Rules of Procedure of the Standing Commissions, but in the sense that in that way (i.e. by means of *postanovlenia*) the recommendations and decisions *(reshenia)* of the respective Comecon organs are adopted.
52. In his memoirs *Ostblock intern. 13 Jahre Dolmetscher für die polnische Partei- und Staatsführung,* Hoffmann und Campe Verlag, Hamburg, 1970, Erwin Weit relates (pp. 265–266) how touchy—though evidently not always successful—Ulbricht sometimes was concerning the use of the German language in intra-bloc relations. Regarding Weit's book see my review in *Soviet Studies,* vol. XXIV, No. 3 (January) 1973.
53. See J. Ptaszek, *op. cit.,* p. 284.

118

means of contributions of the governments of the member countries.[54] There is a range of solutions as to the establishment of the scales of these contributions, and, especially in the case of bigger international bodies (with regard to the Communist international organizations see especially the discussion on the scale of contributions to the budget of Comecon and the Joint Institute for Nuclear Research in Chapters II and IV of this study), there are tremendous differences in the percentages of the total contributions paid by individual member countries.

In the case of smaller international bodies the contracting parties may agree on equal contributions of all member countries, big or small. This simplified solution is often used in the case of Comecon's specialized agencies (see Article VII, para. 1 of the Agreement on the Central Control Office for the Combined Power Systems; Article III, para. 8 of the Agreement on the Common Waggon Pool; Article VIII, para. 1 of the Agreement on the Organization for Cooperation of the Ball-bearing Industry; and Article IX, para. 1 of the Agreement on Intermetall); it is also (Article XII, para. 1) the initial solution provided for in the case of 'Interkhim.' But para. 3 of the same Article XII stipulates that "the Contracting Parties agree to provide for a gradual changeover to payment for the services of 'Interkhim,' carried out on the orders of the individual member countries of 'Interkhim,' and the gradual transition to *khozraschet.*

The latter term, taken over from Soviet economic terminology, was, after 1945, translated into the languages of the "people's democracies" (e.g. *rozrachunek gospodarczy* in Polish); it can be roughly translated into English as "self-financing operation." It signifies a financial system under which expenditures of a unit have to be fully covered by its revenues, and, what is more, a profit should be achieved. The application of this principle distinguishes the financial system of enterprises from that of institutions financed out of the state budget.

In the concrete case of "Interkhim," the provision stipulating the gradual transition from the system of contributions paid by member

54. In the case of an international organization having revenue resulting from its activities, this, of course, lowers the contributions of the member countries. But it is only in exceptional cases of typical service bodies such as international governmental banks that financial needs may be covered totally by revenues. The case of the European Communities, given their "own" sources of revenue, gradually making them independent of contributions, is also unique. For a more detailed discussion of financial problems of international governmental organizations see Richard Szawlowski *Les Finances et le Droit financier d'une Organisation internationale intergouvernementale*, Editions Cujas, Paris, 1971.

states to *khozraschet* means that gradually that body will be transforming itself from a classical "administrative" international governmental organization like, say, Comecon itself or Intermetall, to an international governmental business-type organization, like "Interatominstrument," dealt with in this chapter under point 9.

8. *The International Investment Bank*

The Agreement on the creation of the International Investment Bank was signed in July 1970[55] between seven Comecon countries. Rumania acceded in January 1971. Cuba was admitted in January 1974,[56] and, in April 1974, Yugoslavia signed an agreement on cooperation with the Bank.[57] This agreement gives Yugoslavia the possibility of obtaining loans for her enterprises and for projects "which open prospects of increasing trade with socialist countries."

The main aim of the Bank, according to Article II, para. 1 of the Agreement, is the granting of long- and medium-term loans, primarily for the realization of ventures connected with the international socialist division of labour, specialization and cooperation of production, investments for the broadening of the raw material and combustible basis in the common interest and the construction of objects in other branches of economy, in both the international and national interest.

The Bank has to be extremely "exigent" in its crediting: objects for which credits are granted must represent the highest technical level, guarantee the production of goods conforming to world standards of quality and price, etc.

The headquarters of the Investment Bank are in Moscow. Its highest organ is a Council, composed of representatives of all member countries, each of them having one vote, irrespective of his country's share in the Bank's capital (an unusual provision, identical to the relevant provision in the case of the International Bank for Economic Cooperation). According to Article XIX, last paragraph, of the Agreement, and Article 22, para. 2 of the Bank's Charter, the only category of resolutions passed by the Council are decisions. On basic questions listed in the Charter (e.g. on the approval of the annual report, the balance sheet and the distribution of the Bank's profit or on the admission of new members), decisions have to be adopted unanimously. On other questions not considered as being of top

---

55. For the text in an English translation see our Annexes (No. XV).
56. See, e.g., *Zycie Warszawy*, January 23, 1974.
57. See *Pravda*, April 27, 1974 and *Życie Warszawy*, April 30, 1974.

importance, decisions are taken with a qualified majority of "not less" than 3/4 of the votes. The introduction of majority decisions in certain cases contrasts with the solution in force in the other Comecon Bank. The quorum, both in the case of decisions on "basic questions" and on other questions, is "not less" than 3/4 of the members of the Bank.

The executive of the Bank is its Board of Management, consisting of a Chairman (the Russian Vorobev, who died in March 1975) and his three deputies, appointed from among the nationals of the member countries for a period of five years. The Bank is divided into departments and sections, and may have field offices and representations.[58] Russian is the only working language.

Apart from the capital stock of the Bank formed by Members' quotas, under Article VI, para. 1 of the Agreement "The Bank may attract funds in...convertible currencies by obtaining financial and bank credits and loans..." The latter was reflected in 1973 by a loan to the amount of 50 million dollars, granted to the International Investment Bank by the National Westminster Bank in London for a period of seven years.[59] In 1974 the Bank was given consultative status with the UN Conference for Trade and Development (UNCTAD).[60]

Concerning the practical activities of the Bank, it granted, during 1971–1974, 39 loans, to the total amount of almost 800 million transferable roubles, to eight countries.[61]

Its loan policy seems, in fact, to be very selective. Thus Poland, for example, obtained, up to the end of 1972, seven investment loans to the total amount of 20,750,000 transferable roubles. These loans mean the partial financing, for instance, of a factory of textiles having the resistance of cotton, equipped with French, West German, Dutch, and Swiss machinery. In other cases, loans were granted for the organization of production of brake systems for cars on a British licence, and of electric low-power engines based on Japanese construction and documentation. Hungary is electrifying, with the aid of a loan from the Bank, the railway connecting Rumania with Czechoslovakia, and increasing its traffic capacity.

58. The structure of the Bank is given in A. Ja. Rotlejder, *op. cit.*, p. 108. Evidently no field offices or representations have been established yet.
59. See, e.g., *Życie Warszawy*, March 22, 1973.
60. See *International Investment Bank*, 1974 [Annual Report], published probably in April 1975, p. 17.
61. See *International Investment Bank*, 1974, p. 14. Only a graph is offered, and this does not give an exact figure.

The highest individual loan, until the spring of 1973, in the amount of 77.5 million transferable roubles, was given by the Bank to Czechoslovakia for the construction of a big factory of "Tatra" trucks in Pokshivnica.[62] By the spring of 1974 the record loan was in the amount of 252.4 transferable roubles, given for the building of a mining-metallurgical enterprise in the Soviet Union.[63] Credit terms have been fixed not to exceed twelve years. The interest rate, for loans granted in transferable roubles, was lowered from the initial 4 to 6 to 3 to 5 per cent p.a.[64]

Generally speaking, the activities of the International Investment Bank during the first four years of its existence seem to have started off quite well.[65]

The "Comprehensive Programme" (Chapter VII, para. 25) mentioned the possibility of the creation, within the Bank, of a special fund for the crediting of activities in the field of economic and technical air for developing countries.

The creation of such a special fund was decided upon by the Council of the Bank in April 1973.[66] The total amount of this fund, composed both of transferable roubles and convertible currencies, was fixed at one billion transferable roubles. This would be quite an impressive sum, were it not for the fact that, as was disclosed a month later by the president of the Polish National Bank, the payments to the special fund during the first years of its existence are to be 100 million transferable roubles only.[67]

The Bank's 1974 report reads in connection with the Special fund:[68]

> In 1974 the member countries paid up their first contributions to the Fund in the amount which enables the beginning of the operations. The Bank has carried out necessary organization measures and worked out appropriate regulations concerning the activities of the Special Fund.—From the sources of the Fund the International Investment Bank will grant credits to developing

62. See *Polityka*, March 10, 1973.
63. See *International Investment Bank*, 1973 [Annual Report], p. 19. The 1974 Report does not contain figures on individual loans.
64. See *International Investment Bank*, 1973, p. 12 and 1974, p. 15.
65. A Western account of the International Investment Bank (and the International Bank for Economic Cooperation) for the period up to the second half of 1972 is given in Diethar Stelzl *Die internationalen Banken des Rats für gegenseitige Wirtschaftshilfe*, Olzog Verlag, Munich-Vienna, 1973.
66. See, e.g., *Życie Warszawy*, April 14, 1973.
67. See *Życie Warszawy*, May 19, 1973.
68. See *International Investment Bank*, 1974, p. 16.

countries for a term of up to 15 years to finance construction of new and reconstruction and modernization of operating enterprises in industry, agriculture and other branches of economy.

This Fund is a new thing, as Comecon, until the present—at least officially and in clear contrast with the European Community—did not grant loans to the developing countries. Even so, one should bear in mind that the biggest part of the aid given through the European Development Programme, at present to forty-six developing countries, is of a non-reimbursable character, and that, apart from it, there does exist the EC Food Aid Programme, including at present thirty-five countries. Nothing of this kind is offered by Comecon.[69]

9. *Interatominstrument*

The Agreement creating Interatominstrument was signed on February 22, 1972 by the representatives of six Comecon countries (without Rumania and Mongolia).[70] Independently of the normal ratification process provided for in Article 22, para. 1 of the Agreement, paragraph 2 of the same Article stipulated that the Agreement would enter into force "temporarily" with March 1, 1972.

Interatominstrument is classified as an international economic association (*mezhdunarodnoe khoziaistvennoe obedinenie*). This is to reflect its different character as compared with, say, the Organization of the Common Waggon Pool or the organization for Cooperation of the Ball-bearing Industries. Though there are certain similarities between Interatominstrument and Interkhim (because of the principle of *khozraschet* provided for in both cases, though less precisely in the case of Interkhim, where no relevant deadlines were set), the first is obviously more "revolutionary."

Though the 1972 Agreement was concluded between the governments of the six countries, the members of the Organization are not

69. There are only exceptional, strongly politically-tainted situations where such non-reimbursable aid may be given to a developing non-member country with political affinity. Thus, in connection with the 71st meeting of Comecon's Executive Board in April 1975, it was announced that there took place "an exchange of opinions on the problem of giving material aid, by the members of Comecon, to the population of the liberated regions of South Vietnam"— see *Pravda*, April 25, 1975.
70. For the text of the Agreement in an English translation see our Annexes (No. XVI).

directly countries as such, but national enterprises, economic organizations, research institutes, etc. of the member countries, specializing in the field of equipment for nuclear research and the application of nuclear energy.

In the case of the USSR, for instance, the founding members are the All-Union Association (*obedinenie*) "Isotop," subordinated to the State Committee of the USSR for the Use of Atomic Energy, and the All-Union Export-Import Bureau (*kontora*) "Tekhsnabeksport"; in the case of Poland, the Joint Plants for Nuclear Equipment Construction "Polon" etc. Other national bodies, active in the field, may also accede to Interatominstrument.

Thus, as regards the level of cooperation involved, it ranges lower in this case when compared with the previously discussed international intergovernmental bodies.

The main task of Interatominstrument is to guarantee the supplying of the member countries with the equipment mentioned above. In Comecon countries over 1,000 different varieties of this equipment were drafted and produced in short series, which brought about the necessity for division of labour and specialization in research, production, and trade in that field.

According to Article 3 of the 1972 Agreement, Interatominstrument may, with the agreement of the respective contracting countries, and in conformity with procedure established in those states, open its representations and departments in their territories, and also establish production branches, draft-construction and other organizations.

The leading organ of the Association is its Council. It is composed of representatives of each of the national organizations and enterprises participating in Interatominstrument. But all the representatives from one country have only one "decisive" *(reshajushchij)* vote.

The only type of resolutions passed are decisions. According to the Agreement (Article 8, para, 1) and the Association's Charter (Articles 21–23), decisions of the Council on certain fundamental questions (e.g. the determination of the general direction of the activities of the Association, approval of plans for its activities and its financial plans, and reports on their realization) require unanimity. In other cases (e.g. the appointment and dismissal of the Director, his deputies and the managers of branch offices) a majority of "not less" than 3/4 of the votes is required. Finally, for other problems (especially in the field of decisions on specialization and cooperation) a simple majority of votes is sufficient. In this field, however (but not in the case of problems decided on by 3/4 majorities), such a decision is binding only for those members who voted for it. The quorum is fixed, in all cases, at "not less" than 3/4 of the total votes.

The day-to-day activities of the Association, located in Warsaw, are administrated by a Director and his deputies. The Director acts on the principle of undivided authority (*edinonachalie*). In September 1972 it was stated that the Association would employ 50 people, including 23 foreign specialists.[71]

Interatominstrument, as a business-type organization, is supposed to act on the principle of *khozraschet* (see above, p. 119). As a basis for the Association's economic activity a statutory fund *(ustavnyj fond)* to the amount of 2.1 million transferable roubles was created with equal shares from all countries. In the future it may be increased. The payments are to be made gradually, over a number of years.

As it is planned that the Association will become financially independent only in 1975, during the first three years of its existence its members had to supply, apart from their payments to the statutory fund, additional contributions. The Association may also obtain loans from the banks of the country in which it is located, from the International Bank for Economic Cooperation, the International Investment Bank, as well as from its members.

By 1975 Intratominstrument should thus act as a fully-fledged international multilateral business corporation. This is a new phenomenon in the system of Communist international organizations insofar as these "business-type" bodies were, until quite recently, represented only by a few intergovernmental enterprises.[72]

In January 1974 the Director of Interatominstrument, the Polish engineer Twardoń, stated in a press interview[73] that the Association

71. See *Życie Warszawy*, September 9, 1972. An article entitled "Eastern Europe's Nuclear Cooperative" by Richard Davy (*Times*, April 2, 1973) mentions "about 60 people in the Warsaw office, half local staff and half from member countries."
72. A prime example of such an enterprise is the Polish-Hungarian "Haldex," created in 1959, specializing in the utilization of coal-bins (for its tenth anniversary, see *Życie Warszawy*, April 15, 1969, and for its fifteenth anniversary see *Rynki Zagraniczne*, June 22, 1974). Another example is "Agromash," created in 1965, specializing in the development, production and marketing of machines for the mechanization of labour in the producing of vegetables, vines, and fruit. This enterprise, founded by Bulgaria and Hungary, was later joined by East Germany and the USSR. For an account of "Agromash's" activities see *Pravda*, May 20, 1973. In 1973 the first bilateral Communist business corporation—the Soviet East-German "Assofoto," specializing in the field of the photochemical industry, was established. See, e.g., *Informationen* (Bonn), No. 16/1973.
73. See *Życie Warszawy*, January 19, 1974.

is still at the stage of "getting up speed" and is working hard on the future five-year plan, during which it is hoped to increase the turnover in the relevant equipment between the Comecon countries threefold. The Association organized two big exhibitions in Sofia and Prague, and a similar exhibition was prepared in Warsaw. It was opened in May 1974.[74]

In the process of the gradual application of the principle of *khozraschet*, a "small percentage" of the total amount of the transaction was provided for, in three contracts signed on joint production in the pertinent field, as provision for Interatominstrument. Another point mentioned in the same interview was the fact that preparations were then under way (i.e. the beginning of 1974), on the basis of three plants—in Riga, Toruń and one in Bulgaria—to start production of equipment not yet manufactured in the territories of the contracting countries.

Early in 1975 it was stated[75] that the planned, apparently reduced, pertinent turnover under the five-year plan 1976–1980 will increase two and a half times. Planned specialization is to embrace 25 per cent of the production sortiment and 50 per cent of its total value. Service stations, mostly manned by internationally composed groups of specialists, were planned to open during 1975 in Bulgaria, East Germany, Poland and the USSR.

Many difficulties connected with these and other problems were mentioned, and the Association was referred to as a "guinea pig." Its importance as a testing ground for the recently created new International Economic Associations—Interatomenergo and Intertextilmash—was strongly emphasized, and it was mentioned that experts working on the constitutional documents of the two latter Associations spent many hours in Mr. Twardoń's office.

10. *International Centre for the Training of Civil Aviation Personnel*

In late March 1973 came news about yet another "Comecon family" body being in the organizational stage.[76] This is the Centre for the Training of Civil Aviation Personnel, which is supposed to have the character of an international academic school, located in the USSR. The Soviet Union and East Germany were given the task of organizing the new Centre.

74. See *Rynki Zagraniczne*, May 9, 1974.
75. See *Neues Deutschland*, February 12, 1975.
76. See *Życie Warszawy*, March 25–26, 1973.

The Centre will offer "post-graduate" training of aircraft captains, training of personnel in the use of new types of aircraft and training of flight safety engineers.

In December 1974, at the meeting of Comecon's Standing Commission for Transport, a "general agreement" was signed between eight Comecon countries (save Rumania) on the construction of a common centre in the fields mentioned above.[77] Its headquarters will be located at Ulyanovsk on the Volga river, where a Soviet aviation school has already been in operation for forty years.[78]

It can be assumed that the new Centre may probably start its activities in 1976.

11. *Interelectro, Interatomenergo and Intertextilmash*

In September 1973 came news of preparatory work being done in Comecon on the creation of three new international bodies: "Interelectro," "Interatomenergo" and "Intertextilmash."[79] The respective international agreements were signed in December 1973.[80] The full texts of the treaties do not yet seem to have been published, though some details are already available.[81]

Interelectro was founded by seven countries (Bulgaria, Czechoslovakia, East Germany, Hungary, Poland, Rumania, and the USSR). Its aim is to meet to the fullest the requirements of the member countries in high quality products of the electrotechnical industry. This is to be achieved by the broadening and deepening of economic, production, and scientific and technical cooperation between the partners. Its headquarters are in Moscow.

The first meeting of the Organization's Council was held in March 1974.[82] On the agenda were "basic organizational, internal and structural problems" of the new body. Working groups have been created to deal with the main fields of production of the electrotechnical industry.

Interatomenergo was founded by eight countries (the ones which founded Interelectro plus Yugoslavia). Its field of activity is coopera-

77. See *Życie Warszawy*, December 7, 1974.
78. See *Życie Warszawy*, March 24, 1975 and April 17, 1975.
79. See *Życie Warszawy*, September 29, 1973.
80. See *Pravda*, December 15, 1973. See also the communiqué of the 65th meeting of the Executive Board of Comecon in *Pravda*, December 14, 1973.
81. See, e.g., *Rynki Zagraniczne*, February 28, 1974.
82. See *Życie Warszawy*, March 20 and 22, 1974.

tion in the production of all kinds of equipment, instruments, spare parts and materials for atomic power stations, and the construction of these power stations, as well as pertinent specialization and cooperation, preparation of servicing cadres, aid in starting operations, etc. The production of electric energy by atomic power stations is supposed to increase steadily, though in some member countries they are yet to be constructed (Poland, Rumania and Hungary do not yet have one). The USSR, it was clearly admitted, is not able to cover the increasing demand of the "satellites" in this field, though, one may add, the first Soviet atomic power station, in Obninsk, near Kaluga, was opened already in 1954.

Interatomenergo's headquarters are located in Moscow. The first meeting of its General Council took place in June 1974.[83] The Russian Maltsev was appointed Director-General. A group of over ten Polish specialists was sent to work at the headquarters.[84] It was disclosed on the same occasion that the USSR is the "main shareholder" in Interatomenergo, Poland and Czechoslovakia being second in importance.

Finally, Intertextilmash was founded by seven countries, the same as those cooperating in the case of Interelectro. Its aim is to organize cooperation and specialization in production, common scientific research and draft-construction work, and the organization of technical servicing in the field of the textile industry. This is necessary in view of the fact that there is a deficit of textile machinery in the Comecon countries. Apart from the USSR, East Germany and Czechoslovakia, the production capabilities in the other countries are insufficient in this particular field, and supply is short of all types of machinery.

The headquarters of the new body are located in Moscow. It will include about fifteen national production associations in the field of the textile machinery industry, a few big production units, and construction and drafting bureaux of the participating countries. They will retain their "legal independence" and remain the property of the individual countries.[85]

As follows from the December 1973 communiqué, the first of the bodies mentioned in this sub-chapter—Interelectro—is supposed to be an "administrative" international governmental organization, whereas the two other ones—Interatomenergo and Intertextilmash— are conceived as international economic associations of the Interatominstrument type.

83. See *Pravda*, June 21, 1974.
84. See *Życie Warszawy*, December 8–9, 1974.
85. See *Życie Warszawy*, February 1, 1974.

They will really start their activities probably only in 1976.

12. *Interkhimvolokno*,   *Interetalonpribor*,   *Intergasoochistka*   and
     Intervodoochistka

A new international economic Association, apart from Interatomenergo and Intertextilmash created half a year earlier, is "Interkhimvolokno." It was established by virtue of an agreement signed during
the XXVIII Session of Comecon in June 1974.[86] The signatories were
seven Comecon countries (without Cuba and Mongolia) plus
Yugoslavia. Its declared aim is a more rapid development of the
production of deficitary chemical (synthetic) fibres.

Yet another body, called "Interetalonpribor," specializing in the
field of production, supplies and "operative exchange" of specialized
apparatus, equipment and analytical standards for scientific research
and drafting organizations, was created probably earlier in 1974.[87]
Reporting on a four-day meeting of the Council of Plenipotentiaries of
that body in August 1974, a Polish paper referred to it as a "scientific-
productive association."[88]

In July 1974 another Association, classified as "scientific-
economic"—"Intergasoochistka"—was planned to be established. The
drafts of the respective agreement and the Association's Charter were
agreed upon in July 1974 during a conference of experts from Comecon
countries in the field of environmental protection.[89] But it seems that
no action was taken on the new Association during 1974 or up to
the late summer of 1975.

And in November 1974 mention was also made of plans to create a
similar body specializing in fighting water pollution—"Intervodoochistka."[90] Here again, nothing seems to have materialized by
September 1975.

Generally speaking, the phenomenon of multilateral Communist
international economic associations is almost brand new, and this
form of cooperation is just starting. These bodies will certainly
proliferate in the years to come.[91]

86. See communiqué in *Pravda*, June 22, 1974.
87. See mention, in passing, in *Pravda*, June 13, 1974.
88. See *Życie Warszawy*, August 22, 1974.
89. See *Trybuna Ludu*, July 14, 1974.
90. See *Życie Warszawy*, November 23, 1974.
91. See, in this connection, three papers delivered at the already-mentioned

Referring to the initial difficulties, the remark was made in mid-1974:[92]

> Of course, during the first period there may result, as in any beginnings, complications in the work of the international associations. A great deal has to be learned, experience must be gathered, and optimal methods and forms of practical activities have to be worked out.

June 1974 Bergisch-Gladbach Conference: those by Andreas Bilinsky (Munich), Vladimir Koutikov (Sofia), and Lothar Rüster (Potsdam-Babelsberg).
92. See *Pravda*, June 13, 1974.

Chapter IV

THE REMAINING ORGANIZATIONS OF THE SYSTEM

With the obvious exception of the Warsaw Treaty Organization discussed in Chapter I, most of the bodies forming the system of the Communist international governmental organizations may be classified as belonging to the "Comecon family"; we dealt with them in Chapters II and III.

But there remain a few other organizations belonging to the same system, especially the Joint Institute for Nuclear Research and, recently, Intersputnik, which form a distinct sub-group within the system, independent of that of the "Comecon family" (let alone the WTO), and are therefore treated separately in this chapter. In the pertinent Eastern literature, interestingly enough, a certain confusion can be observed in this field.[1]

1. *The Joint Institute for Nuclear Research*

The Agreement creating the Joint Institute for Nuclear Research was signed in March 1956.[2] In spite of a provision of Article II, para. 3

1. Thus there were, on the one hand, attempts to treat the Joint Institute for Nuclear Research simply as one of Comecon's bodies—see, e.g., Ludwig Ciamaga *Od współpracy do integracji: Zarys organizacji i działalności RWPG w latach 1949–1964* ("From Cooperation to Integration: An Outline of the Organization and Activities of Comecon in the years 1949–1964"), Warsaw, 1965, Chapter 2. On the other hand there was even denial of any "superiority" of Comecon among the international economic organizations of the Communist countries—see P. A. Tokareva, "The Formation of the System of International Organizations of the Socialist Countries"—*Sovetskoe gosudarstvo i pravo*, No. 10/1967, pp. 68–69.
2. English text of the agreement was published in the *United Nations Treaty Series*, Vol. 259 (1957), No. 3686. Text reproduced in our Annexes (No. XVII). The Charter of the Joint Institute, provided for in Article II, para. 1 of the Agreement, is published in *Sbornik dieistvuyushchikh dogovorov, soglashenij i konventsij zakliuchennykh SSSR s inostrannymi gosudarstvami*, Vypusk XVII and XVIII. Moscow, 1960, pp. 339–347. We give an English translation of this Charter in our Annexes (No. XVII).

of that Agreement, providing for the location of the Institute in the Kalinin region, it is in fact located at Dubna, in the Moscow region.

The aim of the Institute, according to the Agreement, is joint theoretical and experimental research in the field of nuclear physics by scientists of the member countries, exclusively for peaceful purposes. The September 1956 Charter of the Institute mentions in its Article 4, in addition to that, a few extra points: promoting of the development of nuclear physics in the member countries; keeping in contact with interested national and international scientific research and other institutions; promoting of all-round development of the scientific research cadres of the member countries.

The original membership of the Joint Institute comprised the USSR and the European "people's democracies," China, Mongolia, and North Korea. North Vietnam joined in September 1956. Cuba is not a member. In Article VIII the Agreement provides for the withdrawal of members, and China, followed by Albania, did so around 1965.[3]

The highest organ of the Joint Institute is the Committee of the "Authorized Representatives of the States Members of the Institute." It has developed more in practice than is provided for in the Agreement itself, where, without even being referred to as a "Committee," the "authorized representatives" are mentioned in Article V, para. 2 in connection with the election of the Director of the Institute and his two Duputies. The meetings of this body take place once a year. It is the Institute's highest policy-making organ, scrutinizes the Director's annual reports, approves the Institute's research plans and its yearly budgets, etc.[4]

There are also two other organs. One of them is the Scientific Council of the Institute, the other its Financial Committee. In actual fact both of these bodies have had to cede important prerogatives provided for them in the Agreement and the Charter to the Committee of the "Authorized Representatives of the States Members of the Institute," and probably act mostly in an advisory capacity for the latter.

---

3. Communist literature only rarely mentions it—see, e.g., the Polish Almanach *Świat w Przekroju 1972*, Wiedza Powszechna, Warsaw, 1972, p. 560, mentioning that Albania and the People's Republic of China "at present do not participate in the work of the Institute." In 1962 there were still seventy Chinese scholars working in the Institute—see report on the Dubna Institute in *Życie Warszawy*, May 20–21, 1962.

4. See, e.g., short notes on the meetings of the Committee in 1970 and 1975 in *Życie Warszawy*, January 15, 1970 and February 21–23, 1975. The latter meeting approved the Institute's development plan for the period 1976–1980.

In a Soviet publication one reads the following in this connection:[5]

> In 1956 the Authorized Representatives of the States-Members of the JINR decided to create the Committee of the Authorized Representatives of the Governments of the States Members of the Joint Institute for Nuclear Research. At the meetings of this Committee (which have been taking place starting with 1957) the report of the Directorate on the activities of the Institute is heard, the Directorate of the Institute is elected, the budget is approved and other questions are dealt with. At present [1967] work is being carried out in the JINR on the putting in of amendments to certain articles of the Charter of the Joint Institute for Nuclear Research.

The Joint Institute is, incidentally, the only international organization belonging to the system discussed in this study in which the scale of contributions of the member countries to the budget was provided for in the Agreement (apart from some minor "Comecon family" bodies, in which the principle of equal contributions applies).[6]

The original scale of assessments was fixed in Article VI of the 1956 Agreement (see Annex No. XVII). When North Vietnam joined six months later, her contribution was settled at 0.05 per cent. But according to Eastern sources it was decided by the Institute's member countries (no exact date was given, but perhaps only in the early sixties) that "at present" North Vietnam would be exempted from payments "in connection with the fight against US aggression."[7] She may have been asked to pay again starting with 1974 or 1975.

The original scale had to be changed, of course, after China and Albania left the Joint Institute in the mid-sixties. Only the withdrawal of China was evidently of consequence here, as she had had to contribute, until then, 20 per cent of the budget. In this connection a change had to take place in the scale. We do not have at our disposal the full

5. See *Mnogostoronnieje ekonomičheskoe sotrudnichestvo...*, *op. cit.*, 1967, p. 248, footnote 1. In the second, 1972 edition of the same collection (pp. 409–410), the same footnote may be found, but without the last sentence about the preparatory work on amendments to the Charter. The document seems to have remained unchanged.
6. Concerning the scale of contributions in the case of Comecon, see Chapter II, p. 68.
7. See *Mnogostoronnieje ekonomičheskoe sotrudnichestvo...*, *op. cit.*, 1967, p. 237, footnote 1. This footnote does not exist in the second (1972) edition of the same collection, which also misses out, incidentally, the whole passage of Article VI of the Agreement giving the original scale of assessments of the members.

present scale. Nevertheless it is known that the USSR, which paid 47.25 per cent previously, now contributes "over 50 per cent," and Poland, which previously paid 6.75 per cent, now contributes "about 8 per cent."[8] The respective contributions (perhaps with the exception of North Korea and Mongolia) were thus increased; the Soviet contribution at present could be over 60 per cent, as is the case in Comecon.

The Joint Institute is headed by a Director and two Deputy Directors, elected by a (simple) majority of the Member States from amongst the scientists of these states. The Director is elected for a term of three years, the Deputy Directors for two years. The Director has always been a Russian (Professor Blochintsev, now Professor Bogolubov) and the posts of the two Deputy Directors rotate between the nationals of the "younger brothers."

In 1962 the total staff of the Joint Institute was already about 2,700[9]; at present it is over 3,000, of whom more than 600 are scientists.[10] One of the Institute's most prominent collaborators is Professor Bruno Pontecorvo, whose defection from the West in 1950 caused considerable alarm.[11]

There is no provision, either in the Agreement or in the Institute's Charter, concerning the working language. It is, of course, Russian, perhaps with a possibility of the kind provided for in the case of the International Mathematical Centre (see below, p. 146).

The Institute has developed fairly broad cooperation with national and international nuclear research institutes, e.g. with the US Atomic Energy Commission and with the Geneva-based CERN.[12] In July 1974 there was news of a "big group" of French researchers who arrived at Dubna and started a series of joint experiments. Cooperation

8. See J. Ptaszek, *op. cit.*, p. 223.
9. See *Życie Warszawy*, May 20–21, 1962. In 1968 the same paper (August 14, 1968) gave the lower figure of "over 2,400." It was also stated on the same occasion that "in connection with personnel changes six scholars were dismissed or left the Institute at their own request." It is possible that these were Jews.
10. See article by Prof. I. D. Morokhov in the *Bulletin* of the International Atomic Energy Agency, vol. 16, No. 3 (June 1974), p. 5.
11. On Pontecorvo's case see, e.g., Alan Moorehead *The Traitors. The Double Life of Fuchs, Pontecorvo, and Nunn May*, Hamish Hamilton, London (1952). Pontecorvo's stay in the USSR was officially disclosed by himself only as late as in 1955, when he published an article in *Pravda*, March 1, 1955 entitled "Ban Atomic Weapons." He signed as Stalin Prize Winner, attacked the "imperialists" and praised the USSR in every respect.
12. Some member countries of the Joint Institute, e.g. Poland, have observer status in CERN—see, e.g., *Życie Warszawy*, July 16, 1974.

of this kind is based on an agreement between the Joint Institute and the French Institute for Nuclear Physics and Elementary Particles.[13]

During a Scientific Conference in Heidelberg in the summer of 1969 a delegation of the Joint Institute reported the discovery, in the Institute, of new isotopes in light elements; in reactions with heavy ions were obtained, synthetically, oxygen-22, nitrogen-21 and carbon -18. These nuclei have an abnormally high number of neutrons.[14]

In 1972 a team at Dubna artificially obtained an element, which takes 105th place in the Mendeleyev table. Work on the synthesis of this element went on starting with 1967, and the result was achieved slightly before the Americans managed to do the same.[15]

The Joint Institute, around which a whole town has grown up from nothing,[16] will be considerably developed in the years to come.[17]

2. *"Intercosmos" and "Intersputnik"*

The present writer indicated the possibility of the creation of an international organization of the Communist countries in the field of outer space already in the mid-sixties.[18]

As early as the autumn of 1965 the Eastern press reported a conference on cooperation in the field of research and the use of outer space for peaceful purposes, which took place in Moscow between 15 and 20 November.[19] Those participating were Bulgaria, Czechoslovakia, Cuba, East Germany, Hungary, Mongolia, Poland, Rumania, and the USSR. The participants discussed, *inter alia*, problems

13. See *Pravda*, July 29, 1974.
14. See *Życie Warszawy*, August 2, 1969.
15. See *Życie Warszawy*, May 18, 1972.
16. See, e.g., Jerzy Kraszewski and Jerzy Redlich *Moskiewskie ABC* ("The ABC of Moscow"), Iskry, Warsaw, 1973, pp. 207–210. The Institute is classified as "gigantic." The name "Dubna" was given to the new town from the name of a small river flowing there. The authors say that scholars of world renown sit on the town council, and that individual council committees are led by professors. The local newspaper "For Communism" has the privilege of being first to publish communiqués on new discoveries by the physicists.
17. Thus, in June 1973, a fifteen-year plan for the further development of the Institute was discussed during a session of its Scientific Council; under discussion came the construction of new scientific facilities and the modernization of the already existing ones—see *Życie Warszawy*, June 8, 1973. The same is confirmed by Kraszewski and Redlich, *op. cit.*, p. 210.
18. See Richard Szawlowski "The International Organizations of the 'Comecon Family,'" *op. cit.* (1966), p. 126.
19. See, e.g., *Życie Warszawy*, November 24, 1965.

connected with the creation of a programme of common research, joint construction and launching of satellites, etc. The timing of that Conference indicates that it was the first reaction to the 1962 Western treaties on the European Launcher Development Organization (ELDO) and the European Space Research Organization (ESRO), which had come into force in 1964 (these organizations were, incidentally, amalgamated into the European Space Agency—ESA— in May 1975), and the creation of INTELSAT by a treaty signed in July 1964, which came into force in 1965.

In the spring of 1967 the same press[20] reported a new conference which took place in Moscow between 5 and 13 April, to discuss cooperation in space research and the peaceful uses of outer space. The same countries participated as were at the 1965 conference. The launching of satellites and rockets, and the creation of an international communications system via artificial earth satellites for transmitting television programmes, telephone messages and other types of information were decided upon.

A third conference of this kind took place in June 1968,[21] and in August of the same year the Communist countries came forward with the proposal of creating a universal international organization in that field within the UN system.[22] This idea had been discussed in Vienna during the same month at the UN Conference on the Exploration and Peaceful Uses of Outer Space, at which "a number of speakers expressed the view that there should be a centralized UN space agency, although some felt that the time was not yet ripe for such action."[23] Finally nothing along these lines materialized.

During 1969 and 1970 a few "joint" research satellites were launched, starting with Intercosmos-1 in October 1969[24] and Intercosmos-2 in December of the same year.[25] Communist international cooperation in this field is taking place within the "Intercosmos" group—the so-called "Council for International Cooperation for Research and Exploitation of Cosmic Space," created in 1967.

This is not a fully-fledged international organization. Two Polish authors refer to "Intercosmos" as a "specialized Agency attached to the Academy of Science of the USSR"[26] (a sort of international

20. See, e.g., Życie Warszawy, April 16–17, 1967.
21. See, e.g., Życie Warszawy, June 18, 1968.
22. See, e.g., Życie Warszawy, August 14, 1968.
23. See U.N. Press Release, WS/360, August 23, 1968, p. 6.
24. See, e.g., Życie Warszawy, October 15, 1969.
25. See, e.g., Pravda, December 28, 1969.
26. See W. Krauze and T. Wujek Współpraca naukowa Polski Ludowej z zagranicą

coordination centre?). It should be classified as a Communist counter-part, though much less institutionalized, of ESRO.

In November 1971 the Eastern press announced the creation of Intersputnik. The communiqué read:[27]

An agreement to create an international system and an organization of cosmic communications, 'Intersputnik,' was signed on the 15th of November in Moscow. The aim of this new organization is to satisfy the needs of the joining countries in channels of telephone-telegraphic communications, and colour and black-and-white television for the transmission of all kinds of information. Empowered by their governments, the representatives of Bulgaria, Hungary, the German Democratic Republic, Cuba, Mongolia, Poland, Rumania, the Soviet Union, and Czecho-slovakia signed the agreement. The document allows for the joining of other states.

The international system of communications includes a cosmic complex consisting of communication satellites with translating relays, means of self-propulsion and earth-bound systems of controls, as well as ground stations which keep up mutual communications by means of artificial earth satellites.

Thus a Communist counterpart of INTELSAT has been created.[28] The programme of Intersputnik provides for the construction, during 1974–1976, of earth stations in the countries belonging to the Organization.[29]

In connection with Brezhnev's visit to Cuba, it was reported in January 1974[30] that a station of cosmic communications called "Caribe," belonging to the international "Intersputnik" system, was

("Scientific Cooperation of People's Poland with Foreign Countries"), Książka i Wiedza, Warsaw, 1974, p. 105.

27. See, e.g., *Pravda*, November 16, 1971.

28. For the text in an English translation see our Annexes (No. XVIII). The Agreement came into force in July 1972.

29. See Stanisław Ryżka "Common Satellites" in *Polityka*, February 10, 1973. This initial stage apparently requires much more time than was initially planned: Ivan Petrov (Deputy Chief of the USSR Space Communication Administration), in his earlier article "'Intersputnik'-international space communication system and organization" in *Telecommunication Journal* (monthly magazine of the International Telecommunication Union), November 1972, p. 680, wrote that "the first stage is scheduled for completion at the end of 1973." This was obviously over-optimistic.

30. See *Pravda*, January 31, 1974.

constructed near Havana with the help of Soviet technicians, and is working with Soviet equipment. TV programmes connected with the Brezhnev visit were relayed by this station through the system of Soviet satellites "Molnia-2" to an analogous station near Moscow, and then beamed by Soviet TV and the "Intervision" system.

It was mentioned on that occasion that similar stations will be opened, during 1974, in Czechoslovakia and Poland, and in the years following in East Germany, Bulgaria, Hungary, Rumania, and "other countries." The opening, for "experimental exploitation," of such a station in Czechoslovakia, near Prague, was announced in May 1974.[31] The first Polish station was started in July 1974[32] and officially opened in October 1974.[33] On the latter occasion it was announced that "in the nearest future the bringing into exploitation is envisaged of a cosmic station installed on a 'stationary' satellite which will make possible the transmission of from several to over ten television programmes broadcast and received simultaneously, and of from several to hundreds, and even thousands of radiophonic programmes and telephone conversations—received and broadcast simultaneously."

The second stage will be concerned with the practical operations of the earth stations of the members with Soviet satellites using leased channels. Finally, in the third stage, a space segment will be owned by Intersputnik; the alternative of just leasing the whole of the space segment from members of Intersputnik is also provided for.

The structure of Intersputnik, located in Moscow, looks, briefly, as follows.[34] Its policy-making organ is the Council, its executive one—the Directorate.

The Council is composed of representatives of all member countries, one from each member and each having one vote. The Council, according to Article 12, para. 7 of the Agreement, has "to attempt" to adopt its decisions unanimously (an original provision also to be found in the case of the International Mathematical Centre). If this is not achieved, a decision is adopted if it receives not less than two-thirds of the votes of all members of the Council. This is followed by the proviso that decisions are not binding for members who do not vote for their adoption and who have stated their reservation in writing;

31. See *Pravda*, May 2, 1974.
32. See *Trybuna Ludu*, July 18, 1974.
33. See *Życie Warszawy*, October 18, 1974.
34. Apart from the 1971 Agreement, see also Mieczysław Grzegorczyk *Prawo Kosmiczne* ("Outer Space Law"), Państwowe Wydawnictwo Naukowe, Warsaw and Cracow, 1973, p. 77.

they may, however, subsequently subscribe to such a decision.

The Directorate is headed by a Director-General, who acts on the principle of *edinonachalie*. A Deputy Director-General is also provided for. Both are elected by the Council for a period of four years. According to Article 13, para. 5 of the Agreement, the Deputy Director-General (not so the Director-General) may be elected "in principle" for one term only. The rationale of this provision, seen in connection with the following provision that the Director-General and his deputy cannot be citizens of the same country, is obvious. As the Director will in practice always be a Russian, there are no limitations in this case, whereas systematic and frequent rotation is provided for citizens of the "satellites." The staff is appointed from among the nationals of the member states "on the basis of their professional competence and the principle of equitable geographical distribution."

In the future Intersputnik will be financed from a statutory fund (fixed assets and working capital) based on members' contributions, whose amounts will be determined by the extent to which they use the communication channels provided. Until this fund is created, Intersputnik operates with a special budget established for each calendar year. The staff costs and other administrative expenditure are financed by the members as agreed upon by them in accordance with a proposal by the Council, and are set out in a special protocol. These financial documents, as in the case of other organizations of the System, are not published.

Member countries may withdraw from the Organization, advising it three months before the end of the current financial year. The dissolution of Intersputnik may take place on the basis of the agreement of all member countries.

What is, generally speaking, striking in the case of Intersputnik is the attempt to make it an absolutely open international body, conceived "in the spirit of the United Nations."

This is reflected, among other things, by the fact that the government of any state which did not sign the 1971 Agreement may accede to it, the Council "taking note" (the two-thirds rule applying if necessary). Resolution 1721 (XVI) of the UN General Assembly (dealing with "International Cooperation in the Peaceful Uses of Outer Space"), and the 1967 treaty on the Principles of Activities of States in the Exploration and Exploitation of Outer Space, including the Moon and other Celestial Bodies, are referred to in the preamble. Coordination of activities with the International Telecommunication Union (a UN Specialized Agency) is provided for in Article 7 of the Agreement.

Finally, not only was the 1971 Agreement concluded in Russian, English, Spanish, and French versions, but, even more unusual for the Organizations of the System under discussion in this study, its Article 19 provides that "the languages of the Organization" are English, Spanish, Russian, and French. No distinction is made, purposefully, it seems, between official and working languages. The question of the actual use of these languages is dealt with in the second part of Article 19, reading "the degree of the use of the languages shall be decided by the Council depending on the actual needs of the Organization."

As it seems out of the question that, because of the participation of tiny Cuba, Spanish will be used, the only working language is Russian. But the above-mentioned provision indicates "aspirations of growth." And it is probable that in the years to come some other countries, especially from among the underdeveloped ones, but also perhaps Finland, may join Intersputnik.

Independently of the Intersputnik venture (as a matter of fact there is, in 1975, no proof of the "physical" establishment of that organization), cooperation is continuing under the "Intercosmos" programme. Thus, for instance, "Intercosmos-5" was launched in December 1971[35] and "Intercosmos-6" in April 1972.[36] "Intercosmos-7" was launched in June 1972.[37] In June, 1972 an international symposium on Cosmic medicine, with the participation of scholars from eight "Intercosmos" countries, took place in Warsaw.[38]

Referring to the launching of "Intercosmos-8" on December 1, 1972, the Soviet Chairman of the "Intercosmos" group, Academician Boris Petrov, mentioned that scholars of the socialist countries will continue, during the coming years, scientific experiments using artificial satellites and geophysical rockets.[39]

In April 1973, "Intercosmos-Kopernik 500" was launched,[40] the ninth artificial satellite in this series, in October 1973—"Intercosmos-

35. See, e.g., *Życie Warszawy*, December 3, 1971.
36. See, e.g., *Pravda*, April 8, 1972.
37. See *Życie Warszawy*, June 17, 1972.
38. See, e.g., *Życie Warszawy*, July 1, 1972.
39. Here quoted after *Życie Warszawy*, December 3–4, 1972.
40. See, e.g., *Pravda*, April 20, 1973. Management of the work of the scientific equipment on board the satellite was done by an "operative group" composed of Polish and Soviet specialists. This satellite burned up in October 1973—see *Życie Warszawy*, March 5, 1974.

10,"[41] and in May 1974—"Intercosmos-11."[42] The two latest have been "Intercosmos-12" in October 1974, and "Intercosmos-13" in March 1975.[43] The speed seems to be high, even when compared with the ELDO/ESRO ventures. In 1975, Swedish scientific equipment for solar research is going to be placed on board artificial satellites of the "Intercosmos" series.[44]

In February 1974 a meeting of the leaders of the national coordination groups of the countries participating in the Intercosmos programme was held in Havana. Discussed were the results of cooperation in the field of cosmic physics, cosmic communications, cosmic meteorology and cosmic biology and medicine. The meeting determined means of preparation for cooperation during the 1976–1980 period.[45] A similar meeting in Prague in December 1974[46] dealt with the prospects of cosmic research during the period 1976–1980, the problem of increasing cooperation between the national Intercosmos Committees and the Committee for Scientific and Technical Cooperation of Comecon, etc.

3. *The Organization for Cooperation of Railways and the Telecommunications and Postal Communications "Organization"*

The Organization for Cooperation of Railways was created in 1956, with headquarters in Warsaw. Its first statute, adopted in 1957 in Peking, was replaced by a new one, agreed upon in Ulan Bator in June 1962.[47] Membership includes the USSR and the European "people's democracies" (including Albania), China, Mongolia, North Korea, and North Vietnam. There is conflicting information on the participation of China (and Albania) in the Organization.[48]

In spite of its name, this body is not only involved in fostering cooperation in the field of railways, but, according to Article 1 of its Statute, should also be involved in problems of the development

41. See *Pravda*, November 1, 1973.
42. See *Pravda*, May 18, 1974.
43. See *Pravda*, November 2, 1974 and March 29, 1975.
44. See *Życie Warszawy*, August 11, 1973.
45. See *Pravda*, February 6, 1974.
46. See *Życie Warszawy*, December 10, 1974.
47. The text of the 1962 Statute in an English translation is given in our Annexes (No. XIX).
48. Thus, for instance, in December 1969 China participated in a conference in Ulan Bator which led to the signing of a protocol about the circulation of passenger trains and direct cars from, among other places, Moscow to Peking

and exploitation of automobile transport and highways.

The Organization's policy-making organ is the Conference of Ministers (of Transport), meeting once a year; the executive organ is the Committee of the Organization. The Committee has a number of Commissions, specializing in particular sub-fields within the Organization's realm. Chinese, German and Russian are the official and at the same time the working languages of the Organization.

The Organization for Cooperation of Railways signed, in 1962, a protocol "on the character and the forms of cooperation" with Comecon.[49] Representatives of the Organization participate in the meetings of Comecon's Standing Commission on Transport Problems, also located in Warsaw, and representatives of the latter, in turn, participate in the meetings of the Organization, in both cases in an advisory capacity.

A few years ago it was stated that the main direction of the Organization's activities is work on the solution of the problem of the adaptation of railway cars to circulate on rails having different gauges.[50]

Concerning the Telecommunications and Postal Communications "Organization," it was created in December 1957.[51] The original members were the postal and telecommunication administrations of the USSR, the seven European "people's democracies" (with Albania), China, Mongolia, North Korea, and North Vietnam. At present, China and Albania do not cooperate with that body.[52] The relevant

---

Peking-Hanoi, Peking-Phenian and Peking-Ulan Bator—see *Yezhegodnik Bol'shoi Sovetskoi Ensiklopedii* ("Yearbook of the Great Soviet Encyclopaedia"), 1970, p. 447. On the other hand the *Encyklopedia Organizacji Międzynarodowych, op, cit.*, 1975, p. 419 affirms that China and Albania have not participated in the work of the Organization since 1965.

49. The Russian text of this protocol is reproduced in *Mnogostoronnieje ekonomicheskoe sotrudnichestvo...*, *op. cit.*, 1972, pp. 224–225. Polish translation in B. W. Reutt (ed.), *op. cit.*, pp. 191–192.

50. See I. Tarski (ed.), *op. cit.*, p. 95. It is well known that Soviet railways have broader gauges than those in other member countries (e.g., Poland, etc.).

51. The text of the Agreement in an English translation is given in our Annexes (No. XX).

52. See *Pravda*, October 2, 1971. From the list of countries whose ministers participated in the VIII Conference (Session) of the "Organization," which had just taken place in Bulgaria, it follows that China and Albania were not represented.

administration of Cuba joined in 1965.[53]

We refer to this body as "Organization" in quotation marks, as it is not a "full-scale" international body, comparable with those discussed above. This is the case because it comprises only a policy-making body—the Conference of Ministers in charge of Postal and Telecommunications services of the Member States—but does not have any executive organ (secretariat) of its own. According to Article IV of the 1957 agreement, the functions of the "Organization" are—in the intervals between the Conferences of Ministers—realized by the competent administration of the Member Country in which the next regular Conference of Ministers is scheduled to take place.[54]

Chinese, German, Russian, and French are generally enumerated (Article VI, para. 1 of the Agreement) as the languages to be used in the work of the "Organization." But paragraphs 2, 3, and 4 of the same Article stipulate that the working documents of the Conference of Ministers be prepared only in German and Russian; the final acts of the Conference, which have to be signed by the participants, are to be drawn up in Chinese, German and Russian; and for oral interpretations all four languages are to be used.

4. *The International Laboratory of Strong Magnetic Fields and Low Temperatures, the International Mathematical Centre and the International Centre for Electron Microscopy*

The International Laboratory of Strong Magnetic Fields and Low Temperatures was created by virtue of an Agreement signed on May 11, 1968 by the Academies of Science of four countries: the USSR, Poland, East Germany, and Bulgaria.[55] It is located in Wrocław, Poland.

The initiative to create this international body came from the Polish side. It deals with research in the field of solid state physics. The importance of this field has increased rapidly in the last fifty years, and it is—side by side with nuclear physics—one of the more important fields in the discipline.[56]

53. See *Mnogostoronnieje ekonomicheskoe sotrudnichestvo...*, *op. cit.*, 1972, p. 376, footnote 1.
54. What D. L. Williams says in Z. Brzezinski, *op. cit.*, p. 466 about the alleged existence of "a secretary and a secretariat" in the case of this body is simply untrue.
55. The text of the Agreement in an English translation is given in our Annexes (No. XXI).
56. See J. Ptaszek, *op. cit.*, pp. 224–225.

In spite of the fact that the relevant Agreement was not signed on behalf of the governments of the countries concerned but their Academies of Science (having, for all practical purposes, the status of national ministries), the International Laboratory is a fully-fledged international organization. This is, among other things, reflected by the fact that it enjoys legal capacity and has its own staff and budget.

The formal structure of the International Laboratory consists of a Council and a Director. The Council is composed of "not more than two" representatives of each member of the International Laboratory. Each member has only one vote. According to paragraph 6 of the Charter of the International Laboratory, adopted in November 1968, decisions of the Council regarding the admission of new members, financial problems, amendments to the Charter and other questions provided for by the Agreement and the Charter have to be adopted unanimously. Decisions on all other questions are taken by (simple) majority of votes of the members of the Council participating in a meeting, if nothing else is provided for by the Agreement and the Charter.

Probably because the International Laboratory is based on the Institute of Low Temperatures and Structural Research of the Polish Academy of Sciences, the latter presents the candidate for the post of Director. He is elected by the Council for a three-year term and may be re-elected. He may be relieved of his post by a decision of the Council. The Deputy Director is elected by the Council upon the proposal of the members, for a term of two years. No mention is made of re-election.

The only working language of the International Laboratory is Russian.

The International Mathematical Centre was created by an agreement signed on January 13, 1972 by the Academies of Science of seven countries: the USSR, Poland, East Germany, Czechoslovakia, Rumania, Hungary, and Bulgaria.[57] It is located in Warsaw and named after Stefan Banach, a famous mathematician, founder and organizer of the Polish school of functional analysis.

The International Centre functions on the basis of the Institute of Mathematics of the Polish Academy of Science. In contrast to the International Laboratory of Strong Magnetic Fields and Low Temperatures, the International Mathematical Centre is not a fully-fledged

57. The text of the Agreement in an English translation is given in our Annexes (No. XXII).

144

international organization. This is reflected in the fact that it does not enjoy legal capacity (it is represented in legal intercourse by the Mathematical Institute of the Polish Academy of Science), and does not have a staff and budget of its own. There is a certain analogy here between the International Centre and the Telecommunications and Postal Communications "Organization."

What is "international" in the case of the Centre is its Scientific Council, composed of two representatives appointed by the Academies of Science of each member country, each Academy having one vote. According to Article 8, para. 3 of the 1972 Treaty (similar to the relevant provision in the case of the Council of Intersputnik), the Scientific Council has to "attempt" to adopt its decisions unanimously. If this is not achieved, a decision is adopted if it receives "not less" than two-thirds of the votes of the Academies of Science participating in the Treaty.[58] Decisions are not binding for those Academies which do not vote for their adoption, though they may later accede to them.

The Director of the International Centre is *ex officio* the Director of the Mathematical Institute of the Polish Academy of Science. "In case of necessity" there may be one or two deputies, appointed on a rotating basis by the Scientific Council upon the proposal of the Academies of Science parties to the Treaty.

Financial problems, in a situation where there is no provision for the International Centre of a budget of its own, are solved in the following way.

The Polish Academy of Science provides the necessary premises, administrative services, and upkeep and development of the library. It also bears the expenses connected with the conducting of the meetings of the Scientific Council, and furnishes living quarters and free medical assistance to those participating in the work of the Centre. Expenses connected with the sending out on missions of members of the Scientific Council, and the sending out and upkeep of those participating in the work of the Centre, are borne by the respective Academies of Science.

58. The rule of looking for consensus in the first place, but agreeing on two-thirds decisions if "general agreement" proves impossible to reach, was recently adopted in the Rules of Procedure of the Third UN Conference on the Law of the Sea—see *Third United Nations Conference... Rules of Procedure (adopted at its 20th meeting on 27 June 1974 and amended at its 40th meeting on 12 July 1974)*, A/CONF. 62/30/Rev. 1. The provision of Rule 37, stipulating that "Before a matter of substance is put to a vote, a determination that all efforts at reaching general agreement have been exhausted shall be made by a two-thirds majority of the representatives present and voting," does not apply to the adoption of the text of the Convention as a whole.

Russian is the working language of the International Centre, with the additional provision of the second sentence of Article 12 of the Treaty, stipulating that "in cases of necessity other languages may also be used as a working language." This is warranted by the fairly frequent presence of scholars from countries where Russian is not by any means considered to be the *lingua franca*.

In January 1973 the first academic year was inaugurated at the Centre, though already in 1972 a symposium lasting a few months, devoted to the mathematical foundations of economics, took place.[59]

During the first academic year, over 200 young mathematicians studied and did research in the field of mathematical logics and the theory of optimal changement. Apart from scholars from the member countries, lectures were also delivered by scholars from the United States, France, West Germany and Britain. During the two semesters, 35 scholarly publications were prepared. The first 1974 semester was devoted to mathematical problems of computer science.[60]

The International Mathematical Centre is, it seems, unique on a world-wide scale.

Finally, in March 1975 it was reported[61] that representatives of the Academies of Science of six countries (Bulgaria, Czechoslovakia, East Germany, Hungary, Poland and the USSR) signed an agreement providing for the creation of the International Centre of the Academies of Science of the Socialist Countries for the Advanced Training of Scientific Cadres in the Field of Electron Microscopy. The Centre is located in the Institute of Solid State and Electron Microscopy of the East German Academy of Science in Halle. The Institute's Director, Professor Heinz Bethge, was appointed first Director of the new International Centre.

59. See *Zycie Warszawy*, January 7–8, 1973.
60. See *Pravda*, May 9, 1974.
61. See *Neues Deutschland*, March 19, 1975.

Chapter V

THE SYSTEM OF THE INTERNATIONAL ORGANIZATIONS OF THE COMMUNIST COUNTRIES: PAST, PRESENT, AND PROSPECTS

The history of the international organizations of the Communist countries, which started formally with the creation of Comecon in January 1949, is over twenty-six years old.

This history may also be divided, independently of the break-up offered in our Introduction, into three periods roughly corresponding to the rules of Stalin (end of the forties until 1953), Khrushchev (1954–1964) and Brezhnev (1965 until the present).

There was very little room for international governmental organizations in Stalin's philosophy of international relations. This was the case not only with respect to universal international bodies,[1] but even more so concerning these bodies in intra-bloc relations, where, almost exclusively, "bilateralism" was practiced.

Bilateral treaties "on friendship, cooperation and mutual assistance" existed on the legal side. But, much more important, there was the tremendous personal authority and terror Stalin was able to exert vis-à-vis the political leaders of the "people's democracies," mostly Moscow trained, and frequently summoned to the Kremlin (only Tito proved able to rebel after a few years). There were also the Soviet troops in most of these countries, and the thousands of "advisers," agents, and secret policemen dispatched to them. And there was also growing economic dependence and exploitation.

With external relations kept strained to the utmost (coup d'état in Czechoslovakia, blockade of Berlin, meddling in Finland, territorial claims on Turkey, invasion in Korea), with the leaders of the

---

1. Trygve Lie, first Secretary-General of the United Nations, in his memoirs, *op. cit.*, relates, in connection with his trips to Moscow—in 1946 and 1950—how Stalin did not want to send more Russians to work in the UN Secretariat, did not want to commit himself concerning any Soviet contributions to U.N. Technical Assistance, and passed over the matter of Soviet membership in the Specialized Agencies (see pp. 230, 301–302).

"satellites" frightened by the prospect of World War III, and with the possibility always there of their easily losing their power (and lives), absolute "bilateral" control over them did not pose great problems. Comecon was created in 1949 principally as a façade, mainly to prove that the Communist bloc is not "worse" than the West with its OEEC.

The new Soviet leadership after Stalin, involved in serious internal strife during at least 1953–1957/8; experimenting with some reforms and (very limited) liberalization at home; and confronted with growing trouble symptoms coming from some of the "satellites"—changed certain policies on the "external front." Some emphasis on détente was evident in the mid-fifties,[2] and certain concessions were made vis-à-vis individual "people's democracies" (especially Poland in 1956); the considerable increase in Soviet cooperation in universal international organizations at this point has already been mentioned.[3]

It is against this background that one has to view the evident switch towards "multilateralism"—within the framework of "classical" governmental regional organizations—in relations between the Communist countries. It was only then that Comecon was revived and developed more and more; and the Warsaw Treaty Organization,[4] the Joint Institute for Nuclear Research, and two smaller organizations (the Organization for Cooperation of Railways and the Telecommunications and Postal Communications "Organization") created between 1955 and 1957.

The second "eruption" in the same field came during the last years of Khrushchev's rule, in the early sixties. It could be connected with the growing awareness of the Soviet leadership (substantiated by the trips to the West of Khrushchev, Mikoyan, Kozlov, etc.) of the capitalist

2. In chronological sequence: renunciation of Soviet territorial claims on Turkey, signing of the Korean armistice, the Geneva Indochina Conference, the giving up of Port Arthur to China, signing of the Austrian State Treaty, relinquishing of the naval base of Porkkala to Finland, dissolution of the Cominform. The normalization of relations with Yugoslavia, West Germany and Japan should also be mentioned.
3. See Introduction, p. xxiii.
4. The WTO was, incidentally, during the first seven years of its existence, considered in the East as a sort of "senior" organization even vis-à-vis Comecon (this was connected with the interpretation of Article 8 of the Warsaw Treaty). Only in the summer of 1962 was it stated (Khruschev) that the Warsaw Treaty is a military and political alliance; and Comecon started to be considered as an "equal partner," each organization having its specific field. It may be added, though, that very recently Gromyko referred to the WTO as a mechanism embracing not only political and military, but also economic cooperation—see *Pravda*, May 15, 1975.

world's economic strength in general, and the success of West European economic integration in particular. The break with Red China must also have been a strong contributing factor.

The attempt, at this time, to give strong, new impetus to the more rapid economic development of the "camp" could also have been connected with the very far-reaching promises given in the Third (1961) Programme of the CPSU (still in force) for the next two decades. One may quote the promises concerning the achievements planned for 1961–1970:

> In the current decade . . . the Soviet Union, in creating the material and technical basis of Communism, will surpass the strongest and richest capitalist country, the U.S.A., in production per head of population; the people's standard of living and their cultural and technical standards will improve substantially; everyone will live in easy circumstances; all collective and state farms will become highly productive and profitable enterprises; the demand of the Soviet people for well-appointed housing will, in the main, be satisfied; hard physical work will disappear; the U.S.S.R. will have the shortest working day.

How far these "prophecies" of the CPSU, which, in the same 1961 Party programme, calls itself "a party of scientific communism," remain unfulfilled even in 1975, is obvious.[5]

However that may be, Khrushchev undertook the abortive 1962–1963 attempt to introduce "supranational" economic planning within Comecon. This failed, but Comecon was further developed, Mongolia was included, and five new international economic organizations were created between 1962 and 1964.

5. W. Morawiecki, in his article "Lenin's Concept of Peaceful Coexistence"— *Polish Yearbook of International Law*, vol. III (1970), Ossolineum, Wrocław, etc., 1972, pp. 33–34, refers, in this connection, to "certain over-optimistic judgements made in the years 1957–1961 about the overtaking of the United States by the USSR in science and technology or the dates when the Soviet Union will run ahead of America in per capita production and win in economic competition with capitalism." He then quotes, among other things, the 1969 World Communist Conference which stated "more realistically" in its resolution: "Practice has shown that socialist transformations and the formation of a new society are a complicated and long-lasting process...." Concerning the crucial problem of the housing situation, a recently published book by Witold Nieciusiński *O systemach socjalistycznej gospodarki mieszkaniowej* ("On the Systems of the Socialist Housing Economy"), Książka i Wiedza, Warsaw 1974, p. 28, admits that the housing conditions of the Soviet population are "still difficult." What is more, on p. 134 (footnote) two Soviet authors are quoted

149

The Brezhnev era was characterized, during its first few years, by a continuation—with an attempt at a certain intensification and "improvements"[6]—of the system of international organizations inherited from the previous period. But starting with 1968, certainly in connection with the shock of the events in and around Czechoslovakia, considerable re-thinking evidently took place in Moscow and tremendous pressure was brought to bear, especially in 1969, on the "junior partners" in the field here under discussion.

Within the Warsaw Treaty Organization, there took place the integration of a part of the operative troops of the member countries—on a permanent basis and even in normal peacetime; the whole Organization was reinforced and built up. All this was coupled with theories of the "class interpretation of sovereignty" kind.

Within the organizations of the "Comecon family" the strongest emphasis was put on the economic integration of the member countries. The very word "integration," which Moscow (not so Warsaw) reserved, until then, for the processes taking place in the "imperialist camp," suddenly became completely acceptable, started to be used in Soviet publications, and was used for the first time in an official document of Comecon in the communiqué of the XXIII Session of April 1969.

Already at the end of 1968 the ever officious G. Sorokin,[7] in an article entitled "Problems of the economic integration of the countries of socialism,"[8] stated that:

> ...in the economic field the objective necessity and the strategic aim of integration...is one world socialist economy with one economic plan.

And the late Andrzej Kruczkowski, Moscow trained Polish Deputy

---

as having voiced the opinion that a separate flat for each family may be achieved in the USSR only about the year 2000.

6. Already in September 1965 Brezhnev declared, during Novotny's visit to Moscow, that the organization of the Warsaw Treaty should be improved and that "a permanent and prompt mechanism for the considering of urgent problems should be created"—see *Pravda*, September 15, 1965. And at the 23rd Congress of the CPSU in March 1966 Brezhnev stated *inter alia*: "In the realm of military cooperation, in the face of the intensified aggressive actions of the imperialist forces headed by the United States of America, the process of further strengthening our connections with the socialist countries and the process of further strengthening and improving the mechanism of the Warsaw Treaty have continued"—see *Pravda*, March 29, 1966.
7. For his services in 1963 in connection with Khruschchev's abortive plans see footnote 91 in chapter II.
8. See G. Sorokin in *Voprosy Ekonomiki*, No. 12/1968.

Minister of Foreign Affairs, was even more specific:[9]

> ...One should say openly that there is no other way towards a permanent annihilation of the centrifugal tendencies in our camp, towards a permanent settling of the frontier of the Elbe as a frontier of peace, without the elimination of the deficiencies of our own understanding of the realities of the modern world, of the deficiency of a clear vision of the perspectives of our action in the field of the creation of the basis for the unity of the economic interests of the states in our bloc.

This whole preparatory work was finally crowned by the adoption of the July 1971 "Comprehensive Programme for the Further Deepening and Perfecting of Cooperation and Development of Socialist Economic Integration of Member Countries of Comecon." Over a dozen new international economic and scientific organizations (or "international economic associations")—and some forty research and coordination centres—were created after 1968. Cuba was included into Comecon in 1972. "Non-institutionalized" multilateral cooperation of the Communist countries also developed in a host of fields.[10] Some of these may,

9. See *Życie Warszawy*, January 7, 1969.
10. See, e.g., some of the multilateral conferences and meetings which took place during 1969 alone (in chronological order).

1. Meeting of Representatives of top-level cooperative organs.
2. Meeting of the Chief Public Prosecutors of the Socialist countries.
3. 2nd Conference of the Heads of Committees and Ministries of Science and Technology.
4. 1st Conference of the Ministers of Internal Trade.
5. Meeting of the writers of the socialist countries.
6. Conference of the Ministers of Agriculture.
7. Conference of the Press Agencies.
8. 2nd Conference of the Chairmen of the State Arbitration Commissions.
9. 11th Conference of the Chiefs of the Water Resources Authorities.
10. 10th Conference of the Ministers of Public Health.
11. Conference of the Research Institutes of the Cooperative Sector.
12. Meeting of experts in the field of textile industries.
13. Consultative meeting of Parliamentarians (in connection with an Interparliamentary Union meeting).
14. 6th meeting of the Academies of Science.
15. Conference of senior representatives of Foreign Ministries (in connection with the UN General Assembly).
16. 4th Conference of Ministers of Academic Schools.
17. Conference of representatives of the Publishing Houses of the Socialist Countries.

Most of these meetings still take place every year (some of them being already institutionalized), and some other ones may be added. One may thus note,

in the future, result in the creation of new international organizations. Pertinent developments, as they look in the mid-seventies, are characterized by the following passage of Brezhnev's message to the XXVIII Session of Comecon in June 1974:[11]

> "The historic process of the rapprochement of the socialist states, the strengthening of their cohesion, continues to gather momentum."

And a little political client (member of the Bulgarian Politbureau and first deputy chairman of the Council of Ministers of that country) declared:[12]

> ...Bulgaria will develop as a constitutent and inseparable part of a single world socialist cooperative, will strengthen all-round fraternal cooperation with the country of the Soviets, together with which, speaking in the words of the First Secretary of the CC of the BCP T. Zhivkov, we will 'act as one organism, which has one set of lungs and one blood system.'

The Bulgarian Communist leadership is, as a matter of fact, already almost publicly offering the USSR full integration. During the festivities in Sofia in September 1974 in connection with the 30th anniversary of the country's "socialist way," Zhivkov, in a flow of superlatives vis-à-vis the Soviet Union, referred, *inter alia*, to the movement towards "all-sided cooperation and ever closer rapprochement between Bulgaria and the USSR," proudly mentioning the fact that two Bulgarians had been Secretaries-General of the Comintern.

---

for instance, a conference in 1973 of the representatives of the banks of the socialist countries; a conference of representatives of the UN Associations of the same countries; or a conference of their Ministers of Justice, and, in 1974, a conference of the representatives of the Trade Unions of the socialist countries; the first meeting of representatives of the political science associations of the seven communist countries; or a conference of the representatives of the national UNESCO committees of those countries (see *Pravda*, June 12 and 30, and November 30, 1973, *Neues Deutschland*, February 27, 1974, and *Życie Warszawy*, September 21 and 26, 1974, respectively). In January 1975 the first conference of the vice-presidents of the Academies of Science of the socialist countries in charge of the social sciences was held in Moscow—see *Pravda*, January 9, 1975; and in February 1975 there took place, also in Moscow, the first conference of their Ministers of Education—see *Pravda*, February 15, 1975. Also in February 1975, a conference of the chiefs of cinematography of the socialist countries took place in Warsaw—see *Życie Warszawy*, February 12, 1975.

11. See *Pravda*, June 19, 1974.

12. See Tano Tsolov in *Problemy Mira i Sotsialisma*, No. 1/1974, p. 58.

The assembled shouted slogans of the "with the Soviet Union for eternal time" type.[13]

At that juncture the basic question comes to mind: what can the process of many-sided integration and constant "rapprochement" finally lead to? The speculative nature of such a discussion should not deter us from venturing into political futorology in this important field.

It may, I submit, be taken almost as a truism that the future of the Soviet bloc depends mainly on developments in the Soviet Union itself. Any ideas or dreams, such as they were, of the West inducing the Soviet Union to "pull back" are long forgotten; and any far-reaching reform developments within the minor partners of the bloc, dramatized especially by Hungary, and, twelve years later, Czechoslovakia, have been forcibly corrected by the "big brother."

Thus my thesis is that it is *internal* developments within the USSR that will mainly determine the basic future evolution of the Soviet bloc.[14]

Very roughly speaking, these internal Soviet developments may go in two directions. One could be a situation in which a clear-cut, large-scale process, similar to what was called the "Polish October" or the "Prague spring," would one day start in the USSR itself. Supposing the dissident movement were gradually to gain momentum and catch on with broad circles of students, the intelligentsia, and perhaps the young workers, this could lead to a fairly radical transformation in the political life of the country and to reforms that no outsider would quash. In such a case the whole model of the entity called the "Soviet bloc" could also change fairly radically. It may, for instance, to use Etzioni's terminology, become transformed into a system in which the hegemonial core state would base its prerogatives on the exercise of *identitive* and *utilitarian* rather than *coercive* powers.

Should such an ideal situation—from the point of view of the West (and of the nations of Poland, Czechoslovakia, etc.)—occur, the following arguments would obviously be superfluous.

But, unfortunately, one strongly has to reckon with the possibility that the second hypothesis will come true, which would mean that no serious political change, let alone "Solzhenitsynization" of the USSR will take place. This would be a situation in which the leadership—in

13. See *Pravda*, September 9, 1974.
14. A similar idea was offered by Ernest Mandel in his lecture which the author attended in May 1974 at the University of Glasgow.

the sense of names—would be changed; a new constitution would replace the one of 1936, still in force; living standards would be certain to rise considerably, etc. But the *basics* of the system—totalitarian party rule, the lack of elementary civil and political rights (in spite of laudable provisions in the constitution and the ratification, in 1974, of the 1966 International Covenant on Political and Civil Rights), the considerable role of the secret police and the top military establishment, etc.—would prevail. Should *this* situation continue, and the chances are at least fifty per cent in favour of that being the case, then—and only then—will our speculations which follow apply.

Let us now, under the latter hypothesis, trace some of the main facts, developments and trends that may well determine the future polity from Moscow to East Berlin in one direction and from Moscow to Ulan Bator in the other.

First, brief mention should be made of relevant Marxist-Leninist teaching. This teaching refers basically to a vision of a Communist-controlled world *as a whole*, but it could well be used *(argumentum a maiori ad minus)* in a prolonged situation with only a *part* of the world under such control.[15]

There are many quotations from Lenin's writings starting with 1915 that preach this idea, as for instance the following one of 1919:[16]

> We are opposed to national enmity and discord, to national exclusiveness. We are internationalists. We stand for the close union and the complete amalgamation of the workers and peasants of all nations in a single world Soviet republic.

This idea was fully reflected in the successive statutes of the Comintern, the latest one, that of 1928, providing for the fight for "the formation of a world union of Socialist Soviet Republics."[17]

15. A very good review of the pertinent Marxist-Leninist teaching up to 1959/60 is given by Elliot R. Goodman in *The Soviet Design for a World State*, Columbia University Press, New York, 1960.
16. See V. I. Lenin, *Collected Works*, Lawrence & Wishart, London—Progress Publishers, Moscow, 1965, vol. 30, p. 293.
17. See in this connection also the first Statute of the Comintern of August 4, 1920, Article 1—"The new international association of workers is established to organize joint action by the proletariat of the different countries which pursue the one goal: the overthrow of capitalism, the establishment of the dictatorship of the proletariat *and of an international Soviet republic....*" (our italics). For texts see, e.g., *The Communist International 1919–1943. Documents*, selected and edited by Jane Degras, Oxford University Press, London-New York-Toronto, Vol. I (1956), pp. 161–166 (1920); and Vol. II (1960), pp. 117–122 (1924) and 464–471 (1928).

And it is interesting to note that even during the first half of the forties the idea of just incorporating previously sovereign members of the international community into the USSR as constituent republics was very much alive. It was not only a question of the incorporation of the three Baltic countries in 1940 and of Tannu-Tuva in 1944, with the incorporation of Outer Mongolia seriously considered, according to reliable sources.[18] There was also the idea of the incorporation, after the War with Germany was won, of Poland and other countries.

Thus, for instance, when Germany attacked the USSR in 1941, a small group of Polish army officers captured by the Soviets in 1939 (a fraction of those that escaped the fate of the thousands assassinated by them at Katyn and elsewhere), evidently under pressure from the NKVD, sent a letter to the People's Commissar for Internal Security—a letter later well-publicized by the Soviet media—declaring, *inter alia:* "...we see the only way to the liberation of the Polish nation in cooperation with the USSR, within the framework of which [USSR] our fatherland will have a chance to develop to the fullest."[19]

And as late as June 1945, Kardelj, then Yugoslav Foreign Minister, declared to the Soviet Ambassador that he would like the Soviet Union to regard the Yugoslavs "as representatives of one of the future Soviet Republics, and the Communist Party of Yugoslavia as a part of the All-Union Communist Party, that is, that our relations

18. Concerning Mongolia, a former corresponding member of the Soviet Academy of Science and the most prominent Soviet expert in that field, Nikolaus Poppe (who cooperated during 1943–1945 with the Gestapo-run *Wannsee-Institut* in Berlin and was professor at the University of Seattle between 1949 and 1969), wrote in 1956 that "On the eve of World War II, the Mongolian People's Republic was ripe for incorporation in the USSR, and a plan was under discussion to merge it with the Buryat-Mongolian Autonomous Soviet Socialist Republic. The plan was dropped when war broke out..." See "The Facts on Outer Mongolia," *New Leader* (New York), February 20, 1956. One should also mention the incorporation, in the autumn of 1944, of the "People's Republic of Tannu-Tuva" into the RSFSR as an autonomous region.
19. See *Dokumenty i Materialy do Historii Stosunków Polsko-Radzieckich* ("Documents and Material Relating to the History of Polish-Soviet Relations"), jointly prepared by the Institute of the History of Polish-Soviet Relations of the Polish Academy of Science and the Institute of Slavistics and Balkan Studies of the Soviet Academy of Science, Książka i Wiedza, Warsaw, Vol. VII, 1973, p. 220.
Also at that time (1941), the leadership of the Slovakian Communist Party put forward the slogan "for a Soviet Slovakia," in the sense of Slovakia being, in the future, a constituent republic of the USSR. This idea was not dropped until the end of 1943. See, e.g., the collective work *Europejskie kraje demokracji ludowej 1944–1948* ("The European Countries of People's Democracy 1944–1948"), Książka i Wiedza, Warsaw, 1972, p. 123.

should be based on the prospect of Yugoslavia becoming in the future a constituent part of the USSR" (declaration disclosed only after the break between Moscow and Belgrade).[20]

In the autumn of 1950, when the Korean aggression was taking a disastrous turn, in the atmosphere of "closing the ranks," Stalin evidently toyed with the idea of incorporating the East European people's democracies into the USSR. Jerzy Putrament, member of the Central Committee of the Polish United Workers' Party for over 25 years now, clearly alludes to this in his memoirs published in Warsaw in 1970:[21]

> That autumn [1950] at a mass meeting in Katowice, one of the [Polish Communist] leaders delivering a speech terminated with the exclamation: long live the great leader of the Polish nation, Generalissimo Stalin! It was not a slip of the tongue. At that level one does not commit such slips, it costs too much. This was some cross-road moment and one did not know too well in which direction the river of history would flow.

The post-Stalinist period, between 1953/54 and 1968, was characterized by rather strong centrifugal tendencies in some of the "people's democracies." The main task for Moscow was thus to keep things under control, using pressure and even force if necessary, but at the same time trying to tranquillize the minor partners by small concessions and by issuing reassuring declarations on respect of sovereignty.

Typical of this was the October 30th, 1956 declaration of the Soviet government "on the basis for the development and further strengthening of friendship and cooperation between the Soviet Union and other socialist states."[22] This, of course, did not prevent it, just a few days later, from intervening militarily in Hungary.

It was precisely the situation in the second half of the fifties, and the sixties until 1968, that induced certain Western observers, such as Brzezinski, to offer a rather over-optimistic picture (from our point of view) of relations within the Soviet bloc and of its political future,

20. When this was quoted in a Soviet note to Yugoslavia in May 1948, the Soviet side "indignantly" remarked "We leave aside the primitive and fallacious reasoning of Comrade Kardelj about Yugoslavia as a future constituent part of the USSR and the CPY as a part of the CPSU." See *The Soviet-Yugoslav Dispute*, Royal Institute of International Affairs, London and New York, 1948, p. 38.
21. See Jerzy Putrament, *op. cit.*, Vol. IV, p. 35.
22. See *Pravda*, October 31, 1956.

characterized by what they classified as pluralization, diversity and erosion. This opinion, repeated by many minor Western analysts, is still offered even today. Students in the Anglo-Saxon world are, for instance, still presented, as their main fare, with Brzezinski's main work in its 1967 edition (1971 printing).[23]

Granted, the breaking off of China dominated the scene during the sixties. But it must be kept in mind that China, because of her sheer size alone, was never actually a full member of the Moscow-controlled part of the world. And as for the six European "people's democracies," the situation, even until as late as 1968, was not, I believe, so clear-cut.

What was not sufficiently noted during the pre-1968 period were, I think, such things as Khrushchev's speech in Leipzig in March 1959, with its overtones,[24] and his attempt of 1962–1963, abortive though it was, to have supranational economic planning introduced within Comecon, only to be stalled, rather surprisingly, by the *deus ex machina* of the Rumanian opposition.

But even though the supranational idea did not materialize, there took place, during that period, certain events that clearly prepared the ground for future developments. We are referring here to the serious build-up of intra-bloc multilateralism, almost non-existent before 1955. Especially important were the creation of the WTO, the serious, almost constant development of Comecon (previously dormant) and the creation of its numerous "specialized agencies," the adoption, in 1962, of the "Basic Principles of International Socialist Division of Labour," and so on.

Many of these developments were certainly very much prompted by two outside events: the spectacular progress of West European integration on the "Western front," and the dramatic deterioration of relations on the "Far Eastern front" with China.

However that may be, the shock of the events in Czechoslovakia in 1968, coupled with Moscow's considerable loss of face internationally because of the invasion, etc., constituted, as already stated, a clear

---

23. See Zbigniew Brzezinski *Soviet Bloc: Unity and Conflict, op. cit.,* 1967 edition, 1971 printing.
24. Khruschev had, among other things, this to say: "(....) Speaking of the future, it seems to me that the further development of the socialist countries will in all probability follow the line of the consolidation of a single world socialist economic system. The economic barriers dividing our countries under capitalism will be removed one after another. The common economic basis of world socialism will strengthen, finally making the question of boundaries pointless." See *Pravda,* March 27, 1959.

turning-point in her concept vis-à-vis the bloc. There was, obviously, the feeling that a repetition of the 1968 débâcle had to be ruled out at any price, and it was precisely for this reason that *integration* within the bloc in the military, economic, technical, and scientific fields, and in some other fields as well, was given top priority.

This feeling was well reflected by Erich Honecker, who stated that the realization of socialist economic integration and the consolidation of "our fraternal alliance" is the revolutionary task of our epoch.[25]

Independently of all this, one notes certain political overtones which might set the scene for the future. Thus, e.g., the bilateral treaty of May 1970 between the USSR and Czechoslovakia refers to the aim of "deeper mutual acquaintance with one another and the rapproachement of the people of the two countries"; and in connection with the opening of the Polish-East German border in 1972 there are frequent references to the historic process of strengthening of friendship and continuous mutual rapproachement of neighbouring [Communist] nations.

There is also a marked attempt at intensifying the propagation and teaching of the Russian language as the *lingua franca* at least of the élites of the bloc. Perhaps the most intensive work is going on in this respect in East Germany. The opinion has been repeatedly voiced there, in print, that the Russian language should be mastered as a "second native tongue."[26] From March 1973, the second programme of the East German TV has been transmitting a whole evening's programme in Russian (on Thursdays); and in October 1973, the second programme began to transmit yet another two hour Russian programme on Sundays. Members of the Soviet Forces in East Germany and their wives are active in thousands of Russian language classes, etc.[27]

25. Erich Honecker, quoted in Gerhard Schürer "Revolutionary Task of the Epoch," *Pravda*, May 5, 1973.
26. At the Students' Conference in Leipzig in 1971, the Secretary of the Central Council of the *Freie Deutsche Jugend* demanded that the Russian language should be mastered "as a second native tongue"—see Wolfgang Herder *Jeden zu politischem Denken erziehen*, in *Forum* (East Berlin), No. 7/1971.
The same periodical, No. 1/1975 printed an article entitled *Die zweite Muttersprache*, where the importance of Russian is extolled, and mention is made, among other things, of academic schools in East Germany, where instructors deliver a few lectures in Russian, Russian-language "Olympics" are organized, etc. Similar "Olympics" are also organized in senior high schools in Poland, and the second international competition of the national Russian-language chamption teams was scheduled to take place in Moscow in 1975—see *Życie Warszawy*, March 10, 1975.
27. See *Informationen*, Bonn, No. 19/1973, p. 6.

Let us now ponder upon *future* developments in integration through the main Communist international bodies.

First of all, concerning the Warsaw Treaty, concluded in 1955, it will probably be replaced by a new one during the second half of the seventies, as it is not likely that Moscow would like to make full use of the clause providing for an automatic extension for a further 10-year period for those countries which did not serve notice of withdrawal one year before the lapse of the original twenty years. If the 1955 treaty was not replaced by a new one already by May 1975, this is only because Moscow did not want to upset the "delicate" remaining part of the CSCE negotiations.[28]

It is obvious that the Warsaw Treaty No. II will, in many respects, go further, if not much further, than the 1955 document. A strong attempt will be made to incorporate in the new text those "achievements" already included, for instance, in the five previously mentioned bilateral 1967–1975 treaties between the USSR and Bulgaria, Hungary, Czechoslovakia, Rumania and East Germany.

Thus there may be introduced a provision about automatic full-scale military help, and an attempt will probably be made by Moscow to arrange that the *casus foederis* be geographically unlimited. The principle of "proletarian (socialist) internationalism" (the Brezhnev doctrine) may be put into the text. Additional "improvements" may also be included, on both the military and the political side, e.g. some new provisions on military integration,[29] a build-up of institutionalized political cooperation (for instance the creation of a Committee of Ministers of Foreign Affairs), etc.

Concerning Comecon, the "Comprehensive Programme" of 1971 provides, as already mentioned, for its implementation during a period of 15 to 20 years. When this is executed, though perhaps with delay and not a hundred per cent, it will mean far-reaching integration of the respective national economies, specialization and cooperation in production, research, etc., numerous common enter-

28. Regarding the bilateral treaties on friendship, cooperation and mutual assistance, good examples of situations in which the USSR decided to have a new treaty concluded—or a previous one extended—many years before the old ones expired, are the already mentioned May 1970 treaty with Czechoslovakia, and the October 1975 treaty with East Germany. On the other hand, the story of the July 1970 treaty with Rumania is quite exceptional.
29. According to Reuter's report from Bucharest (see *The Christian Science Monitor*, June 28, 1974), already at the April 1974 meeting of the Political Consulative Committee of the WTO there was considerable tension when Ceaucescu rejected "Soviet attempts to establish a more tightly coordinated joint military command structure."

prises, convertibility of national currencies, the opening, perhaps, of all—or almost all—frontiers, large-scale exchange of manpower, and so on and so forth. And, as one reads time and again in Soviet literature:[30]

> Integration processes...should end in the merging of states and nations into one world economy....The solving of the above-mentioned task of the development of human society is the historical mission of socialism. 'The aim of socialism,' said Lenin, 'is not only the elimination of the splitting up of mankind into small states and of all isolation of nations, not only the rapprochement of nations, but also their merging.'—Such is the ultimate aim of socialism, such is the ultimate point in the general process of integration, after the attainment of which the process will exhaust itself and leave the historical scene. It is necessary to keep in mind this ultimate aim of integration as the general perspective.

While integration processes will proceed in the Soviet bloc, one must not forget that *West* European integration will also go on. The declarations of the Paris and Copenhagen "summits" of October 1972 and December 1973 respectively proclaimed the aim of achieving the stage of European Union before 1980. The December 1974 Paris "summit" was more cautious in setting dates. It seems clear that because of various setbacks, European Union may be achieved only later, say around 1985 or 1990.[31] But it is almost certain to come. This

30. See, e.g., E. T. Usenko "International-Legal Problems of Socialist Economic Integration," in *Sovetskij Yezhegodnik Mezhdunarodnovo Prava* 1970, Izdatel'stvo "Nauka," Moscow, 1972, pp. 16–17. Comecon's Secretary Faddeev, also, quotes in his 1974 book (*op. cit.*, pp. 10–11) Lenin's well-known statement about a "one world cooperative," and continues: "All the experience of the Council of Mutual Economic Assistance demonstrates that our cooperation is developing in this direction. The embodiment of this course is the Comprehensive Programme..."

31. In June 1974 the West German Finance Minister Apel voiced the opinion that because of great structural differences it would not be possible to achieve European economic and monetary union by 1980 (see, e.g., *Die Welt*, June 6, 1974). One should note, though, that at the same time (see *Le Monde*, June 6, 1974) the new French Prime Minister Chirac declared in the National Assembly that the realization of European Union before the end of the present decade is, in the eyes of the government and the president of the Republic, a task of special importance. The December 1974 Paris "summit" decided, among other things, that starting with 1978 the European Parliament could be elected by universal suffrage, and the Belgian prime minister was charged with studying the consruction of European Union and reporting back by the end of 1975 (see, e.g., *Le Monde*, December 12, 1974).

fact alone would, I suggest, be a strong stimulus—and, at the same time, pretext or justification—for Moscow to take some dramatic initiatives leading to constitutional integration within the Soviet bloc.[32]

Such a final decision, with extremely far-reaching consequences, would not, of course, be taken easily. Certainly a careful weighing of all the "pros" and "cons" would take place at that crucial moment.

Briefly, the evident "pros" from Moscow's point of view (and these considerations evidently lie behind the spectacular "preparatory work" in the form of the many-sided integration now going on) would be the firm hope of the elimination, "once and for all," of any repetition of the 1956 and 1968 situations, requiring forms of military intervention extremely painful internationally, an end to any Rumanian-type "antics," etc. Further, it would mean serious "rationalization," streamlining of the whole huge *Grossraum*, and better economic exploitation especially of Poland, East Germany and Czechoslovakia. It would be a clear and almost indispensable logical retort to the political integration of Western Europe. It would also be a logical closing of the ranks in the event of a continuation, let alone potential escalation, of Chinese "aggressive attitudes." Finally, it would be a welcome practical confirmation of Marxist-Leninist theory, and could also satisfy psychological empire-building ambitions.

The main, immediate "cons," again from the Moscow viewpoint, would certainly lie in the reduction of the Great Russian element. Whereas the proportion within the present confines of the USSR

In May 1975, Giscard d'Estaing, in an interview with *Business Week* (quoted here after *The Times*, May 30, 1975) declared that, in his opinion, within the European Community "we have exhausted the possibility of purely technical and economic steps.... What we need is some political coordination, and with political coordination we will give a new push to political union." Certain actions, like the July 22, 1975 treaty giving the European Parliament greater budgetary powers and creating the EC Court of Auditors (see, e.g., *The Times*, July 23, 1975), are small steps in the right direction.

32. The fact that certain developments and solutions adopted by the European Community may be used by Moscow to put pressure on the minor partners to have similar things introduced in their own bloc may be illustrated by something that seems to be shaping up in the mid-seventies. While, starting with January 1, 1975, the foreign trade policy of the European Community members is taken care of by the Community, Moscow would like to use this as an argument for forcing the same on the minor Comecon partners: the unity of the Brussels group vis-à-vis outsiders, so it is argued, must be met by similar unity of the Moscow group. Already by the autumn of 1974 it was allegedly mentioned by some Soviets that the pertinent present situation could be changed by the Comecon governments—see, e.g., *Die Presse* (Vienna), October 22, 1974.

161

now stands, according to the 1970 census, at over 53 per cent in favour of the Russians,[33] (and is probably, very slowly, still going down), it would change, in the event of the inclusion of over 100 million East Europeans, to some 37/38 per cent. Nevertheless the Russians would still form by far the strongest single nation, inhabiting a territory bigger than that of all the non-Russian nations put together.

Thus, if the nationalities' problems in the "core territory" (at present especially the Ukrainians, but recently, it seems, also the Lithuanians and Azerbaijanis) do not escalate excessively during the few decades to come, Moscow may feel able to "digest" the new republics, or at least keep them effectively under control. Then the calculated risk of the considerable dilution of the Russian element already indicated, and potential strong ferment among the populations of some of the new "accessions" (e.g. the Poles), etc., may indeed be taken in view of all the real or even imagined "pros" sketched above. Recently, some publicists of the biggest—from the point of view of population and size—of the potential European candidates for Moscow-imposed constitutional integration, Poland, have proved that they grasp the main danger connected with "comprehensive integration" in all fields.[34]

Should such a final decision be taken in Moscow, most of the respective national "parliaments," simple appendices to the Central Committees of their Communist parties, would probably, singing the International, pass the pertinent resolutions—petitions to be formally addressed to the Supreme Soviet of the USSR.

But national feeling evidently does exist, is sometimes strong and should by no means be neglected.[35] Any potential armed resistance,

33. Percentage calculated on the basis of figures given in *Itogi Vsesojuznoj Perepisi Naselenia 1970 goda* ("Results of the All-Union Population Census 1970"), published by the Central Statistical Department of the Council of Ministers of the USSR, vol. IV, "Statistika," Moscow, 1973, p. 9.
34. In a series of short articles under the heading "The Prospects for Poles," published by the Warsaw weekly *Polityka* in connection with the 30th anniversary of "People's Poland" in the summer of 1974, several authors strongly emphasized the capital importance of the "saving and consolidation of Polish statehood" (Wiesław Górnicki), claiming that "after the independent existence of a state is safeguarded," the satisfaction of the nation is determined by the rank of the state among others, and the living standards (Witold Lipski)—see *Polityka*, July 20, 1974. The Catholic writer Andrzej Wielowieyski even risked praising the serious achievements of the young Polish state and its army in the inter-war period, and their importance for the achievements in post-World War II Poland—see *Polityka*, July 6, 1974.
35. Again, one may use the Polish example as an illustration. The results of an enquette, administered in the senior high school class (of 32 students) in a

e.g., by Rumania, but also spontaneous active resistance of the population, say, in Poland, may, it is true, be quickly suppressed by the use of force. Whether, though, such an unprecedented large-scale venture would not, in the long run, have detrimental consequences for Moscow herself (e.g. extensive and protracted passive resistance, "ideological infection" of the original Soviet citizens, etc.), is a question on which the next generation of Soviet leaders must rack its brains.

Summing up, some twenty years from now, with the *rebus sic stantibus* proviso, if there are no far-reaching, let alone dramatic, changes within the USSR (if she "survives until 1994" looking politically roughly as she does now), it seems probable that the Soviet Union may, as the final result of a long integration process in literally every important field, try to increase the number of her constituent republics by all—or almost all—of the present European members of the bloc, plus Mongolia. In this way the old aim of the Comintern would, if only partially (because regionally rather than on a world-wide scale), materialize.

At that point the regional international organizations now forming that System would, after fulfilling their integration (or rather incorporation) aims—to borrow Engel's well-known saying—belong to the museum, along with the stone axe and the spinning wheel—and along with the now allegedly sovereign smaller partners of the USSR in the bloc she has under her control.

To terminate, the following should be said: we are not trying to assert that what has just been sketched is almost a certainty. What is suggested is rather that there are strong chances of developments going in that direction, one that could be highly dangerous for the national survival of the smaller members of the Soviet bloc[36] and also highly undesirable for the West.

---

provincial city, showed that national feelings run high: "We should show the world what we are able to do...A Pole should be the symbol of the most perfect, best man...I am seized by the desire to render glorious the name of Poland, so that it may resound throughout the world"—see *Polityka*, November 2, 1974. Strong oppositional feelings among University-level students, because of the "permanent humiliation of our national dignity," are well reflected in an anonymous article sent in from Poland, entitled "Youth about itself," published by *Na Antenie* in *Orzeł Biały*, December 1974.
36. A shocking example here is the case of Riga. Soviet statistics are blatantly trying to conceal the percentage of Russians in the Latvian capital.
A most characteristic example in this connection is the publication entitled *Riga. Statisticheskij Sbornik* ("Riga. Statistical Collection"), published by the Statistical Office of the city of Riga in 1968. In this publication of over 250

Not to see this, or to dismiss it lightheartedly and not take it into account in long-range political planning, would be tantamount to political blindness.[37]

---

pages this problem is simply not referred to at all! According to *Latvijskaya SSR v tsifrakh v 1971 godu* ("The Latvian SSR in figures in 1971"), published by the Central Statistical Department of the Council of Ministers of the Latvian SSR in 1972, p. 26, Russians made up, in 1970, almost 30 per cent (exactly: 29.8) of the population in Latvia. The case of Riga is not elaborated on. But it is obvious that most of the Russians are concentrated in the capital and that their percentage there is thus much higher, over 50 per cent. In fact, according to a letter of protest of the summer of 1971 by 17 Latvian Communists (see *Arkhiv Samizdata*—AS, Nr. 1042, wypusk 3/72, January 21, 1972), some 25,000–35,000 Russians settle in Riga each year, and the percentage of Latvians there has shrunk to just 40 per cent (!). By now, probably, it is already less.

37. We formulated this hypothesis in our lectures on the system of the Communist International Governmental Organizations in December 1971 at the School of Advanced Studies, Australian National University in Canberra, and in July 1972 at the School of Political Science (Otto-Suhr-Institut) of the *Freie Universität* in West Berlin. It is probably characteristic that the trend projected found much more acceptance in Berlin than in Canberra, the latter being perhaps too far away from the Soviet and East European scene.

SELECTED BIBLIOGRAPHY

A. *Books*

This bibliography contains mostly those books that are directly referred to in our work as a source of information, plus some additional ones that seemed worth listing. It does not include certain less important publications, especially some of the older Western ones, partially outdated, and sometimes containing a considerable number of mistakes.

Acheson, Dean, *Present at the Creation. My Years with the State Department*, Norton and Company, New York, 1969.

Agoston, Istvan, *Le Marché Commun communiste. Principes et pratique du Comecon*, Droz, Geneva, 1964.

Amundsen, Gunnar L., *Le Conseild'Entraide économique. Structure, réalisations, perspectives*, Universite des Sciences Humaines Strasbourg II, Strasbourg, 1971.
    Problèmes de Coordination monétaire dans la Région du CAEM (Comecon): Exigences fondamentales et implications théoriques, Norwegian Institute of Foreign Policy, Oslo, 1973.

Ausch, Sandor, *Theory and Practice of CMEA Cooperation*, Akademiai Kiadó, Budapest, 1972.

Bagramian, Marshal Ivan, *Tak nachinalas' vojna*, Vojenizdat, Moscow, 1970. Polish translation *Taki był początek wojny*, Publishing House of the Ministry of National Defence, Warsaw, 1972.

Basic Principles of International Socialist Division of Labour, published by the Secretariat of Comecon, Moscow 1962.

Boguslavskij, M. M., *Pravovoe regulirovanie mezhdunarodnykh khozjajstvennykh otnoshenij. Ocherki teorii i praktiki ekonomicheskovo sotrudnichestva stran sotsializma*, Izdatel'stvo Nauka, Moscow, 1970.

Bożyk Paweł and Wojciechowski, Bronisław, *Handel Zagraniczny Polski 1945–1969*, Państwowe Wydawnictwo Ekonomiczne, Warsaw, 1971.

Brzezinski, Zbigniew K., *Soviet Bloc: Unity and Conflict*, Harvard University Press, Cambridge, Mass., 1967 edition, 1971 printing.

Bykov, A. N., *Nauchno-tekhnicheskaya integratsia sotsialisticheskikh stran*, Izdatel'stvo "Mezhdunarodnye Otnoshenya," Moscow 1974.

Caillot, Jean, *Le C.A.E.M.*, Librairie générale de Jurisprudence, Paris, 1971.

Ciamaga, Lucjan, *Od Współpracy do integracji. Zarys organizacji i działalności RWPG w latach 1949–1964*, Ksiażka i Wiedza, Warsaw, 1965.

Comprehensive Programme for the Further Extension and Improvement of Co-operation and the Development of Socialist Economic Integration by the CMEA Member-Countries, published by the Secretariat of Comecon, Moscow, 1971.

Crozier, Brian (ed.), *"We Will Bury You." A Study of Left-Wing Subversion today*, Tom Stacey Ltd., London, 1970.

Degras, Jane (ed.), *The Communist International 1919–1943. Documents*, Oxford University Press, London—New York—Toronto, three volumes 1956–1965.

165

Dokumenty i materiały do historii stosunków Polsko-Radzieckich, eight volumes, Książka i Wiedza, Warsaw, 1962–1974.

Drabowski, Eugeniusz, *Rubel transferowy—międzynarodowa waluta krajów RWPG*, Państwowe Wydawnictwo Naukowe, Warsaw, 1974.

Etzioni, Amitai, *Political Unification. A Comparative Study of Leaders and Forces*, Holt, Rinehart and Winston, New York etc., 1965.

Europejskie kraje demokracji ludowej 1944–1948, Książka i Wiedza, Warsaw, 1972.

Faddeev, N. V., *Sovet Ekonomicheskoi Vzaimopomoshchi.*, Izdatel'stvo "Ekonomika," Moscow, 1974.

Fontaine, André, *Histoire de la guerre froide*, Fayard, Paris, 1967. English translation, Random House, New York, 1969.

Goodman, Elliot R., *The Soviet Design for a World State*, Columbia University Press, New York, 1960.

Góra, Stanisław and Knyziak, Zygmunt, *Międzynarodowa specjalizacja produkcji krajów RWPG*, Państwowe Wydawnictwo Ekonomiczne, Warsaw, 1974.

Grzegorczyk, Mieczysław, *Prawo kosmiczne*, Państwowe Wydawnictwo Naukowe, Warsaw and Cracow, 1973.

Griffith, W. E., *Albania and the Sino-Soviet Rift*, The MIT Press, Cambridge. Mass., 1963.

Gumpel, Werner and Hacker, Jens, *Comecon und Warschauer Pakt*, Schriftenreihe der Bundeszentrale für politische Bildung, Bonn, 1966.

Hacker, Jens and Uschakow, Alexander, *Die Integration Osteuropas 1961 bis 1965*, Verlag Wissenschaft und Politik, Cologne, 1966.

Hewett, Edward A., *Foreign Trade Prices in the Council for Mutual Economic Assistance*. Cambridge University Press, 1974.

Istoria Vsesojuznoi Kommunisticheskoi Partii (bol'shevikov). Kratkij kurs, Moscow, 1952.

Itogi Vsesojuznoi Perepisi Naselenia 1970 goda, Central Statistical Department of the Council of Ministers of the USSR, vol. IV, "Statistika," Moscow, 1973.

Jain, J. P., *Documentary Study of the Warsaw Pact*, Asia Publishing House, New York, 1973 [though published in 1973, the Introduction to the book, curiously enough, covers events to the early sixties only, and the reproduced documents stop at January 1965].

Jakubowski, Jerzy, *Prawo jednolite w międzynarodowym obrocie gospodarczym. Problemy stosowania*. Państwowe Wydawnictwo Naukowe, Warsaw, 1972.

Jurek, M. and Skrzypkowski, E., *Układ Warszawski*, Publishing House of the Ministry of National Defence, second edition, Warsaw, 1971.

Kamiński, Z. and Ruszkowski, A., *Prace normalizacyjne w RWPG*, Wydawnictwa Normalizacyjne, Warsaw, 1965.

Kaser, Michael, *Comecon. Integration Problems of Planned Economies*, Oxford University Press, first ed. 1965, second ed. 1967.

Kasprzycki, Jerzy, *Widziane w Brukseli*, Iskry, Warsaw, 1974.

Kiss, Tibor, *International Division of Labour in Open Economies. With Special Regard to the CMEA*, Akadémiai Kiadó, Budapest, 1971.
Hol all a KGST—integratio? Kossuth Konjoerado, Budapest 1972.

Klepacki, Zbigniew M. (ed.), *Encyklopedia Organizacji Międzynarodowych*, Książka i Wiedza, Warsaw 1975.

Kormnov, Ju. F., *Spetsializatsia i kooperatsia proizvodstva stran SEV*, Izdatel'stvo "Ekonomika," Moscow, 1972.

Kormnov, Ju. F. and Leznik, A. D., *Soglashenia o spetsializatsii i kooperatsii v proizvodstve mezhdu stranami-chlenami SEV (osnovnye elementy). Obzor.* International Centre for Scientific and Technical Information, Moscow, 1973.

Kraje RWPG 1950–1973, Główny Urząd Statystyczny, Warsaw, 1974.

Kraszewski, Jerzy and Redlich, Jerzy, *Moskiewskie ABC*, Iskry, Warsaw, 1973.

Krauze, W. and Wujek, T., *Współpraca naukowa Polski Ludowej z zagranicą*, Książka i Wiedza, Warsaw, 1974.

Kurs mezhdunarodnovo prava, six volumes, Izdatel'stvo "Nauka," Moscow, 1967–1973.

Lenin, V. I., *Collected Works*, Lawrence and Wishart, London—Progress Publishers (initially Foreign Languages Publishing House), Moscow, 45 volumes, 1963–1970.

Librach, Jan, *The Rise of the Soviet Empire*, Pall Mall Press, London—Dumnow, 1965.

Lie, Trygve, *In the Cause of Peace. Seven Years with the United Nations*, The Macmillan Company, New York, 1954.

Madej, Tadeusz, *Ekonomiczne problemy specjalizacji i kooperacji w przemyśle krajów RWPG*, Państwowe Wydawnictwo Naukowe, Warsaw, 1972.

Marer, Paul, *Postwar Pricing and Price Patterns in Socialist Foreign Trade (1946–1971)*, International Development Research Centre, Indiana University, 1972.

Meissner, Boris, *Der Warschauer Pakt. Dokumentensammlung*, Verlag Wissenschaft und Politik, Cologne, 1962.

Die "Breshnev-Doktrin." Dokumentation, Verlag Wissenschaft und Politik, Cologne, 1969.

Metera, J., *Współpraca naukowo-techniczna krajów RWPG*, Państwowe Wydawnictwo Ekonomiczne, Warsaw, 1969. Second edition, with Z. Ziółkowski, Warsaw, 1972.

Mezhdunarodnye organizatsii sotsialisticheskikh stran (pravovye voprosy organizatsii i diejatel'nosti), Izdatel'stvo Mezhdunarodnye Otnoshenia, Moscow, 1971.

Molnár, Miklós, *Budapest 1956. A History of the Hungarian Revolution*, George Allen and Unwin, London, 1971.

Monat, Pawel with Dille, John, *Spy in the U.S.*, Harper and Row, New York, 1961.

Moorehead, Alan, *The Traitors. The Double Life of Fuchs, Pontecorvo, and Munn May*, Hamish Hamilton, London, 1952.

Nieciusiński, Witold, *O systemach socjalistycznej gospodarki mieszkaniowej*, Książka i Wiedza, Warsaw, 1974.

Orth, Robert, *Hilfsorganisationen des Weltkommunismus*, Ilmgau Verlag, Pfaffenhofen/Ilm, 7th edition, 1971.

Ptaszek, Jan, *Polska-ZSRR. Gospodarka, Współpraca*, Państwowe Wydawnictwo Ekonomiczne, Warsaw, 1972.

Putrament, Jerzy, *Pół Wieku*, vol. IV—*Literaci*, Czytelnik, Warsaw, 1970.

Quilitzsch, Siegmar and Kruger Joachim (eds.). *Sozialistische Staatengemeinschaft. Die Entwicklung der Zusammenarbeit und der Friedenspolitik der sozialistischen Staaten*, Staatsverlag der DDR, Berlin (East), 1972.

167

Rada Wzajemnej Pomocy Gospodarczej. Wybór materiałów i dokumentów, Książka i Wiedza, Warsaw, 1964

Ransom, Charles, *The European Community and Eastern Europe*, Butterworths, London, 1973.

Remington, Robin Allison, *The Warsaw Pact. Case Studies in Communist Conflict Resolution*, The MIT Press, Cambridge, Mass. and London, 1971.

Reutt, Bogusław W. (ed.), *Podstawowe dokumenty RWPG i organizacji wyspecjalizowanych*, Książka i Wiedza, Warsaw, 1972.

Ribi, Rolf C., *Das Comecon. Eine Untersuchung über die Problematik der wirtschaftlichen Integration sozialistischer Länder*, Polygraphischer Verlag, Zürich and St. Gallen, 1970.

Riga. Statisticheskij Sbornik, Statistical Office of the City of Riga, 1968.

Rotleider, A. Ja., *Mezhdunarodnye kreditnye organizatsii stran-chlenov SEV*, Izdatel'stvo Finansy, Moscow, 1973.

Seton-Watson, Hugh, *The New Imperialism*, Capricorn Books edition, New York, 1967.

Soviet-Yugoslav Dispute. Royal Institute of International Affairs, London and New York, 1948.

Sovremennye problemy razoruzhenya, Izdatel'stvo Mysl', Moscow, 1970.

Spaak, Paul-Henri, *Les combats inachevés*, two volumes, Fayard, Paris, 1969. English translation: *The Continuing Battle. Memoirs of a European, 1936–1966*, Weidenfeld and Nicolson, London, 1971.

Stelzl, Diethar, *Die internationalen Banken des Rats für gegenseitige Wirtschaftshilfe*, Olzog Verlag, Munich-Vienna, 1973.

Stepanenko, S. I., *Sotrudnichestvo stran-chlenov-SEV v oblasti standardizatsii*, second edition, Izdatel'stvo Standartov, Moscow, 1972.

Sovershenstvovanie nauchno-technicheskovo sotrudnichestva stran SEV, Izdatel'stvo Mysl', Moscow, 1974.

Sutton, Anthony C., *Western Technology and Soviet Economic Development 1917–1930*, three vols., Hoover Institution, Stanford, California, 1969.

National Suicide. Military Aid to the Soviet Union, Arlington House, New Rochelle, N. Y., 1973.

Szawlowski, Richard, *Les Finances et le Droit financier d'une Organisation internationale intergouvernementale*, Editions Cujas, Paris, 1971.

Szulc, Tad, *Czechoslovakia Since World War II*, The Viking Press, New York, 1971.

Tarski, Ignacy (ed.), *Współpraca krajów RWPG w zakresie transportu*, Państwowe Wydawnictwo Ekonomiczne, Warsaw, 1970.

Tinbergen, Jan, *Economic Policy. Principles and Design*, North-Holland Publishing Company, Amsterdam 1956, third printing 1966.

International Economic Integration, second revised edition, Elsevier, Amsterdam—London—New York, 1965.

Tokareva, P. A., Kudrjashov, M. D., Morozov, V. I. (eds.), *Mnogostoronnieje ekonomicheskoe sotrudnichestvo sotsialisticheskikh gosudarstv. Sbornik dokumentov*, Izdatel'stvo Juridicheskaya Literatura, Moscow, 1967.

Tokareva, P. A. (ed.), *Mnogostoronnieje ekonomicheskoe sotrudnichestvo sotsialisticheskikh gosudarstv. Sbornik dokumentov*, second amplified edition, Juridicheskaya Literatura, Moscow, 1972.

Truman, Harry S., *Memoirs*, vol. II, *Years of Trial and Hope*, The New American Library, New York, 1965.

Tyranowski, Jerzy, *Traktaty sojusznicze Polski Ludowej*, Ksiazka i Wiedza, Warsaw, 1972.

Uschakow, Alexander, *Der Rat für Gegenseitige Wirtschaftshilfe*, Verlag Wissenschaft und Politik, Cologne, 1962.

— *Der Ostmarkt im Comecon. Eine Dokumentation*. Nomos Verlagsgesellschaft, Baden-Baden, 1972.

Usenko, E. T., *Formy regulirovania sotsialisticheskovo mezhdunarodnovo razdelenia truda*, Izdatel'stvo Mezhdunarodnye Otnoshenya, Moscow, 1965.

— (ed.)., *Miezhviedomstviennye swiazi v usloviakh sotsialisticheskoj integratsii. Pravovoj aspekt*. Juridicheskaya Literatura, Moscow, 1973.

Wasilkowski, Andrzej, *Zalecenia Rady Wzajemnej Pomocy Gospodarczej*, Państwowe Wydawnictwo Naukowe, Warsaw, 1969.

Weit, Erwin, *Ostblock intern. 13 Jahre Dolmetscher für die polnische Partei- und Staatsführung*, Hoffmann und Campe Verlag, Hamburg, 1970. English translation: *At the Red Summit: Interpreter Behind the Iron Curtain*, Macmillan Publishing Co., Inc., New York, 1973.

Wolfe, Thomas W., *Soviet Power and Europe 1945–1970*, The Johns Hopkins Press, Baltimore—London, 1970.

Wybrane Problemy Międzynarodowe, Książka i Wiedza, Warsaw, 1972.

Zolotarev, W. I., *Programma ekonomicheskovo sotrudnichestva sotsialisticheskikh stran*, Izdatel'stvo Mezhdunarodnye Otnoshenia, Moscow, 1973.

B. Periodicals and newspapers

Only those periodicals and newspapers used in this book, and referred to in the footnotes, are listed below.

Adelphi Papers (London).
Annuaire français de droit international (Paris).
Arkhiv Samizdata (Munich).
Armeerundschau (East Berlin).
Aussenpolitik (Freiburg i. B.).
Bulletin of the International Atomic Energy Agency (Vienna).
Christian Science Monitor, The (Boston).
Canadian Slavonic Papers (Ottawa).
Commerce du Levant, Le (Beirut).
Daily Telegraph, The (London)
Dziennik Polski (London).
Economist, The (London).
Einheit (East Berlin).
Ekonomicheskaya Gazeta (Moscow).
Ekonomicheskoe sotrudnichestvo stran-chlenov SEV (Moscow).

Europa-Archiv (Bonn).
Figaro, Le (Paris).
Financial Times, The (London).
Forum (East Berlin).
Frankfurter Allgemeine Zeitung (Frankfurt a. M.).
Gospodarka Planowa (Warsaw).
Guardian, The (London and Manchester).
Hindu, The (Madras)
Horizont (East Berlin).
Informationen (Bundesminister für innerdeutsche Beziehungen, Bonn).
International Affairs (Moscow).
International Herald Tribune, The (Paris).
Internationales Recht und Diplomatie (Hamburg).
Izvestia (Moscow).

Junge Welt (East Berlin).
Kommunist Estonii (Tallin).
Krasnaya Zvezda (Moscow).
Kurier, Der (Vienna).
Monde, Le (Paris).
Na Antenie (London).
Nachrichten für Aussenhandel (Frankfurt a. M.).
Neue Zürcher Zeitung (Zurich).
Neues Deutschland (East Berlin).
New Leader, The (New York).
New York Times, The (New York).
New Yorker, The (New York).
Newsweek (New York).
Nouvelle Revue des deux mondes, La (Paris).
Nowa Kultura (Warsaw).
Nowe Drogi (Warsaw).
OAS Chronicle (Washington, D. C.).
Orbis (Philadelphia).
Orzeł Biały (London).
Osteuropa-Recht (Stuttgart).
Peking Review (Peking).
Planovoe Khoziajstvo (Moscow).
Polish Yearbook of International Law (Warsaw).
Politicheskoe Obrazovanie (Moscow).
Polityka (Warsaw).
Pravda (Moscow).
Presse, Die (Vienna).
Problems of Communism (Washington, D.C.).
Revue belge de droit international (Brussels).
Rocznik Polityczny i Gospodarczy (Warsaw).
Rudé Pravo (Prague).
Rynki Zagraniczne (Warsaw).

Scinteia (Bucharest).
Soviet and East European Foreign Trade (White Plains, N.Y.).
Soviet Military Review (Moscow).
Soviet News (London).
Soviet Studies (Oxford).
Sovetskij Yezhegodnik Mezhdunarodnovo Prava (Moscow).
Sovetskoe Gosudarstvo i Pravo (Moscow).
Spiegel, Der (Hamburg).
Sprawy Międzynarodowe (Warsaw).
Staat und recht (East Berlin).
Strategic Review (Washington, D. C.).
Studia Nauk Politycznych (Warsaw).
Telecommunications Journal (Geneva).
Time (New York).
Times, The (London).
Times of India, The (Bombay).
Trybuna Ludu (Warsaw).
UNDP Business Bulletin (New York).
United Nations. General Assembly. Official Records (New York).
United Nations Treaty Series (New York).
Voprosy Ekonomiki (Moscow).
World Affairs (London).
World Marxist Review (Toronto).
Yearbook on International Communist Affairs (Stanford, Calif.).
Yearbook of International Organizations (Brussels).
Yezhegodnik Bol'shoi Sovetskoi Entsiklopedii (Moscow).
Zeit, Die (Hamburg).
Życie Gospodarcze (Warsaw).
Życie Warszawy (Warsaw).

ANNEXES

I. TREATY OF FRIENDSHIP, CO-OPERATION AND MUTUAL ASSISTANCE BETWEEN THE PEOPLE'S REPUBLIC OF ALBANIA, THE PEOPLE'S REPUBLIC OF BULGARIA, THE HUNGARIAN PEOPLE'S REPUBLIC, THE GERMAN DEMOCRATIC REPUBLIC, THE POLISH PEOPLE'S REPUBLIC, THE ROMANIAN PEOPLE'S REPUBLIC, THE UNION OF SOVIET SOCIALIST REPUBLICS AND THE CZECHOSLOVAK REPUBLIC. SIGNED AT WARSAW, ON 14 MAY 1955*

The Contracting Parties,

Reaffirming their desire to create a system of collective security in Europe based on the participation of all European States, irrespective of their social and political structure, whereby the said States may be enabled to combine their efforts in the interests of ensuring peace in Europe;

Taking into consideration, at the same time, the situation that has come about in Europe as a result of the ratification of the Paris Agreements, which provide for the constitution of a new military group in the form of a "West European Union", with the participation of a remilitarized West Germany and its inclusion in the North Atlantic bloc, thereby increasing the danger of a new war and creating a threat to the national security of peace-loving States;

Being convinced that in these circumstances the peace-loving States of Europe must take the necessary steps to safeguard their security and to promote the maintenance of peace in Europe;

Being guided by the purposes and principles of the Charter of the United Nations;

In the interests of the further strengthening and development of friendship, co-operation and mutual assistance in accordance with the principles of respect for the independence and sovereignty of States and of non-intervention in their domestic affairs;

Have resolved to conclude the present Treaty of Friendship, Co-operation and Mutual Assistance and have appointed as their plenipotentiaries:

The Presidium of the National Assembly of the People's Republic of Albania: Mehmet Shehu, President of the Council of Ministers of the People's Republic of Albania;

The Presidium of the National Assembly of the People's Republic of Bulgaria: Vylko Chervenkov, President of the Council of Ministers of the People's Republic of Bulgaria;

The Presidium of the Hungarian People's Republic: András Hegedüs, President of the Council of Ministers of the Hungarian People's Republic;

The President of the German Democratic Republic: Otto Grotewohl, Prime Minister of the German Democratic Republic;

Council of State of the Polish People's Republic: Józef Cyrankiewicz President of the Council of Ministers of the Polish People's Republic;

The Presidium of the Grand National Assembly of the Romanian People's Republic: Gheorghe Gheorghiu Dej, President of the Council of Ministers of the Romanian People's Republic;

The Presidium of the Supreme Soviet of the Union of Soviet Socialist

---

* *United Nations Treaty Series*, Vol. 219 (1955), No. 2962.

Republics: Nikolai Aleksandrovich Bulganin, President of the Council of Ministers of the Union of Soviet Socialist Republics;
The President of the Czechoslovak Republic: Viliam Široký, Prime Minister of the Czechoslovak Republic;

who, having exhibited their full powers, found in good and due form, have agreed as follows:

Article 1

The Contracting Parties undertake, in accordance with the Charter of the United Nations, to refrain in their international relations from the threat or use of force and to settle their international disputes by peaceful means in such a manner that international peace and security are not endangered.

Article 2

The Contracting Parties declare that they are prepared to participate, in a spirit of sincere co-operation, in all international action for ensuring international peace and security and will devote their full efforts to the realization of these aims.

In this connexion, the Contracting Parties shall endeavour to secure, in agreement with other States desiring to co-operate in this matter, the adoption of effective measures for the general reduction of armaments and the prohibition of atomic, hydrogen and other weapons of mass destruction.

Article 3

The Contracting Parties shall consult together on all important international questions involving their common interests, with a view to strengthening international peace and security.

Whenever any one of the Contracting Parties considers that a threat of armed attack on one or more of the States Parties to the Treaty has arisen, they shall consult together immediately with a view to providing for their joint defence and maintaining peace and security.

Article 4

In the event of an armed attack in Europe on one or more of the States Parties to the Treaty by any State or group of States, each State Party to the Treaty shall, in the exercise of the right of individual or collective self-defence, in accordance with Article 51 of the United Nations Charter, afford the State or States so attacked immediate assistance, individually and in agreement with the other States Parties to the Treaty, by all the means it considers necessary, including the use of armed force. The States Parties to the Treaty shall consult together immediately concerning the joint measures necessary to restore and maintain international peace and security.

Measures taken under this article shall be reported to the Security Council in accordance with the provisions of the United Nations Charter. These measures shall be discontinued as soon as the Security Council takes the necessary action to restore and maintain international peace and security.

Article 5

The Contracting Parties have agreed to establish a Unified Command, to which certain elements of their armed forces shall be allocated by agreement between the Parties, and which shall act in accordance with jointly established principles. The Parties shall likewise take such other concerted action as may be necessary to reinforce their defensive strength, in order to defend the peaceful labour of their peoples, guarantee the inviolability of their frontiers and territories and afford protection against possible aggression.

Article 6

For the purpose of carrying out the consultations provided for in the present Treaty between the States Parties thereto, and for the consideration of matters arising in connexion with the application of the present Treaty, a Political Consultative Committee shall be established, in which each State Party to the Treaty shall be represented by a member of the Government or by some other specially appointed representative.

The Committee may establish such auxiliary organs as may prove to be necessary.

Article 7

The Contracting Parties undertake not to participate in any coalitions or alliances, and not to conclude any agreements, the purposes of which are incompatible with the purposes of the present Treaty.

The Contracting Parties declare that their obligations under international treaties at present in force are not incompatible with the provisions of the present Treaty.

Article 8

The Contracting Parties declare that they will act in a spirit of friendship and co-operation to promote the further development and strengthening of the economic and cultural ties among them, in accordance with the principles of respect for each other's independence and sovereignty and of non-intervention in each other's domestic affairs.

Article 9

The present Treaty shall be open for accession by other States, irrespective of their social and political structure, which express their readiness, by participating in the present Treaty, to help in combining the efforts of the peace-loving States to ensure the peace and security of the peoples. Such accessions shall come into effect with the consent of the States Parties to the Treaty after the instruments of accession have been deposited with the Government of the Polish People's Republic.

Article 10

The present Treaty shall be subject to ratification, and the instruments of ratification shall be deposited with the Government of the Polish People's Republic.

The Treaty shall come into force on the date of deposit of the last instrument of ratification. The Government of the Polish People's Republic shall inform the other States Parties to the Treaty of the deposit of each instrument of ratification.

Article 11

The present Treaty shall remain in force for twenty years. For Contracting Parties which do not, one year before the expiration of that term, give notice of termination of the Treaty to the Government of the Polish People's Republic, the Treaty shall remain in force for a further ten years.

In the event of the establishment of a system of collective security in Europe and the conclusion for that purpose of a General European Treaty concerning collective security, a goal which the Contracting Parties shall steadfastly strive to achieve, the present Treaty shall cease to have effect as from the date on which the General European Treaty comes into force.

Done at Warsaw, this fourteenth day of May 1955, in one copy, in the Russian, Polish, Czech and German languages, all the texts being equally authentic. Certified copies of the present Treaty shall be transmitted by the Government of the Polish People's Republic to all the other Parties to the Treaty.

In faith whereof the Plenipotentiaries have signed the present Treaty and have thereto affixed their seals.*

* Here, as in the other legal documents reproduced in our Annexes, the names of those signing the respective treaties have been missed out.

II. CONVENTION CONCERNING THE JURIDICAL PERSONALITY, PRIVILEGES AND IMMUNITIES OF THE STAFF AND OTHER ADMINISTRATIVE ORGANS OF THE JOINT ARMED FORCES OF THE STATES PARTIES TO THE WARSAW TREATY*

The Governments of the People's Republic of Bulgaria, the Hungarian People's Republic, the German Democratic Republic, the Polish People's Republic, the Socialist Republic of Rumania, the Union of Soviet Socialist Republics and the Czechoslovak Socialist Republic,

Being guided by the principles of the Treaty on friendship, cooperation and mutual assistance signed in Warsaw on 14 May 1955,

Taking into consideration the Decision of the States Parties to the Warsaw Treaty, taken at the conference of the Political Consultative Committee of 17 March 1969 in Budapest,

Noting that the general tasks and the role of the Staff and other administrative organs of the Joint Armed Forces are determined by documents accepted by the States Parties to the Warsaw Treaty,

Taking into account the Statute of the Joint Armed Forces and the Joint Command of the States Parties to the Warsaw Treaty,

Bearing in mind that for the fulfilment of the tasks with which the Staff and other administrative organs of the Joint Armed Forces are charged, they have to be accorded juridical personality, privileges and immunities,

Have agreed as follows:

Article 1

1. The Staff of the Joint Armed Forces shall consist of generals, admirals and officers of the States Parties to the Warsaw Treaty who shall, during the fulfilment of their official duties, be accorded privileges and immunities in accordance with the present Convention.

In the Staff of the Joint Armed Forces there shall also work employees detached *(vydelennye)* by the country in which the Staff is located, some of whom shall enjoy privileges and immunities under conditions set forth in the present Convention. The categories and number of employees who shall enjoy privileges and immunities shall be agreed upon by the Staff of the Joint Armed Forces and the General (Main) staffs of the armies of the States Parties to the Convention. A list of names of these employees shall be communicated yearly by the Staff of the Joint Armed Forces to the General (Main) staffs of the armies of the States Parties to the Convention.

2. For the purposes of the present Convention the term "Staff of the Joint Armed Forces" shall also stand for other administrative organs of the Joint Armed Forces of the States Parties to the Warsaw Treaty.

3. The headquarters of the Staff of the Joint Armed Forces shall be in Moscow.

Article 2

The Staff of the Joint Armed Forces of the States Parties to the Warsaw

* Translation by the author. Russian text published in *Krasnaya Zvezda*, April 27, 1973

Treaty shall posses juridical personality, and, in order to fulfil the tasks for which it was created, shall have the capacity:

(a) to enter into agreements;

(b) to acquire, lease and alienate property;

(c) to appear in court.

Article 3

1. The Staff of the Joint Armed Forces shall enjoy, on the territory of every State Party to the present Convention, the juridical personality, privileges and immunities set forth in the present Convention.

2. The premises of the Staff of the Joint Armed Forces, its property, assets and documents, wherever located, shall enjoy immunity from every form of administrative and legal process except in so far as the Staff itself waives immunity in any individual case.

3. The Staff of the Joint Armed Forces shall be exempt from direct taxes and duties in the territory of every State Party to the Convention. This exemption shall not apply to charges for concrete categories of services and public utilities.

4. The Staff of the Joint Armed Forces shall be exempt from customs duties and restrictions on imports and exports of articles intended for official use.

5. The Staff of the Joint Armed Forces shall enjoy, in the territory of every State Party to the present Convention, conditions not less favourable than those enjoyed in that country by the national military command or diplomatic representations in the matter of priorities, tariffs and rates on postal, telegraph and telephone communications.

Article 4

1. Officials of the Staff of the Joint Armed Forces shall be accorded, in the territory of each state-party to the present Convention, while exercising their official functions, the following privileges and immunities:

(a) inviolability for all papers and documents;

(b) the same customs facilities in respect of their personal baggage as are accorded to officials of diplomatic missions in the country concerned;

(c) exemption from national service obligations and from direct taxes and duties on the rate of pay (salary) paid to the personnel of the Staff of the Joint Armed Forces by the country which sends them;

(d) immunity from personal arrest or detention and also from the jurisdiction of judicial and administrative institutions in respect of any acts done by them in their capacity as officials.

The provisions of paragraphs b) and c) shall apply to members of family residing with officials of the Staff of the Joint Armed Forces.

2. The Chief of Staff of the Joint Armed Forces and his deputies shall enjoy, in the territories of all States Parties to the present Convention, in addition to the privileges and immunities specified in paragraph 1 of the present article, privileges and immunities accorded in the country concerned to diplomatic representatives. The above-mentioned persons shall receive diplomatic passes.

3. The privileges and immunities provided for in this article are accorded to the persons specified therein solely in the interests of the fulfilment by these persons of their official functions.

178

The Commander-in-Chief of the Joint Armed Forces, in agreement with the Minister of Defence of the country concerned, shall have the right and the duty to waive the immunity of an official of the Staff in any case where the immunity would impede the course of justice and can be waived without prejudice to the purpose for which it was accorded.

4.   Officials of the Staff of the Joint Armed Forces and members of their families shall be issued, by the Staff, special certificates of identity, confirming the right to privileges and immunities.

Officials of the Staff of the Joint Armed Forces and members of their families shall be exempt from compulsory visas and registration. They shall be registered by the Staff of the Joint Armed Forces.

5.   The provisions of paragraphs 1, 2, 3, and 4 of this article shall not apply as between officials of the Staff of the Joint Armed Forces and members of their families and the authorities of the country of which they are nationals or of the country on whose territory they reside permanently.

6.   Persons who enjoy the privileges and immunities provided for by the present Convention shall be obliged to observe the laws of the state on whose territory they find themselves, and not to interfere in the internal affairs of the state concerned.

Article 5

In the case of a waiver by the Commander-in-Chief of the Joint Armed Forces of the immunity of an official of the Staff, provided for by article 4 of the present Convention, against such a person, who committed a penal or administrative breach of law, shall be applied the legislation of the country on whose territory the breach of law took place, and action shall be taken by its military justice authorities competent in questions of prosecution of punishable acts.

The military justice authorities of the States Parties to the present Convention may mutually address one another with a request for granting legal aid in individual cases. Such requests shall be considered in a friendly spirit.

Article 6

1.   The present Convention shall be ratified by the States which sign it, in accordance with their constitutional procedures.

2.   The instruments of ratification shall be deposited with the Government of the Union of Soviet Socialist Republics, which is designated depositary of the present Convention.

3.   The Convention shall enter into force on the date of the deposit of instruments of ratification by three states. With respect to other States which sign the Convention, it shall enter into force on the date of the deposit by them of their instruments of ratification.

4.   Potential questions of dispute arising out of the interpretation and application of the present Convention shall be settled by the States Parties to this Convention by way of negotiations between national commands or through diplomatic channels, or by any other means agreed upon.

5.   The present Convention has been drawn up in a single copy in the Russian language. The Convention shall be deposited with the Government of the Union of Soviet Socialist Republics, which shall send certified true copies

of it to the governments of all the other States which sign it, and shall also notify those governments and the Staff of the Joint Armed Forces of the deposit of each instrument.

In witness whereof the undersigned, duly authorized to do so, have signed the present Convention.

Done at Moscow, on 24 April 1973.

III. CHARTER OF THE COUNCIL FOR MUTUAL ECONOMIC ASSISTANCE. SIGNED AT SOFIA, ON 14 DECEMBER 1959*

The Governments of the People's Republic of Albania, the People's Republic of Bulgaria, the Hungarian People's Republic, the German Democratic Republic, the Polish People's Republic, the Romanian People's Republic, the Union of Soviet Socialist Republics and the Czechoslovak Republic,

Bearing in mind that the economic co-operation which is successfully taking place between their countries helps to promote the most rational development of the national economy, to raise the level of living of the people and to strengthen the unity and solidarity of those countries;

Determined to continue the development of comprehensive economic co-operation based on consistent implementation of the international socialist division of labour in the interests of the building of socialism and communism in their countries and the maintenance of lasting peace throughout the world;

Convinced that the development of economic co-operation between their countries contributes to the achievement of the purposes set forth in the Charter of the United Nations;

Affirming their readiness to develop economic relations with all countries, irrespective of their social and political structure, on the basis of equality, mutual advantage and non-intervention in each other's domestic affairs;

Recognizing the increasing importance of the part played by the Council for Mutual Economic Assistance in the organizing of economic co-operation between their countries,

Have agreed, to these ends, to adopt the present Charter.

Article I

Purposes and principles

1. The purpose of the Council for Mutual Economic Assistance is to promote, by uniting and co-ordinating the efforts of the member countries of the Council, *the further deepening and perfecting of cooperation and the development of socialist economic integration*, the planned development of the national economies and the acceleration of the economic and technical progress of those countries, the raising of the level of industrialization of the countries with a less-developed industry, a continual growth in the productivity, *the gradual approximation and equalization of the levels of economic development*, together with a steady increase in the well-being of the peoples, of the member countries of the Council.

2. The Council for Mutual Economic Assistance is based on the principle of the sovereign equality of all the member countries of the Council.

Economic and scientific-technical co-operation between the member countries of the Council shall take place in accordance with the principles of *socialist internationalism, on the basis of* respect for *state* sovereignty, *independence*

---

* *United Nations Treaty Series*, Vol. 368 (1960), No. 5245. The passages in italics, translated by the author, are the 1962 and 1974 amendments. Illegal as they are (see pp. 50–51), they nevertheless apply in actual fact.

and national interest, *non-interference in the internal affairs of countries*, complete equality of rights, mutual advantage and friendly mutual aid.

Membership

1. The original members of the Council for Mutual Economic Assistance shall be the countries which have signed and ratified the present Charter.

2. Membership in the Council shall be open to other countries which subscribe to the purposes and principles of the Council and declare that they agree to accept the obligations contained in the present Charter.

New members shall be admitted by a decision of the Session of the Council, on the basis of official requests by countries for their admission to membership in the Council.

3. Any member country of the Council may leave the Council, after notifying the depositary of the present Charter to that effect. Such notice shall take effect six months after its receipt by the depositary. Upon receiving such notice, the depositary shall inform the member countries of the Council thereof.

4. The member countries of the Council agree:

(a) To ensure implementation of the recommendations, accepted by them, of organs of the Council;

(b) To render to the Council and its officers the necessary assistance in the execution of the duties laid upon them by the present Charter;

(c) To make available to the Council the material and information essential to the fulfilment of the tasks entrusted to it;

(d) To keep the Council informed of progress in the implementation of the recommendations *of the organs of the* Council adopted *by them*.

Article III

Functions and powers

1. In conformity with the purposes and principles set forth in article I of the present Charter, the Council for Mutual Economic Assistance shall:

(a) Organize:

Comprehensive economic and scientific-technical co-operation among the member countries of the Council, with a view to the most rational use of their natural resources and the more rapid development of their productive forces, *and promote the development of socialist economic integration;*

(b) *Assist in the perfecting of the international socialist division of labour by means of the co-ordination of plans for the development of the national economy, and by specialization and co-operation in production of the member countries of the Council;*

(c) *Undertake measures for the study of economic and scientific-technical problems of interest to the member countries of the Council;*

(d) Assist the member countries of the Council in the preparation, *co-ordination* and execution of joint measures regarding:

The development of industry and agriculture in the member countries of the Council;

The development of transport, for the primary purpose of ensuring the conveyance of the increasing volume of export-import and transit freight between member countries of the Council;

The most effective use of *the basic investments allocated by the member countries of the Council for the development of the extractive and processing branches of industry and also for the construction of major projects of interest to two or more countries;*

The development of the exchange of goods and services between member countries of the Council and with other countries;

The exchange of experience in the matter of scientific-technical achievements and advanced methods of production;

(e) Undertake other action required for achieving the purposes of the Council.

2. The Council for Mutual Economic Assistance, in accordance with the present Charter:

(a) Is authorized to adopt recommendations and decisions through its organs acting within their competence;

(b) *May conclude international agreements with member countries of the Council, with other countries, and with international organizations.*

Article IV

Recommendations and decisions

1. Recommendations shall be adopted on questions of economic and scientific-technical co-operation. Such recommendations shall be communicated to the member countries of the Council for consideration.

Recommendations adopted by member countries of the Council shall be implemented by them through decisions of the Governments or competent authorities of those countries, in conformity with their laws.

2. Decisions shall be adopted on organizational and procedural questions. Such decisions shall take effect, unless it is specified otherwise in them, *or follows from the nature of the decisions,* from the date on which the record of the meeting of the Council organ concerned is signed.

3. All recommendations and decisions of the Council shall be adopted only with the consent of the member countries concerned, each country being entitled to state its interest in any question under consideration by the Council.

Recommendations and decisions shall not apply to countries which state that they have no interest in the question at issue. Nevertheless, each such country may subsequently associate itself with the recommendations and decisions adopted by the remaining member countries of the Council.

Article V

Organs

1. For the discharge of the functions and the exercise of the powers mentioned in article III of the present Charter, the Council for Mutual Economic Assistance shall have the following principal organs:

The Session of the Council,
The Executive Board of the Council,
The Committees of the Council,
The Standing Commissions *of the Council,*
The Secretariat *of the Council.*

2. Other organs may be established, as necessary, in conformity with the present Charter.

Article VI
The Session of the Council

1. The Session of the Council shall be the highest organ of the Council for Mutual Economic Assistance. It shall be authorized to discuss all questions falling within the competence of the Council, and to adopt recommendations and decisions in accordance with the present Charter.

2. The Session of the Council shall consist of delegations from all the member countries of the Council. The composition of the delegation of each country shall be determined by the Government of the country concerned.

3. The regular sessions of the Council shall be convened *not less than once a year* in the capital of each member country of the Council in turn, under the chairmanship of the head of the delegation of the country in which the session is held.

4. A special session of the Council may be convened at the request or with the consent of not less than one third of the member countries of the Council.

5. The Session of the Council shall:

(a) Consider:

Basic questions of economic and scientific-technical co-operation and shall determine the principal directions of the activities of the Council;

The report *of the Executive Board* on the activities of the Council;

(b) Perform such other functions as may be found necessary for achieving the purposes of the Council.

6. The Session of the Council is authorized to establish such organs as it may consider necessary for the discharge of the functions entrusted to the Council.

7. The Session of the Council shall establish its own rules of procedure.

Article VII
The Executive Board of the Council

1. *The Executive Board* of the Council for Mutual Economic Assistance shall consist of representatives of all the member countries of the Council *at the level of deputy heads of government,* one for each country.

The Executive Board shall be the principal executive organ of the Council.

2. *The Executive Board* shall hold its meetings *as a rule once every quarter.*

3. *The Executive Board* shall have the right, within its field of competence, to adopt recommendations and decisions in conformity with the present Charter. *The Executive Board* may submit proposals for consideration by the Session of the Council.

4. *The Executive Board* shall:

(a) *Direct the totality of work connected with the realization of the tasks facing the Council in accordance with the decisions of the Session of the Council, and carry out systematic supervision over the fulfilment by member countries of the Council of the obligations arising from the recommendations of organs of the Council adopted by them;*

(b) *Direct the work of co-ordination of plans for the development of the national economy, of specialization and co-operation of the production of the member countries of the Council, and organize the working out of the basic directions of rational division of labour in the most important branches of production of those countries;*

(c) *Consider the proposals of member countries of the Council and of the corresponding organs of the Council, on questions of economic and scientific-technical co-operation, analyze the state of that co-operation and work out measures for its further development;*

(d) *Work out the basic directions and measures for the development of: Exchange of goods and services between the member countries of the Council; Scientific-technical co-operation between member countries of the Council;*

(e) *Direct the work of the Committees, of the Standing Commissions, and of the Secretariat of the Council, and also of other corresponding organs of the Council, and determine the basic questions and directions for their activities.*

(f) Approve:

The personnel *of the Secretariat of the Council, the* budget *of the Council,* and the report of the Secretariat on the execution of the budget;

The regulations for *the Committees,* the Standing Commissions, and the Secretariat of the Council, *and also of other organs of the Council;*

(g) Establish control organs for supervising the financial activity of the Secretariat of the Council;

(h) Perform other functions arising from the present Charter and from the recommendations and decisions of the Session of the Council.

5. *The Executive Board may establish such organs as it may consider necessary for the realization of its functions.*

6. *The Executive Board* shall establish its own rules of procedure.

Article VIII

The Committees of the Council

1. *Committees of the Council shall be set up by the Session of the Council to ensure comprehensive consideration and solution, on a multilateral basis, of the most important problems of co-operation between the member countries of the Council in the sphere of the economy, science and technology.*

The Committees of the Council shall carry out the functions specified in their regulations, and also other functions arising from the recommendations and decisions of the Session of the Council and the Executive Board of the Council.

2. *The Committees shall consist of the chiefs of the corresponding competent organs of the member countries of the Council, one from each country.*

3. *The Committees of the Council shall have the right, within the limits of their competence:*

(a) *To adopt recommendations and decisions in accordance with the present Charter;*

(b) *To submit proposals for consideration by the Session of the Council and the Executive Board of the Council;*

(c) *To establish working organs to prepare individual questions within the competence of the Committees to be considered and agreed upon by the Committees, and also convene scientific-technical conferences and other meetings;*

(d) *To ask the Standing Commissions, and other corresponding organs of the Council, for material, observations and proposals on questions connected with their activities.*

4. *The Committes of the Council shall present annual reports on the work done to the Executive Board of the Council.*

5. *The Committees of the Council shall establish their own rules of procedure.*

The Standing Commissions *of the Council*

1. Standing Commissions of the Council for Mutual Economic Assistance shall be set by the Session of the Council for the purpose of promoting the further development of economic relations between the member countries of the Council and organizing comprehensive economic and scientific-technical co-operation in the various sectors of the national economies of those countries.

The Standing Commissions shall work out measures and prepare proposals for implementing the economic and scientific-technical co-operation mentioned *above, including the preparation of the corresponding multilateral agreements, and also* perform other functions arising from the present Charter and from the recommendations and decisions of the Session of the Council, *the Executive Board and the Committees of the Council.*

2. *The Standing Commissions shall consist of delegations appointed by the member countries of the Council.*

3. The Standing Commissions shall have the right, within their field of competence:

(a) To adopt recommendations and decisions in conformity with the present Charter;

(b) To submit proposals for consideration by the Session of the Council and *the Executive Board of the Council, and also to send, upon request or on their own initiative, material, observations, and proposals to other corresponding organs of the Council;*

(c) *To establish working organs to prepare individual questions within the competence of the Commissions to be considered and agreed upon by the Commissions, and also convene scientific-technical conferences and other meetings.*

4. The Standing Commissions shall submit to *the Executive Board of the Council* annual reports on the work done and on their future activities.

5. The Standing Commissions shall establish their own rules of procedure.

Article X

The Secretariat *of the Council*

1. The Secretariat of the Council for Mutual Economic Assistance shall consist of the Secretary of the Council, his deputies and such personnel as may be required for the performance of the functions entrusted to the Secretariat.

The Secretary of the Council shall be appointed by the Session of the Council, and his deputies by the Executive Board of the Council.

The Secretary of the Council and his deputies shall direct the work of the Secretariat of the Council. The personnel of the Secretariat shall be recruited from citizens of the member countries of the Council, in accordance with the regulations for the Secretariat of the Council.

The Secretary of the Council shall be the chief officer of the Council. He shall represent the Council vis-à-vis officials and organizations of the member countries of the Council and other countries, and vis-à-vis international organizations. The Secretary of the Council may authorize his deputies, as well as other members of the Secretariat to act on his behalf.

The Secretary and his deputies may take part in all meetings of the organs of the Council.

2. The Secretariat of the Council shall:

(a) *Organize the preparation and assist in the conducting of meetings of the organs of the Council and sessions held within the framework of the Council, prepare material or assist in the preparation of material for meetings of the organs of the Council in accordance with the work plans of these organs, and ensure the carrying out of the functions of secretariat of the other organs of the Council;*

(b) *Work out economic surveys and conduct economic studies on the basis of material from the member countries of the Council, prepare and publish information, reference and other material on questions of economic and scientific-technical co-operation between member countries of the Council, and also prepare other surveys and studies;*

(c) Prepare proposals on *individual* problems of the work of the Council for consideration in the appropriate organs of the Council;

(d) *Work out, or assist in the working out of,* the drafts of multilateral agreements on questions of economic and scientific-technical co-operation, *in accordance with* recommendations and decisions *of the organs of the Council;*

(e) *Organize and keep a record of the implementation of recommendations and decisions of the organs of the Council, and prepare appropriate proposals for their consideration.*

(f) Undertake other action arising out of the present Charter, the recommendations and decisions adopted in the Council, and the regulations for the Secretariat of the Council.

3. The Secretary of the Council, his deputies and the personnel of the Secretariat, when fulfilling the duties entrusted to them, act as international officials.

4. The headquarters of the Secretariat of the Council shall be in Moscow.

Article XI

Relations of the Council with other Countries

The Council for Mutual Economic Assistance may invite countries which are not members of the Council to take part in the work of the organs of the Council, *or realize co-operation with them in other forms.*

The conditions under which *the countries which are not members of the Council* may participate in the work of the organs of the Council, *or under which they may cooperate with the Council in other forms,* shall be determined by the Council in agreement with the countries concerned, *as a rule by means of concluding agreements.*

Article XII

Relations of the Council with international organizations

The Council for Mutual Economic Assistance may establish and maintain relations *with organs* of the United Nations, *and with specialized* and other international organizations.

The nature and form of such relations shall be determined by the Council in agreement with the corresponding *organs of the United Nations* and with international organizations, *in particular by means of concluding agreements.*

Article XIII

Financial questions

1. *All income and expenditure of the Council shall be envisaged in the budget of the Council.* The member countries of the Council shall bear the expenditures *connected with* maintaining the Secretariat and financing its activities, *and other expenditure of the Council, in accordance with its budget. The amount of the contribution shares of the member countries to the budget of the Council* shall be determined by the Session of the Council.

2. The Secretariat of the Council shall submit to the *Executive Board of the Council the draft budget of the Council for each calendar year,* and a report on the execution of the budget.

Audit of the financial activities of the Secretariat of the Council shall be carried out every year.

3. The maintenance expenses of participants in the meetings of *organs of the Council,* and in all meetings held within the framework of the Council, shall be borne by the country sending its representatives to those meetings and sessions.

4. The expenses *involved in the provision of premises, and also of the technical means necessary for* the meetings and sessions indicated in paragraph 3 of the present Article, shall be borne by the country in which these meetings and sessions are held, *with the exception of cases when such meetings and sessions are held on the premises of the Council.*

Article XIV

Miscellaneous provisions

1. The Council for Mutual Economic Assistance shall enjoy, on the territories of all member countries of the Council, the legal capacity essential to the performance of its functions and the achievement of its purposes.

2. The Council, as also the representatives of the member countries of the Council and the officers of the Council, shall enjoy, on the territory of each of those countries, the privileges and immunities which are necessary for the performance of the functions and the achievements of the purposes set forth in the present Charter.

3. The legal capacity, privileges and immunities mentioned in this article shall be defined in a special Convention.

4. The provisions of the present Charter shall not affect the rights and obligations of the member countries of the Council arising out of their membership of other international organizations, or out of international treaties which they have concluded.

5. *The representatives of countries on the Executive Board of the Council shall be, at the same time, permanent representatives of their countries in the Council. A permanent representative of a country in the Council shall have, at the headquarters of the Secretariat of the Council, a deputy, the necessary number of advisers, and other employees.*

Article XV

Languages

The official languages of the Council for Mutual Economic Assistance shall be the languages of all the member countries of the Council.

The working language of the Council shall be Russian.

Article XVI

Ratification and entry into force of the Charter

1. The present Charter shall be ratified by the signatory countries, in accordance with their constitutional procedure.

2. The instruments of ratification shall be deposited with the depositary of the present Charter.

3. The present Charter shall enter into force immediately after the deposit of instruments of ratification by all the countries which have signed the Charter, and the depositary shall notify those countries thereof.

4. With respect to each country which in accordance with article II, paragraph 2, is admitted to membership in the Council for Mutual Economic Assistance and which ratifies the Charter, this Charter shall enter into force *provisionally from the date on which the Session of the Council decides to admit the given counter to membership of the Council, and finally* from the date of the deposit by such country of its instrument of ratification of the Charter, and the depositary shall notify the other member countries of the Council thereof.

Article XVII

Procedure for amendment of the Charter

Each member country of the Council for Mutual Economic Assistance may make proposals for the amendment of the present Charter.

Amendments to the Charter, when approved by the Session of the Council, shall come into force immediately after the ratifications of those amendments have been deposited with the depositary by all member countries of the Council.

Article XVIII

Final provisions

This Charter has been drawn up in a single copy, in the Russian language. It shall be deposited with the Government of the Union of Soviet Socialist Republics, which shall send certified true copies of the Charter to the Governments of all the other member countries of the Council and shall notify those Governments, and the Secretary of the Council, of the deposit of the instruments of ratification with the Government of the USSR.

In witness whereof the representatives of the Governments of the member countries of the Council for Mutual Economic Assistance have signed the present Charter.

Done at Sofia, on 14 December 1959.

IV. CONVENTION BETWEEN ALBANIA, BULGARIA, HUNGARY, THE GERMAN DEMOCRATIC REPUBLIC, POLAND, ROMANIA, THE UNION OF SOVIET SOCIALIST REPUBLICS AND CZECHOSLOVAKIA CONCERNING THE JURIDICAL PERSONALITY, PRIVILEGES AND IMMUNITIES OF THE COUNCIL FOR MUTUAL ECONOMIC ASSISTANCE. SIGNED AT SOFIA, ON 14 DECEMBER 1959*

The Governments of the People's Republic of Albania, the People's Republic of Bulgaria, the Hungarian People's Republic, the German Democratic Republic, the Polish People's Republic, the Romanian People's Republic, the Union of Soviet Socialist Republics and the Czechoslovak Republic,

Having regard to article *XIV* of the Charter of the Council for Mutual Economic Assistance which provides:

That the Council for Mutual Economic Assistance shall enjoy, on the territories of all member countries of the Council, the legal capacity essential to the performance of its functions and the achievement of its purposes;

That the Council, as also the representatives of the member countries of the Council and the officers of the Council, shall enjoy, on the territory of each of those countries, the privileges and immunities which are necessary for the performance of the functions and the achievement of the purposes set forth in the said Charter;

That the legal capacity, privileges and immunities mentioned shall be defined in a special Convention;

Have agreed as follows:

Article I

Juridical personality

The Council for Mutual Economic Assistance shall possess juridical personality and shall have the capacity
(a) To enter into agreements;
(b) To acquire, lease and alienate property;
(c) To appear in court.

Article II

Property, assets and documents

1. The premises of the Council for Mutual Economic Assistance shall be inviolable. Its property, assets and documents, wherever located, shall enjoy immunity from every form of administrative and legal process except in so far as in any particular case the Council has waived its immunity.

2. The Council for Mutual Economic Assistance shall be exempt from all direct taxes and duties levied either by State or by local authorities. This exemption shall not apply to charges for public utility and similar services.

* *United Nations Treaty Series*, Vol. 368 (1960), No. 5244. The passages in italics, translated by the author, are the 1962 and 1974 amendments. Illegal as they are (see pp. 50–51) they nevertheless apply in actual fact. The Russian text of the 1974 version of the Convention was kindly furnished to us by Dr. Alexander Uschakow, University of Cologne.

3. The Council for Mutual Economic Assistance shall be exempt from customs duties and restrictions on imports or exports of articles intended for official use.

Article III

Privileges in respect of communications

The Council for Mutual Economic Assistance shall enjoy, in the territories of each member country of the Council, treatment not less favourable than that enjoyed by diplomatic missions in that country in the matter of priorities, rates and taxes on post, cable and telephone communications.

Article IV

Representatives of member countries of the Council

1. Representatives of member countries of the Council for Mutual Economic Assistance to organs of the Council and to conferences convened under the auspices of the Council shall while exercising their official functions be accorded in the territory of each member country of the Council the following privileges and immunities:

(a) Immunity from personal arrest or detention and from the jurisdiction of judicial institutions in respect of any acts done by them in their capacity as representatives;

(b) Inviolability for all papers and documents;

(c) The same customs facilities in respect of their personal baggage as are accorded to members of comparable rank of diplomatic missions in the country concerned;

(d) Exemption from national service obligations and from direct taxes and duties on salaries paid to them by the countries which appointed them.

2. In addition to the privileges and immunities specified in paragraph 1 of this article, *permanent* representatives of countries to the Council and their deputies shall enjoy the privileges and immunities accorded to diplomatic envoys in the country concerned.

3. The privileges and immunities provided in this article are accorded to the persons specified therein solely in the interests of their official functions. Each member country of the Council shall have the right and the duty to waive the immunity of its representative in any case where in the opinion of that country the immunity would impede the course of justice and can be waived without prejudice to the purpose for which it was accorded.

4. The provisions of paragraphs 1 and 2 shall not apply as between a representative and the authorities of the country of which he is a national.

5. In this article the expression "representatives" *in para. 1* shall be deemed to include *permanent* representatives to the Council, their deputies, heads, members and secretaries of delegations, advisers and experts.

Article V

Officials of the Council

1. *The Executive Board* of the Council for Mutual Economic Assistance, on the recommendation of the Secretary of the Council, shall specify the cate-

gories of officials to which the provisions of this article shall apply. The names of such officials shall be communicated periodically by the Secretary of the Council to the member countries of the Council.

2. Officials of the Council shall, on the territory of each member country of the Council:

(a) Be immune from legal and administrative process in respect of all acts performed by them in their official capacity;

(b) Be exempt from national service obligations;

(c) Be exempt from direct taxes and duties on the salaries paid to them by the Council;

(d) Have the right to the same customs facilities in respect of their personal baggage as are accorded to members of comparable rank of diplomatic missions in the country concerned.

3. In addition to the privileges and immunities specified in paragraph 2 of this article, the Secretary of the Council and his deputies shall enjoy the privileges and immunities accorded to diplomatic envoys in the country concerned.

4. The privileges and immunities provided in this article are accorded to the persons specified therein solely in the interests of the Council and in order to ensure the independent exercise of their official functions. The Secretary of the Council shall have the right and the duty to waive the immunity of any official in any case where in his opinion the immunity would impede the course of justice and can be waived without prejudice to the interests of the Council. In the case of the Secretary of the Council and his deputies, the right to waive immunity shall be vested in the *Executive Board of the Council.*

5. The provisions of paragraph 2 (b) and (c) of this article shall not apply to officials of the Council who are nationals of the country which is the seat of the organ of the Council in which they are employed.

Article VI

Final provisions

1. The present Convention shall be ratified by the member countries of the Council, in accordance with their constitutional procedures.

2. The instruments of ratification shall be deposited with the depositary of the present Convention.

3. The present Convention shall enter into force immediately after the deposit of instruments of ratification by all the member countries of the Council which have signed the Convention, and the depositary shall notify those countries thereof.

4. With respect to each country which in accordance with article II, paragraph 2, of the Charter of the Council for Mutual Economic Assistance is admitted to membership in the Council, *and gives notice of its agreement to join the present Convention, it shall enter into force provisionally from the date on which the Session of the Council decided to admit the given country to membership in the Council, and finally* on the date of the deposit by such country of its instrument of ratification of the Convention, and the depositary shall notify the other member countries of the Council thereof.

5. This Convention has been drawn up in a single copy in the Russian language. It shall be deposited with the Government of the Union of Soviet

Socialist Republics, which shall send certified true copies of the Convention to the Governments of all the other member countries of the Council and shall notify those Governments, and the Secretary of the Council, of the deposit of the instruments of ratification with the Government of the USSR.

In witness whereof the representatives of the Governments of the member countries of the Council for Mutual Economic Assistance have signed the present Convention.

Done at Sofia, on 14 December 1959.

V. STATUTE OF THE SECRETARIAT OF THE COUNCIL FOR MUTUAL ECONOMIC ASSISTANCE.*

Approved by the Conference of the Representatives of the Countries in the Council on March 3, 1961 and revised by the Executive Board of the Council on July 12, September 28 and December 20, 1962, and on February 2, 1965.

The Secretariat of the Council for Mutual Economic Assistance is an economic and executive—administrative organ of the Council and functions in conformity with the Charter of the Council and the present Statute.

I. Functions and Powers

1. The Secretariat of the Council shall:

(a) prepare material or assist in the preparation of material for meetings of the organs of the Council in conformity with the working plans of these organs, including the preparation for the Executive Board of material and research necessary for work on coordination of the national economic plans of the member countries of the Council;

(b) draw up economic reports and carry out economic research on the basis of material of the member countries of the Council; prepare and publish informatory and source material and other material dealing with questions of economic and scientific-technical cooperation between the member countries of the Council, and also prepare other reports and research;

(c) prepare proposals on individual questions concerning the work of the Council for examination in the competent organs of the Council;

(d) organize the preparation for, and assist during meetings of organs of the Council and conferences called within the framework of the Council.

For these purposes the Secretariat of the Council shall:

prepare drafts of working plans of organs of the Council and draft agendas for the meetings of these organs in accordance with their rules of procedure;

undertake measures necessary to ensure punctual preparation and dispatching of material to meetings of organs of the Council, and also to conferences held within the framework of the Council;

carry out the functions of secretariats of the organs of the Council. The functions of the secretariats of Standing Commissions of the Council shall be carried out by corresponding divisions of the Secretariat of the Council;

perform other functions arising out of the rules of procedure of the organs of the Council;

(e) organize, on the basis of the material of member countries of the Council, the exchange of information between them about bilateral and multilateral economic agreements of these countries;

(f) work out, together with the Standing Commissions of the Council, drafts of multilateral agreements on cooperation in the field of specialization of production and on other questions of economic and scientific-technical cooperation in conformity with the recommendations and decisions of the organs of the Council.

* Translation by the author. Russian text in P. A. Tokareva (ed.), *Mnogostoronnieje ekonomicheskoe sotrudnichestvo . . .*, *op. cit.*, pp. 175–187; Polish text in B. Reutt (ed.), *Podstawowe dokumenty . . .*, *op. cit.*, pp. 144–159.

(g) organize and keep a record of the recommendations and decisions of organs of the Council, and also a record of their implementation; generalize information of the member countries of the Council on how the carrying out of recommendations by the organs of the Council which they have accepted is being realized, and prepare relevant proposals for examination by the Executive Board and the Standing Commissions of the Council;

(h) carry out supervision of the timely realization by the Standing Commissions of the Council and by the Bureau of the Executive Board for Integrated Problems of the Economic Plans* of the decisions of the Sessions of the Council and of the Executive Board of the Council;

(i) study and generalize the experience of the economic and scientific-technical cooperation of the member countries of the Council;

(j) prepare, if necessary, on the basis of an analysis of the activities of the Standing Commissions of the Council, proposals on the basis of the material of these Commissions, submitted by them for consideration by the Session of the Council and the Executive Board of the Council, and also proposals on the ensuring of coordination of work of the organs of the Council on related questions;

(k) assist in the organization of economic and scientific-technical cooperation of the member countries of the Council on questions not falling within the scope of the activities of the Standing Commissions of the Council;

(l) undertake, in conformity with the decision of the Session of the Council or of the Executive Board of the Council, measures aimed at establishing and maintaining ties with countries which are not members of the Council, and also with international organizations;

(m) present, for confirmation by the Executive Board of the Council, a draft list of basic problems to be dealt with by the Secretariat of the Council;

(n) draw up projects of the staffing plans and budget of the Secretariat of the Council, as well as reports on the execution of the budget for each calendar year, and submit them for approval to the Executive Board of the Council;

(o) carry out the functions of depositary of multilateral agreements concluded by member countries of the Council, if this is provided for by such agreements;

(p) carry out financial and economic functions related to the activities of the Council;

(q) undertake other activities arising out of the Charter of the Council, and also from recommendations and decisions of the organs of the Council.

In the carrying out of its functions the Secretariat of the Council shall do independent economic work, including the preparation of its own opinions, recommendations and views on the questions under consideration, and ensure the necessary coordination of the work of the organs of the Council on related questions.

2. In order to carry out the above functions, the Secretariat of the Council shall be authorized:

(a) to ask for and receive, from the member countries of the Council, and also from the Standing Commissions of the Council, necessary material and information;

(b) to call, in accordance with decisions of the organs of the Council,

---

* At present: the Committee for Cooperation in the Field of Planning.

conferences of experts of the member countries of the Council, and also, in cases in which this is needed, to invite, on its own initiative or on the proposal of individual countries, experts from these countries for the preparation, or preliminary consideration, of material for meetings of organs of the Council. In this it shall be taken into consideration that member countries of the Council may, if they wish, participate in the work on material which is prepared by the Secretariat of the Council;

(c) to submit proposals for consideration by organs of the Council on questions of economic and scientific-technical cooperation of member countries of the Council, especially proposals on questions concerning the coordination of plans for the development of the national economy of member countries of the Council, the ensuring of the carrying out of recommendations and decisions of organs of the Council, and the coordination of the activities of the Standing Commissions of the Council;

(d) to communicate with officials and organizations of member countries of the Council and of other countries, and also with international organizations.

II. Staff

1. The Secretariat of the Council consists of the Secretary of the Council, who is the highest official in the Council, the deputies of the Secretary of the Council, specialists in the field of the economy of the member countries of the Council and of other countries, in the basic branches of the national economy of the member countries of the Council, in international legal questions, in statistics, financial and other questions, and also of the essential technical and service personnel.

2. The Secretary of the Council, his deputies and other specialist staff members shall be appointed from among citizens of member countries of the Council recommended by these countries. The question of filling vacancies in the Secretariat with specialists of this or other member country of the Council shall be considered by the Executive Board of the Council upon being submitted by the Secretary of the Council.

Specialists recommended for work in the Secretariat of the Council must have the necessary theoretical preparation, practical experience in the work, organizational aptitude and a satisfactory knowledge of the working language of the Council.

On recommendation, and equally on appointment, transfer to another position or promotion in office, one should be guided first of all by the necessity of securing a high level of efficiency, competence and conscientiousness of the apparatus of the Secretariat of the Council.

The Secretary of the Council and his deputies shall be responsible for ensuring that from the specialists recommended by the member countries of the Council only those are accepted who fulfil the set requirements from the point of view of professional qualifications.

3. The Secretary of the Council shall be appointed and discharged by the Session of the Council, and his deputies by the Executive Board.

The Secretary of the Council and his deputies shall be appointed for a period of four years. This appointment may be renewed for another term.

Other staff members of the Secretariat of the Council shall be appointed and discharged from work in accordance with the Rules appended to the present

Statute concerning the conditions of work of the staff of the Secretariat of the Council.

4. The structure of the Secretariat of the Council and its staffing plan, by which are defined the service categories and the numerical composition of the personnel of the Secretariat of the Council, shall be approved by the Executive Board of the Council.

5. The Secretary of the Council and his deputies shall direct the work of the Secretariat of the Council. The Secretary of the Council shall allot duties between himself and his deputies. The Secretary of the Council shall determine, together with his deputies, the duties of the structural units of the Secretariat of the Council, and take other measures which will ensure the proper fulfilment of the functions with which the Secretariat is charged.

6. The Secretary of the Council, his deputies and other staff members of the Secretariat of the Council shall act, in the carrying out of their official duties, as international officials, independent of the organizations and public servants of the countries which recommended them for work in the Secretariat of the Council. Staff members of the Secretariat of the Council may not combine work in the Secretariat of the Council with work outside it and engage in activities which are incompatible with the carrying out of their official duties.

7. With the aim of enabling the staff members of the Secretariat of the Council to fulfil their duties independently, privileges and immunities shall be accorded to them in conformity with the Convention on the Juridical Personality, Privileges and Immunities of the Council for Mutual Economic Assistance.

III. Headquarters

The headquarters of the Secretariat of the Council shall be the city of Moscow.

ANNEX to the Statute of the Secretariat of the Council for Mutual Economic Assistance

[Rules concerning the conditions of work of the staff of the Secretariat of the Council for Mutual Economic Assistance]

General Provisions

The present Rules shall apply to all staff members of the Secretariat of the Council, irrespective of the place of their permanent employment in the Secretariat of the Council; in this connection the words "place where the Secretariat is located," used below, should be understood depending upon the place where the given staff member is working.

Appointment

1. Staff members of the Secretariat, with the exception of technical and service personnel, shall be appointed on the recommendations of the member countries of the Council.

2. The country which recommends a specialist for work in the Secretariat shall supply data on this specialist, according to the forms established in the Council. These data shall be transmitted to the Secretary of the Council.

3. Specialists recommended for work in the Secretariat may be invited by the Secretary of the Council or by his deputy for a personal talk, in which event, if specialists are invited who reside outside the place where the Secretariat is located, they shall be refunded pertinent expenses, equivalent to amounts established for corresponding service categories of personnel of the Secretariat in accordance with points 36 and 37 of the present Rules.

4. The question of filling vacant posts in the Secretariat with specialists of a given member country of the Council shall be examined by the Executive Board of the Council upon the proposal of the Secretary of the Council.

5. The Secretary of the Council shall inform member countries of the Council, if possible simultaneously with proposals on the distribution among the countries of posts to be filled, about the basic requirements which the specialists must fulfil on taking up particular posts in the Secretariat, and about approximate deadlines for filling the given posts.

6. When it is impossible for a country to present a candidate for a particular post, that country shall inform the Secretary of the Council about it within three months from the date the Executive Board of the Council made the decision on filling the posts in the Secretariat, in accordance with point 4 of the present Rules. The Secretary of the Council may in that case present proposals for consideration by the Executive Board of the Council on the filling of the given post by a specialist from another member country of the Council.

7. The head of the division of integrated economic problems and the chiefs of the groups within this division, as well as the heads of other divisions of the Secretariat of the Council, shall be appointed by the Executive Board of the Council on the proposal of the Secretary of the Council, in mutual agreement with the Bureau of the Executive Board for Integrated Problems of the Economic Plans* or with the Standing Commissions of the Council, respectively.

Other staff members of the Secretariat shall be appointed by the Secretary of the Council in accordance with the approved staffing plan.

Staff members who are specialists shall be appointed for a period of four years. When this period expires the respective member country of the Council or the Secretary of the Council may propose an extension of the period of the appointment of the staff member for a further four years or for a shorter period agreed upon by the Secretary of the Council and the given country.

8. Technical personnel of the Secretariat shall be appointed, as a rule, from among the citizens of the country where the Secretariat is located. Appointment and discharge of technical staff who are citizens of the country where the Secretariat is located shall be carried out in accordance with the legislation of that country.

Service personnel shall be appointed from among persons who reside permanently in the country where the Secretariat is located. Appointment, discharge and other conditions of work of service personnel shall be determined by the labour laws of the country where the Secretariat is located, and also by points 27, 32, 48 and 56 of the present Rules.

9. Appointment of staff members shall be made by letter of appointment from the Secretariat. The letter of appointment shall contain the date of appointment, the post and the salary. The appointed staff member must be acquainted

*At present: the Committee for Cooperation in the Field of Planning.

with the documents of the Council in which are defined the rights and duties of staff members of the Secretariat. The appointed staff member shall be given a copy of his letter of appointment.

Duties of Staff Members

10. Staff members of the Secretariat must fulfil their duties honestly and conscientiously, observe work discipline, strictly carry out the instructions given by the Secretariat and the rules relating to the internal organization of work, and treat Council property with care; they must show initiative at work and improve their professional qualifications.

11. Staff members of the Secretariat shall be subordinate to the Secretary of the Council and his deputies, and also to the heads of the corresponding structural units of the Secretariat of the Council.

Staff members shall be responsible for the carrying out of their official duties to the Secretary of the Council and his deputies, and also to the heads of the corresponding structural units of the Secretariat of the Council.

12. Missed out.

Working Time and Leave of Absence

13. The length of the working day of staff members of the Secretariat, and and also days of rest (days of leave) and holidays shall be established by the law in force in the country where the Secretariat is located.

Staff members who are not citizens of the country where the Secretariat is located shall have the right to receive during the year an additional two paid days free from work for celebrating the holidays of their countries.

14. Overtime work on week-days, and also work on days of leave and holidays, shall be allowed as an exception in extreme and urgent circumstances.

As overtime work shall be considered all work carried out by staff members over and above the normal duration of the working day by order of the Secretary of the Council, his deputies and the heads of the divisions of the Secretariat of the Council.

The duration of overtime work for technical personnel and the system of compensation for this work shall be determined by the labour legislation of the country in which the Secretariat is located.

15. For work on leave days or on holidays, carried out by order of the Secretary of the Council, his deputies and the heads of the divisions of the Secretariat of the Council, staff members shall be compensated by leave of equal duration.

Leave

16. Staff members of the Secretariat shall be due, once during the working year, regular leave of thirty calender days' duration. The right to the regular leave shall be given six months after a staff member commences employment in the Secretariat.

If the staff member, because of circumstances beyond his control, did not use up the whole or part of the regular leave due to him during the current working year, the unused leave shall be carried forward to the following working year, and this leave can be used up by the staff member together with the regular leave for the new working year. However, it shall not be allowable to accumulate leave for more than two years.

17. In determining the length of leave for an uncompleted working year, its calculation shall be made by counting 2.8 days for every month of work.

18. Female staff members shall have the right to paid maternity and natal leave of a hundred and twenty six calender days, this being inclusive of the pre-natal and post-natal periods. This leave shall be given on the basis of a certificate from a medical institution or an official doctor's certificate.

Female staff members shall have the right, after terminating their maternity and natal leave, to a supplementary leave of up to three months' duration, without pay.

After giving birth mothers shall be allowed two paid breaks per day of forty five minutes' duration each during the feeding period of the child. On the wish of the nursing mother the two breaks may be joined into one, joined onto the lunch break or carried forward to the end of the working day.

19. While the staff member is on leave, days of illness shall not be counted as part of the leave. The duration of the illness should be confirmed by a certificate from a medical institution or by an official doctor's certificate from the place in which the leave was spent.

20. In the event of a staff member spending his leave in his own country, which is not that in which the Secretariat is located, the time spent on the journey shall not be counted as part of the leave, but not more than two days in both directions.

21. Staff members of the Secretariat shall have the right to leave for sitting examinations in educational institutions, and also for the writing and defence of diploma projects and dissertations. The duration of such leaves, and also the order in which they are given and the pay, shall be determined according to the legislation of the country in which the examinations are taken and the diploma projects and dissertations defended.

22. Regular leaves given to staff members, and also other leaves with retention of pay, shall be paid in accordance with points 28, 29 and 30 of the present Rules.

23. A staff member may not be recalled from leave unless this is caused by important circumstances. In the event of recall of a staff member from leave he shall be refunded the actual expenses which he incurs in connection with the recall from leave, including the expense of travelling to the place where he was spending his leave and back, if he continues his leave, after being recalled, in the same place where he had been spending it prior to being recalled.

On the wish of the staff member the remaining leave not used up may be used either in the current or in the following year.

24. In the event of a staff member spending his regular leave in a member country of the Council which is not his permanent place of residence or the country where the Secretariat of the Council is located, he shall have the right to change into the currency of that country a sum which is not higher than his official monthly salary, at the rate established for such payments by the state bank of the country where the Secretariat is located.

In the event of a staff member spending the above-mentioned leave with his family, he shall have the right to change into the currency of the given country an additional 75% of his monthly official salary, if he did not obtain for himself or for the members of his family a place in that country in a sanatorium or rest house with payment in the currency of his own country or of the country where the Secretariat is located.

25. A staff member shall have the right to paid leave in the event of:
(a) the staff member's marriage—three days;
(b) the death of a member of his family—three days;
(c) the birth of a child—two days.

In such cases, in the event of the necessity of a long journey (to a country where the Secretariat is not located, or to a point which is not less than five hundred kilometres from the place where the Secretariat is located), the time spent on the journey shall not be included in the above-mentioned duration of leave of absence, but not above two days in both directions.

26. At the discretion of the Secretary of the Council or of his deputies, and also of the heads of the divisions of the Secretariat of the Council, a staff member may, under special circumstances, be given supplementary leave without retention of salary.

27. Staff members of the Secretariat shall receive, on going on their regular leave, a single allowance equivalent to 75% of their official monthly salaries.

For staff members who are not citizens of the country where the Secretariat is located, the allowance paid shall be equivalent to 75% of their official monthly salaries inclusive of the supplements established for these staff members to their salary.

The single allowance shall be payable once within the working year.

Salary

28. Staff members shall receive salary equivalent to the rate of remuneration which is established for them in accordance with the posts they hold. The classification of posts in the Secretariat with an indication of the salaries for each category of post shall be determined by the staffing plan of the Secretariat.

Staff members who are not citizens of the country where the Secretariat is located shall receive a supplement to their pay equivalent to 25% of their official salary.

29. Salary shall be paid to staff members in the currency of the country in which the Secretariat is located. Staff members shall have the right to change into the currency of their own country up to 50% of their salary at the rate established for such payments by the state bank of the country in which the Secretariat is located.

30. In the settlement for an incomplete month the calculation of salary shall be derived from 1/30 of the monthly salary of the staff member (together with the supplements provided for by point 28) for each calendar year.

31. Salary of staff members who are not citizens of that country in which the Secretariat is located shall be free from direct taxes and levies in that country. Retentions from the salary of these staff members may be effected upon the decisions of the judicial organs of the member countries of the Council.

The payment of direct taxes and levies, and also of other sums out of the salary of staff members who are citizens of the country in which the Secretariat is located, shall be effected in accordance with the legislation in force in that country.

32. In the event of illness, staff members of the Secretariat shall retain full salary for the entire duration of the illness. The duration of the illness must be confirmed by a certificate from a medical institution or by an official doctor's certificate.

33. In the event of temporary replacement of a staff member (due to illness, leave of absence, a mission, etc.), the person replacing him shall have the right to receive the difference between his own official salary and the salary of the staff member whom he is replacing, on the condition, however, that the person replacing is not the official deputy of the person replaced, and that such replacement lasts not less than one month and is decided upon by a respective decision of the Secretariat.

34. A staff member who does not reside permanently in the country where the Secretariat is located shall be paid or refunded by the Secretariat on being appointed or on being transferred to a new place of work in the Secretariat:

(a) travel expenses for the staff member and members of his family to the place of work in the Secretariat to the equivalent of the cost of a first class ticket on an express train or of an aeroplane tourist class ticket.

In special cases, with the agreement of the Secretary of the Council or of his deputies, and also of the heads of the divisions of the Secretariat of the Council, travel expenses may be paid by the Secretariat to the equivalent of the cost of a first class sleeping car ticket (for travel by rail) or of a first class air fare;

(b) transport expenses for not more than 250 kg. of luggage per staff member and 80 kg. for every member of his family at the tariff for rail or sea transport, independent of the quantity of luggage which may be transported free with the ticket;

(c) daily travel allowances at the rates established for respective service categories for staff of the Secretariat, for every day of the journey, in which case the day of departure from the place of work or from the permanent place of residence and the day of arrival at the place of work in the Secretariat shall be counted as one day;

(d) pay for every day on the journey, calculated at the rate of 1/30 of the monthly salary established for the staff member in the Secretariat (taking into consideration supplements to his pay provided for by point 28);

(e) a single allowance equivalent to his monthly salary. The allowance shall be paid, as a rule, in the currency of the country where the Secretariat is located and after the staff member's arrival at the place of work. However, the staff member shall have the right to receive 50 percent of the allowance before departure for work in the currency of his own country.

35. Staff members who are discharged from work in the Secretariat shall be paid or refunded:

(a) daily travel allowances;

(b) travel expenses of the staff member and members of his family to the permanent place of residence;

(c) cost of transport of luggage.

The mentioned payments or refunds shall be made in the way provided for by point 34 of the present Rules.

36. While the staff member is on a mission in a country which is not that in which the Secretariat is located, he shall be paid or refunded:

(a) a daily travel allowance for every day spent on the mission at the rates established for respective service categories of staff of the Secretariat. For the

Secretary of the Council and his deputies there shall be established a supplement equivalent to 40%, and for heads of divisions of the Secretariat of the Council and for counsellors—equivalent to 20 per cent of the stated rates. The day of departure from a mission and the day of arrival from the mission shall be counted as one day. If staff members on a mission are secured free board, their travel allowance shall be derived from the equivalent of 30% of the above-mentioned rates per day, taking into consideration the supplements provided for over and above them for individual categories of posts;

(b) housing expenses equivalent to the actual cost of residence in a single room of a first class hotel;

(c) travel expenses equivalent to the cost of a first class ticket on an express train or of an air tourist class ticket.

In particular cases travel expenses may be refunded, with the agreement of the Secretary of the Council or of his deputies, and also of the heads of the divisions of the Secretariat of the Council, to the equivalent of the cost of a first class sleeping car ticket or a first class air ticket.

37. In the case of missions within the country in which the Secretariat is located, payments shall be effected in accordance with the legislation in force in that country.

38. A staff member shall retain for the whole duration of his mission his full pay.

39. In the event of illness of a staff member while on a mission, he shall retain the pay provided for by points 36, 37 and 38 of the present Rules.

40. The rates of daily travel allowances during the above-mentioned journeys from one country to another shall be established by the Executive Board of the Council upon the proposal of the Secretary of the Council.

Incentives and Disciplinary Measures

41. A staff member of the Secretariat, depending upon his professional qualifications, his conscientiousness and diligence in the carrying out of his duties, may be given an increase of salary for the post held, within the limits of the maximum rate of salary established for the given post.

42. Gratitude may be expressed to a staff member who shows special ability, diligence and initiative in the carrying out of his duties.

43. For unconscientious and unsatisfactory carrying out of his duties a staff member may receive punishment (mention, reprimand).

Discharge from Work

44. The head of a division of integrated economic problems and the chiefs of groups in this division, and also the heads of other divisions of the Secretariat of the Council, shall be discharged from work upon the decision of the Executive Board of the Council.

The discharge from work of other staff members shall be effected by order of the Secretary of the Council.

45. A staff member may be discharged from work in the Secretariat:

(a) in the event of recall of the staff member by the country of which he is citizen, in which case the country shall inform the Secretary of the Council about this not less than one month in advance and shall take care that the recalled staff member be replaced by a new one at least ten days before he is discharged.

(b) as the result of the abolition of the post which the given staff member held, and the impossibility of appointing him to another post which is suited to his knowledge and experience;

(c) in view of the unsuitability of the staff member for the post held by him;

(d) in the event of the staff member committing an offence incompatible with work in the Secretariat.

46. If temporary inability on the part of the staff member to work lasts for longer than four consecutive months, the question may be raised with his country of replacing him by another specialist from that country.

47. In all cases of discharge from work not on the initiative of the staff member himself, except in the case of dismissal in accordance with point 45 "d" of the present Rules, he must be notified of this not less than one month prior to discharge from work. If the staff member is discharged from work before this time has elapsed, he shall be paid his salary for the period beginning with the day he is discharged from work until the expiry of the notice period for discharge from work.

48. If the staff member has not, at the time he is discharged from work, used up the regular leave due to him, he shall receive financial compensation for this leave and also a single allowance at the time of departure for his leave of absence, to be paid in proportion to the leave due to him.

49. On being discharged from work every staff member shall receive an official attestation stating the length of service in the Secretariat, the post held and the salary received.

Miscellaneous Provisions

50. Disability and old age pensions shall be assessed and paid to staff members of the Secretariat by those member countries of the Council which sent the staff members to work in the Secretariat, in accordance with the legislation in force of these countries and taking into consideration the work of the staff members on the Secretariat.

Pensions in the case of loss of the family provider as a result of the death of a staff member of the Secretariat shall be assessed and paid in the same way.

51. Staff members of the Secretariat and the members of their families shall be guarateed free medical services.

52. In the case of the fulfilling, on being required to do so by his country, of personal obligations involving the interruption of his work in the Secretariat, a staff member shall be paid his salary by the Secretariat in full for the time spent in fulfilling these obligations. This provision shall not apply in the case of the drafting of the staff member for active military service.

The country shall inform the Secretary of the Council in good time of the summoning of a staff member to fulfil his personal obligations.

53. Staff members who are not citizens of the country in which they reside while working in the Secretariat shall pay their rent themselves to the competent organizations. In cases where the rent of these staff members in the country of residence is established at a higher rate, the difference between the raised rates of rent and the rates existing for local citizens shall be refunded to the above-

mentioned staff members of the Secretariat. If such staff members reside in a hotel, the cost of residing in the hotel shall be covered by the Secretariat. In this case the staff members shall return to the Secretariat the appropriate sums, consisting of the rents and local rates which are usual for the country of residence.

Payment for the use of furniture provided by the Secretariat shall be collected to the equivalent of 0.75% of its purchase value for every month of usage.

Current renovation of apartments (the removal of small defects resulting from usage,—white-washing or painting of ceillings, walls, frames, doors, putting in of window panes, repair of floors, heating, water, gas and bath equipment, etc.) shall be carried out by the staff members residing in them at their own expense.

54. In particular cases, under special and extraordinary circumstances, the staff member may be accorded, on the decision of the Secretary of the Council or of his deputies, material and possibly other aid.

55. For reasons connected with official needs and with the raising of professional qualifications of staff members, it may be suggested to them, or they may be allowed to study, at the expense of the Secretariat, the working language of the Council and also other languages.

The conditions of work of teachers hired by the Secretariat to teach the staff members languages shall be determined by the labour legislation of the country in which the Secretariat is located, and the teachers included in the staff of the Secretariat shall be affected by points 27, 32, 48 and 56 of the present Rules.

56. In the event of the death of a staff member, his heirs shall have the right to a single allowance equivalent to his monthly salary. They shall also have the right to financial compensation for the unused leave which was due to the staff member who had died, including the single allowance given on going on leave, which shall be paid in this case in proportion to the leave due to the staff member.

57. The Secretary of the Council, his deputies and the heads of the divisions of the Secretariat of the Council shall take care of cultural and social amenities for staff members within the limits of the funds allotted for those purposes in the budget of the Secretariat.

58. On all questions arising out of the application of the current Rules, the staff members shall have the right to approach personally the Secretary of the Council, his deputies, and also the heads of the divisions of the Secretariat of the Council.

59. The present Rules may be supplemented or amended by the Executive Board of the Council.

VI. BASIC PROVISIONS GOVERNING THE FINANCIAL ACTIVITIES OF THE SECRETARIAT OF THE COUNCIL FOR MUTUAL ECONOMIC ASSISTANCE*

Approved by the Meeting of Representatives of the Countries in the Council for Mutual Economic Assistance on 15 December 1961 and amended by the Executive Board of the Council on 28 September 1962.

1. All receipts and expenditure connected with the maintenance of the Secretariat of the Council and the financing of its activities shall be provided for in the budget of the Secretariat of the Council.

2. The draft budget shall be prepared by the Secretariat of the Council for each calender year in the currency of the country in which the Secretariat of the Council is located. In cases of necessity the draft budget may provide for expenditure in the currency of other countries, including freely convertible currency.

3. The Secretariat of the Council shall present the draft budget together with an explanatory note for approval by the Executive Board of the Council not later than sixty days before the expiry of the current year.

The budget shall be approved for the global amount of income, with the singling out of the amount of the contribution of each member country of the Council, and for the global amount of expenditure, with the singling out of appropriations for salaries and other basic expenditure items of the budget.

4. The member countries of the Council shall transfer the amounts of contributions due by them, according to the approved budget, in the proper currency, to the Secretariat of the Council in equal parts during the first month of each quarter of the calendar year for which the budget is approved, the amounts which were not used up in the budget of the preceding year being included in these amounts.

In the case where the budget is not approved before the current year has expired, the member countries of the Council shall transfer to the Secretariat of the Council in the following year, on account of the budget for that year, in conformity with the procedure established above, amounts equal to those which they transferred to the budget for the previous year.

5. In order to ensure the uninterrupted financing of its activities, the Secretariat of the Council shall have a working capital fund whose amount shall be determined by the Executive Board of the Council.

6. Budgetary funds shall be used by the Secretariat of the Council to cover obligations and effect payments as a rule during the calendar year to which they pertain.

7. The Secretary of the Council and his deputies shall administer the financial resources of the budget of the Secretariat of the Council.

The Secretary of the Council and his deputies may, if necessary, use up the remaining unspent resources under one budgetary item to cover expenses under another budgetary item. They shall also determine the amounts of expenditure for the divisions of the Secretariat of the Council and may authorize the heads of

* Translation by the author. Russian text in P. A. Tokareva, M. D. Kudrjashov, V. I. Morozov (eds.), *Mnogostoronnieje ekonomicheskoe sotrudnichestvo...*, *op. cit.*, pp. 109–111; Polish text in B. Reutt (ed.), *Podstawowe dokumentry...*, *op. cit.*, pp. 160–161.

the divisions of the Secretariat of the Council to administer the financial resources, within the limits of this expenditure.

8. The Secretariat of the Council shall keep financial resources in one of the banks of the country in which it is located.

The Secretariat of the Council may exchange financial resources in the currency of one member country of the Council into the currency of another member country of the Council in the amounts necessary for the performance of functions entrusted to the Secretariat of the Council.

9. Financial documents, presented to the bank by the Secretariat of the Council for the purpose of making use of financial resources, are signed by two persons. The Secretary of the Council and his deputies, and also, with the authorization of the Secretary of the Council or his deputies, the heads of the divisions of the Council, shall have the right to first signature. The accountants and the persons discharging their duties, authorized to do so by the Secretary of the Council or his deputies, or the heads of the divisions of the Secretariat of the Council who have the rights to first signature, shall have the right to second signature.

10. The Secretariat of the Council shall present a report on the execution of the budget for approval to the Executive Board of the Council not later than the 15th of May of each year.

11. The Secretary of the Council and his deputies shall:

(a) establish the principles ensuring the proper use of financial and material resources;

(b) appoint the employees of the Secretariat of the Council authorized to receive financial resources, undertake obligations and make payments;

(c) determine the procedure for conducting internal financial audit, including audit of the financial activities of the divisions of the Secretariat of the Council, which is conducted by the Secretariat of the Council with the participation, in cases of necessity, of the proper experts from the member countries upon agreement with these countries.

VII. STATUTE OF THE AUDIT COMMISSION FOR THE AUDIT OF THE FINANCIAL ACTIVITIES OF THE SECRETARIAT OF THE COUNCIL FOR MUTUAL ECONOMIC ASSISTANCE*

Approved by the Meeting of Representatives of the Countries in the Council on 16 February, 1962 and amended by the Executive Board of the Council on 28 September, 1962.

An Audit Commission shall be created by the Executive Board of the Council for Mutual Economic Assistance in conformity with article VII of the Charter of the Council for the audit of the financial activities of the Secretariat of the Council for Mutual Economic Assistance.

Composition, Functions and Powers

1. An Audit Commission shall be established consisting of three specialists appointed for this purpose by the member countries of the Council, one from each country, in order of the names of the countries according to the Russian alphabet.

The members of the Audit Commission shall be appointed for three calendar years.

The country appointing a specialist to the Audit Commission shall notify the Secretariat of the Council of this within sixty days from the date on which the Secretariat of the Council requests that country to appoint a specialist. The Secretariat shall immediately inform other member countries of the Council of the appointment.

If a specialist appointed by a country becomes unable to perform his functions, the given country shall see to it in good time that he is replaced by another specialist, notifying the Secretariat of the Council of this.

2. The members of the Audit Commission shall elect from among themselves the chairman of the Commission and shall establish its work procedure.

3. In performing their duties, the members of the Audit Commission shall act in the capacity of international officials and shall be guided by the Charter of the Council for Mutual Economic Assistance, the Convention concerning the juridical personality, privileges and immunities of the Council, the Statute of the Secretariat of the Council, the present Statute and other legal documents of the Council, including the decisions of the organs of the Council.

4. The Audit Commission shall be responsible to the Executive Board of the Council and shall be accountable to it.

5. Expenses connected with the performance by the members of the Audit Commission of their duties shall be covered by the countries which appoint them.

6. The members of the Audit Commission may participate in the meeting of the Executive Board of the Council when the protocol of the Audit Commission on the audit of the financial activities of the Secretariat of the Council is discussed, and may take the floor on this matter.

---

* Translation by the author. Russian text in P. A. Tokareva (ed.), *Mnogostoronnieje ekonomicheskoe sotrudnichestvo...*, *op. cit.*, pp. 187–189; Polish text in B. Reutt (ed.), *Podstawowe dokumenty...*, *op. cit.*, pp. 162–164.

7. The Audit Commission shall conduct the audit of the financial activities of the Secretariat of the Council once a year. It shall conduct such audit for the expired year, as a rule in the month of May of every following year. The Audit Commission may also audit the course of the execution of the budget of the Secretariat of the Council for any period of the current year.

8. The Audit Commission shall audit:

(a) the regularity of execution of the budget of the Secretariat of the Council;

(b) the conformity of financial operations with the regulations and rules in force in the Council and also with decisions of organs of the Council;

(c) the availability of financial resources deposited in banks and kept in the Secretariat of the Council, and also the availability in the Secretariat of the Council of material resources and their conformity with book-keeping evidence;

(d) the conformity of financial documents with book-keeping evidence of the Secretariat of the Council;

(e) the regularity of the drawing up by the Secretariat of the Council of financial documents.

9. The members of the Audit Commission shall have free access to all account books and entries whose examination is, in the view of the Commission, necessary for the proper conducting of audit. They shall also have the right to obtain from the Secretariat of the Council the necessary explanations and information on matters arising during the conducting of audit.

10. The Audit Commission shall draw up an audit protocol about the results of the audit of financial activities, in which should be reflected the results of the audit in conformity with paragraph 8 of the present Statute, the conclusion on the report of the Secretariat of the Council on the execution of the budget, and also proposals of the Commission on the improvement of financial activities of the Secretariat of the Council. Before signing the protocol the Audit Commission should make it possible for the Secretariat of the Council to become acquainted with the content of the protocol and, if necessary, to give explanations to the Commission on matters raised in the protocol.

11. The audit protocol shall be drawn up in the Russian language in one copy, and shall be signed by all members of the Audit Commission. This protocol shall be conveyed to the Secretariat of the Council to be submitted for examination by the Executive Board of the Council.

The original copy of the audit protocol shall be kept in the Secretariat of the Council. The Secretariat of the Council shall immediately send certified true copies of the protocol to the member countries of the Council.

12. The Secretary of the Council or his deputy may make any observations in connection with the protocol. The members of the Audit Commission should be notified about these observations, and they should also be presented to the Executive Board of the Council together with the audit protocol.

Approved by the Executive Board of the Council on 20 December 1962.

Article I

General Provisions

The Standardization Institute of the Council for Mutual Economic Assistance is an organ of the Council established in pursuance of a decision of the XVI (extraordinary) session of the Council for Mutual Economic Assistance for the conducting of common and important research and the working out of proposals on the unification of existing standards and the creation of new standards with the aim of promoting the development of standardization in member countries of the Council. The Institute functions in conformity with the Charter of the Council and the present Provisional Statute.

Article II

Functions and Powers

1. The Standardization Institute of the Council for Mutual Economic Assistance shall perform the following functions:

(a) conduct theoretical and experimental research connected with the solution of scientific-technical problems important to the member countries of the Council in the sphere of standardization and unification;

(b) work out draft recommendations on the unification of national standards and the creation of new standards;

(c) submit for consideration by pertinent Standing Commissions of the Council draft recommendations worked out in conformity with point 1 (b) of the present article;

(d) prepare proposals on:

common problems of the development of standardization in member countries of the Council;

the standardization of the most important types of production of interest to the member countries of the Council;

the introduction into the national economy of member countries of the Council of the most advanced standards, worked out in various countries, and also of recommendations of international organizations in the field of standardization;

(e) study and determine the economic effectiveness of the introduction of standards, and also work out general principles and new methods of work in the field of unification and standardization;

(f) periodically inform member countries of the Council, and also the Standing Commissions and the Secretariat of the Council, about research conducted in the Institute;

(g) undertake other measures arising from the work plan of the Institute.

---

* Translation by the author. Russian text in P. A. Tokareva (ed.), *Mnogostoronnieje ekonomicheskoe sotrudnichestvo...*, *op. cit.*, pp. 190–194; Polish text in Reutt (ed.), *Podstawowe dokumenty...*, *op. cit.*, pp. 167–171.

2. To perform the functions indicated above the Institute may:

(a) submit proposals for consideration by the Standing Commission of the Council on Standardization and other organs of the Council;

(b) request material essential to its work from standardization organs of the member countries of the Council, and also from the Standing Commissions of the Council;

(c) communicate with respective officials, organizations and institutions of member countries of the Council;

(d) conclude agreements with respective organizations and institutions of member countries of the Council on the performance by them of specific work envisaged by the work plan of the Institute;

(e) call, in conformity with the work plan of the Institute, conferences of experts for the consideration of specific problems being worked out by the Institute.

Article III

The Board of Directors of the Institute

1. The Standardization Institute of the Council for Mutual Economic Assistance is headed by the Board of Directors of the Institute composed of the Director of the Institute and his deputies.

2. The Board of Directors of the Institute shall:

(a) perform the function of directing the activities of the Institute in conformity with the work plans of the Institute approved by the Standing Commission on Standardization of the Council, and also with the recommendations and decisions of this Commission on methodological questions of the work of the Institute;

(b) submit to the Standing Commission of COMECON on Standardization for consideration:

— draft annual work plans, drawn up on the basis of proposals from member countries of the Council, the Standing Commissions and the Secretariat of the Council;

— annual reports on the activities of the Institute;

(c) submit draft estimates of expenditure and of the staffing plan of the Institute to the Secretariat of the Council;

(d) perform the necessary administrative-economic and financial functions connected with the work of the Institute, in conformity with the procedure established in the Council.

3. The Director of the Institute is the chief administrative officer of the Institute. He represents the Institute vis-à-vis officials and organizations of the member countries of the Council.

The Director of the Institute and his deputies shall direct the work of the Institute. Duties shall be distributed between the Director and his deputies by the Director. The Director of the Institute together with his deputies shall determine the duties of the structural units of the Institute and take other measures to ensure proper performance of functions entrusted to the Institute.

4. Appropriations provided for the Institute in the budget of the Secretariat of the Council by the Executive Board of the Council shall be managed by the Director of the Institute or his deputies.

Article IV

The Council of the Institute

1. The Council of the Standardization Institute of the Council for Mutual Economic Assistance shall consist of appropriate specialists from the member countries of the Council concerned. The Council of the Institute shall also include the Director of the Institute, his deputies and the head of the standardization division of the Secretariat of the Council.

The composition of the Council of the Institute shall be approved by the Standing Commission of the Council on Standardization upon presentation by the Director of the Institute, agreed upon with the countries concerned.

2. The Council shall be the consultative organ of the Board of Directors of the Institute and shall meet under the chairmanship of the Director of the Institute.

3. The Council of the Institute shall:

(a) consider the draft annual work plans of the Institute and the drafts of the annual reports on the activities of the Institute;

(b) consider questions connected with the progress of execution of work plans of the Institute and of individual research, and also of draft estimates of expenditure and of the staffing plan of the Institute;

(c) consider in a preliminary way proposals submitted by the Board of Directors of the Institute for consideration by the Standing Commission of the Council on Standardization and by other organs of the Council.

4. The Council shall establish itself the course of its work.

Article V

Composition of the Institute

1. The Standardization Institute of the Council for Mutual Economic Assistance shall consist of appropriate specialists and technical and service personnel, who are citizens of the member countries of the Council.

Specialists from other countries shall be able to participate in the work of the Institute and its Council in conformity with Article X of the Charter of the Council for Mutual Economic Assistance.*

2. The structure of the Institute and its staffing plan which define categories of officials and the numerical composition of the staff of the Institute, are approved by the Executive Board of the Council upon submission by the Secretary of the Council.

3. The Director of the Institute and his deputies shall be appointed by the Executive Board of the Council from among citizens of the member countries of the Council upon presentation by the Secretary of the Council for Mutual Economic Assistance, agreed upon with the Standing Commission of the Council on Standardization.

The Director of the Institute and his deputies shall be appointed for a period of four years. This appointment may be renewed for a new period.

Other staff members of the Institute shall be appointed and discharged by the Director of the Institute in accordance with procedure established by the Rules concerning the conditions of work of the staff of the Secretariat of the Council.

* At present Article XI.

4. Staff members of the Institute shall be subordinate to the Director of the Institute and his deputies, to whom they shall be responsible for the fulfilment of their official duties. Staff members of divisions, laboratories and the shop shall be subordinate also to the heads of these structural units of the Institute.

In other respects the provisions of the Rules concerning the conditions of work of the staff of the Secretariat of the Council shall apply to the staff members of the Institute.

5. Categories of officials of the Institute, to whom the provisions of article V of the Convention on Juridical Personality, Privileges and Immunities of the Council apply, shall be determined by the Executive Board of the Council upon submission by the Secretary of the Council.

Article VI

Financial Questions

1. The financing of the activities of the Standardization Institute of the Council for Mutual Economic Assistance shall be done out of the budget of the Secretariat of the Council, in which, for this purpose, provisions shall be made for the necessary appropriations in a separate section.

2. In conformity with decisions of the Executive Board of the Council the cost of equipment, apparatus and material, and work carried out by them for the Institute may be included in the contributions of individual member countries of the Council to the budget of the Secretariat of the Council.

3. The amount of contributions of countries which are not members of the Council which participate in the work of the Institute in conformity with Article X of the Charter of the Council,* and also the procedure for payment of these contributions, shall be determined by agreement between the Council and these countries.

4. The procedure for carrying out the audit of expenditure of financial resources allotted to the Institute shall be determined by the Secretary of the Council or his deputies in conformity with the provisions in force in the Council on this question.

5. The Board of Directors of the Institute shall present an annual report to the Secretariat of the Council according to procedure established by the latter on the use of financial resources allotted to the Institute.

Article VII

Miscellaneous Provisions

1. The Institute shall be located in Moscow, USSR.

2. The Provisional Statute of the Standardization Institute of the Council for Mutual Economic Assistance may be amended or supplemented by the Executive Board of the Council upon the proposal of member countries of the Council, the Standing Commission of the Council on Standardization and the Secretariat of the Council.

* At present Article XI.

IX. AGREEMENT ON COOPERATION BETWEEN THE COUNCIL FOR MUTUAL ECONOMIC ASSISTANCE AND THE FINNISH REPUBLIC*

The Council for Mutual Economic Assistance and the Finnish Republic,

proceeding from the policy of peaceful coexistence of states with differing social and state systems pursued by the CMEA countries and the Finnish Republic,

noting that the Charter of the Council for Mutual Economic Assistance confirms the readiness of the CMEA countries to develop their economic ties with other countries on the principles of equality, mutual advantage and non-interference in domestic affairs,

desiring to promote the development of mutually advantageous multilateral economic, scientific and technical cooperation between the CMEA countries and the Finnish Republic,

convinced that the development of such cooperation on the basis of the international division of labour will help to accelerate economic and technical progress in the CMEA countries and the Finnish Republic and to achieve the aims defined by the Charter of the United Nations,

have decided to conclude the present Agreement on the following:

Article 1

1. The purpose of the present Agreement shall be to develop multilateral economic, scientific and technical cooperation between the member states of the Council for Mutual Economic Assistance and the Finnish Republic.

2. Cooperation in accordance with the present Agreement will be carried on in matters of mutual interest to the CMEA countries and the Finnish Republic in various spheres of the economy, including industry, science and technology.

Article 2

1. For the purpose of making a systematic study of the potentialities in developing multilateral economic, scientific and technical cooperation, specified in Article 1 of the present Agreement, and organising work in implementing such cooperation, a Commission on Cooperation Between the Council for Mutual Economic Assistance and the Finnish Republic, hereinafter referred to as the Commission on Cooperation, shall be set up.

2. The Commission on Cooperation shall consist of representatives of the CMEA countries appointed by the appropriate agencies of these countries, and representatives of the Finnish Republic appointed by the President of the Finnish Republic.

Article 3

1. To fulfil its tasks, the Commission on Cooperation may adopt recommendations for the CMEA countries and the Finnish Republic on matters of

* Text reproduced from *International Affairs* (Moscow), No. 10/1973.

economic, scientific and technical cooperation and decisions on organisational and procedural questions in its work.

2. The recommendations and decisions shall be adopted by the Commission on Cooperation with the consent of the interested CMEA countries and the Finnish Republic.

3. The recommendations of the Commission on Cooperation adopted by the interested CMEA countries and the Finnish Republic shall be implemented through the conclusion of multilateral or bilateral agreements between them, their agencies, organizations and institutions or in any other manner agreed upon by them.

Article 4

The CMEA countries and the Finnish Republic will render the Commission on Cooperation the necessary assistance in its work and also, by agreement within the framework of the Commission on Cooperation, present to the Commission material and information required for the performance of its tasks.

Article 5

The Commission on Cooperation shall carry on its activity in accordance with the Statute, which is an integral part of the present Agreement.

Article 6

The provisions of the present Agreement shall not affect the obligations of the CMEA countries and the Finnish Republic which follow from their membership of the international organizations or from the international agreements concluded by these countries and CMEA.

Article 7

In the event of any questions arising from the implementation of the present Agreement, these will be settled through negotiations between the Council for Mutual Economic Assistance and the Finnish Republic through the appropriate representatives of the Parties.

Article 8

1. The present Agreement, following its approval by the CMEA countries, shall be subject to ratification by the Council for Mutual Economic Assistance and the Finnish Republic.

The Agreement shall enter into force within 30 days of the exchange of the instruments of its ratification.

2. By mutual consent of the Council for Mutual Economic Assistance and the Finnish Republic the present Agreement, including the Statute of the Commission on Cooperation, may be amended or enlarged with the observance of the procedure indicated in Point 1 of the present Article.

Article 9

1. The Agreement has been concluded for an unlimited period. However, each of the Parties may abrogate the Agreement, giving due notice to the other Party not less than 6 months in advance.

Cooperation between the CMEA countries and the Finnish Republic, implemented on the basis of the recommendations of the Commission on Cooperation adopted by them, will be continued even upon the expiration of the above mentioned 6-month period if no country participating in the cooperation demands its termination or limitation. In that event, the period and terms for terminating or limiting the said cooperation will be determined by agreement between the CMEA countries concerned and the Finnish Republic.

2. Withdrawal of any of the Parties from the present Agreement shall not affect the validity of the agreements concluded between the CMEA countries and the Finnish Republic, their agencies, organizations and institutions in accordance with Article 3, Point 3 of the present Agreement.

Done at Moscow, this 16th day of May, 1973, in two original copies, each in the Russian and the Finnish languages, both texts being equally authentic.

ANNEX to the Agreement on Cooperation Between the Council for Mutual Economic Assistance and the Finnish Republic of May 16, 1973

STATUTE of the Commission on Cooperation of the Council for Mutual Economic Assistance and the Finnish Republic

The Commission on Cooperation Between the Council for Mutual Economic Assistance and the Finnish Republic, hereinafter referred to as the Commission on Cooperation, has been set up in accordance with Article 2 of the Agreement on Cooperation between the Council for Mutual Economic Assistance and the Finnish Republic of May 16, 1973, for the purpose of organising multilateral cooperation between the CMEA countries and the Finnish Republic on matters of mutual interest.

I. Composition

1. The Commission on Cooperation shall consist of representatives of the CMEA countries and of the Finnish Republic.

2. The representatives of the CMEA countries on the Commission on Cooperation shall be appointed by the appropriate agencies of these countries.

The representatives of the Finnish Republic on the Commission on Cooperation shall be appointed by the President of the Finnish Republic.

II. Functions and Powers

1. The Commission on Cooperation shall perform the following functions:

(a) study the possibility for developing multilateral economic, scientific and technical cooperation between the CMEA countries and the Finnish Republic, work out measures for developing such cooperation and promote their implementation;

216

(b) determine and consider questions of multilateral economic, scientific and technical cooperation of mutual interest for the CMEA countries and the Finnish Republic;

(c) organise the formulation of multilateral agreements on matters of economic, scientific and technical cooperation between the interested CMEA countries and the Finnish Republic, their agencies, organisations and institutions;

(d) consider matters relating to the fulfilment by the CMEA countries and the Finnish Republic of the recommendations of the Commission on Cooperation adopted by them, and also of the multilateral agreements concluded on the recommendation of the Commission;

(e) promote the organisation of mutual consultations and the exchange of information between the CMEA countries and the Finnish Republic and their competent agencies, organizations and institutions on matters of multilateral economic, scientific and technical cooperation which are of mutual interest;

(f) perform other acts necessary for the fulfilment of its tasks.

2. The Commission on Cooperation is empowered to adopt recommendations for the CMEA countries and the Finnish Republic on matters of economic, scientific and technical cooperation and decisions on organisational and procedural aspects of its work.

3. For the purpose of fulfilling its tasks, the Commission on Cooperation may set up standing and ad hoc working agencies.

III. Recommendations and Decisions

1. The Commission on Cooperation shall adopt its recommendations and decisions with the consent of the interested CMEA countries and the Finnish Republic. They shall not apply to CMEA countries announcing their lack of interest in a given matter. However, each of these countries may subsequently accede to the recommendations and decisions adopted by the interested CMEA countries and the Finnish Republic on the terms agreed by them.

2. The representatives of the CMEA countries and the Finnish Republic on the Commission on Cooperation shall present the recommendations it adopts for consideration by the competent agencies of their countries and shall, within 60 days after the signing of the Protocol at a meeting of the Commission on Cooperation, inform each other of the results of such considerations. This shall be done through the Secretaries of the Parties appointed by them in accordance with Section IV, Point 7 of the present Statute.

Whenever necessary, the Commission on Cooperation may also set up some other time-limit during which the CMEA countries and the Finnish Republic shall inform each other of the results of consideration of this or that recommendation.

3. Recommendations of the Commission on Cooperation adopted by the interested CMEA countries and the Finnish Republic shall be implemented in accordance with Article 3, Point 3 of the Agreement of May 16, 1973.

4. Decisions of the Commission on Cooperation shall come into force from the date of signing of the protocol of its session, unless the Commission takes other decisions.

5. Recommendations and decisions adopted by the Commission on Cooperation shall be entered in the protocols of the sessions of this Commission,

signed by the representatives of the CMEA countries and the Finnish Republic.

IV. Procedure of work

1. The Commission on Cooperation shall adopt a plan of work for a period of no less than one year. The Commission on Cooperation shall also define the procedure of preparing questions included in the plan and the volume and deadlines for presenting necessary materials by the CMEA countries and the Finnish Republic.

2. The sessions of the Commission on Cooperation shall be held whenever necessary, but at least once a year.

The date, place and preliminary agenda of the coming session shall be determined by the Commission on Cooperation at its previous session.

Whenever necessary, extraordinary sessions of the Commission may be called by the Chairman of the Commission on Cooperation by agreement with the Parties.

3. Chairmanship at sessions of the Commission on Cooperation shall be exercised alternately by a representative of the CMEA countries and the representative of the Finnish Republic.

The Chairman shall enter upon his duties on the termination of the current session of the Commission on Cooperation and shall perform these until the end of the next regular session of the Commission.

4. The sessions of the Commission on Cooperation shall be attended by the Secretary of the Council for Mutual Economic Assistance or another official person of CMEA authorised by the Secretary of the Council.

Representatives of CMEA agencies and other international organisations of the CMEA countries having contractual relations with CMEA may participate in the sessions of the Commission on Cooperation at its invitation.

5. A country participating in the work of CMEA agencies in accordance with the Agreement between CMEA and that country may participate in the work of the Commission on Cooperation on the terms to be determined by agreement between the Commission on Cooperation and that country.

6. The Commission on Cooperation shall be duly assembled in the presence at its session of the representatives of all the interested CMEA countries and the representatives of the Finnish Republic.

7. Organisation of the sessions of the Commission on Cooperation and its working agencies, the circulation of material for these sessions, the drafting of plans for the work of the Commission on Cooperation and also the fulfilment of other tasks of an organisational character connected with the activity of the Commission shall be performed by Secretaries appointed by each of the Parties. For the purpose of fulfilling these tasks, the two Secretaries shall be in constant contact with each other.

8. The costs of maintenance for the participants in the sessions of the Commission on Cooperation and its working agencies shall be borne by the country dispatching its representatives to the sessions. Whenever sessions of the Commission on Cooperation or its working agencies are not held in the CMEA building, the country where the sessions are held shall make available to the Commission on Cooperation premises and also technical facilities necessary for these sessions and shall bear the incidental costs.

In the event of other expenses arising from the implementation of the

Agreement of May 16, 1973, these shall be borne by the Council for Mutual Economic Assistance and the Finnish Republic. The shares of CMEA and the Finnish Republic in covering such expenses shall be established by agreement between them.

X. PROTOCOL CONCERNING THE CHARACTER AND FORMS OF COOPERATION BETWEEN THE COUNCIL FOR MUTUAL ECONOMIC ASSISTANCE AND THE INTERNATIONAL BANK FOR ECONOMIC COOPERATION*

The Council for Mutual Economic Assistance (COMECON) and the International Bank for Economic Cooperation (IBEC),

Bearing in mind that their organs are engaged in the study of a range of problems in the sphere of monetary and financial relations of the member countries of COMECON and the IBEC and that cooperation is already realized between them in the field of some of these problems,

Recognizing mutual interest in the development and perfecting of such cooperation and

Governed by relevant provisions of the Charter of the Council for Mutual Economic Assistance and the Agreement concerning multilateral settlements in transferable roubles and the establishment of the IBEC,

Have agreed as follows:

Article 1

Cooperation between COMECON and the IBEC shall be realized on the principle of reciprocity in the sphere of monetary and financial questions and questions of foreign trade and other matters, if these relate to monetary and financial relations of the member countries of COMECON and the IBEC. The questions mentioned shall be defined by the proper organs of these organizations.

Article 2

Cooperation between COMECON and the IBEC in the sphere of questions mentioned in article 1 of the present Protocol shall be realized by the proper Standing Commissions and the Secretariat of COMECON on the one hand, and by the Council and the Board of Management of the IBEC on the other.

Article 3

The relevant Standing Commissions of COMECON and the Council of the IBEC and the Secretariat of COMECON and the Board of Management of the IBEC, acting in conformity with the legal documents of COMECON and the IBEC, and depending upon the character of questions being studied by them, shall:

(a) undertake measures propitious to coordination of work of the organs of COMECON and the IBEC in the sphere of questions of mutual interest and necessitating common study and shall keep up essential contacts during preparation of material in the sphere of these questions.

* Translation by the author. Russian text in P. A. Tokareva (ed.), *Mnogostoronnieje ekonomicheskoe sotrudnichestvo...*, *op. cit.*, pp. 227–229; Polish text in B. Reutt (ed.), *Podstawowe dokumenty...*, *op. cit.*, pp. 196–198.

With this aim the relevant organs of COMECON and the IBEC shall keep themselves mutually informed, in particular, about plans drawn up by them for the following calendar year and for other periods and, when it is agreed to study any questions of mutual interest to COMECON and the IBEC, they shall coordinate the procedure, time limits and sphere of study of these questions;

(b) exchange protocols (or excerpts from them) of relevant meetings and consultations, at which questions of mutual interest are considered in conformity with article 1 of the present Protocol, and, on the basis of mutual agreement, other material and documents in the sphere of these questions, including material for meetings and consultations called by one of the Parties, to which representatives of the proper organs of the other Party are invited;

(c) make proposals, prepared by the proper organs of one Party, for consideration by the proper organs of the other Party, assuring, in this, the mutual participation of representatives of the proper organs of both Parties.

Article 4

On the condition that provisions of the legal documents of COMECON and the IBEC in force are observed, the proper organs of these organizations shall mutually convey to each other proposals on the matter of the participation of their representatives at meetings and consultations called within the framework of these organizations during the consideration of questions of mutual interest.

Article 5

COMECON and the IBEC shall undertake measures necessary to safeguard the confidential character of documents and information not to be published that organs of COMECON and the IBEC shall exchange among themselves.

Article 6

Should questions connected with the realization of the present Protocol arise, these questions shall be resolved by representatives of COMECON and the IBEC. In this sphere the representative of COMECON shall be the Secretary of COMECON, and the representative of the IBEC—the Chairman of the Board of Management of the IBEC.

Article 7

The present Protocol may be supplemented or amended on the basis of mutual agreement between authorized representatives of COMECON and the IBEC.

Each Party may at any time give notice to this Protocol, notifying the other Party of this not later than within six months.

Done at Moscow, on 20 July 1970, in two copies in the Russian language.

XI. AGREEMENT CONCERNING THE CREATION AND JOINT EXPLOITATION OF THE COMMON WAGGON POOL*

The Governments of the People's Republic of Bulgaria, the Hungarian People's Republic, the German Democratic Republic, the Polish People's Republic, the Romanian People's Republic, the Union of Soviet Socialist Republics and the Czechoslovak Socialist Republic,

Having regard to the continuous increase in rail freight transport between their countries and in accordance with recommendations of organs of the Council for Mutual Economic Assistance regarding better exploitation of freight cars and increasing the economy of transport,

Have decided to conclude an agreement as follows:

Article I

1. For the purposes of creating the necessary conditions for reducing empty freight car runs in international and inland communications, speeding up turnover and raising the economic effectiveness of freight car exploitation, and also for lowering freight density and better usage of main international railway lines, and border and sorting stations, the Contracting Parties have agreed to create a common freight waggon pool, henceforth called the "common pool."

2. The common pool shall be created out of two-axle and four-axle freight cars (covered and open-top) for rails of 1435 mm. gauge.

3. The type and number of cars transferred to the common pool by the Contracting Parties which have railways with a gauge of 1435 mm. shall correspond to the actual needs of international freightage on their railways, taking into consideration the usage of these cars in inland communications.

4. The number of cars transferred to the common pool by the Union of Soviet Socialist Republics should correspond approximately to the number of cars from the common pool which are daily on the railways of the USSR.

Article II

1. To settle matters connected with the creation and joint exploitation of the common pool in accordance with the conditions defined in the present Agreement, there shall be established a Council of the Common Waggon Pool, henceforth called "the Council."

2. The Council shall consist of authorized representatives of all the Contracting Parties—one from each Party. The Council shall meet as often as necessary, but not less than once a year.

3. The Council shall be authorized to examine all matters connected with the realization of the present Agreement, and to make decisions on them. Decisions shall be made by the Council only with the agreement of the representatives of all the Contracting Parties.

* Translated by the author. Russian text in P. A. Tokareva (ed.), *Mnogostoron-nieje ekonomicheskoje sotrudnichestvo...*, *op. cit.*, pp. 349–354; Polish text in B. Reutt (ed.), *Podstawowe dokumenty...*, *op. cit.*, pp. 469–476.

4. The Council shall approve the rules of procedure of its work itself.

Article III

1. To ensure the implementation of decisions of the Council, and the carrying out of all current work connected with the exploitation of the common pool, and also for supervision over international freight and passenger train traffic, the work of border stations and the undertaking of measures agreed upon regulating the lending of aid to the railways of the Contracting Parties in ensuring the transport of export and import freight, the Council shall have an executive apparatus functioning continuously—the Bureau for the Exploitation of the Common Waggon Pool, henceforth called "the Bureau," located in the capital of the Czechoslovak Socialist Republic, the city of Prague.

2. The Bureau shall consist of the director of the Bureau, his deputy, the necessary number of specialists, and technical and service personnel.

3. The director of the Bureau and his deputy shall be appointed and released from their posts by the Council. Other employees of the Bureau shall be appointed and released from their posts by the director of the Bureau in accordance with the Statute of the Bureau, and employees who are specialists shall be appointed and released from their posts by the director of the Bureau after coming to an agreement with the representative of the country concerned in the Council.

4. The work of the Bureau shall be directed by the director of the Bureau, who shall be responsible to the Council.

5. In the performance of their official duties the director of the Bureau, his deputy and the specialist of the Bureau shall act as international officials.

6. The Bureau shall enjoy juridical personality.

The Bureau, and also its officials, shall enjoy the same privileges and immunities as are enjoyed by the Council for Mutual Economic Assistance and its officials in accordance with article II and paragraphs 2, 4 and 5 of article V of the Convention concerning the Juridical Personality, Privileges and Immunities of the Council for Mutual Economic Assistance. The director of the Bureau shall have the right and the duty to waive the immunity of any official of the Bureau in cases where, in his opinion, the immunity would impede the course of justice and can be waived without prejudice to the interests of the Bureau. In the case of the director of the Bureau and his deputy, the right to waive immunity shall be vested in the Council.

7. The functions and powers of the Bureau, its composition, work procedure, and other matters connected with the activities of the Bureau, shall be defined by the Statute of the Bureau approved by the Council.

8. Expenses connected with the upkeep of the Bureau shall be borne equally by the railways of the Contracting Parties.

Article IV

1. The Contracting Parties have agreed that cars transferred by them to the common pool should be standard cars. However, during the transitional period necessary for the carrying out of standardization of cars, exploitation shall be permitted, in the common pool, of cars meeting the specific technical requirements of the period, which are defined in the Regulations on the joint

use of the common waggon pool, henceforth called "the Regulations of the CWP."

2. The Regulations of the CWP shall also establish, apart from the technical requirements which should be met by cars transferred to the common pool, the mode of use of these cars, the methods of determining the settlement share of the railways of the Contracting Parties in the common pool, the procedure of drawing cars into the common pool and the procedure of withdrawing them from the pool, and the method of settlements between the railways for use of the cars of the common pool, and settle other questions connected with the use of the common pool. The mode of utilization of cars transferred by the USSR to the common pool shall be established taking into account conditions resulting from the difference between the gauge of USSR railways and the railways of the other Contracting Parties.

3. The Regulations of the CWP shall be approved by the Council.

4. The type and number of cars transferred by the Contracting Parties to the common pool shall be determined periodically by the Council, with due regard for the provisions of paragraphs 3 and 4 of article I of the present Agreement.

Article V

1. Cars included in the common pool shall remain the property of the Contracting Party which transferred these cars. Cars included in the common pool shall, in addition to the initials of the railway to which they belong, be marked with a special sign.

2. Cars of the common pool shall be used by the railways of the Contracting Parties primarily in international communications between these Parties. These cars may also be used in inland communications of the Contracting Parties and with countries which are not participants in the present Agreement.

3. In cases when the railways of one of the Contracting Parties load cars of the common pool assigned to be directed to the railways of countries which do not participate in the present Agreement, the settlement share of the railways of that Party shall be lowered accordingly.

4. All conditions under which cars of the common pool shall be directed to the railways of countries which do not participate in the present Agreement shall be defined in the Regulations of the CWP.

Article VI

1. The Contracting Parties agree that the necessary maintenance, upkeep and current repairs of the cars of the common pool shall be carried out by the railways of the Party which uses these cars.

2. Periodic repairs of the cars of the common pool shall be carried out by the railways of the Contracting Party to which these cars belong, at times established in the common timetables of planned repairs envisaged in the Regulations of the CWP. In the transitional period, however, timetables of planned repairs established by the respective railways may be applied.

3. In order to carry out the periodic repairs, cars of the common pool shall be directed to the railway of the Contracting Party to which they belong, calculated in such a way that they arrive at that railway not later than on the date set for the periodic repairs.

4. The conditions and the types of repairs, the procedure for providing the railways of the Contracting Parties using cars of the common pool with spare parts for repairs of these cars, and also the procedure for directing the cars of the common pool for periodic repairs, shall be defined in the Regulations of the CWP.

Article VII

The railway which uses a car shall be responsible, in accordance with the Regulations of the CWP, for its loss, serious damage requiring repair of the extent of a periodic repair, or damage as a result of which the car of the common pool is subject to exclusion from the inventory of the railway pool of the Contracting Party which owns the car.

Article VIII

1. The railways of the Contracting Parties shall use the cars of the common pool free of charge if the number of cars used by them does not exceed their settlement share.
2. The settlement share of the railways of each of the Contracting Parties shall be determined according to the type of cars, taking as the basis the actual share of the given Party in the common pool and those divergences from the share which are envisaged in the Regulations of the CWP. The settlement share shall be determined by the Bureau.
3. The Bureau shall regulate the number of cars of the common pool to be available between the railways of the Contracting Parties, compensating for differences in numbers and types of cars in accordance with the Regulations of the CWP.
4. For the use of cars over and above the settlement share, the railways of the Contracting Parties shall transfer, in conformity with the calculations of the Bureau and in accordance with the Regulations of the CWP, payment for every twenty-four hours of car use to the railways which have available to them a smaller number of cars of the common pool than their settlement share. The rate of payments for every twenty-four hours of car use shall be determined by the Council.
5. If the Bureau receives a demand from the railway of one of the Contracting Parties that its pool be replenished with cars in conformity with the settlement share of that railway, the Bureau shall immediately notify these railways which have available to them a higher number of cars of the common pool than their settlement share, and also the transit railways, of this. It shall agree with them upon the transfer of the necessary number of cars, calculated in such a way that the railway which made the demand receives the respective replenishment of cars of the common pool from neighbouring railways within forty eight hours from the date the Bureau was notified (counting from the beginning of the following twenty-four hour period).
6. The railways of the Contracting Parties which fail to carry out the instructions of the Bureau shall make payment for use of the cars which they should have transferred, in accordance with rates which rise progressively depending upon the period of time for which the cars were withheld, and which are different in the first and second halves of the year. The scale of these rates shall be determined in the Regulations of the CWP.

7. If the railways of one of the Contracting Parties do not accept the cars of the common pool transferred to them, the railways which transferred them shall be freed from payment for the respective number of twenty-four hour periods of car use, in accordance with the Regulations of the CWP.

8. The Bureau shall determine, in accordance with the Regulations of the CWP, the number of cars of the common pool to be available, shall keep stock of cars of the common pool on the railways of individual Contracting Parties, and shall also settle accounts between these railways.

Article IX

1. Mutual assistance in the field of cars shall be given on the basis of agreement between the railways of the Contracting Parties concerned, if possible with cars of the common pool.

2. The Bureau shall be notified immediately by the railways of the respective Parties of agreement reached among the railways of the Parties concerned regarding the lending of assistance with cars of the common pool. In that case the settlement share of cars of the common pool shall increase correspondingly for railways which have received assistance, and shall decrease for railways which have lent assistance.

3. The conditions of lending mutual assistance in the field of cars shall be agreed upon among the railways of the Parties concerned.

Article X

The Russian language shall be the working language of the Council and the Bureau. All documents connected with meetings of the Council and the activities of the Bureau shall be drawn up in the working language.

Article XI

The present Agreement has been made for an indefinite period of time. Each Contracting Party may withdraw from participation in the present Agreement, notifying the depositary of the Agreement of this not less than 6 months before the expiry of the current calendar year. Such notification enters into force from the first of January of the following year.

Article XII

Other countries may accede to the present Agreement, with the consent of all the Contracting Parties, by depositing with the depositary of the Agreement an instrument of accession for safekeeping.

Article XIII

The Agreement may be amended or supplemented at any time with the consent of all the Contracting Parties. Proposals that the Agreement be amended or supplemented shall be made by the Party concerned to the depositary of the Agreement, which shall undertake measures to submit them to the Contracting Parties for approval.

Article XIV

The present Agreement shall be subject to approval by the governments of the Contracting Parties.

The Agreement shall enter into force upon the expiry of 30 days after depositing of the last instrument regarding approval of this Agreement with the depositary for safekeeping, of which the depositary shall notify the Contracting Parties.

The present Agreement has been drawn up in a single copy in the Russian language and deposited for safekeeping with the Government of the Czechoslovak Socialist Republic, which shall act as the depositary thereof.

The Government of the Czechoslovak Socialist Republic shall transmit certified true copies of the Agreement to all the Contracting Parties.

In faith whereof the Plenipotentiaries of the Contracting Parties have signed the present Agreement.

Done at Bucharest, on 21 December 1963.

XII. AGREEMENT CONCERNING THE ESTABLISHMENT OF AN ORGANIZATION FOR COOPERATION OF THE BALL-BEARING INDUSTRY*

The Governments of the People's Republic of Bulgaria, the Hungarian People's Republic, the German Democratic Republic, the Polish People's Republic and the Czechoslovak Socialist Republic,

Being guided by the principles of the international socialist division of labour and

Desiring to ensure a speedier development of the ball-bearing industry, raise its technical level and satisfy as fully as possible the requirements of their countries for ball-bearings,

Taking into account that close cooperation on the basis of equality, mutual advantage and comradely mutual assistance will lead to the further development of the industry of ball-bearings,

Have decided to conclude the following Agreement:

Article I

For the purpose of further co-operation in the sphere of the ball-bearing industry, the Contracting Parties hereby establish an Organization for Cooperation of the Ball-bearing Industry (hereinafter called the OCBI), with headquarters in the Polish People's Republic in the city of Warsaw.

Article II

The Organization for Cooperation of the Ball-bearing Industry shall act in accordance with th present Agreement and the Statute of the OCBI, which shall be an integral part of the Agreement.**

Article III

The Organization for Cooperation of the Ball-bearing Industry shall work out measures aimed at the fuller satisfaction of requirements in the sphere of ball-bearings of a suitable range by means of increasing the speed of the growth of production of ball-bearings, the introduction of modern technology and organization of production, and also at the rational exploitation of the production capacities of the ball-bearing industry of the individual Contracting Parties. For these purposes the OCBI shall perform the following functions:

1. The examination of proposals in the sphere of the specialization of production of ball-bearings, and also measures for the implementation of these proposals.

2. Co-ordination of annual plans of production of ball-bearings, taking into account the requirements of the countries, in accordance with long-term trade agreements in force.

---

* Translation by the author. Russian text in P. A. Tokareva (ed.), *Mnogostoronnieje ekonomicheskoe sotrudnichestvo...*, *op. cit.*, pp. 279–283; Polish text in Reutt (ed.), *Podstawowe dokumenty...*, *op. cit.*, pp. 437–442.
** Not reproduced here.

3. The examination of proposals and measures aimed at satisfying the requirements of the Contracting Parties in the sphere of ball-bearings out of their own production, taking into account the export of ball-bearings to countries which do not participate in the Agreement and imports from them.

4. The co-ordination of the nomenclature, volume and time-limits of reciprocal deliveries of ball-bearings and their components, with the participation of organizations for foreign trade, with the aim of subsequently concluding an arrangement reached on reciprocal deliveries in trade agreements.

5. The working out of measures concerning the organization of the production of ball-bearings not produced or produced in insufficient quantity by the Contracting Parties.

6. The organization of mutual operative assistance in deliveries of ball-bearings and their components from warehouse supplies.

7. The co-ordination of scientific research and experimental construction work connected with the production and exploitation of ball-bearings.

8. The working out of standard technological processes, unified assemblies and inner constructions of ball-bearings.

9. The organization, according to a procedure determined in the individual countries, of a more operative exchange of technical documentation and exchange of scientific and technical achievements and advanced experience in the field of production and application of ball-bearings, in particular by means of consultations and the direct familiarization of specialists with production.

10. The analysis of basic problems of the economics of the production of ball-bearings, the working out of measures in the sphere of its perfecting, taking into consideration the world level, and also the organization of the exchange of economic and technical information.

11. The co-ordination of perspective production plans regarding nomenclature of ball-bearing, in accordance with recommendations of organs of COMECON in the sphere of the co-ordination of perspective plans for the economic development of the countries members of the Council for Mutual Economic Assistance.

12. The examination of proposals on the development of the ball-bearing industry, and also, if necessary, of proposals regarding the modernization of existing plants and the building of new ones.

13. The preparation of proposals on the construction of common enterprises producing ball-bearings, and also of enterprises servicing this branch of the industry.

14. The determination of requirements in technological equipment, implements, basic and auxiliary materials essential to the ball-bearing industry, and the working out of appropriate recommendations in this sphere.

15. The co-ordination of problems connected with the purchase and use of licences for the ball-bearing industry.

16. The working out of proposals on the establishment of common construction bureaux, laboratories and institutes.

17. The working out of recommendations on the typification and standardization of ball-bearings, and also on the unification of technical conditions for the receiving of materials and ball-bearings.

Article IV

1. The work of the OCBI shall be directed by the Board of Management,

229

which shall be composed of permanent representatives of all Contracting Parties, one for each Party.

2. The Board of Management shall establish its own Rules of Procedure.

3. The Board of Management shall hold meetings as necessary, but not less than once every six months, at a place determined by the Board.

4. The Board of Management of the OCBI shall discuss questions falling within the sphere of its functions, in accordance with article III of the present Agreement, and shall adopt decisions or recommendations connected with them. Decisions and recommendations shall be adopted by the Board only with the agreement of all Contracting Parties.

5. Meetings of the Board of Management shall be chaired by the representatives of the countries, in turn, in order of the names of the countries according to the Russian alphabet, for a period of one year.

6. The Board of Management shall approve its annual and perspective work plans and shall continuously control the course of their fulfilment.

7. The Board of Management may make amendments to the Statute of the OCBI, in accordance with the provisions of the present Agreement.

Article V

1. The Board of Management shall adopt decisions on points 1–10 of article III, and recommendations on points 11–17 of that article.

2. Decisions shall enter into force if within 30 days from the date of signature of the protocol of a meeting of the Board of Management there are no objections from competent organs of the Contracting Parties, through their representatives in the OCBI.

3. Recommendations shall be acted upon by the Contracting Parties on the basis of decisions of competent organs of individual countries.

The Contracting Parties shall inform the Director of the Secretariat through their representatives on the Board of Management, within 60 days from the date of signature of the relevant protocol, of the results of consideration of recommendations by the competent organs of their countries. The Director of the Secretariat shall inform all representatives on the Board of Management of this without delay.

Article VI

1. The Secretariat of the Board of Management shall be the standing working organ of the OCBI.

2. The Secretariat shall consist of the Director of the Secretariat his deputies, and the essential number of specialists and technical and administrative personnel, who shall be citizens of the Contracting Parties.

3. The rights, duties, work procedure, structure of and posts in the Secretariat, and the working conditions of its personnel, shall be defined in respective Regulations, approved by the Board of Management.

4. The Director of the Secretariat, his deputies and specialists shall be appointed and dismissed by the Board of Management.

5. The headquarters of the Secretariat shall be in the Polish People's Republic, in the city of Warsaw.

Article VII

The Contracting Parties agree that the Government of the Polish People's Republic shall furnish the OCBI with suitable premises and the necessary equipment.

Article VIII

1. The Contracting Parties shall cover equally among themselves expenditure connected with the activities of the OCBI.
2. The financing of the activities of the OCBI and its Secretariat shall be conducted on the basis of a budget, worked out for the period of one year, proceeding basically from the following items of expenditure:

(a) administrative and management expenses, including the upkeep of the personnel of the Secretariat, expenses connected with the operation of the OCBI, and also the payment for work carried out on behalf of the OCBI by other organizations;

(b) amortization deductions for the allocation to the OCBI of suitable premises and their equipment by the Polish People's Republic.

3. Expenditure for the maintenance of the participants in meetings and conferences, held within the framework of the OCBI, shall be covered by the country delegating its representatives to these meetings and conferences. Expenditure connected with the allocation of premises, and also the technical appliances essential for the above-named meetings and conferences, shall be covered by the country in which these meetings and conferences are held.

4. The budget and the report on the use of financial resources shall be approved by the Board of Management. For the audit of the financial activities of the Secretariat of the Board of Management of the OCBI the Board of Management shall establish an Audit Commission, the composition of which shall be regulated by the Statute of the OCBI.

5. Payments intended for the financing of the activities of the OCBI and its Secretariat shall have the character of non-commercial payments and shall be remitted by the Contracting Parties for half-yearly periods on the basis of payment agreements between the Contracting Parties.

6. Rules connected with the financial activities of the OCBI and the activities of the Audit Commission shall be defined in a separate document.

Article IX

The OCBI shall possess juridical personality.

Article X

The official languages of the OCBI shall be the languages of the Contracting Parties. The working language of the OCBI shall be Russian.

Article XI

The present Agreement shall be subject to approval by the Government of each of the Contracting Parties. The Agreement shall enter into force upon the expiry of 30 days from the date of the deposit of the last document on the approval of the Agreement with the depositary, and the depositary shall notify all the Contracting Parties thereof.

Article XII

The present Agreement shall be deposited for safekeeping with the Government of the Polish People's Republic, which shall fulfil the function of depositary of the Agreement.

Article XIII

The Agreement shall be concluded for an unlimited period of time.

Amendments may be made to the Agreement only with the consent of all the Contracting Parties.

Other countries may accede to the present Agreement by depositing with the depositary an instrument of accession, which shall enter into force from the date of consent by all the Contracting Parties.

Any Contracting Party may withdraw from the present Agreement, notifying the remaining Contracting Parties to that effect through the depositary of the present Agreement before the end of February of each year. Withdrawal from the Agreement shall take effect for that country on January 1st of the following year. Withdrawal from the Agreement shall not free the Contracting Party from obligations incurred on the basis of the Agreement.

Article XIV

The Agreement has been drawn up in a single copy in Russian. Certified true copies of the Agreement shall be sent by the depositary to all the Contracting Parties.

In witness whereof the duly authorized representatives of the Contracting Parties have signed the present Agreement.

Done at Moscow, on 25 April 1964.

XIII. AGREEMENT CONCERNING THE ESTABLISHMENT OF AN INTERNATIONAL CENTRE FOR SCIENTIFIC AND TECHNICAL INFORMATION*

The Governments of the People's Republic of Bulgaria, the Hungarian People's Republic, the German Democratic Republic, the Mongolian People's Republic, the Polish People's Republic, the Socialist Republic of Romania, the Union of Soviet Socialist Republics and the Czechoslovak Socialist Republic,

Being guided by the principles of equality, mutual respect for independence and sovereignty, non-interference in internal affairs, mutual benefit and mutual fraternal assistance, and also in the interests of the further expanding and deepening of scientific-technical cooperation,

Desiring to ensure conditions for all possible speeding up of scientific-technical progress and an increase in the efficiency of scientific-technical activities in the countries.

Taking into consideration that the perfecting of scientific and technical information is a necessary condition for the development of science and technology,

Have resolved to conclude the following Agreement.

Article I

The Contracting Parties shall establish an International Centre for Scientific and Technical Information, hereinafter referred to as the "Centre." The Members of the Centre shall be the Contracting Parties.

Article II

The basic tasks of the Centre shall be:

1. The working out of proposals on methods and technical means of scientific-technical information for countries participating in the Agreement (an international system of scientific and technical information). The working out of this should be based upon the national systems of scientific and technical information and should be intended for information servicing of organizations of the Contracting Parties and the perfecting of cooperation between the national systems.

2. The realization, on the basis of wide use of new techniques, of information servicing of organizations of the Contracting Parties, first of all concerning problems which are of important national economic significance for the ensuring of scientific-technical progress.

3. The publication of essential information material and the use of other forms of dissemination of scientific-technical achievements.

4. The carrying out of scientific research work in the field of the theory and practice of scientific-technical information, in particular the working out of methodological material concerning the forms, methods and organization of processes of scientific and technical information at a modern technical level,

* Translation by the author. Russian text in P. A. Tokareva (ed.), *Mnogostoronnieje ekonomicheskoe sotrudnichestvo . . . , op. cit.*, pp. 420–426.

233

and also the preparation of analytical surveys on problems of scientific-technical information of interest to the Contracting Parties.

5. The lending, on request by interested parties, of organizational, methodological and scientific-technical assistance in matters of scientific and technical information.

6. Assistance in the preparation and raising of the qualifications of workers in scientific and technical information of the Contracting Parties, and also the exchange of experience in the field of the preparation and raising of the qualifications of the personnel of organs of scientific and technical information.

Article III

The Centre shall perform the tasks it is charged with:

(a) by its own means, without duplicating the work of national organs of information;

(b) in cooperation with organs of information of national systems, in particular through use by arrangement with them of their data banks and material-technical basis;

(c) through the conclusion of agreements with the corresponding organizations of the Contracting Parties or of third countries.

Article IV

1. The Centre shall be an international organization.

2. The location of the Centre shall be Moscow.

3. The activities of the Centre shall be based upon the present Agreement and shall be realized in conformity with the Statute of the International Centre for Scientific and Technical Information.*

Article V

1. The Centre shall possess juridical personality. On the territories of the Contracting Parties it shall enjoy the legal capacity necessary for the realization of the functions it is charged with. On matters not regulated by the present Agreement, by the Statute of the Centre or by Agreements of the Centre with the country in which it is located, the legal capacity of the Centre shall be defined by the leigislation of the countries in which the Centre and its branches are located.

2. For the performance of the tasks it is charged with, the Centre shall have the authority:

(a) to conclude contracts;

(b) to acquire, lease and alienate property;

(c) to open branches on the territory of the Contracting Parties with the agreement of the corresponding parties;

(d) to appear as plaintiff or defendant in court and in arbitration organs.

Article VI

1. The supreme directing organ over activities of the Centre shall be the

* Not reproduced here.

Committee of Plenipotentiaries, which shall consist of permanent representatives appointed by the Contracting Parties. The representatives of each of the Contracting Parties shall dispose of one decisive vote in the Committee of Plenipotentiaries.

2. The Committee of Plenipotentiaries shall meet not less than once a year.

3. The representatives of the Contracting Parties shall preside over meetings of the Committee of Plenipotentiaries in order of the countries according to the Russian alphabet.

4. The Committee of Plenipotentiaries shall:

(a) approve the Statute of the Centre and make amendments to it;

(b) approve the plan for the development of the Centre, the annual work plans and the report on the activities, and the annual budget and the report on it;

(c) appoint the Director of the Centre and his deputies;

(d) appoint the members of the Audit Commission and determine the procedure for its activities;

(e) approve the structure and the overall number of staff of the Centre;

(f) examine problems concerning the admission of new members and adopt corresponding recommendations;

(g) examine other matters connected with the activities of the Centre.

5. The Committee of Plenipotentiaries shall adopt, in matters concerning the activities of the Centre, decisions which shall enter into force from the date of signature of the protocol of the meeting of the Committee.

6. The Committee of Plenipotentiaries shall adopt, in matters connected with cooperation of national systems of scientific and technical information of the Contracting Parties, within limits defined by the present Agreement and Statute of the Centre, recommendations which shall enter into force after their approval by the competent organs of the Contracting Parties.

7. Approval and amendment of the Statute of the Centre, the plan for the development of the Centre, the total amount of the annual budget, the appointment of the Director of the Centre and his deputies, the appointment of members of the Audit Commission, the approval of the composition of the Scientific Council, the structure and total strength of the Centre, proposals on changes in the scale of contributions and on admission of new members, and the establishment of new branches shall require unanimity. Abstention from voting shall not affect the adoption of a decision.

The procedure for adoption of decisions and recommendations on matters which do not require unanimity shall be defined in the Statute of the Centre.

Each Contracting Party shall have the right to declare that it has no interest in a matter under consideration. Recommendations and decisions adopted on these matters shall not apply to the Contracting Party which states that it has no interest. The Contracting Party which has declared that it has no interest may later join the recommendations and decisions adopted by the Committee of Plenipotentiaries.

Article VII

Supervision over the financial activities of the Centre shall be realized by the Audit Commission.

Article VIII

1. Guidance of the day-to-day activities of the Centre shall be realized by

235

the Director of the Centre, who has deputies. The Director and his deputies shall be appointed by the Committee of Plenipotentiaries: the Director—for a five year, and his deputies for a three year term. The Director shall be appointed upon representation by the country in which the Centre is located. The deputies of the Director shall be appointed in turn from among the citizens of all the Contracting Parties in accordance with the manifested interest of each of these Parties. Re-election for a new term shall be permitted. The Committee of Plenipotentiaries shall have the authority to relieve the Director and his deputies from the posts held by them before their terms expire.

2. In his work the Director of the Centre shall be guided by the present Agreement, the Statute of the Centre and decisions of the Committee of Plenipotentiaries. He shall be accountable in matters concerning the activities of the Centre to the Committee of Plenipotentiaries and shall represent the Centre before other organizations and institutions.

3. The rights and duties of the Director of the Centre shall be defined in the Statute of the Centre.

Article IX

There shall be established, to work with the Director, a Scientific Council, which shall be a consultative organ and shall consist of specialists and scientists of the Contracting Parties. The functions and procedure of work of the Scientific Council shall be defined in the Statute of the Centre.

Article X

The Government of the Union of Soviet Socialist Republics shall place at the disposal of the Centre, on lease terms, the necessary premises.

Article XI

1. The financing of the activities of the Centre shall be realized in conformity with the budget drawn up for one calendar year. The budget of the Centre and its branches shall be drawn up in the currencies of the countries in which they are located. At the same time necessary sums may be provided for in the budget in transferable roubles, and also in freely convertible currency, for the purchase of material valuables and for other expenditures of the Centre.

The budget shall include income received by the Centre for services rendered by it, payments made by the Contracting Parties in accordance with the amount of their contribution share, and also expenses connected with the maintenance of the Centre and the carrying out by it of the programme of work approved for the corresponding year.

2. The amount of the contribution share of the Contracting Parties shall be determined in a Protocol annexed to the present Agreement.

3. The cost of equipment, apparatus, and materials supplied by the Parties, and also of services rendered to the Centre on a contractual basis in transferable roubles at foreign trade prices in effect between the Contracting Parties, may be counted as part of the contribution share of the Contracting Parties.

4. Expenses connected with the maintenance of participants at conferences

and meetings connected with the performance of the tasks of the Centre, including meetings of the Committee of Plenipotentiaries, the Audit Commission and the Scientific Council, shall be covered by the country which sends its representatives to these meetings and conferences.

5. Expenses connected with the provision of premises, and also of the technical facilities necessary for meetings and conferences, shall be covered by the country in which these meetings and conferences are held, with the exception of cases when these meetings and conferences are held on the premises of the Centre; in such cases the above-mentioned expenses shall be included in the budget of the Centre.

6. The results of scientific-research, methodological and other analogous work performed by the Centre in accordance with the approved and mutually financed programme of work shall be given to member countries of the Centre free of charge.

All other services shall be rendered by the Centre for a fee at prices established by the Committee of Plenipotentiarites, taking into consideration the ensuring of the possible profitableness of the Centre.

Article XII

The official languages of the Centre shall be the languages of the Contracting Parties. The working language of the Centre shall be the Russian language.

Article XIII

Admission to membership of the Centre shall be open to other countries which declare their consent to the principles of the present Agreement.

Admission of new members shall be carried out upon the consent of all the Contracting Parties and shall enter into force from the date of deposit with the depositary of the present Agreement of the document concerning the consent of the last of the Contracting Parties.

Article XIV

The provisions of the present Agreement shall not infringe upon the rights and duties of the Contracting Parties arising out of other international agreements concluded by them.

Article XV

1. The present Agreement shall be concluded for an indefinite period and shall enter into force after its approval by all the Contracting Parties in accordance with their legislation and after notification of the depositary of the Agreement of this.

2. The Agreement may be supplemented or amended only upon the consent of all the Contracting Parties.

3. Every Contracting Party may withdraw from the present Agreement at any time, notifying the depositary of the Agreement to that effect. Notification of withdrawal from participation in the Agreement should be sent to the depositary not later than three months before the expiry of the current financial year.

237

Such notification shall enter into force after the expiry of the financial year in which notification of withdrawal from participation in the Agreement is given.

4.   The problem of the amount and procedure of financial compensation for the Contracting Party that is withdrawing from the Centre, taking into consideration the amortization of apparatus, equipment and other property allocated or acquired from the contribution shares of that Party, shall be decided by the Committee of Plenipotentiaries.

5.   When the Centre (branches) is liquidated, all its equipment and other property shall become the property of the country in which the Centre (branches) is located. The other member countries of the Centre shall be paid financial compensation in accordance with the contribution share of each individual country in the capital expenditures on the Centre, taking into consideration the physical and moral depreciation of basic resources. Financial resources (liabilities and assets) should be distributed between the Contracting Parties proportionally to the amounts of financial payments actually made by the Contracting Parties during their participation in the work of the Centre.

Article XVI

The Centre, as well as the representatives of countries in the Committee of Plenipotentiaries and officials of the Centre, shall enjoy, on the territory of each Contracting Party, the privileges and immunities necessary for the performance of the functions and aims provided for by the present Agreement and the Statute of the Centre.

Employees of the Centre shall be workers of an international organization and shall be obliged to further its aims and tasks through their activities. Employees shall be responsible to the Centre and may not receive instructions from national organizations.

The privileges and immunities referred to in the present article shall be established by separate agreements.

Article XVII

The present Agreement shall be deposited for safekeeping with the Government of the Union of Soviet Socialist Republics, which shall fulfil the functions of depositary.

The present Agreement has been signed at Moscow on 27 February 1969. The Agreement has been drawn up in one copy in the Russian language.

Certified true copies of the agreement shall be sent by the depositary to all the Contracting Parties.

In witness whereof the plenipotentiaries of the Contracting Parties have signed the present Agreement.

XIV. AGREEMENT CONCERNING THE ESTABLISHMENT OF AN INTERNATIONAL BRANCH ORGANIZATION FOR COOPERATION IN THE SPHERE OF SMALL TONNAGE CHEMICAL PRODUCTION, "INTERKHIM"*

The Governments of the People's Republic of Bulgaria, the Hungarian People's Republic, the German Democratic Republic, the Polish People's Republic, the Union of Soviet Socialist Republics and the Czechoslovak Socialist Republic,

Being guided by the principles of the international socialist division of labour,

Desiring to ensure, by the application of new, more effective forms of cooperation and the efficacious application of economic principles of cooperation, conditions for the further development of specialization and cooperation in production and the co-ordination of plans for the development of small tonnage chemical production, a more rational development and exploitation of production capacities, raising of the technical and economic level of production, the further development of mutual exchange of small tonnage chemical products, and to ensure by this means that the needs of all the Contracting Parties for small tonnage chemical products are fully met,

Have decided to conclude the following Agreement.

Article I

1. The Contracting Parties shall establish by virtue of the present Agreement an International Branch Organization for economic and scientific-technical cooperation in the sphere of small tonnage chemical production, "Interkhim."
2. The headquarters of "Interkhim" shall be at Halle (Saale, GDR).

Article II

1. The aim of "Interkhim" shall be to meet to the fullest the needs of all the Contracting Parties in the sphere of small tonnage chemical products of high quality by benefitting from the advantages of international socialist division of labour, and by broadening and deepening economic and scientific-technical cooperation between the Contracting Parties, based upon the principles of voluntariness and respect for mutual interests.
2. The activities of "Interkhim" shall be governed by the present Agreement and the Charter of "Interkhim" annexed to the present Agreement**, and shall be realized in accordance with the principles provided for in the Charter of COMECON: full equality of rights, respect for the sovereignty and national interests of the Contracting Parties, mutual advantage and mutual fraternal assistance.

Article III

1. "Interkhim" shall organize comprehensive economic and scientific-

---

* Translation by the author, Russian text in P. A. Tokareva (ed.), *Mnogostoron-nieje ekonomicheskoe sotrudnichestvo...*, *op. cit.*, pp. 298–305; Polish text in B. Reutt (ed.), *Podstawowe dokumenty...*, *op. cit.*, pp. 448–456.
** Not reproduced here.

technical cooperation between the Contracting Parties in the sphere of small tonnage chemical products such as: synthetic dyes and semi-products for their production, auxiliary substances for the textile, leather and paper industries, chemical admixtures for polymers, chemical means of conservation of plants and other products—to be referred to henceforth as "small tonnage chemical production," according to procedure and nomenclature which shall be agreed upon between the appropriate organs of the Contracting Parties, as a rule on the basis of agreements (contracts, protocols), in which the principles of mutual material interest and the application of elements of "self-financing operation" (*khoziajstvennyj raschet*) shall be taken into consideration, in accordance with the experience accumulated by the Contracting Parties.

The Council of "Interkhim" shall determine which groups of small tonnage chemical products "Interkhim" shall begin with, and the order in which it shall realize its activities in the future.

2. In the future the activities of "Interkhim" in the sphere of economic and scientific-technical cooperation may, with the agreement of the Contracting Parties, be extended to other kinds of chemical products, not envisaged in paragraph 1 of the present article.

Article IV

The Contracting Parties express their agreement to:

(1) the ensuring by the appropriate organs of the countries concerned of the implementation of the resolutions of the Council of "Interkhim" adopted with the agreement of the Contracting Parties;

(2) the lending of necessary aid to "Interkhim" and its staff members in their performance of the tasks envisaged in the present Agreement and the Charter of "Interkhim;"

(3) the transmitting to "Interkhim" of material and information necessary for the performing of the tasks entrusted to it;

(4) the informing of the Board of Directors of "Interkhim" of the course and results of the implementation of the resolutions of the Council of "Interkhim."

Article V

Among the basic tasks of "Interkhim" shall be:

(1) The working out of proposals in the sphere of the co-ordination of small tonnage chemical production plans, taking into consideration analyses and prognoses of technical and economic development and the proper balances.

(2) The working out of proposals in the sphere of specialization and co-operation in the production of small tonnage chemical products, the preparation or help in the preparation of contracts (agreements) in the sphere of specialization and cooperation in the production of these products.

(3) The preparation of proposals in the sphere of mutual deliveries of small tonnage chemical products on terms mutually advantageous to the Contracting Parties.

(4) The working out of proposals in the sphere of fuller and more rational utilization of production capacities in existence or being created in small

tonnage chemical production and of co-ordination of plans for the creation of new production capacities.

(5) The preparation of proposals in the sphere of broadening the assortment of products of small tonnage chemical production and the increasing of production of its deficitary kinds.

(6) The working out of proposals in the sphere of the steady raising and attaining of a high technical level in the production of small tonnage chemical products with the aim of improving technical-economic indicators and the quality of these products, on the basis of the scientific data possessed and by means of the co-ordination and common solution of scientific research tasks on principles determined by contracts, also including their exchange free of charge.

(7) The organizing of the exchange of scientific-technical information regarding problems of production and application of products of small tonnage chemistry, making use of the experience of the socialist countries and other countries in this field. The examination of world attainments in the field of small tonnage chemical production and the working out of proposals on the matter of exploitation of these attainments by the Contracting Parties.

(8) The working out of conclusions in the sphere of the unification of norms, technical conditions and methods of examination of products of small tonnage chemistry which are objects of mutual trade exchange between the Contracting Parties.

(9) Research on the conjuncture of the world market with the aim of making use of this research in the solution of production and trade problems in the field of small tonnage chemical production.

(10) The preparation of proposals in the sphere of co-ordination of operations of the Contracting Parties in the field of purchase and sale of licenses for small tonnage chemical products in third countries.

(11) The carrying out of trade functions for particular types of small tonnage chemical products, in the sphere of which the Contracting Parties consider this to be advantageous and purposeful.

Article VI

1. "Interkhim" shall possess juridical personality and shall be authorized to conclude contracts, acquire, lease and alienate property and to appear in court.

2. The legal status and privileges of "Interkhim" and its employees shall be defined in the "Agreement on the Legal Status and Privileges of International Branch Organizations for Economic Cooperation" signed on 9 September 1966 in Warsaw by the countries which are members of "Interkhim."*

Article VII

1. To ensure the realization of its tasks "Interkhim" shall possess the following basic organs:
The Council of "Interkhim,"
The Board of Directors of "Interkhim."

2. The working organs, which may prove to be indispensable, shall be established in accordance with the Charter of "Interkhim."

* Not reproduced in our Annexes.

241

Article VIII

1. The leading organ of "Interkhim" shall be the Council. The Contracting Parties shall be represented in the Council by delegations, each consisting of up to three representatives, of which one shall fulfil the function of chairman of the delegation. Each delegation shall have one vote.

2. The functions of chairman of the Council shall be performed in turn by the chairmen of the delegations of the Contracting Parties.

3. The Council shall be authorized to examine all problems within the sphere of competence of "Interkhim" and to adopt resolutions in the sphere of these problems. The Council shall also be authorized to introduce individual amendments and more accurate formulations to the Charter of "Interkhim," which cannot be at variance with the provisions of the present Agreement.

4. Resolutions of the Council of "Interkhim" shall be adopted only with the agreement of the Contracting Parties, which express their interest in the solution of a given problem.

The Contracting Parties which have not expressed their interest in a given problem shall not take part in the preparation of a resolution. Resolutions of the Council shall not extend to Contracting Parties which are not interested in the given problem. However, each of these Contracting Parties may later join resolutions passed by the remaining Contracting Parties.

5. Resolutions of the Council which may result in obligations for the Contracting Parties shall come into force upon the expiry of fifty days from the date on which the protocol of the session of the Council is signed, if in this period no reservation is submitted by any of the Contracting Parties, or if no other date for their coming into force is provided for the resolutions of the Council. Should, however, one or several of the Contracting Parties notify within fifty days that it is not interested in the resolution passed by the Council of "Interkhim," that resolution shall enter into force as regards the remaining interested Contracting Parties.

Resolutions which come into force and which may result in obligations for the Contracting Parties shall as a rule be realized by means of the conclusion of bilateral or multilateral agreements (contracts, protocols), which then become part of long-term trade agreements and annual protocols on trade exchanges between the Contracting Parties, in the sphere of mutual deliveries. Resolutions of the Council concerning other problems shall enter into force on the date of the signing of the protocol of the session, if it is not provided for otherwise in the resolutions themselves.

Article IX

1. The standing executive organ of "Interkhim" shall be the Board of Directors.

2. The Board of Directors of "Interkhim" shall act within the limits of the powers assigned to it by the Charter of "Interkhim" and in conformity with resolutions of the Council of "Interkhim" as well as on the basis of the Regulations of the Board of Directors approved by the Council of "Interkhim."

3. The Board of Directos shall consist of the Director, his deputies, the necessary number of specialists, appointed from among the citizens of the Contracting Parties, and of the necessary administrative-technical and service

personnel, employed in conformity with the Regulations of the Board of Directors.

The Director of the Board of Directors and his deputies shall be appointed and recalled by the Council of "Interkhim."

4. The head of the Board of Directors shall be the Director. The Director of the Board of Directors shall direct the activities of the Board and shall be responsible to the Council for the carrying out of resolutions of the Council pertaining to the activities of the Board and for the work of the Board of "Interkhim" as a whole.

The Director shall represent "Interkhim" before official persons and organizations of the Contracting Parties and other countries, and before international organizations.

The rights and responsibilities of the Director of the Board of Directors shall be defined by the Charter of "Interkhim."

Article X

"Interkhim" may establish and maintain relations with other international organizations, in the first place with the Council for Mutual Economic Assistance and other international economic organizations of the Socialist countries.

Article XI

1. The Contracting Parties express their agreement to the Government of the German Democratic Republic putting accommodation, the necessary appliances and dwellings for employees of the organization at the disposal of "Interkhim."

2. Problems connected with the headquarters of "Interkhim" on the territory of the German Democratic Republic, including relations resulting from paragraph 1 of the present article, shall be regulated by means of agreement between the Government of the German Democratic Republic and "Interkhim."

Article XII

1. The Contracting Parties shall bear expenses connected with the creation and activities of "Interkhim" in equal shares.

2. Payments appropriated to cover expenses connected with the establishment of "Interkhim" and payments appropriated to cover expenses connected with current activities of "Interkhim" shall have the character of non-commercial payments and shall be remitted by the Contracting Parties every half year, in accordance with the agreements in force concerning payments between the Contracting Parties.

3. The Contracting Parties shall agree to provide for the gradual transition to paying for services of "Interkhim" carried out on order of individual member countries of "Interkhim" and for the gradual transition to "self-financing operation" *(khoziajstvennyj raschet)*

4. In the acquisition by "Interkhim" of property necessary for the fulfilment of its tasks, envisaged in the Agreement, settlements shall be made in transferable roubles.

Article XIII

The provisions of the present Agreement shall not infringe upon the rights and responsibilities of the Contracting Parties resulting from their membership in other international organizations and from international agreements concluded by them.

Article XIV

The official languages of "Interkhim" shall be the languages of all the Contracting Parties. The working languages shall be Russian and German.

Article XV

1. The Agreement shall be concluded for an indefinite period of time.
2. The present Agreement may be amended only with the consent of all the Contracting Parties.
3. Any Contracting Party may withdraw from the present Agreement, notifying the remaining Contracting Parties to that effect through the depositary of the Agreement before the end of February of each year. Withdrawal from the Agreement shall take effect on 1 January of the following year.

The Contracting Party which withdraws from the Agreement shall be paid compensation in cash based on the contribution of that Party to the capital expenditures of "Interkhim." The exact amount of compensation in cash shall be determined by the Council of "Interkhim."

Article XVI

"Interkhim" may be dissolved by agreement between the Governments of all the member countries of "Interkhim."

Upon the dissolution of "Interkhim," all its equipment and property shall become the property of the German Democratic Republic, in whose territory "Interkhim" is situated. The other member countries of "Interkhim" shall be paid compensation in cash in equal shares.*

Upon the dissolution of "Interkhim," the financial resources, with the exception of the portion required to defray the obligations of "Interkhim," shall be distributed among the member countries of "Interkhim" in equal shares. The exact amount of compensation in cash shall be determined by the Council of "Interkhim."

Article XVII

1. Other countries may accede to the present Agreement with the consent of all the Contracting Parties. The country wishing to accede to the present Agreement shall notify the depositary to that effect in writing.
2. The date on which the Agreement shall enter into force for the countries acceding to the Agreement shall be the date on which consent is expressed by all the Contracting Parties to the accession of the given countries to the Agreement.

* The word printed in the Polish translation (*różnych*—different) is obviously a printing mistake and should read *równych*—equal.

244

Article XVIII

The present Agreement shall be subject to approval by the Government of each of the Contracting Parties and shall enter into force upon the expiry of thirty days from the date of deposit with the depositary of the last instrument concerning the approval of the Agreement, of which the depositary shall inform all the Contracting Parties.

Article XIX

The present Agreement shall be deposited with the Government of the German Democratic Republic, which shall act as the depositary thereof.

Article XX

The present Agreement has been drawn up in a single copy in the Russian language. Certified copies of the Agreement shall be transmitted to all the Contracting Parties by the depositary.

In witness thereof the duly authorized representatives of the Contracting Parties have signed the present Agreement.

Done at Moscow, on 17 July 1969.

XV. ARTICLES OF AGREEMENT OF THE ESTABLISHMENT OF THE INTERNATIONAL INVESTMENT BANK*

The Governments of the People's Republic of Bulgaria, the Hungarian People's Republic, the German Democratic Republic, the Mongolian People's Republic, the Polish People's Republic, the Union of Soviet Socialist Republics, and the Czechoslovak Socialist Republic

in order to promote further the economic development of national economies of the Contracting Parties

agreed as follows:

Article I

To establish the International Investment Bank hereinafter referred to as "the Bank".

The founders of the Bank are the above mentioned Contracting Parties.

Membership in the Bank shall be open to other countries in accordance with Article XXIII of the present Agreement.

The activities of the Bank are performed on the basis of full equality and respect of the sovereignty of all member countries of the Bank.

The location of the Bank is the city of Moscow.

The Bank is established and shall operate in accordance with the following provisions:

Article II

The fundamental task of the Bank shall be to grant long-term and medium-term credits primarily for carrying out projects connected with the international Socialist division of labour, specialisation and co-operation of production, expenditures for expansion of raw materials and fuel resources for the members' collective interest, and the construction of enterprises of mutual concern to member states in other branches of the economy, as well as construction of projects for development of national economies of the countries and for other purposes, established by the Council of the Bank and consistent with the aims of the Bank.

In its activities of the Bank will proceed from the principle that efficient use must be made of resources, provision must be made to guarantee that all obligations can be met, and strict responsibility must be accepted for the return of finance granted by the Bank.

Credits will be provided to finance the construction only of such objects as conform to the advanced technological standards, and promise high quality output with minimum wastage, while the prices of goods produced must be competitive on the world market.

The Bank shall grant credits for carrying out measures and constructing projects of common interest to several member countries provided a long-term agreement or any other undersanding is available on measures and constructing projects and realization of production in the interests of member countries with

* Translation by the Bank, Moscow 1971. The author is not responsible for its obvious linguistic shortcomings.

due regard to the recommendations on co-ordination of national economic plans of member countries.

The Bank's activities must be organically linked to other measures which promote the further development of Socialist economic co-operation and the gradual elimination of disparities between levels of economic development among member countries. At the same time the principle that the Bank's credits must be put to efficient use must remain in force. By agreement with the Council for Mutual Economic Assistance, the Bank will participate in the work of the Council for Mutual Economic Assistance organs examining questions connected with the co-ordination of members' national economic development plans in the field of capital investment.

Article III

1. The authorised capital stock of the Bank is 1,000 mn. transferable roubles.*

It is formed in the collective currency (transferable roubles) and in convertible currencies or gold.

The gold content of the transferable rouble is fixed at 0,987412 grams of fine gold.

2. Members' quotas in the authorised capital are fixed according to the share of their exports in members' total mutual trade and make for

the People's Republic of Bulgaria	85,1 mn. transferable rbls.
the Hungarian People's Republic	83,7 mn. transferable rbls.
the German Democratic Republic	176,1 mn. transferable rbls.
the Mongolian People's Republic	4,5 mn. transferable rbls.
the Polish People's Republic	121,4 mn. transferable rbls.
the Union of Soviet Socialist Republics	399,3 mn. transferable rbls.
the Czechoslovak Socialist Republic	129,9 mn. transferable rbls.

The authorised banks of those countries deliver obligations to the Bank for the amount of shares (quotas) of member countries.

3. 70% of the authorised capital to be paid in transferable roubles and 30% in convertible currencies or gold.

4. Of the authorised capital, the sum of 175 mn. transferable roubles is to be paid up initially, followed by another 175 mn. in the course of the second year of the Bank's activities. The remaining capital will be called up as the Bank's operations and its need for funds develop.

The terms and conditions of payments shall be determined by the Council of the Bank.

5. The authorised capital can be increased with the agreement of the member countries' respective governments, on the recommendation of the Bank's Council, which determines the method and timing of increasing the issued capital.

6. The authorised capital is also increased on acceptance of a new member by the amount of the new participant's quota.

* The authorised capital was increased by 52,6 mn. transferable roubles and now totals 1052,6 mn. transferable roubles as the Socialist Republic of Rumania joined the Bank.

The amount, method and timing of an instalment shall be determined by the Council of the Bank upon agreement with the country concerned.

Article IV

The Bank shall have reserve capital.

The Bank can create its own special funds.

Purposes, amounts, terms and conditions of creating and using the reserve capital and own special funds shall be determined by the Council of the Bank.

Article V

Special funds can be created out of resources of interested countries.

Article VI

The Bank may attract funds in transferable roubles, national currencies of interested countries, and convertible currencies by obtaining financial and bank credits and loans, accepting medium and long-term deposits, and also by other means.

The Bank's Council can take decisions on the issue of interest-bearing bond loans placed on international money markets.

The conditions of issuing bond loans shall be determined by the Council of the Bank.

Article VII

1. The Bank shall grant long-term and medium-term credits for the purposes provided for in Article II of the present Agreement.

2. Credits shall be granted to:

(a) banks, economic organisations and enterprises of member countries officially authorised to receive credits;

(b) international economic organisations and enterprises of member countries;

(c) banks and economic organisations of other countries. The procedure for this is established by the Bank's Council.

3. The Bank may issue guarantees. The procedure for this is established by the Council of the Bank.

Article VIII

The way of credit planning, time limits, terms of granting, employment and repayment of credits, issuing guarantees as well as imposition of sanctions in case of violation of terms of credits or guarantees are regulated by the Statutes and decisions of the Council of the Bank.

Article IX

The Bank can place surplus funds with other banks, and buy and sell currencies, gold and securities as well as conduct other banking operations appropriate to the aims and purposes of the Bank.

248

Article X

The Bank's activities must be economically viable.

Article XI

The Bank shall be entitled to co-operate with bodies of the Council for Mutual Economic Assistance, International Bank for Economic Co-operation and other economic organisations of member countries.

The Bank may on terms of equality contact and establish business relations with international financial and credit institutions as well as other banks.

The character and forms of these relations are determined by the Council of the Bank.

Article XII

Participation in the International Investment Bank provides no obstacle whatever to the realisation and development of member countries' direct financial and business links, whether between themselves, with other countries, or with international financial and banking organisations.

Credit operations of the Bank are not intended to supercede the established principles and procedure for granting credits on the basis of bilateral inter-governmental agreements on economic co-operation and mutual assistance.

Article XIII

1. The Bank shall possess full juridical personality.

The Bank shall have the legal capacity necessary for the fulfilment of its functions and achievement of the aims and purposes with which it is entrusted by the present Agreement and Statutes.

2. In the territory of each member country the Bank itself, representatives of the countries in its Council and officials of the Bank shall enjoy privileges and immunities necessary to carry out their functions and attain the purposes provided for in the present Agreement and Statutes of the Bank.

The above mentioned privileges and immunities are determined in Articles XV, XVI and XVII of the present Agreement.

3. The Bank may open branches and representative offices in the territory of the Bank's domicile as well as in the territories of other countries.

Legal relations between the Bank and the country of its location, its branches and representative offices are determined by appropriate agreements.

4. The Bank bears responsibility under its obligations within the limits of its property.

The Bank shall not be responsible under obligations of member countries and member countries shall not be responsible under obligations of the Bank.

Article XIV

The activities of the Bank shall be governed by the present Agreement, the Statutes of the Bank attached hereto as well as by the rules and regulations issued by the Bank within its competence.

Some modifications may be introduced into the Statutes of the Bank with the approval of the governments of member countries on the recommendation of the Council of the Bank in the interests of further development and improvement of Bank's activities, and deepening of international Socialist economic integration.

Article XV

1. The property of the Bank, assets and documents wherever located as well as operations of the Bank shall be immune from any form of administrative or juridical process, except when the Bank waives its immunity. The Bank's premises as well as premises of its branches and representative offices in the territory of any member country shall be inviolable.

2. In the territories of member countries the Bank:

(a) shall be immune from all direct taxes and charges whether national or local. This provision shall not apply to the charges for public utilities and other services;

(b) shall be immune from customs duties and restrictions on the import and export of articles destined for official use;

(c) shall enjoy privileges in respect of priorities, tariffs and rates of postal, telegraphic, and telephone communications which are accorded to diplomatic representations in those countries.

Article XVI

1. Representatives of the countries in the Council of the Bank while in their official capacity are granted the following privileges and immunities in the territory of member countries:

(a) immunity from arrest or detention as well as legal process with respect to acts performed by them in their official capacity;

(b) inviolability of papers and documents;

(c) the same customs exemptions as regards their personal effects which are accorded to officials of comparable rank of diplomatic representations in the given country;

(d) release from national service obligations, direct taxation and charges in respect of sums paid to the representatives by the country which appointed them.

2. Privileges and immunities provided for in the present Article are granted to the above mentioned persons solely in the interests of the Bank. Each member country has the right and is obligated to waive the immunity of its representatives in all cases when in the opinion of that country the immunity prevents to administer justice and waiving the immunity shall not prejudice the aims for which it was granted.

3. Provisions of paragraph 1 of the present Article shall not refer to relations between a representative and bodies of the country of which he is a citizen.

Article XVII

1. The Council of the Bank upon presentation by the Chairman decides

which categories of the Bank's officials will enjoy the provisions of the present Article.

The names of the above officials shall be periodically communicated by the Chairman to the competent authorities of member countries.

2. Officials of the Bank while in official capacity in the territory of each member country:

(a) shall be immune from juridical and administrative process for all acts performed by them as officials of the Bank;

(b) shall be accorded immunities from national service obligations, taxation and charges on salary received from the Bank. This provision shall not apply to the officials of the Bank who are citizens of the country in which territory the Bank, its branches or representative offices are located;

(c) shall be granted the same customs exemptions in respect of their personal effects as are accorded to officials of comparable rank of diplomatic representations in the given country.

3. Priviliges and immunities provided for in the present Article are granted to the officials of the Bank solely in the interests of the Bank.

The Chairman of the Board has the right and is obligated to waive the immunity accorded to the officials of the Bank in all cases when in his opinion the immunity prevents to administer justice and waiving the immunity shall not prejudice the aims for which it was given. The right to waive the immunity as regards the Chairman and members of the Board belongs to the Council of the Bank.

Article XVIII

The officials of the Bank in their official capacity act as international officials.

They are subject only to the Bank and are independent from any officials or bodies of their own countries. Each member country should respect the international character of those duties.

Article XIX

The highest authority of the Bank is the Council of the Bank. It carries out general management of the Bank's activities.

The Council of the Bank consists of the representatives from all member countries appointed by the governments of those countries.

Each member country, irrespective of the amount of its quota, has one vote in the Council of the Bank.

Major decisions must be taken by the Council unanimously, while for other questions a majority of at least three-quarters if sufficient. The Bank may make decisions provided not less than three-quarters of member countries are represented at the meeting.

Article XX

The executive body of the Bank is the Board.

The Board is accountable to the Council of the Bank.

The Board consists of the Chairman and three Deputies appointed by the Council of the Bank from citizens of member countries for a period of five years.

251

The basic task of the Board is the supervision over the Bank's activities in accordance with the Agreement, Statutes and decisions of the Council of the Bank.

The Chairman administers the current affairs of the Bank and of the Board on the principle of undivided authority within his competence and power determined by the Statutes and decisions of the Council of the Bank.

Article XXI

For auditing purposes an Auditing Committee shall be appointed by the Council of the Bank.

Article XXII

Claims against the Bank can be lodged within two years after the date of origin of the right to sue.

Article XXIII

Any country wishing to join the present Agreement and become a member of the Bank may file with the Council of the Bank an official application indicating that it shares in the aims and principles of the Bank's activities and accepts all the obligations arising from the Agreement and Statutes of the Bank.

Acceptance of new members is by decision of the Council of the Bank.

A duly certified copy of the Council's decision on adoption of a new member will be sent to the country concerned and to the depository of the present Agreement.

A country shall be considered to have joined the Agreement and become a member of the Bank on the date the above document with the application attached hereto is received by the depository whereof the latter informs member countries and the Bank itself.

Article XXIV

Any member may withdraw from the Bank and participation in the present Agreement after giving the Council of the Bank at least six month's notice.

During the mentioned period all relations between the Bank and the country concerned are to be settled under their mutual obligations.

The depository of the present Agreement is officially notified by the Council of the withdrawal of a country from the Bank.

Article XXV

The present Agreement is to be ratified and shall enter into force from the date when the last of the Contracting Parties transmits its instrument of ratification to the depository of the present Agreement.

The Agreement will provisionally come into action on January 1, 1971 unless it has not come into effect by that date under the terms of paragraph 1 of this Article.

Article XXVI

The present Agreement may be amended only with the consent of all member countries of the Bank.

The present Agreement shall lapse if not less than two-thirds of member countries declare their non-participation in the Bank in accordance with Article XXIV of the Agreement and denunciation of the Agreement.

In this case the Bank shall suspend permanently its operations in the manner and at the time determined by the Council of the Bank.

Article XXVII

The present Agreement shall remain deposited with the Secretariat of the Council for Mutual Economic Assistance which shall act as the depositary of the Agreement.

Done at the city of Moscow on July 10, 1970 in a single copy in Russian.

Certified copies of the present Agreement shall be transmitted by the depositary to all Contracting Parties.

STATUTES OF THE INTERNATIONAL INVESTMENT BANK

The International Investment Bank is established on the basis of the Agreement among the governments of the People's Republic of Bulgaria, the Hungarian People's Republic, the German Democratic Republic, the Mongolian People's Republic, the Polish People's Republic, the Union of the Soviet Socialist Republics, and the Czechoslovak Socialist Republic.

GENERAL PROVISIONS

Article 1

The International Investment Bank, hereinafter referred to as "the Bank", organises and conducts long-term and medium-term credit as well as other banking operations in accordance with the Agreement on the establishment of the International Investment Bank (hereinafter referred to as "the Agreement") and its Statutes.

Article 2

The Bank shall possess full juridical personality. Its name is "International Investment Bank".

The aims and purposes of the Bank, its capacity, including competence and limits of its responsibility, provisions concerning the legal regulations of the Bank's activities, as well as privileges and immunities accorded to the Bank, to the representatives of member countries in the Council and officials of the Bank are determined by the Agreement and the Statutes of the Bank.

The Bank shall have power to:

(a) conclude international and other agreements as well as to sign contracts within its competence;

253

(b) purchase, rent or alienate property;

(c) appear in legal and arbitration bodies;

(d) open branches and representative offices in the country of its domicile and in the territory of other countries;

(e) issue instructions and regulations on matters within its competence;

(f) take other actions aimed at fulfilment of the functions with which it is entrusted.

Article 3

The Bank shall bear responsibility under its obligations within the limits of the property it possesses.

The Bank shall not hold responsibility under obligations of member countries as well as member countries shall not be responsible under obligations of the Bank.

Article 4

The Bank has a seal bearing the inscription "International Investment Bank". Branches and representative offices and subdivisions of the Bank have a seal with the same inscription plus the name of the branch, representative office or corresponding subdivision.

Article 5

The Bank guarantees secrecy of operations, documents, accounts and deposits of its clients and correspondents.

Bank's officials and employees are required to maintain secrecy as regards banking operations, documents, accounts and deposits of the Bank, its clients and correspondents.

MEMBERSHIP

Article 6

The founders of the Bank are the countries which signed and ratified the Agreement.

Other countries may also become members of the Bank.

Any country wishing to join the Bank may file with the Council of the Bank an official application indicating that it shares in the aims and principles of the Bank's activities and accepts all the obligations arising from the Agreement and Statutes of the Bank.

Acceptance of new members is by decision of the Council of the Bank.

Any country may withdraw from the Bank by transmitting a notice at the Council of the Bank not less than six months in advance.

During that period the relations between the Bank and the country concerned are to be settled under their mutual obligations.

Article 7

Whenever institutions or organisations of member countries violate provisions of the Agreement or the Statutes of the Bank, in particular, if they fail to fulfill their obligations to the Bank, the Council of the Bank shall inform competent bodies of member countries and, if necessary, governments of those countries.

RESOURCES OF THE BANK

Article 8

The resources of the Bank include contributions of member countries to its authorised capital, interested countries' contributions to their special funds, the attraction of funds from member countries of the Bank and international money markets, and the transfer of a proportion of profits to the reserve capital of the Bank and its own special funds.

Article 9

The authorised capital stock is 1,000 mn. transferable roubles.

It is formed in collective currency (transferable roubles) and in convertible currencies or gold.

The authorised capital shall be used for the purposes set out in the Agreement and the Statutes of the Bank and shall serve as security of Bank's obligations.

The authorised capital may be increased in accordance with provisions of the Agreement.

Contributions to the authorised capital shall be made in conformity with provisions of the Agreement and decisions of the Council of the Bank.

The country which paid its instalment into the authorised capital receives a certificate from the Bank which serves as an acknowledgement and evidence of the payment made.

In case of withdrawal from the Bank the amount paid to the authorised capital shall be taken into account when regulating relations between that country and the Bank under their mutual obligations.

Article 10

The Bank forms reserve capital and can also create its own special funds. The reserve capital and special funds are made out of the Bank's profit.

Article 11

Special funds of the Bank can be created from resources of interested countries, including a fund for financing construction of joint projects in member countries and a fund for financing programmes relating to economic and technical assistance to developing countries.

Purposes, amounts, terms and conditions of making and using those special funds are determined by corresponding agreements between interested countries and the Bank.

Article 12

The Bank may attract funds in transferable roubles, national currencies of interested countries, and in convertible currencies by obtaining financial and

255

banking credits and loans, accepting medium and long-term deposits, and also by other means.

The Council of the Bank can take decisions on the issue of interest-bearing bond loans placed on international money markets.

The conditions of issuing bond loans shall be determined by the Council of the Bank.

CREDIT OPERATIONS OF THE BANK

Article 13

The Bank grants long-term and medium-term credits to the borrowers indicated in the Agreement out of its own resources and attracted funds in the currencies agreed upon between the Bank and the borrower for the purposes provided for in the Agreement, takes part with other banking institutions in granting such credits and issues guarantees under obligations of economic organizations and enterprises in the manner established by the Council of the Bank.

Article 14

Financing of projects provided for in the Agreement shall be carried out on the basis of current and long range credit plans. The way of drawing up credit plans is determined by the Council of the Bank.

Article 15

Long and medium-term credits, whether representing a project's sole source of finance or being complemented by the borrower's own resources, are granted from the Bank's own capital, reserves and borrowings.

Each credit or guarantee granted by the Bank must be the subject of an agreement.

Economic criteria characterising high efficiency of financed projects, terms of granting, using and repayment of credits are provided for in a credit contract.

Credits are provided primarily for carrying out projects of high efficiency.

Economic efficiency criteria are:

a high technical standard must be ensured in construction; the enterprise must achieve optimum volume of production and represent efficient use of capital for the industry concerned; its output must conform to world standards in respect of quality and price; availability of the appropriate raw materials, the market for the product; the duration of the construction of the enterprise and a number of other economic and financial considerations determined by the Council of the Bank and depending on the character and purpose of the investment.

The Bank at its discretion can carry out an appraisal or send the plan of a project, technical documentation and estimate for an appraisal to the competent national organisations or international groups of specialists. Data necessary for carrying out an appraisal are provided for with the help of beneficiaries of credits.

When giving credits and guarantees the Bank may require provision with appropriate security.

The manner of granting and repayment of credits, security, terms and conditions which are to be stipulated in credit contracts are determined by the Council of the Bank.

Article 16

Medium-term credits are made as a rule for up to 5 years, long-term credits—for a maximum term of up to 15 years.

Article 17

Repayment of credits granted by the Bank is effected by the borrower in accordance with the schedule prescribed in the credit contract. Repayment starts as a rule not later than six months after the date fixed in the contract of putting the project into operation.

Repayment of credits is made as a rule in the currencies in which it is granted or in other currencies upon agreement between the Bank and the borrower.

Article 18

1. The Bank shall take necessary measures to ensure that credits and guarantees are used only for the purposes they are granted and that they are used efficiently.

For this purpose the Bank shall be authorised:

(a) when carrying out credit and guarantee operations to permit the borrower to draw on a credit only for the purposes stipulated in the contract;

(b) to exercise strict control over adherence to terms of credit contracts during the preparatory period and during the construction of a project and repayment of a credit by the borrower;

(c) to send its specialists and specialists of international groups of experts, invited by the Bank, to the places of building projects during preparatory works and the process of construction and repayment of a credit for supervision. In these cases the countries involved will assist the above mentioned specialists to fulfill their duties and may appoint their representatives to participation in supervision.

2. If the borrower violates the terms of a contract the Bank shall have the right to impose the following sanctions:

(a) to limit or suspend permanently granting credits to the borrower;

(b) to raise interest rate for the use of a credit during violation by the borrower the terms of a contract;

(c) to demand reimbursement of corresponding amounts to the Bank by such borrowers and their guarantors, and if borrowers or their guarantors keep their funds with the Bank—to effect prior to maturity recovery from their accounts;

(d) to take other measures for defending the interests of the bank in accordance with the principles established by the Council of the Bank.

Limitation and suspension of financing are conduced in accordance with the manner established by the Council of the Bank.

Measures and sanctions which shall be applied by the Bank in case of violation of a credit contract or terms of a guarantee issued in favour of the Bank are determined in a corresponding contract or guarantee.

In the event of essential violation of the terms of a credit contract by a borrower or terms of a guarantee by a guarantor the Bank shall inform competent bodies of the country of the borrower or guarantor, and in case of necessity—the government of the country concerned.

OTHER OPERATIONS
Article 19

The Bank can place surplus funds with other banks, buy and sell currency, gold and securities, and conduct other banking operations corresponding to the purposes of the Bank.

INTEREST AND CHARGES
Article 20

The Bank will charge interest on the credit it grants.

The Bank will pay interest on attracted funds, receive commission for providing guarantees and carrying out instructions from its clients and correspondents.

The basic principles of the Bank's policy with regard to interest rates, commission and other charges will be established by the Council of the Bank.

Interest rates will vary according to the length of credit being provided and the currency in which it is made.

ORGANISATION AND MANAGEMENT
Council of the Bank
Article 21

1. The highest authority of the Bank responsible for the general management of its activities is the Council of the Bank.

The Council of the Bank consists of representatives from all member countries of the Bank appointed by the respective governments.

Each member country irrespective of the amount of its quota in the authorised capital has one vote in the Council of the Bank.

2. The Council of the Bank shall hold meetings as frequently as it may be required but not less than twice a year.

3. Meetings shall be presided over in succession by representatives of each member country.

The Council of the Bank establishes procedure for the work.

Article 22

1. The Council of the Bank:

(a) determines the general trend of the Bank's activities on financing, attraction of funds and interest rate policy of the Bank, commission and other charges under Bank's operations, principles of co-operation with banks of member countries and other similar institutions;

(b) on the basis of suggestions of the Chairman of the Board, approves a list of projects to be financed by the Bank with indication of amounts for each project and determines general conditions which are to be stipulated in credit contracts concluded by the Bank. The Council fixes a total amount and maximum amount of credit for each project within the limits of which the Board has the right to give credits;

(c) approves credit plans, annual report, balance sheet and allocation of profits of the Bank, its structure, staff schedule and estimate of administrative expenses;

258

(d) appoints the Chairman and members of the Board;

(e) appoints the Chairman and members of the Auditing Committee, hears its reports and passes resolutions;

(f) takes decisions on opening branches and representative offices of the Bank in member countries and in other countries or suspension of their activities;

(g) approves Employment Regulations;

(h) takes decisions on purposes, size, terms and conditions of creation and use of the reserve capital and special funds as well as the manner of formation of special funds of interested countries;

(i) passes recommendations on:

— increase in the authorised capital of the Bank;

— amendments of the Statutes of the Bank;

(ii) takes decisions on:

— issue of bond loans;

— admission of new members;

— method and timing of contributions into the authorised capital of the Bank;

— terms and procedure for permanent suspension of the Bank's activities;

(iii) carries out other functions resulting from the present Agreement and Statutes of the Bank necessary for fulfilment of the functions with which it is entrusted.

2. The Council of the Bank must take decisions unanimously on the following matters:

— approval of the annual report, balance-sheet and allocation of profits of the Bank;

— recommendations regarding increase in the authorised capital of the Bank;

— method and dates of contributions into the authorised capital;

— issue of bond loans;

— opening or closing down branches and representative offices;

— appointment of the Chairman, members of the Board, Chairman and members of the Auditing Committee;

— admission of new members to the Bank;

— recommendations on amendments of the Bank's Statutes;

— method and timing of permanent suspension of the Bank's activities in accordance with Article XXVI of the Agreement.

For other questions a majority of at least three-quarters is sufficient.

3. The Council of the Bank has the right to handle over to the Board some of the matters which, according to the Statues of the Bank, are in the competence of the Council.

The Board

Article 23

The executive body of the Bank is the Board. The Board is accountable to the Council of the Bank.

The Board consists of the Chairman and three Deputies appointed by the Council of the Bank from citizens of member countries for a term of five years.

The basic task of the Board is the supervision over the Bank's activities in accordance with the Agreement, Statutes and decisions of the Council of the Bank.

The Chairman administers the current affairs of the Bank and of the Board on the principle of undivided authority within his competence and power determined by the Statutes and decisions of the Council of the Bank.

The Chairman of the Board is authorised to:

(a) manage the property and assets of the Bank in accordance with the Statutes of the Bank and decisions of the Council;

(b) implement credit plans approved by the Council of the Bank;

(c) organise the work for attracting and placing of surplus funds;

(d) submit to the Council of the Bank a list of projects to be financed stating merits of the proposals;

(e) take decisions on granting credits for investment projects within the credit limits given to him by the Council of the Bank;

(f) take decisions on issuing guarantees within competence granted by the Council of the Bank;

(g) fix interest rates and terms for granting credits and guarantees according to the principles and conditions determined by the Council of the Bank;

(h) prepare necessary material and suggestions for consideration by the Council of the Bank;

(i) represent the Bank in its dealings with third parties, lodge claims and institute proceedings in court and arbitration in the name of the Bank;

(k) issue orders and take decisions on current questions of the Bank's activities;

(l) sign contracts, obligations and procurations in the name of the Bank;

(m) organise and exercise business and correspondent relations of the Bank with other banks and organisations;

(n) approve rules and regulations of the Bank on conducting credit and banking operations in accordance with the principles determined by the Council of the Bank;

(o) appoint and dismiss officers and staff of the Bank except members of the Board, approve office regulations, fix salary in accordance with the staff schedule and administrative expenses confirmed by the Council of the Bank, and rewards for distinguished services;

(p) determine the number of employees, salary for service staff and technicians within the limits of the salary fund approved by the Council, assign employees to departments and sections;

(q) authorise officials of the Bank to represent the Bank in its dealings with third parties, sign contracts, obligations and procurations in the name of the Bank;

(r) discharge other functions in accordance with the Agreement, the Statutes and resolutions of the Council of the Bank.

The Chairman takes decisions on matters under items b, c, d, e, f, g, h, m, n, p, after they have been discussed at a Board meeting.

The results of discussions at Board meetings shall be registered in minutes.

If some members of the Board disagree with the decision taken by the Chairman they may require that their opinion be recorded in the minute and if they find it necessary they may inform thereof the Council of the Bank.

Members of the Board supervise the departments assigned to them and are responsible to the Chairman.

Article 24

The Chairman, members of the Board and other officials when performing their duties are international officials. They submit to the Bank and are independent of authorities or officials of the country citizens of which they are.

BANK'S AUDITING

Article 25

Auditing of the Bank's activities including checking of implementation of the Council's decisions, annual reports, cash and property, records, accounts and book-keeping of the Bank, its branches and agencies shall be made by the Auditing Committee appointed by the Council of the Bank for a period of five years. The Auditing Committee will be composed of the Chairman and three members.

The Chairman and members of the Auditing Committee cannot hold any positions with the Bank.

The procedure of auditing shall be fixed by the Council of the Bank.

The Chairman of the Board shall furnish the Auditing Committee with necessary documents.

Audit reports shall be submitted to the Council of the Bank.

STRUCTURE OF THE BANK

Article 26

The Bank has departments, sections and may have representative offices.

The structure of the Bank is approved by the Council of the Bank.

The staff of the Bank is appointed from the citizens of member countries of the Bank in conformity with the Employment Regulations of the Bank.

SETTLEMENT OF DISPUTES

Article 27

Claims against the Bank can be lodged within two years after the date of origin of the right to sue.

Article 28

Disputes between the Bank and its clients shall be submitted to arbitration being either an existing institution or established anew, subject to agreement of both parties.

In the absence of an agreement the dispute shall be referred to the Arbitration commission at the Chamber of Commerce in the country of Bank's domicile.

ACCOUNTING

Article 29

The financial year of the Bank is from January 1 to December 31 inclusive.

Annual balance sheets shall be published in the manner established by the Council of the Bank.

ALLOCATION OF PROFITS

Article 30

The Bank's activities must be economically viable.

After approval of an annual report net profits shall be distributed by the Council of the Bank and may be allocated to the reserve capital, own special funds, distributed among member countries or used for other purposes.

AMENDMENTS OF THE STATUTES

Article 31

In accordance with Article XIV of the Agreement any modifications may be introduced into the Statutes of the Bank with the consent of the governments of member countries of the Bank upon recommendation of the Council of the Bank.

Article 32

Amendments to the Statutes of the Bank may be proposed to the Council of the Bank for consideration by each member of the Bank as well as by the Board.

SUSPENSION OF OPERATIONS

Article 33

The Bank may suspend permanently its operations in conformity with Article XXVI of the Agreement.

The timing and procedure of cessation of the Bank's activities and liquidation of business shall be determined by the Council of the Bank.

XVI. AGREEMENT CONCERNING THE ESTABLISHMENT OF AN INTERNATIONAL ECONOMIC ASSOCIATION FOR THE CONSTRUCTION OF NUCLEAR INSTRUMENTS "INTERATOMINSTRUMENT"*

The Governments of the People's Republic of Bulgaria, the Hungarian People's Republic, the German Democratic Republic, the Polish People's Republic, the Union of Soviet Socialist Republics and the Czechoslovak Socialist Republic,

In the interest of the further broadening and deepening of cooperation and the uniting of efforts in the field of the construction of nuclear instruments,

Governed by the principles confirmed in the Comprehensive Programme for the Further Deepening and Perfecting of Cooperation and Development of Socialist Economic Integration of the Member Countries of COMECON,

Have resolved to conclude the present Agreement.

Article 1

By the present Agreement the Contracting Parties are establishing the international economic association for the construction of nuclear instruments "Interatominstrument," hereinafter referred to as "the Association."

The location of the Association shall be the city of Warsaw in the Polish People's Republic.

Article 2

The basic purpose of the Association shall be to meet to the fullest the requirements of the Contracting Parties in instruments and equipment of nuclear technology of high quality, corresponding to a world scientific-technical level.

To achieve this purpose the Association shall conduct scientific-research, experimental, draft-construction and production activities in the field of instruments and equipment of nuclear technology, organize scientific-technical, production and commercial cooperation in this field between the economic organizations of the Contracting Parties, and also promote the expansion of trade with other countries.

Article 3

The Association may open, with the agreement of the respective Contracting Parties and in conformity with procedure established in their states, its representations and departments on the territories of these states, and also establish production branches, draft-construction and other organizations, hereinafter referred to as "branches and departments" of the Association.

The Association may open its branches and departments on the territories of other states in conformity with procedure established in them.

Article 4

1. The Association shall possess juridical personality in the country

* Translation by the author. Russian text in P. A. Tokareva (ed.), *Mnogostoronnieje ekonomicheskoe sotrudnichestvo . . .*, *op. cit.*, 617–625.

in which it is located and shall carry out its activities in accordance with the legislation in force in that country, apart from the provisions stipulated in the present Agreement, and also in the Charter of the Association, which is an integral part of the present Agreement.*

The Association shall have the competence to conclude contracts, acquire, lease and alienate property, and also appear in court and in arbitration organs.

2. The branches and departments of the Association shall carry out their activities in accordance with the legislation of the countries in which they are located apart from the provisions stipulated in the present Agreement and in the Charter of the Association.

The branches and departments which are established by the Association as juridical persons shall enjoy the rights of national juridical persons in the countries in which they are located.

3. The legal capacity of the Association, its branches and departments necessary for the carrying out of the functions they are entrusted with shall be recognized on the territory of the Contracting Parties.

Issues which are not regulated by the present Agreement and the Charter of the Association shall be duly regulated in necessary cases by the Association, with the agreement of the competent organs of the countries in which the Association and its branches and departments are located.

Article 5

1. Economic organizations of the Contracting Parties, including enterprises, trusts, industrial and foreign trade associations, groups of enterprises, scientific-research institutes, draft-construction and other economic organizations, acting in accordance with national legislation in economic transactions in their own names and themselves assuming responsibility, may be members of the Association.

2. The original members of the Association are the economic organizations mentioned in the annex to the present Agreement.

3. The procedure for amendment of the composition of members of the Association shall be defined by the Charter of the Association.

Article 6

1. The Association shall bear material responsibility for its commitments within the limits of the property it possesses.

The composition of property of the Association and its sources shall be defined in the Charter.

The Association shall not bear material responsibility for the commitments of the Contracting Parties and the members of the Association, just as the Contracting Parties and members of the Association shall not be responsible for the commitments of the Association.

2. The present Agreement shall not affect the legal position of the economic organizations which are members of the Association in the countries in which they are located. These economic organizations shall retain to the full their economic and juridical independence.

* Not reproduced here.

Article 7

1.   The activities of the Association shall be carried out on the principles of "self-financing operation" (*khoziajstvennyj raschet*).

2.   To maintain the economic activities of the Association a statutory fund in the amount of two million one hundred thousand transferable roubles shall be established.

The participation of the Contracting Parties in the establishment of this fund shall be determined in equal shares.

The amount of the statutory fund and the criteria for determining the participation for the Contracting Parties in its establishment may be revised when necessary, taking into account the experience accumulated and the perspectives of the development of the Association, its branches and departments.

3.   Payment of the contributions to the statutory fund of the Association shall be made by its members in accordance with the procedure provided for in the Charter of the Association.

Should several economic organizations of one country participate in the Association, the amount of the contribution of each of them shall be determined by the competent organs of the respective country.

4.   Contributions shall be made in the amount of ten per cent in the first year of the activities of the Association, and in the second year in the amount of up to twenty-five per cent of the statutory fund.

The remaining part of the statutory fund shall be paid taking into account the development of the economic activities of the Association and its requirements in resources in conformity with the procedure determined by the Council of the Association and by dates established by it.

5.   The statutory fund may be raised with the agreement of the Contracting Parties upon the proposal of the Council of the Association.

6.   The statutory fund may be raised upon accession to the present Agreement of the governments of other states.

The amount of the contribution share of the governments of other states which accede to the present Agreement shall be determined upon agreement with them.

7.   Before the transition of the Association to full self-support, during the first three years of its activities, the members of the Association shall pay, over and above the amounts envisaged in paragraph 4 of the present article, additional payments necessary to cover the current expenditures of the Association.

The amount of these payments shall be determined by the financial plans of the Association in accordance with the provisions of paragraph 2 of the present article.

Article 8

1.   The leading organ of the Association shall be the Council, consisting of representatives appointed by the members of the Association. In the composition of the Council there shall be one permanent representative from each member of the Association.

All the representatives of the economic organizations of one country which are members of the Association shall have one deciding vote in the Council.

On the fundamental questions of the activities of the Association enumerated in the Charter of the Association, the Council shall adopt decisions unanimously, and on other questions—by a qualified majority of not less than 3/4 of the votes or by a simple majority of votes.

Decisions on the coordination of the economic activities of the members of the Association, including decisions on specialization and cooperation of scientific-research, draft-construction and other work, and also production in the field of the construction of nuclear instruments, shall be binding only for those members who voted for their adoption.

The Council shall have the right to adopt decisions when members of the Association representing not less than 3/4 of the votes on the Council attend its session. The absence from a session of the Council of representatives of members of the Association who have one deciding vote in the Council, and who were notified in time of its date and agenda, shall not deprive the decision adopted at the given session of its force with regard to these members.

2. The directing of the operative activities of the Association shall be realized by the Director and his deputies. The Director and his deputies shall be appointed by the Council from among citizens of the countries whose economic organizations are members of the Association.

The Director shall realize direct effective guidance of the activities of the Association on the basis of one-man management within the framework of his competences and rights, defined by the Charter and the decisions of the Council.

3. There shall be established an Audit Commission, appointed by the Council, for the audit of the financial and economic activities of the Association.

4. Upon the decision of the Council there may be established other organs of the Association necessary for the performance of the tasks facing it.

Article 9

1. The Association shall carry out its activities on the basis of annual and long-term plans approved by the Council of the Association.

These plans shall be coordinated with the national economic plans of the countries whose economic organizations are members of the Association, to the extent necessary to maintain the normal activities of the Association, its branches and departments.

2. The Association, its branches and departments shall be included in the system of material and technical supplies of the countries in which they are situated. For production distributed according to plan or set as quotas, the Association shall be allotted the necessary material and technical resources and funds.

Article 10

The Association may obtain loans from the respective banks of the country in which it is located, the International Bank for Economic Cooperation and the International Investment Bank, in conformity with the regulations and instructions of these banks.

The Association may also obtain loans from its members, on terms established according to an arrangement between the Association and the respective members.

266

Article 11

1. For the duration of the first three years of the activities of the Association, the Association, its branches and departments shall be exempted in the countries in which they are located from all direct State and local taxes and dues, with the exception of payments for municipal and other services.

2. After the transition of the Association to full self-support, matters concerning the payment by the Association, its self-financing branches and departments of taxes, including taxes on profit, shall be regulated by a supplementary agreement between the Contracting Parties.

Article 12

1. Material commodities and valuables provided by the members of the Association as part of their contributions on the territory of the countries in which the Association, its branches and departments are located, shall be exempted from the levying of customs duties, taxes and dues.

2. On the territories of the Contracting Parties, the Association, its branches and departments shall:

(a) be exempted from customs dues and all restrictions in the import and export of goods intended for the activities of the Association;

(b) enjoy all the preferences and privileges which are granted to the corresponding state economic organizations and enterprises.

3. The property of the Association, its branches and departments shall not be subject to being alienated for state or public needs, and also to removal or confiscation by administrative precedure.

4. Profit due to the members of the Association as a result of its distribution shall not be subject to imposition of taxes, and may be used for the purchase of commodities in the country in which the Association is located or freely transferred to the country in which the respective member of the Association is located.

Article 13

1. Workers and employees of the Association, its branches and departments, who are not citizens of the respective country in which they are located, shall be exempted from:

(a) personal obligations established by the legislation of the country in which the Association, its branches and departments are located;

(b) imposition of customs duties on goods imported and exported for personal needs upon their arrival for regular work at the Association, its branches and departments or upon their departure to their country of permanent residence after completing their work at the Association, its branches and departments.

2. Workers and employees of the Association, its branches and departments who are not citizens of the countries in which they are located shall be given the right to transfer their savings to their countries of permanent residence in conformity with the currency regulations of the country in which the Association, its branches and departments are located.

3. The conditions of work of personnel of the Association, its branches and departments shall be determined by the legislation of the country in which

they are located, the present Agreement, and also the Statute concerning the staff of the Association approved by the Council of the Association.

Article 14

Workers and employees of the Association, its branches and departments and also members of their families who are not citizens of the country in which the Association, its branches and departments are located, shall be furnished with living quarters, municipal services and medical assistance upon terms applicable to citizens of the country in which the Association, its branches and departments are located.

Article 15

The Association shall maintain contacts with the respective organs of the Council for Mutual Economic Assistance, and may also establish business contacts with international economic organizations and other organizations concerning problems arising from the activities of the Association.

Article 16

The provisions of the present Agreement shall not effect the rights and obligations of the Contracting Parties, arising out of other international agreements concluded by them.

Article 17

The languages of the countries whose economic organizations are members of the Association shall be the official languages of the Association.

The working language of the Association shall be Russian.

Article 18

The governments of other states which share its aims and principles and take upon themselves the obligations arising out of the present Agreement may, with the consent of all the Contracting Parties, accede to the present Agreement.

The government which desires to accede to the present Agreement shall notify the depositary of this in writing, indicating the economic organizations which are proposed as members of the Association.

Accession to the Agreement shall be considered to have taken place after the depositary receives the consent of all the Contracting Parties.

Article 19

Each Contracting Party may denounce the present Agreement, notifying the depositary of this not less than six months in advance.

During this period relations between the Association and the members withdrawing from it regarding their mutual obligations should be regulated.

Article 20

The Association may be liquidated upon the consent of all the Contracting Parties.

The procedure and time limits of liquidation of the Association shall be determined by consent between the Contracting Parties.

Article 21

The present Agreement has been concluded for an unlimited period.

The Agreement may be amended with the consent of all the Contracting Parties.

Article 22

1.   The present Agreement shall be subject to ratification in accordance with the legislation in force in the states whose governments sign the present Agreement, and shall enter into force on the date on which the depositary receives the last document concerning the ratification of the Agreement, of which the depositary shall notify all the Contracting Parties.

2.   The present Agreement shall be put into force temporarily from 1 March, 1972, if it does not enter into force on that date according to the first paragraph of the present article.

Article 23

The present Agreement shall be deposited for safekeeping with the Government of the Polish People's Republic, which shall fulfil the functions of depositary.

The Present Agreement had been concluded at the city of Warsaw on 22 February, 1972.

The Agreement has been drawn up in a single copy in Russian.

True certified copies of the present Agreement shall be sent by the depositary to all the Contracting Parties.

ANNEX to the Agreement concerning the establishment of the International Economic Association for the Construction of Nuclear Instruments "Inter-atominstrument"

List of the economic organizations—original members of the Association
The People's Republic of Bulgaria
The State Economic Association "RESPROM," Sofia
The Hungarian People's Republic
The group of enterprises "GAMMA," Budapest
The trade enterprise in instruments and organizational techniques "MIGERT," Budapest
The German Democratic Republic
VEB RVT Messelektronik "OTTO SCHON," Dresden
The enterprise in external trade "ELEKTROTECHNIK EKSPORT-IMPORT," Berlin

The enterprise in external and internal trade "ISOKOMMERZ," Berlin
The Polish People's Republic
The United Plants for the Construction of Nuclear Instruments "POLON,"
  Warsaw
The Union of Soviet Socialist Republics
The All-Union Association "IZOTOP" of the State Committee on the Use of
  Atomic Energy of the USSR, Moscow.
The All-Union Export-Import Office "TEKHSNABEKSPORT," Moscow
The Czechoslovak Socialist Republic
The production-economic organization "TESLA," Prague
The external trade organization "KOVO," Prague.

XVII. AGREEMENT BETWEEN ALBANIA, BULGARIA, HUNGARY, GERMAN DEMOCRATIC REPUBLIC, PEOPLE'S REPUBLIC OF CHINA, DEMOCRATIC PEOPLE'S REPUBLIC OF KOREA, MONGOLIAN PEOPLE'S REPUBLIC, POLAND, ROMANIA, UNION OF SOVIET SOCIALIST REPUBLICS AND CZECHOSLOVAKIA CONCERNING THE ORGANIZATION OF A JOINT INSTITUTE FOR NUCLEAR RESEARCH. SIGNED AT MOSCOW, ON 26 MARCH 1956*

The Governments of the People's Republic of Albania, the People's Republic of Bulgaria, the Hungarian People's Republic, the German Democratic Republic, the People's Republic of China, the Democratic People's Republic of Korea, the Mongolian People's Republic, the Polish People's Republic, the Romanian People's Republic, the Union of Soviet Socialist Republics and the Czechoslovak Republic,

Attaching great importance to the use of atomic energy for peaceful purposes for the benefit of all mankind, and
Recognizing the necessity for co-operation between scientists in different countries in theoretical and experimental research in the field of nuclear physics, with a view to expanding the possibilities of the use of atomic energy for peaceful purposes,

Have resolved to conclude this Agreement and have appointed as their plenipotentiaries:
The Government of the People's Republic of Albania: Spiro Kolek, Vice-Chairman of the Council of Ministers and Chairman of the State Planning Commission of the People's Republic of Albania;
The Government of the People's Republic of Bulgaria: Ruben Abramov, Minister of Culture of the People's Republic of Bulgaria;
The Government of the Hungarian People's Republic: István Hidás, Vice-Chairman of the Council of Ministers of the Hungarian People's Republic;
The Government of the German Democratic Republic: Ernst Wolf, Secretary of State;
The Government of the People's Republic of China: Liu Sze, Deputy Minister of Geology of the People's Republic of China;
The Government of the Democratic People's Republic of Korea: Dyong Joong Chak, Minister of the Chemical Industry of the Democratic People's Republic of Korea;
The Government of the Mongolian People's Republic: Sodnomyn Avarzid, Deputy Prime Minister of the Mongolian People's Republic;
The Government of the Polish People's Republic: Mieczysław Lesz, Deputy Chairman of the State Economic Planning Commission;
The Government of the Romanian People's Republic: Marin Gaston, First Deputy Chairman of the State Planning Commission and Chairman of the Committee on Nuclear Energy of the Council of Ministers of the Romanian People's Republic;
The Government of the Union of Soviet Socialist Republics: Aleksander

* *United Nations Treaty Series*, Vol. 259 (1957), No. 3686.

Vasilevich Topchiev, Principal Scientific Secretary of the Presidium of the Academy of Sciences of the USSR;

The Government of the Czechoslovak Republic: František Vlasák, Minister of Power of the Czechoslovak Republic,

Who, having exhibited their full powers, found in good and due form, have agreed as follows:

Article I

With a view to permitting joint theoretical and experimental research in the field of nuclear physics by scientists of the States parties to this Agreement, an international scientific research organization, known as the "Joint Institute for Nuclear Research", is hereby constituted.

Article II

The Joint Institute for Nuclear Research shall conduct all its activities on the basis of a Statute to be drafted by the Director of the Institute and approved by the Governments of the States members of the Institute.

The Joint Institute for Nuclear Research shall have legal personality. It may co-operate in its work with appropriate institutes and laboratories in the territory of the States members of the Institute.

The Institute shall be situated in the Kalinin region of the USSR.

Article III

The members of the Joint Institute for Nuclear Research shall be the States which have signed this Agreement.

Other States which may in the future wish to take part in the work of the Joint Institute for Nuclear Research shall declare their assent to the provisions of this Agreement and shall become members of the Institute by decision of the majority of the States members of the Institute.

Article IV

The Joint Institute for Nuclear Research shall include the following scientific research units:

(a) A Laboratory of Nuclear Problems, equipped with a synchro-cyclotron with a proton energy of 680 MeV (formerly the Institute of Nuclear Problems of the Academy of Sciences of the USSR),

(b) A Laboratory of High-Energy Physics, equipped with a synchro-phasotron with a design proton energy of 10,000 MeV (formerly the Electrophysics Laboratory of the Academy of Sciences of the USSR).

On the date of the entry into force of this Agreement, the Government of the Union of Soviet Socialist Republics shall transfer the said Institute of Nuclear Problems and the said Electrophysics Laboratory of the Academy of Sciences of the USSR, together with all their equipment and their basic, auxiliary and administrative installations and buildings, to the Joint Institute for Nuclear Research.

With a view to the further development of research in the field of nuclear physics at the Joint Institute, it is proposed to construct the following:

272

(a) A theoretical Physics Laboratory, with a computing department and electronic computing machines;

(b) A neutron Physics Laboratory, equipped with an experimental high-neutron-flux nuclear reactor;

(c) A cyclotron designed to accelerate multiply charged ions of various elements, for experimental work with those ions, at the Laboratory of Nuclear Problems;

(d) Other experimental installations and laboratories.

Article V

The Joint Institute for Nuclear Research shall be headed by a Director and two Deputy Directors, elected by a majority of the States members of the Institute from amongst the scientists of those States. The Director shall be elected for a term of three years, and the Deputy Directors for a term of two years.

The election of the Director of the Institute and his two deputies shall be duly carried out by the authorized representatives of the States members of the Institute.

The Director of the Institute shall have full authority to deal with the appropriate institutions of the States members of the Institute in all matters relating to the Institute's activities.

The Director of the Joint Institute for Nuclear Research shall be responsible to the Governments of the States members of the Institute for the activities of the Institute and shall report to them at regular intervals.

A Scientific Council of the Institute is hereby constituted to discuss and approve plans for scientific research, the results of their execution and other matters relating to the scientific activities of the Institute. The members of the Scientific Council shall be scientists appointed by the States members of the Institute, not more than three being appointed by each State.

The Director of the Joint Institute shall be the Chairman of the Scientific Council.

The Director of the Institute shall appoint a deputy to deal with matters relating to construction and to the internal affairs of the Institute.

Article VI

Each State member of the Joint Institute for Nuclear Research shall make annual financial contributions towards the maintenance of the Institute and the construction therein of new scientific-research facilities and shall contribute to the material support of the Institute.

The individual contributions of the States which are founding members of the Institute towards the construction and maintenance costs of the Institute shall be determined in accordance with the following scale:

People's Republic of Albania . . . .   .05 per cent
People's Republic of Bulgaria . . . .   3.6 per cent
Hungarian People's Republic   4   per cent
German Democratic Republic . . . .   6.75 per cent
People's Republic of China   20   per cent
Democratic People's Republic of Korea . . . .   .05 per cent

Mongolian People's Republic	....	.05 per cent
Polish People's Republic	....	6.75 per cent
Romanian People's Republic	....	5.75 per cent
Union of Soviet Socialist Republics	....	47.25 per cent
Czechoslovak Republic	....	5.75 per cent

On the accession of new States to membership in the Institute and in the event of the withdrawal of any State from membership in the Institute, the scale of contributions towards the construction and maintenance costs of the Institute shall be reviewed and the new scale shall be submitted to the Governments of States members of the Institute for approval.

The amount of the individual contributions of States members of the Institute shall not be a factor affecting the extent to which any particular member State participates in the scientific activities and administration of the Institute.

Article VII

A Financial Committee composed of representatives of all States members of the Institute is hereby established to approve the budget and review the financial operations of the Institute. Each State member of the Institute shall have one representative in the Financial Committee. The member of the Committee shall be appointed by the Governments of the States concerned. The members of the Financial Committee, each representing a State, shall preside in turn over the meetings of the Committee.

Article VIII

Any State member of the Joint Institute for Nuclear Research may withdraw from the Institute.

Notice of withdrawal from the Institute shall be given in writing to the Director of the Institute by the authorized representative of the Government of the member State wishing to withdraw not later than three months before the expiry of the current financial year.

Article IX

The Joint Institute for Nuclear Research may be dissolved by agreement between the Governments of all the States members of the Institute.

Upon the dissolution of the Institute, all its equipment and basic, auxiliary and administrative installations shall become the property of the Union of Soviet Socialist Republics, in whose territory the Institute is situated. The other States members of the Institute shall be paid compensation in cash in proportion to their individual contributions to the capital expenditures of the Institute.

Upon the dissolution of the Institute, the financial balance, with the exception of the portion required to meet the obligations of the Institute, shall be distributed among the States members of the Institute at the time of its dissolution, in proportion to the total financial contributions actually made by them during the period of their participation in the work of the Institute.

274

Article X

This Agreement shall come into force on the date of its signature by all the States members of the Institute. With respect to each State which subsequently accedes thereto, the Agreement shall come into force as from the date of the decision to admit the State to membership in the Institute in accordance with the procedure prescribed in article III of the Agreement.

This Agreement was signed at Moscow on 26 March 1956, in a single copy, in Russian. Certified true copies of the Agreement shall be sent by the Government of the USSR to all the States parties to the Agreement.

In witness whereof the plenipotentiaries have signed this Agreement and have thereto affixed their seals.

CHARTER OF THE JOINT INSTITUTE FOR NUCLEAR RESEARCH*

Chapter I
Creation of the Institute and its Headquarters

Article 1

The Joint Institute for Nuclear Research, hereinafter referred to as "The Institute," is an international scientific-research organization, created in accordance with the Agreement concerning the organization of a Joint Institute for Nuclear Research, concluded by the Governments of:

The People's Republic of Albania, the People's Republic of Bulgaria, the Hungarian People's Republic, the German Democratic Republic, the People's Republic of China, the Democratic People's Republic of Korea, the Mongolian People's Republic, the Polish People's Republic, the Rumanian People's Republic, the Union of Soviet Socialist Republics, and the Czechoslovak Republic on 26 March 1956.

Article 2

The headquarters of the Institute: the Union of Soviet Socialist Republics, the town of Dubna in the Moscow region.

Postal address: Moscow, Main Post Office, Postal Box No. 79.

Article 3

The Institute shall possess juridical personality and shall enjoy, in accordance with the laws of the host country, legal capacity and the status necessary for the performance of its functions and the achievement of its purposes.

The Institute shall enjoy the right to receive freely printed publications from abroad.

It shall have its own round seal, and an impression of its pattern shall be annexed to the Statute.

---

* Translation by the author. Russian text in P. A. Tokareva (ed.), *Mnogostoronnieje ekonomicheskoe sotrudnichestvo...*, *op. cit.*, pp. 400–410; Polish text in B. Reutt (ed.), *Podstawowe dokumenty...*, *op. cit.*, pp. 348–359.

Chapter II
The Purposes and Tasks of the Joint Institute for Nuclear Research

Article 4

The purpose of the Joint Institute for Nuclear Research shall be:

The ensuring of the common conducting of theoretical and experimental research in the field of nuclear physics by scientists of the States members of the Institute;

The furthering of the development of nuclear physics in the States members of the Institute by means of exchange of experience and achievements in the conducting of theoretical and exprimental research;

The maintaining of contacts with interested national and international scientific-research and other organizations in the matter of the development of nuclear physics and the finding of new possibilities of peaceful application of atomic energy;

The furthering of comprehensive development of the creative aptitudes of scientific-research personnel of the States members of the Institute.

In all its activities the Institute shall further the use of nuclear energy only for peaceful purposes for the good of all humanity.

The results of scientific-research work performed in the Institute shall be published or reported at scientific conferences and meetings in order that all may become acquainted with them.

Reports on work carried out shall be sent out to all States members of the Institute.

Chapter III
Membership of the Joint Institute for Nuclear Research

Article 5

The members of the Joint Institute for Nuclear Research shall be the States which have signed the Agreement concerning the organization of this Institute.

Other States, if they wish to take part in the work of the Institute and declare their consent to the provisions of the Agreement concerning the organization of the Institute and the Charter of the Institute, shall become Members of the Institute by decision of the majority of the States members of the Institute.

The amount of individual contributions towards the maintenance and construction costs of the Institute of States which have newly become Members of the Institute shall be submitted by the Financial Committee for approval by the Governments of the States members of the Institute.

Article 6

All Members of the Institute shall have equal rights to participate in the scientific activities and in the management of the Institute.

Article 7

The question of work in the Institute of scientists from States which are not Members of the Institute shall be decided by the Directorate of the Institute in each individual case, with due regard to the principle of reciprocity.

By arrangement with the State concerned or directly with the scientist himself or with the scientific institution, the Directorate of the Institute shall determine the rate and procedure of compensation for the use of equipment and material of the Institute.

Article 8

Any State member of the Institute may withdraw from membership.

Notice of withdrawal from the Institute shall be given in writing to the Directorate of the Institute by the Government of the State wishing to withdraw not later than three months before the expiry of the current financial year.

Withdrawal from the Institute shall take effect after the expiry of the financial year in which the State gives notice of withdrawal from the Institute. The amount of compensation in cash to States which withdraw from membership of the Institute shall be determined by the Financial Committee according to their individual contributions towards the capital expenditure of the Institute, after a report on the execution of the budget for the financial year in which the State gives notice of withdrawal from membership of the Institute.

Chapter IV
The Financial Committee and the Budget

Article 9

A Financial Committee composed of representatives of all States members of the Institute is hereby established to approve the budget and supervise the financial operations of the Institute.

Each State member of the Institute shall have one representative on the Financial Committee. The members of the Committee shall be appointed by the Governments of the States concerned.

The Financial Committee shall meet for sessions not less than once a year. Representatives from each State shall preside in turn over meetings of the Financial Committee.

Decisions of the Financial Committee shall be adopted by a majority of not less than 2/3 of the votes.

Article 10

The Financial Committee shall examine and approve:

(a) The estimates of financing expenditures for the scientific and economic activities of the Institute;

(b) The structure, posts and official rates of pay of all categories of employees of the Institute;

(c) The plan for financing the capital investment of the Institute;

(d) The amounts and terms of cash payments of States members of the Institute for the maintenance and construction costs of the Institute, in accordance with the scale of individual contributions envisaged in the Agreement between the States members of the Institute.

(e) Carry out supervision over the financial activities of the Institute.

Article 11

The budget of the Institute shall be prepared annually for the period from 1 January to 31 December inclusive.

Article 12

In the budget presented to the Financial Committee the Directorate shall provide for all expenditures of the Institute for the following items:

(a) The financing of scientific-research work and the material support of the employees of the Institute;

(b) Expenditures for the construction of scientific-research and other objects of the Institute;

(c) Resources for incentives for employees of the Institute, bonuses for years of service in the Institute, and the lending of one-time material aid to employees of the Institute;

(d) The financing of other expenditures connected with the activities of the Institute.

Article 13

In accordance with the budget approved by the Financial Committee, every State member of the Institute shall make cash payments on fixed dates for the maintenance costs of the Institute and the construction of objects of the Institute.

Cash payments by States members of the Institute shall be made in the currency of the country in which the Institute is located.

In cases when the Joint Institute for Nuclear Research needs currency for the purchase of equipment, instruments, materials, scientific-technical literature and periodical publications in States non-members of the Institute, the States members of the Institute shall pay, as part of their contribution share established by the Agreement, part of the sum in the currency of these States. The amount of the sums in other currencies shall be determined by the Financial Committee.

The value of deliveries by States members of the Institute of equipment, instruments and materials, and the value of specific jobs carried out by order of the Institute, may be counted as part of the individual contributions.

The modality of settlements shall be established by the Financial Committee.

Article 14

On the accession of new States to membership in the Institute and in the event of the withdrawal of any State from membership in the Institute, the scale of contributions towards the construction and maintenance costs of the Institute shall be reviewed and a new scale shall be submitted to the Governments of the States members of the Institute for approval.

Article 15

During the execution of the budget the Directorate of the Institute may make partial changes in the distribution of resources between items in the budget, separately within the bounds of allocations for capital investment and for operational activities.

Article 16

The report on the execution of the budget shall be presented by the

Directorate of the Institute to the Financial Committee according to the position at the end of every financial year.

The dates of presentation of the report shall be established by the Financial Committee.

Chapter V
The Scientific Council of the Joint Institute for Nuclear Research

Article 17

The Scientific Council of the Institute shall consist of scientists of the States members of the Institute appointed by the States members of the Institute, not more than three being appointed by each State.

The Director of the Institute and the Vice-Directors, elected in accordance with article 20 of the present Charter, shall sit on the Scientific Council, with the right to deciding vote.

The Directors of the Laboratories shall sit on the Scientific Council of the Institute, with the right to an advisory vote, if they are not appointed as members of the Scientific Council by the respective Governments.

Article 18

The Scientific Council of the Institute shall:

(a) Discuss and approve the plans of the scientific-research work of the Institute;

(b) Examine the results of the fulfilment of the plans of the scientific-research work of the Institute, and also the results of individual research projects;

(c) Discuss other questions connected with the scientific activities of the Institute.

The Scientific Council shall assemble for meetings not less than twice a year.

Article 19

The Director of the Institute shall be the Chairman of the Scientific Council.

The Scientific Council of the Institute shall establish its own rules of procedure.

Chapter VI
The Directorate of the Joint Institute for Nuclear Research

Article 20

The Institute shall be headed by the Directorate of the Institute, consisting of the Director of the Institute and two Vice-Directors, elected by a majority of the States members of the Institute from amongst the scientists of those States. The Director shall be elected for a term of three years, and the Vice-Directors for a term of two years.

The election of the Director of the Institute and the two Vice-Directors shall be carried out by the Authorized Representatives of the States members of the Institute.

Article 21

The Director of the Institute shall have full authority to deal with the appropriate institutions of the States members of the Institute in all matters relating to the Institute's activities.

The Institute shall be able to establish direct contact with scientists and scientific organizations of various countries.

The Vice-Directors of the Institute shall be the deputies of the Director in directing the Institute, and shall bear equal responsibility with him for all the activities of the Institute.

Article 22

The Directorate of the Institute shall be responsible to the Governments of the States members of the Institute for the activities of the Institute and shall report to them at regular intervals.

The Directorate of the Institute, in carrying out its functions in the field of managing the Institute, shall be guided only by the decisions of the Financial Committee and the Scientific Council, and shall not accept for implementation any instructions from individual States members of the Institute.

Article 23

The Directorate of the Institute shall present to the Financial Committee every year at fixed dates the draft budget and the report on the execution of the budget.

Article 24

The Directorate of the Institute shall direct the scientific activities of the Institute in accordance with the plan of scientific-research work approved by the Scientific Council of the Institute, and the financial activities in accordance with decisions reached by the Financial Committee.

The Directorate of the Institute shall have the authority to change partially the directions of scientific-research work in individual Laboratories of the Institute.

It shall have to report all changes to the Scientific Council of the Institute.

Article 25

The Directorate of the Institute shall present the collective draft plans of scientific-research work, the draft long-term plans for development of the Institute, and a report on the scientific activities of the Institute every year to the Scientific Council for examination and approval.

Article 26

The Director of the Institute shall be the chief administrator of appropriations of the Institute. He shall administer all resources and property of the Institute.

Article 27

The Director of the Institute shall have the authority:

(a) To employ and dismiss employees in accordance with the Statute concerning the personnel of the Institute;

(b) To establish and change the salaries of employees of all categories within the limits of the official rates of pay approved by the Financial Committee, and also to establish, for highly qualified staff, individual increments to salary of up to 50 percent of the basic rate of pay, within the limits of the sums approved for these purposes by the estimates.

Chapter VII
The Laboratories of the Joint Institute for Nuclear Research
Article 28

The Institute shall include: a Laboratory for Nuclear Problems, a Laboratory for High-Energy Physics, a Neutron Physics Laboratory and a Theoretical Physics Laboratory, each of which covers the respective field of nuclear physics research.

The Laboratories of the Institute shall consist of scientific divisions and sectors.

Depending upon the emergence of new tasks, or when the necessity no longer exists, the number of Laboratories may be changed by decision of the Scientific Council of the Institute, and the number of divisions and sectors by decision of the Directorate of the Institute.

Article 29

To direct the Laboratories the Directorate shall appoint, from amongst the scientists of the States members of the Institute, Directors of the Laboratories, and their appointment shall subsequently be approved by the Scientific Council.

The Directors of the Laboratories shall be responsible for their activities and for the work of the Laboratories to the Directorate of the Institute.

Article 30

The Directors of the Laboratories shall direct all the scientific-research activities of the Laboratories in accordance with the plan of work approved by the Scientific Council of the Institute.

The Directors of the Laboratories shall have the authority, with the agreement of the Directorate of the Institute, to change partially the course of the scientific-research work in the Laboratories.

The Directors of the Laboratories shall be given the authority to carry out, through the Directorate of the Institute: selection of personnel; employment and dismissal of employees of the Laboratories; determining and changing of the rates of pay of the employees of the Laboratories in conformity with the approved maximum rates of pay, depending upon the type and field of the work of each employee; expressing of thanks and imposing of punishment.

Article 31

In the Laboratories, Scientific Councils shall be established whose composition shall be approved by the Scientific Council of the Institute.

The Director of the Laboratory shall be the Chairman of the Scientific Council of the Laboratory.

The Scientific Council of the Laboratory shall:

(a) Prepare the plans of the scientific-research work of the Laboratory;

(b) Examine the results of the fulfilling of plans of scientific-research work and the results of individual research projects;

(c) Confer scientific degrees of doctor and candidate of physico-mathematical and technical sciences;

(d) Discuss other questions relating to the scientific activities of the Laboratory.

Article 32

The Directors of the Laboratories shall submit to the Directorate of the Institute, at fixed dates, the draft plan of scientific research work of the Laboratory, a report on its work, and orders for the necessary equipment and materials.

Chapter VIII
Administrative and Economic Management of the Joint Institute for Nuclear Research

Article 33

The Director of the Institute shall appoint a deputy—an Administrative Director—to direct the administrative and economic activities and construction of the Institute.

Article 34

The Administrative Director shall direct the work of divisions under his charge envisaged in the structure of the Institute. He shall have the authority to employ and dismiss employees of the divisions which he directs.

Article 35

The Administrative Director, empowered by the Director of the Institute, shall have the authority to manage appropriations, and shall be responsible for the proper spending of the funds of the Institute within the framework of the budget approved by the Financial Committee.

In his activities the Administrative Director shall be subordinate to the Director of the Institute and shall be responsible to him.

Chapter IX
The Employees of the Joint Institute for Nuclear Research

Article 36

All persons on the staff of the Institute shall be considered to be employees of an international scientific organization and shall be obliged to further its aims and tasks.

Article 37

Employees of the Institute shall be recruited from among citizens of the States members of the Institute.

Quotas from each State member of the Institute shall be examined by the Directorate of the Institute and submitted for approval to the Scientific Council.

The question of work in the Institute of scientific employees delegated by the States members of the Institute for a short period of time shall be decided by the Directorate of the Institute.

Article 38

The duties and rights of employees of the Institute shall be defined by the Statute concerning the personnel of the Joint Institute for Nuclear Research annexed to the Charter.* Employees of the Institute should respect the legislation of the country in which the Institute is located.

Article 39

The Directorate of the Institute shall be authorized to accept students from academic schools or trainees from among citizens of the States members of the Institute to do practical work in the Laboratories of the Institute. In these cases expenses will be assumed by the States sending the students or trainees for practical work. The procedure and periods of doing practical work shall be defined by the Directorate of the Institute.

Chapter X
Dissolution of the Joint Institute for Nuclear Research

Article 40

The Joint Institute for Nuclear Research may be dissolved by agreement between the Governments of the States members of the Institute.

Upon the dissolution of the Institute, all its equipment and basic, auxiliary and administrative installations shall become the property of the Union of Soviet Socialist Republics, in whose territory the Institute is situated. The other States members of the Institute shall be paid compensation in cash in proportion to their individual contributions to the capital expenditures of the Institute.

Upon the dissolution of the Institute, the financial balance, with the exception of the portion required to meet the obligations of the Institute, shall be distributed among the States members of the Institute at the time of its dissolution, in proportion to the total financial contributions actually made by them during the period of their participation in the work of the Institute.

Chapter XI
Approval of the Charter

Article 41

The present Charter shall be subject to approval at a Meeting of the Authorized Representatives of the Governments of the States members of the Institute.

A certified copy of the Charter shall be kept in the Institute.

Chapter XII
Amendment of the Charter

Article 42

Total or partial amendment of the Charter in the future shall be permitted.

Proposals for the amendment of the Charter shall be submitted to the Directorate of the Institute. The Directorate shall have the authority to make proposals itself for the amendment of the Charter. After these proposals are adopted by the

* Not reproduced here.

majority of the States members of the Institute, the Directorate of the Institute shall be guided by the adopted amendments to the Charter.*

This Charter has been drawn up on 23 September 1956 in a single copy, in the Russian language. Certified true copies of this Charter shall be sent by the Directorate of the Institute to all States members of the Institute.

In witness whereof the Authorized Representatives of the Governments of the States members of the Institute have signed the present document and have affixed to it the seal of the Institute.

* The Russian text reproduced in *Mnogostoronnieje ekonomicheskoe sotrudni-chestvo...* contains the following footnote on pp. 409–410:
"In 1956 the Authorized Representatives of the States members of the JINR created a Committee of Authorized Representatives of the Governments of the States members of the Joint Institute for Nuclear Research. At meetings of this Committee (held from 1957) the direction of the activities of the JINR is determined, a report of the Directorate on the activities of the Institute is heard, the Directorate of the Institute is elected, the budget is approved, and other important questions are examined."

XVIII. AGREEMENT CONCERNING THE ESTABLISHMENT OF AN
INTERNATIONAL SYSTEM AND AN ORGANIZATION FOR COSMIC
COMMUNICATIONS "INTERSPUTNIK"*

The Contracting Parties,

Recognizing the necessity for promoting the strengthening and development of comprehensive economic, scientific-technical, cultural and other relations through the setting up of communications, and also of radio and television broadcasting by artificial Earth satellites;

Recognizing the usefulness of co-operation in theoretical and experimental research, and also in the planning, creation, exploitation and development of an international system of communications by artificial Earth satellites;

In the interests of the development of international co-operation on the basis of respect for the sovereignty and independence of states, of equal rights, non-interference in internal affairs, and also of mutual assistance and mutual benefit;

Basing themselves upon the provisions of resolution 1721 (XVI) of the General Assembly of the United Nations and the Treaty on Principles Governing the Activities of States in the Exploration and Use of Outer Space, including the Moon and other Celestial Bodies, of 27 January 1967,

Have agreed as follows:

Article 1

1. An international system of communications by artificial Earth satellites is hereby established.

2. To ensure co-operation and co-ordination of efforts in the planning, establishment, exploitation and development of a communications system, the Contracting Parties hereby establish an international organization "Intersputnik," hereinafter referred to as the Organization.

Article 2

1. "Intersputnik" shall be an open international organization.

2. The members of the Organization shall be the Governments which have signed the present Agreement and deposited instruments of ratification for safekeeping in accordance with article 20, and also the Governments of other states which have acceded to the present Agreement in accordance with article 22.

Article 3

The Organization shall be situated in Moscow.

Article 4

1. The international system of communications by artificial Earth satellites shall include as its structural components:

* Translation by the author. Russian text in P. A. Tokareva (ed.), *Mnogostoron-nieje ekonomicheskoe sotrudnichestvo...*, *op. cit.*, pp. 387–396.

— a cosmic complex consisting of communications satellites with relay instruments, on-board means of control and ground control systems, ensuring normal functioning of the satellites;

— ground stations, accomplishing mutual communications by artificial Earth satellites.

2. The cosmic complex shall be the property of the Organization or shall be leased from Members of the Organization which have such systems.

3. The ground stations shall be the property of states or of recognized exploitation organizations.

4. The Members of the Organization shall have the right to include ground stations constructed by them in the communications system of the Organization, if these stations conform to the technical requirements of the Organization.

Article 5

The establishment of the international communications system is envisaged in the following stages:

— the stage of carrying out experimental work by the Members of the Organization in their ground stations using communications channels placed at the disposal of the Organization free of charge by the Union of Soviet Socialist Republics on its communications satellites. The duration of this stage is set to last up to the end of 1973;

— the stage of work using communications channels on communications satellites of Members of the Organization under lease terms;

— the stage of commercial exploitation of the communications system using the cosmic system which is the property of the Organization or is leased from its Members. The transition to this stage shall take place when the establishment of the cosmic complex belonging to the Organization or its lease shall be acknowledged by the Contracting Parties to be economically expedient.

Article 6

The launching and sending into orbit of communications satellites which are the property of the Organization, and also their control in orbit shall be carried out by the Members of the Organization which have the proper means for this, on the basis of agreements between the Organization and such Members of the Organization.

Article 7

The Organization shall co-ordinate its activities with the International Telecommunication Union, and also co-operate with other organizations whose activities bear a relation to the use of communications satellites both in the technical respect (the use of the frequency spectrum, the application of technical norms to communications channels and of standards to apparatus), and in problems of international regulation.

Article 8

The Organization shall possess juridical personality and shall have the

286

capacity to conclude contracts, acquire, lease and alienate property and undertake legal actions.

Article 9

1. On the territory of the states whose governments are members of the Organization, it shall enjoy the legal capacity necessary for the achievement of its aims and the fulfilment of its functions. The extent of this legal capacity shall be determined in pertinent agreements with the competent organs of the states on whose territory it carries out its activities.

2. The legislation of the states on whose territory the activities of the Organization are realized shall be applied in matters which are not regulated by the present Agreement and by the agreements indicated in paragraph 1 of the present article.

Article 10

1. The Organization shall bear material responsibility for its commitments within the limits of the property it possesses.

2. The Organization shall not bear material responsibility for commitments of the Contracting Parties, just as the Contracting Parties shall not be responsible for commitments of the Organization.

Article 11

1. To direct the activities of the Organization the following organs shall be established:
— The Council—the leading organ;
— The Directorate—the standing executive and administrative organ headed by the Director-General.
The time of the establishment and commencement of activities of the Directorate shall be determined by the Council.

2. Until the commencement of activities of the Directorate the functions of the Director-General representing the Organization, indicated in paragraph 2 of article 13, shall be performed by the chairman of the Council.

3. An Auditing Commission shall be established to audit the financial activities of the Organization

4. The Council may set up such auxiliary organs as are necessary for the realization of the aims of the present Agreement.

Article 12

1. The Council shall be composed of one representative from each Member of the Organization.

2. Each Member of the Organization shall have one vote in the Council.

3. The Council shall meet for regular sessions not less than once a year. A Special session may be called at the request of any Member of the Organization or of the Director-General, if not less than one third of the Members of the Organization declare for calling it.

4. Sessions of the Council shall be held, as a rule, in the place where the

Organization is located. The Council may take the decision to hold sessions in the territory of other states, whose Governments are Members of the Organization, upon the invitation of these Members of the Organization.

Until the commencement of activities of the Directorate the Council shall meet in turn in the states whose governments are members of the Organization according to their names by the Russian alphabet. In such a case expenses connected with the conducting of sessions shall be borne by the host Members of the Organization.

5. Presiding over sessions of the Council shall be performed by representatives of Members of the Organization in turn in order of the names of these Members of the Organization according to the Russian alphabet. The representative of the Member of the Organization which follows according to the alphabet shall be appointed deputy chairman. The Chairman and his deputy shall retain their full powers until the next regular session of the Council.

6. Matters covered by the present Agreement shall be within the competence of the Council. The Council shall:

(1) examine and approve measures connected with the establishment, acquisition or lease, and also the exploitation of the cosmic complex;

(2) approve plans for the development and perfecting of the communications system of the Organization;

(3) determine the technical requirements for communications satellites of the Organization;

(4) examine and approve the programme of the launching into orbit of communications satellites of the Organization;

(5) approve the plan of distribution of communications channels between the Members of the Organization, and also the procedure and conditions governing the use of communications channels by other users;

(6) determine the technical requirements for ground stations;

(7) determine conformity with the technical requirements of ground stations offered for inclusion in the communications system of the Organization;

(8) elect the Director-General and his deputy and control the activities of the Directorate.

(9) elect the chairman and the members of the Auditing Commission and approve the work procedure of that Commission;

(10) approve the structure and staffing plan of the Directorate and also the Staff Regulations of the Directorate;

(11) approve the work plan of the Organization for the forthcoming calendar year;

(12) examine and approve the budget of the Organization and the report on its execution, and also the balance-sheet and the distribution of profits of the Organization;

(13) examine and approve the annual reports of the Director-General on the activities of the Directorate;

(14) approve the report of the Auditing Commission;

(15) take note of the official applications of governments wishing to accede to the Agreement;

(16) determine the procedure and time-limits for payment of contributions and also the redistribution of contributions in accordance with paragraph 5 of article 15;

(17) determine the dues for the transmission of units of information or the

cost of lease of a channel on communications satellites of the Organization;

(18) examine proposals on the introduction of amendments to the present Agreement and present them to the Contracting Parties for approval in accordance with the procedure established by article 24;

(19) adopt the rules of procedure for its work;

(20) examine and decide upon other matters arising from the Agreement.

7. The Council should aim at unànimous adoption of its decisions. If this is not achieved, decisions of the Council shall be considered adopted when not less than two thirds of all Members of the Council vote for them. Decisions of the Council shall not be mandatory for those Members who do not declare for their adoption and state their reservations about them in written form; these Members may, however, later accede to the decisions adopted.

8. In the fulfilment of its functions, envisaged in paragraph 6 of the present article, the Council shall act within the limits of the resources established by the Contracting Parties.

9. The first session of the Council shall be called by the Government of the state in which the seat of the Organization is fixed, not later than three months after entry into force of the present agreement.

Article 13

1. The Directorate shall consist of the Director-General, his deputy and the necessary staff.

2. The Director-General, acting on the principles of undivided authority, *(edinonachalie)*, shall be the chief administrative officer of the Organization and shall represent it in that capacity in relations with the competent organs of Members of the Organization in all matters concerning its activities, and also in relations with states whose Governments are not members of the Organization and with international organizations with which the Council deems it necessary to co-operate.

3. The Director-General shall be responsible to the Council and shall act within the limits of the full powers granted to him by the present Agreement and by decision of the Council.

4. The Director-General shall realize the following functions:

(1) ensure the carrying out of decisions of the Council;

(2) conduct talks with the communications administrations, draughting organizations and industrial enterprises of Members of the Organization on problems of draughting, preparation and delivery of elements and signals for the apparatus on board communications satellites of the Organization;

(3) conduct talks on problems of launching of communications satellites for the Organization;

(4) upon the instructions of the Council within the framework of the powers established by the Council, conclude international and other agreements;

(5) draw up the draft budget for the next financial year, present it to the Council for approval, and render an account to the Council on the execution of the budget for the expired financial year;

(6) prepare a report on the activities of the Directorate for the expired year for presentation to the Council;

(7) work out the draft work plans of the Organization, and also the draft

plans of the development and perfecting of the communications system and present them to the Council for approval;

(8) ensure the preparation, summoning and conducting of sessions of the Council.

5. The Director-General and his deputy shall be elected from among citizens of the states whose Governments are Members of the Organization, for a term of four years. The deputy of the Director-General can be elected, as a rule, for one term only. The Director-General and his deputy cannot be citizens of one and the same state.

6. The staff of the Directorate shall be recruited from among citizens of the states whose Governments are Members of the Organization, taking into consideration professional competence and an equitable geographical representation.

Article 14

1. The Auditing Commission shall consist of three members, elected by the Council for a term of three years from among citizens of different countries whose Governments are Members of the Organization.

The Chairman and Members of the Auditing Commission can not hold any posts in the Organization.

2. The Director-General shall place at the disposal of the Auditing Commission all material and documents necessary for the realization of audit.

3. The report of the Auditing Commission shall be furnished to the Council of the Organization.

Article 15

1. To maintain the activities of the Organization a statutory fund (fixed and working capital) shall be established. The decision on the establishment of the statutory fund and on its amount shall be made by the Contracting Parties upon the proposal of the Council and shall be formalized in a special protocol. The amount of contributions of Members of the Organization to the formation of the statutory fund shall be fixed proportionally to the extent to which communications channels are used by them.

2. If in the process of perfecting the communications system the necessity manifests itself to increase the statutory fund, the amount of additional payments shall be subject to distribution between the Members of the Organization which expressed their agreement to that increase.

3. The following expenses of the Organization shall be covered out of payments of Members of the Organization into the statutory fund:

(1) for scientific-research and experimental-construction work on the cosmic complex and on ground stations;

(2) for the designing, construction, acquisition or lease of the cosmic complex;

(3) for payment for the launching and sending into orbit of communications satellites of the Organization;

(4) for other purposes connected with the activities of the Organization.

4. Until the formation of the statutory fund the activities of the Organization shall be maintained in conformity with a special budget drawn up for

each calendar year. Expenditure provided for in the budget for the upkeep of the staff of the Directorate, the conducting of sessions of the Council and other measures of an administrative nature, shall be covered by the Members of the Organization in amounts established by the Contracting Parties on the proposal of the Council and formalized in a special protocol.

5. Upon joining of the Organization by new Members or in the case of a Member leaving the Organization, the contribution shares of the other Members of the Organization shall change accordingly.

6. The currency in which contributions are made to the statutory fund and to the budget of the Organization shall be determined by the Contracting Parties on the proposal of the Council.

7. On amounts unpaid by members of the Organization by the established date the Organization shall charge an additional 3% annually.

8. In the case of Members of the Organization not fulfilling their financial obligations within one year, the Council shall decide the question of partial or full suspension of rights arising from membership in the Organization.

9. Profit obtained from exploitation of the communications system shall be distributed among Members of the Organization proportionally to the amount of their contributions. Upon the decision of the Members of the Organization the profit may be utilized to increase the statutory fund or to establish any special funds.

10. Expenditure for the upkeep of participants in conferences and meetings connected with the carrying out of tasks of the Organization, including meetings of the Council, shall be covered by the Contracting Countries with delegate their representatives to such conferences or meetings.

Article 16

1. The Organization shall exploit the cosmic complex, offering communications channels to its Members and to other users, in accordance with the provisions of the present Agreement.

2. The communications channels which are at the disposal of the Organization shall be distributed among the Members of the Organization according to their need for channels. Communications channels over and above the general needs of all Members of the Organization may be leased to other users.

3. Communications channels shall be furnished for payment according to tariffs established by the Council. The amount of the tariffs should be at the level of average world tariffs calculated in gold francs.

The procedure for the settlement (of accounts) for communications services shall be determined by the Council.

Article 17

1. Any Contracting Party may denounce the present Agreement, sending written notification of this to the depositary government.

The denunciation of the Agreement by such a Contracting Party shall enter into force after the expiry of the financial year in which the term of a year expires from the date of notification of the depositary Government of that denunciation. Such a Contracting Party should pay, by the dates established by the Council, the amount of the contributions determined for it for the financial year in which the denunciation enters into force, and also fulfil all other financial obligations which it has taken upon itself.

2. The amount of financial compensation to the Contracting Party which has denounced the Agreement shall be determined by the Council in accordance with the amount of the contributions of that Contracting Party to the statutory fund of the Organization, taking into consideration the physical and moral using up of basic resources. The financial compensation shall be paid after approval by the Council of the report on the budget for the financial year in which the denunciation enters into force.

Article 18

1. The present Agreement may be terminated with the agreement of all the Contracting Parties.

Termination of the Agreement means the liquidation of the Organization.

The procedure for liquidation of the Organization shall be determined by the Council.

2. In the case of liquidation of the Organization its basic resources shall be realized and the Members of the Organization shall be paid financial compensation in accordance with their contribution share in the capital expenditure for the establishment of the communications system, taking into consideration the physical and moral using up of basic resources. The working capital on hand, with the exception of the portion allotted for paying off of obligations of the Organization, shall be distributed between the Members of the Organization proportionally to the actual financial contributions made by the date of liquidation of the Organization.

Article 19

The languages of the Organization shall be English, Spanish, Russian and French.

The extent to which the languages are used shall be decided by the Council depending upon the actual needs of the Organization.

Article 20

1. The present Agreement shall be open for signature until 31 December 1972 at Moscow.

2. The Agreement shall be subject to ratification. The instruments of ratification shall be deposited for safekeeping with the Government of the USSR, which shall be appointed depositary of the present Agreement.

Article 21

The Agreement shall enter into force after the deposition for safekeeping of six instruments of ratification.

Article 22

1. The Government of any state that has not signed the present Agreement

may accede to it. In such a case the Government shall make an official declaration to the Council of the Organization that it shares the aims and principles of the activities of the Organization and takes upon itself the responsibilities arising from the present Agreement.

2. Documents concerning accession to the Agreement shall be deposited with the depositary Government.

Article 23

For Governments which deposit the instruments of ratification or documents concerning accession for safekeeping after entry into force of the present Agreement, it shall enter into force on the date of deposition of the indicated acts for safekeeping.

Article 24

Amendments to the present Agreement shall enter into force for each Contracting Party which adopts these amendments after approval by two thirds of the Contracting Parties. The amendment which has entered into force shall become mandatory for other Contracting Parties after they have adopted such an amendment.

Article 25

1. The depositary Government of the present Agreement shall notify all the Contracting Parties of the date of every signature, the date of deposition for safekeeping of each instrument of ratification and each document concerning accession, the date of entry into force of the Agreement, and also of all other notifications received by it.

2. The present Agreement shall be registered by the depositary Government in accordance with article 102 of the Charter of the United Nations.

Article 26

The present Agreement, the Russian, English, Spanish and French texts of which shall be equally authentic, shall be deposited for safekeeping in the archives of the depositary Government. Certified true copies of the Agreement shall be dispatched in the proper manner to the Contracting Parties by the depositary Government.

In witness whereof the duly authorized plenipotentiaries have signed the present Agreement.

Done at Moscow, on 15 November 1971.

XIX. STATUTE OF THE ORGANIZATION FOR COOPERATION OF RAILWAYS*

With the purpose of the further development of international contacts and scientific-technical cooperation in the sphere of rail and automobile transport and highways, the Ministers in charge of railways in the following countries:

The People's Republic of Albania, the People's Republic of Bulgaria, the Hungarian People's Republic, the Democratic Republic of Vietnam, the German Democratic Republic, the Chinese People's Republic, the Democratic People's Republic of Korea, the Mongolian People's Republic, the Polish People's Republic, the Rumanian People's Republic, the Union of Soviet Socialist Republics and the Czechoslovak Socialist Republic,

Have established by this Statute the Organization for Cooperation of Railways (OCR).

Article I

Tasks of the Organization

The basic tasks of the Organization for Cooperation of Railways shall be:

1. The conducting of business arising out of Agreements on international passenger and freight communications (AIPC—AIFC) and out of regulations and official instructions connected with them.

The drawing up of tariffs of international railway communications, the organization of working out of the most rational international routes, the co-ordination of international transport plans, the improvement of the working of boundary railway stations and their development, and also the co-ordination of problems connected with the building and reconstruction of railway lines and highways of international importance.

2. The solution of problems concerned with the most economical utilization of rolling-stock, the speeding up of traffic flow and the improvement of train time-tables in international communications.

3. The organization of scientific and technical co-operation and exchange of experience in the field of railway transport, automobile transport and highways, including the co-ordination of the activities of scientific research institutes and construction project bureaux.

4. The study and co-ordination of problems connected with the unification of the gabarits of rolling-stock, the outer construction of rails, equipment of the SCB, and signals and rules of usage, and the conducting of work on the introduction of the most perfect kinds of traction.

5. The working out of problems connected with the development and exploitation of automobile transport and highways.

6. Cooperation with other international organizations concerned with problems of rail and automobile transport and highways.

---

* Statute signed in June 1956, as amended in June 1962. Translation by the author. Russian text in P. A. Tokareva (ed.), *Mnogostoronnieje ekonomicheskoe sotrudnichestvo* . . . , *op. cit.*, pp. 322–325; Polish text in B. Reutt (ed.), *Podstawowe dokumenty* . . . , *op. cit.*, pp. 360–363.

Article II

The Conference of Ministers

1. The leading organ of the Organization for Cooperation of Railways shall be the Conference of Ministers.

2. The Conference of Ministers shall hold a session each year for the purpose of consideration and adoption of decisions in the sphere of the questions named in article I and other matters which arise in international co-operation and in scientific and technical co-operation in the field of rail and automobile transport and highways.

The Conference of Ministers shall approve the programme of work of the Committee of the Organization for Cooperation of Railways, the staffing plan and the annual budget.

3. Sessions of the Conference of Ministers shall be held in turn in each of the countries named in the preamble.

4. The Ministers shall implement the decisions adopted by the Conference of Ministers within the limits of the powers granted them by the legislation of their countries. Decisions regarding questions lying beyond the limits of the powers granted to the Ministers shall be subject to approval by the Governments concerned.

5. Decisions at a session of the Conference of Ministers shall be adopted unanimously by the participating Ministers.

Article III

The Committee of the Organization for Cooperation of Railways

1. The Committee of the Organization for Cooperation of Railways (henceforth called "the Committee") shall be the executive organ of the Conference of Ministers.

2. The Committee shall ensure the activity of the Organization in periods between sessions of the Conference of Ministers.

3. The membership of the Committee shall include one representative of each country member of the OCR.

The Committee shall be headed by the Chairman, Deputies of the Chairman and the Secretary, approved by the Conference of Ministers from among the members of the Committee. The distribution of the positions of Chairmen of the Commissions and counsellors among the members of the OCR shall be determined by the session of the Conference of Ministers.

4. The Committee shall publish a Bulletin of the Organization for Co-operation of Railways.

5. The organizational structure, the purview of rights and duties, the order of work and adoption of decisions of the Committee shall be approved by the Conference of Ministers upon submission by the Committee.

Article IV

The Commissions and other Organs of the Committee

1. For the fulfilment of the tasks named in article I, the following Commissions of the Committee shall be established:

for International Passenger Communications;
for International Freight Communications;
for Tariff-Economic Problems;
for Problems of Exploitation;
for Problems of Gabarits and Wagons;
for Problems of Equipment of the SCB and Signal Equipment;
for Problems of Traction and Electrification;
for Problems of Rails and Engineering Installations;
for Problems of Automobile Transport and Highways.

2. For the solution of individual problems, the Committee shall have the right, with the agreement of the Conference of Ministers, to establish other Commissions and permanent working groups. It may establish on its own temporary working groups of experts.

Article V

Financial Questions

1. The financing of the upkeep of the Committee and its Commissions and the publication of the Buletin of the OCR shall be carried out by the members of the OCR, who shall make membership contributions for this purpose.

2. The amount of membership contributions shall be determined by the Conference of Ministers, taking into consideration the length of the railways.

3. The budget of the Committee shall be drafted for a year and approved by the Conference of Ministers together with the work programme of the Committee. The report on the execution of the budget for the expired year shall be subject to approval by the Conference of Ministers.

4. Each member of the OCR shall pay its membership contribution not later than two months after receiving pertinent notification from the Committee.

5. The Chairman shall be the administrator of appropriations of the Committee, and in his absence one of the Deputies of the Chairman or the Secretary.

Article VI

The Headquarters of the Committee

The Committee shall be located in one of the countries named in the preamble.

The Headquarters of the Committee shall be determined by the Conference of Ministers every five years.

Article VII

Procedure for Acceptance of New Members

The acceptance of new members shall be carried out by the Conference of Ministers upon the proposal of the Committee.

Article VIII

Entry into force of the Statute

The present Statute shall be subject to ratification by all the Governments of the countries named in the preamble. It shall enter into force three months after the date on which it is ratified by the Governments.

Article IX

Procedure for Amendment of the Statute and Withdrawal from the Organization

1. Amendments to the present Statute may be made by the Conference of Ministers.
2. Any member of the OCR shall have the right to withdraw from the present Organization.
3. Notice of withdrawal from the Organization shall be given to the Committee at least six months before the expiry of the calendar year.

Article X

Final Provision

The present Statute has been drawn up in the Chinese, German and Russian languages. The texts in those languages are equally authentic. In the case of varying interpretation of the texts, the precise meaning shall be arrived at on the basis of the text in the Russian language.

XX. AGREEMENT CONCERNING THE ESTABLISHMENT OF AN ORGANIZATION FOR COOPERATION OF THE SOCIALIST COUNTRIES IN THE FIELD OF TELECOMMUNICATIONS AND POSTAL COMMUNICATIONS*

Recognizing the necessity for the further expanding and strengthening of cooperation between socialist countries in the field of communications with a view to developing telecommunications and postal communications, the Ministers in charge of communications problems in the People's Republic of Albania, the People's Republic of Bulgaria, the Hungarian People's Republic, the Democratic Republic of Vietnam, the German Democratic Republic, the People's Republic of China, the Democratic People's Republic of Korea, the Mongolian People's Republic, the Polish People's Republic, the Rumanian People's Republic, the Union of Soviet Socialist Republics and the Czechoslovak Republic, have deemed it expedient to establish an "Organization for Co-operation of the Socialist Countries in the Field of Telecommunications and Postal Communications," called the "OCC."

Article I

Tasks of the Organization

The tasks of the Organization are:

1. The improvement of exploitation and extending of telegraph and telephone communications between the socialist countries.

2. The perfecting of the organization of the existing networks of tele-communications and postal communications between the socialist countries.

3. The co-ordination of problems relating to the planning and construction of radio relay, cable and aerial communications lines; the working out of technical conditions, standards and norms for communications equipment and cables.

4. The working out and execution of technical measures ensuring reciprocal interchange of television and radio broadcasts and also the most economic methods of radiophonization.

5. The expanding of postal exchange and the preparation of recommendations on the introduction into the postal service of advanced methods of work organization and mechanization.

6. The co-ordinating of tariffs for communications services between the socialist countries.

7. The co-ordinating of activities in the field of scientific-technical co-operation and scientific research work, including the activities of scientific research institutes and design and construction bureaux.

8. The co-ordinating of activities in the sphere of distribution and use of radio frequency.

9. The co-ordinating of activities in the field of ionospheric service and

---

* Translation by the author. Polish text in B. Reutt (ed.), *Podstawowe dokumenty...*, *op. cit.*, pp. 477–481. The Russian text in P. A. Tokareva (ed.), *Mnogostoronnieje ekonomicheskoe sotrudnichestvo...*, *op. cit.*, pp. 373–377 does not reproduce the complete agreement.

of the organization of regular mutual exchange regarding data on the ionosphere and data in the sphere of transmitting radio waves.

10. The rendering of help in the perfecting and development of communications facilities of individual members of the Organization at their request.

11. The co-ordinating of activities in international communications organizations.

Article II

Membership

The members of the Organization shall be the communications administrations of the socialist countries which have expressed the desire to participate in its work and have signed the present Agreement or acceded to it.

Article III

Conference of Ministers

1. The activities of the Organization shall be directed by the Conference of Ministers in charge of communications problems in the socialist countries.

2. Sessions of the Conference shall be convened every year, if necessary, to examine problems on the agenda and to pass respective resolutions. Each session shall determine the place and date of the convocation of the next session of the Conference.

In determining the dates of the convocation of the regular session of the Conference, the work schedule of the other international organizations should be taken into consideration.

3. In the event of necessity special sessions of the Conference may be convened by consent of two-thirds of the members of the Organization.

4. Ordinary sessions of the Conference shall be held in countries whose communications administrations are members of the Organization. The communications administration extending the invitation shall carry out the preparation of problems for the agenda and the organization of the conducting of the session of the Conference.

The special sessions of the Conference shall be held in the country whose communications administration submits the proposal to convene such a Conference.

5. Regional Conferences of Ministers may be convened in order to examine individual problems of regional significance upon the recommendation of the session of the Conference or on the initiative of communications administrations of members of the Organization.

Agreement upon the place and date of convocation of such a Conference shall be realized through the intermediary of the communications administration of the country in which the regular session of the Conference is scheduled to take place.

6. Decisions at sessions of the Conference shall be passed unanimously. Recommendations on technical problems and problems of exploitation shall be passed by majority of votes.

7. The Ministers shall carry out decisions passed by the Conference within the bounds of the competences and rights granted to them by internal legislation.

Decisions on problems outwith the bounds of their competences and rights shall be subject to approval by the Governments.

8.   The Conference will work in accordance with the accepted rules of procedure.

Article IV

The activities of the Organization between sessions

1.   In the period between sessions of the Conference of Ministers the activities of the Organization shall be assured by the communications administration of the country in which the regular session is to be convened.

2.   Any communications administration that is member of the Organization may, on its own initiative or on the instructions of the session of the Conference, take upon itself the preparation of individual questions envisaged in the agenda for the next session.

3.   On the decision of the session of the Conference the preparation of individual technical questions may be entrusted to *ad hoc* working commissions created for that purpose.

4.   For help and the preparation of the regular session or of a special session of the Conference, the communications administration which extends the invitation will, if necessary, convene a Co-ordinative Commission. The Commission shall consist of representatives of the communications administrations that are members of the Organization which express the wish at a session to participate in its work.

The Chairman of the Co-ordinative Commission shall be the Minister in charge of communications problems in the country in which the regular session of the Conference is to be convened.

Article V

Expenses of the Organization

1.   Expenses connected with the conducting of a session of the Conference shall be borne by the communications administration of the country in which the session takes place.

2.   Expenses connected with the realization of scientific-technical co-operation, the co-ordination of the activities of scientific research institutes, ionospheric services and the lending of other kinds of assistance shall be determined by agreement between the interested communications administrations.

3.   Expenses connected with the upkeep of participants in the sessions of the Conference of Ministers, *ad hoc* working commissions, and the Co-ordinative Commission, and expenses connected with the delegating of specialists, shall be borne by each communications administration which delegates its representatives.

Article VI

Languages

1.   In the work of the Organization the Chinese, German, Russian and French languages shall be used.

2.   The working documents of the session of the Conference shall be drawn up in the German and Russian languages.

3. The final acts of the sessions of the Conference, subject to signature by its participants, shall be drawn up in the Chinese, German and Russian languages.

4. For oral translations the Chinese, German, Russian and French languages shall be used. Every delegation shall also have the right to use other languages.

In such a case the delegation shall itself undertake measures to provide a translation of speeches into one of the above-mentioned languages.

Article VII

Cooperation with other international organizations

The Organization shall realize cooperation and keep contacts with other international organizations of the socialist countries which have a common sphere of activities.

Article VIII

Procedure for admission of new members

Admission of new members shall be carried out at a session of the Conference of Ministers.

Article IX

Withdrawal from the Organization

Any member of the Organization may terminate its participation in the Organization by means of written notification of this of other members. Such notification shall come into force three months after the date of its transmission.

Article X

Final provisions

1. Amendments and supplements to the present Agreement shall be made by the Conference of Ministers.

2. This Agreement is concluded for an indefinite period of time and shall enter into force after its approval by the Governments of the countries enumerated in the preamble to the Agreement. The members of the Organization shall notify the communications administration of the country in which the regular session of the Conference is held of the approval which has taken place, and the session shall notify all the other members of the Organization.

3. The Agreement shall be kept in the archives of the Ministry of Communications of the USSR, which will send, as soon as possible, certified true copies of the Agreement to all its participants.

Drawn up in the Chinese, German and Russian languages. In the case of differences regarding the interpretation of the Agreement the Russian text shall be considered authentic.

Signed at Moscow, on 21 December 1957.

XXI. AGREEMENT CONCERNING THE ESTABLISHMENT OF AN INTERNATIONAL LABORATORY OF STRONG MAGNETIC FIELDS AND LOW TEMPERATURES*

With the aim of conducting theoretical and experimental research in the field of static magnetic fields under conditions of low temperatures,

The Contracting Parties: the Bulgarian Academy of Science, the German Academy of Science in Berlin of the German Democratic Republic, the Polish Academy of Science, the Academy of Science of the Union of Soviet Socialist Republics,

Have agreed as follows:

Article I

1. By the present Agreement the Contracting Parties shall establish an International Laboratory of Strong Magnetic Fields and Low Temperatures, hereinafter referred to as "the International Laboratory."
2. The location of the International Laboratory shall be the city of Wrocław in the Polish People's Republic.

Article II

The activities of the International Laboratory shall be realized in accordance with the present Agreement, signed by all the Contracting Parties, and the Charter of the International Laboratory, approved by its Council.

Article III

The basic tasks of the International Laboratory shall be:

The study of the properties of solid superconductors;
Listing of new superconducting systems;
Research on the form of the surfaces of trusses of metals;
Research on the electronic structure of magnetic materials;
Research on the interactions of magnetic moments of nuclei in a solid body;
Obtaining the lowest temperatures and the development of methods of adiabatic demagnetizing;
The development of methods of creating strong magnetic fields;
The working out of the constructions of non-pivotal electromagnets cooled by water or condensed gases;
The conducting of meteorological work in the field of strong magnetic fields and low temperatures.

The primary task of the International Laboratory shall be the creation of solenoids with a magnetic field intensity of above 100 kOe.

---

* Translation by the author. Russian text in P. A. Tokareva (ed.), *Mnogostoronnieje ekonomicheskoe sotrudnichestvo . . .*, *op. cit.*, pp. 592–598.

Article IV

1. The original members of the International Laboratory shall be the Contracting Parties which have signed the present Agreement.

2. Membership of the International Laboratory shall be open to the scientific organizations of other countries which declare their consent to the provisions of the present Agreement and the Charter* of the International Laboratory and consent to join it.

New members shall be admitted by a unanimous decision of the Council on the basis of official declarations of scientific organizations to the Director of the International Laboratory after obtaining the consent of all the members of the International Laboratory.

Article V

1. All the members of the International Laboratory shall enjoy equal rights to participation in the scientific activities and the management of the International Laboratory.

2. All the members of the International Laboratory pledge to promote its development and the fulfilment of the basic tasks defined in article III of the present Agreement.

Article VI

1. All the activities of the International Laboratory shall be directed by the Council of the International Laboratory and its Director.

2. There shall be not more than two representatives from each member of the International Laboratory on the Council of the International Laboratory. Each member of the International Laboratory shall have one deciding vote in the Council.

The Director and the Deputy Director of the International Laboratory shall sit on the Council with the right to a deliberative vote.

3. The Council may establish its own rules of procedure.

Article VII

1. The Director shall be responsible to the Council for the activities of the International Laboratory and shall be guided by its decisions.

2. The Director shall be elected by the Council upon presentation by the Polish Academy of Science for a term of three years, and may be re-elected for a new term. He may be relieved of the post he holds by decision of the Council.

3. The Deputy Director of the International Laboratory shall be elected by the Council upon presentation by the members of the International Laboratory for a term of two years.

4. The Director and the Deputy Director shall be elected from amongst scientific workers who are citizens of the countries whose scientific organizations are members of the International Laboratory.

Article VIII

1. In the International Laboratory there shall be conducted joint scientific

* Not reproduced here.

303

research, carried out by all its members, and research according to the programmes of one or several members of the International Laboratory on the basis of their requests.

The joint plan of scientific research shall be approved by the Council of the International Laboratory.

2. Publications on the results of all the research conducted in the International Laboratory should contain an indication of the place in which it was conducted.

3. The results of scientific research work shall be set forth in an annual report on the scientific activities of the International Laboratory. The report shall be communicated to the members of the International Laboratory after its acceptance by the Council.

4. Legal protection of inventions and discoveries made in the International Laboratory in connection with the carrying out of joint scientific research, the transfer of such inventions, encouragement and reward of the authors of such inventions and discoveries, and the solution of other problems concerning joint inventions and discoveries shall be realized in accordance with the "Recommendations on Certain Problems of Invention Connected with the Joint Carrying out of Scientific and Technical Research" approved by the X meeting of the Standing Commission of COMECON on the Coordination of Scientific and Technical Research (annex 8 to the protocol of the X meeting of the Commission), and other regulations in force in relations between countries whose scientific organizations are members of the International Laboratory.

5. Legal protection of inventions and discoveries made in connection with the carrying out of research following the programmes of the members of the International Laboratory shall be regulated in accordance with the national legislation of the countries of which the authors are citizens.

Article IX

1. The financing of joint scientific research work carried out in the International Laboratory shall be realized according to the estimates of expenditures approved for each calendar year by the Council of the International Laboratory.

2. Expenditures connected with the carrying out of joint scientific research realized by all the members of the International Laboratory shall be covered on the principle of the contribution shares of all the members of the International Laboratory. The amount of the contribution shares of the Contracting Parties shall be fixed by a special protocol.

The Council of the International Laboratory shall present for approval by the members of the International Laboratory changes in the amounts of contribution shares in cases of the acceptance of members or withdrawal from membership in the International Laboratory.

3. Expenditures connected with the activities of the International Laboratory shall embrace:

(a) the remuneration of the Director, the Deputy Director, the permanent personnel of the International Laboratory and the scientific workers sent to carry out joint work;

(b) the preparation and acquisition of materials, equipment and apparatus necessary for the carrying out of research work;

(c) the repair of equipment;

(d) the cost of electrical energy, heat and water for scientific purposes;

(e) expenditures connected with the obtaining of liquefied gases (nitrogen and helium);

(f) the remuneration of scientific workers and specialists invited to carry out work determined by the Council and give consultations and expert opinions connected with the activities of the International Laboratory;

(g) administrative-management expenses;

(h) other expenditures connected with the activities of the International Laboratory, including: management expenses and expenditures for the repair of buildings and installations.

4. Expenditures connected with the carrying out of research following the programmes of one or several members of the International Laboratory shall be covered solely by the countries concerned on conditions determined by the Council.

5. Each member of the International Laboratory may, with the consent of the Council or the Director, cede the time for work in the International Laboratory planned for it to another member.

6. Questions of the utilization of income obtained as a result of the activities of the International Laboratory shall be decided upon by the Council.

7. The estimates of expenditures of the International Laboratory shall be drawn up in Polish zlotys.

The calculation of Polish zlotys into transferable roubles shall be carried out in accordance with the recommendation of the IV meeting of the Standing Commission of COMECON on Monetary and Financial problems "On the Procedure for the Realization of Settlements of Expenditures incurred at Internal Prices and Tariffs of the Member States of COMECON for the Construction of Separate Objects and the Maintenance of Scientific Research Institutions and other Organizations" (annex 4 to the protocol of the IV meeting of the Commission).

8. The cost of equipment, apparatus, and materials supplied by the Parties, in accordance with the plan approved by the Council and at foreign trade prices in effect between the countries whose scientific organizations are members of the International Laboratory, may be counted as part of the contribution shares of the members of the International Laboratory in expenditures connected with its activities.

Article X

1. Expenses connected with the sojourn of scientific workers sent to conduct joint work shall be covered by the International Laboratory. The amount of expenses for workers who are not citizens of the country in which the International Laboratory is located shall be determined in accordance with regulations applied in relations between the Polish Academy of Science and the respective member of the International Laboratory.

2. Expenses connected with the sojourn in the International Laboratory of scientific workers and specialists sent to conduct scientific research in accordance with the programmes of one or several of the members of the International Laboratory shall be covered by those members of the International Laboratory which sent them.

3.   The number of scientific workers sent in accordance with the programme of each member of the International Laboratory, and also the duration of their work in the International Laboratory, shall be established by the Council.

Article XI

To realize audit of the financial and economic activities of the International Laboratory, the Council shall appoint an Audit Commission.

Article XII

1.   The Polish Academy of Science shall place at the disposal of the International Laboratory the premises necessary for its activities and also equipment in accordance with annex I to the present Agreement.*

2.   The Bulgarian Academy of Science, the German Academy of Science in Berlin of the German Democratic Republic and the Academy of Science of the Union of Soviet Socialist Republics shall place single contributions in transferable roubles, in accordance with annex 2 to the present Agreement,** at the disposal of the International Laboratory to ensure that it is put into operation. The indicated single contributions shall be earmarked for the acquisition of equipment, apparatus and materials.

3.   The list of equipment, apparatus and materials necessary to put the International Laboratory into operation, which should be acquired at the expense of the single contributions, shall be determined by the Council of the International Laboratory.

4.   The above-mentioned Parties may put on account of their single contribution apparatus, instruments and materials, whose value shall be determined according to foreign trade prices in effect between countries whose scientific organizations are members of the International Laboratory.

5.   The Council of the International Laboratory shall determine the amount of initial single contributions of new members of the International Laboratory.

Article XIII

The International Laboratory shall possess juridical personality.

Article XIV

In matters connected with the activities of the Interntional Laboratory on the territory of the Polish People's Republic, the legislation of the Polish People's Republic shall apply, unless it is otherwise provided for by the present Agreement and the Charter of the International Laboratory.

Article XV

The official languages of the International Laboratory shall be the languages

---

*   Not reproduced here.
**   Not reproduced here.

of the countries whose scientific organizations are members of the International Laboratory.

The working language shall be Russian.

Article XVI

1. The Agreement has been concluded for an indefinite period.

2. Each member of the International Laboratory may withdraw from participation in the Agreement. Notice of withdrawal from membership in the International Laboratory shall be given in writing to the Director of the International Laboratory not later than six months before the expiry of the calendar year. Membership shall cease on 31 December of that year.

The Council shall settle the problem of the amount and procedure of compensation in cash for the Party withdrawing from membership of the International Laboratory, taking into consideration the depreciation of the apparatus, machines and equipment furnished or acquired as part of the contributions of that Party.

Article XVII

1. The International Laboratory may be dissolved by consent of all its members.

2. The Council shall settle all problems connected with the dissolution of the International Laboratory.

Article XVIII

1. The present Agreement shall come into force on the date of its signature by all the Contracting Parties.

2. With respect to each Party which is subsequently admitted for the first time, the Agreement shall come into force as from the date of the taking of the decision by the Council to admit the Party to membership of the International Laboratory.

3. Each member of the International Laboratory may make proposals for the amendment of the present Agreement.

The Agreement may be amended only with the consent of all members of the International Laboratory.

Article XIX

1. The present Agreement has been drawn up in a single copy in the Russian language.

2. The Agreement shall be deposited with the Polish Academy of Science, which shall send true certified copies of the Agreement of all the Contracting Parties and perform the other functions of depositary.

In witness whereof the representatives of the Contracting Parties have signed the present Agreement.

Done at Wrocław, on 11 May 1968.

XXII. AGREEMENT CONCERNING THE ESTABLISHMENT OF THE INTERNATIONAL MATHEMATICAL CENTRE "STEFAN BANACH" IN WARSAW FOR THE RAISING OF THE QUALIFICATIONS OF SCIENTIFIC CADRES*

The Bulgarian Academy of Science, the Hungarian Academy of Science, the German Academy of Science in Berlin, the Polish Academy of Science, the Academy of the Socialist Republic of Rumania, the Academy of Science of the Union of Soviet Socialist Republics, the Czechoslovak Academy of Science,

Mindful of the benefits of the development of scientific cooperation between the socialist countries in the field of mathematics and its applications,

Recognizing the usefulness of joint cooperation in the perfecting of mathematical cadres,

Being guided by the common principles of cooperation of the socialist countries, and also bearing in mind the Agreement concerning Multilateral Scientific Cooperation between the Academies of Science of the Socialist Countries, signed at Moscow on 15 December 1971,

Have resolved to conclude the present Agreement.

Article 1

By the present Agreement there shall be established, on the basis of the Mathematical Institute of the Polish Academy of Science, the International Mathematical Centre "Stefan Banach" for the raising of the qualifications of scientific cadres, hereinafter referred to as "the Centre."

The location of the Centre shall be the city of Warsaw in the Polish People's Republic.

Article 2

The basic purpose of the Centre shall be the raising of the qualifications of scientific cadres, already prepared by the countries whose Academies of Science are participants in the present Agreement, in the most urgent fields of mathematics and its applications.

Article 3

In order to achieve the aim indicated in article 2, the Centre shall:

Organize short-term and long-term specialized courses, training periods, seminars, symposia, summer schools, colloquia, scientific conferences and other meetings of specialists;

Accept mathematicians, on the basis of proposals from the Academies of Science concerned, for the giving of lectures, participation in seminars and other undertakings, conducting of scientific research and undergoing of a training period;

Engage in research, mindful of the necessity of unity of the processes of teaching and research, and also in scientific-information activities.

* Translation by the author. Russian text in P. A. Tokareva (ed.), *Mnogostoron-nieje ekonomicheskoe sotrudnichestvo . . . , op. cit.*, pp. 612–616.

The subjects, scope and forms of the activities of the Centre shall be determined by its work programme, approved in accordance with article 8 for a period of one year or longer.

Article 4

1. Mathematicians sent by the Academies of Science which are participants in the present Agreement shall take part in the work of the Centre, among them:

Those in charge of seminars and research groups, and those giving lectures;
Those undergoing a training period at the Centre;
Participants in conferences, symposia and other scientific undertakings conducted by the Centre.

2. With the consent of the Scientific Council, mathematicians from other countries may also participate in the work of the Centre.

Article 5

The Academies of Science which are participants in the Agreement shall be under an obligation to further in every way possible the successful development of the activities of the Centre, especially by means of the selection and sending to the Centre of mathematicians from institutions of the Academies of Science, and also from scientific institutions not belonging to the Academies.

Article 6

The Centre shall not possess juridical personality. In legal matters the Mathematical Institute of the Polish Academy of Science shall represent the Centre before other organizations.

Article 7

1. The activities of the Centre shall be directed by the Scientific Council of the Centre and by the Director of the Centre.
2. The Director of the Mathematical Institute of the Polish Academy of Science shall be Director of the Centre. In case of necessity for the realization of his activities, the Director of the Centre may have one or two deputies, appointed in turn by the Scientific Council upon the proposal of the Academies of Science which are participants in the Agreement.
3. The Director of the Centre shall represent the Centre in relations with the Academies of Science which are participants in the Agreement, and also in relations with other respective institutions.
4. The Director of the Centre shall:

Ensure the carrying out of decisions of the Scientific Council;
Work out the draft work plans of the Centre and present them to the Scientific Council;
Prepare a report on the activities of the Centre for the expired year for presentation to the Scientific Council;

Ensure the preparation, summoning and conducting of meetings of the Scientific Council;

Make proposals to the Academies of Science which are participants in the Agreement concerning the delegating of scientists in the field of mathematics to ensure the activities of the Centre in accordance with its programme;

Carry out other work in accordance with the present Agreement and the decisions of the Scientific Council.

Article 8

1. The Scientific Council shall be established by the Academies of Science which are participants in the Agreement with the aim of defining jointly the direction of the activities of the Centre, its scientific-research and instruction programme.

Each Academy of Science which is a participant in the Agreement shall appoint two representatives to the Scientific Council.

The Director of the Centre shall be member of the Scientific Council *ex officio*.

Each Academy of Science which is a participant in the Agreement shall have one vote in the Scientific Council.

The Scientific Council shall choose a chairman from among its own membership. The Chairman of the Scientific Council shall be elected in turn from among the representatives of the Academies of Science which are participants in the Agreement in order of the names of the countries according to the Russian alphabet.

2. The Scientific Council shall:

Determine the most urgent fields of mathematics and its applications for individual periods of specialization;

Approve the work programmes for individual periods presented by the Director of the Centre;

Approve the organizational committees for the individual fields chosen for the periods of specialization and for other undertakings of the Centre;

Examine and approve the annual reports presented by the Director of the Centre;

Examine other questions concerning the activities of the Centre, arising out of the present Agreement.

3. Meetings of the Scientific Council shall be held not less than once a year. The Scientific Council may hold its meetings if not less than two thirds of the Academies of the Science which are participants in the Agreement are represented at them.

The Scientific Council should aim at unanimous adoption of its decisions. If unanimity is not achieved, decisions shall be considered to be adopted when they obtain not less than two thirds of the votes of the Academies of Science which are participants in the Agreement.

Decisions of the Scientific Council shall not be mandatory for those Academies of Science which do not opt for their adoption, but these Academies of Science may, however, later accede to the decisions adopted.

Non-participation of one or several Academies of Science in certain undertakings should not hinder the realization of cooperation between the remaining
Academies of Science.

4. The Scientific Council shall establish the rules of procedure for its
work.

Article 9

1. Mathematicians participating in the work of the Centre shall retain
personal copyright to results obtained in accordance with the legislation of
their country.

2. Publication of the results of research carried out in the Centre should
contain indications of the place in which it was conducted.

Article 10

1. The Polish Academy of Science shall furnish the Centre with the
necessary official premises and administrative services, and also provide for the
maintenance and development of the library of the Centre.

2. Expenses connected with the sending out of members of the Scientific
Council, and the sending out and maintenance of participants in the work of
the Centre, shall be covered by the Academy of Science which sends them.

Expenses connected with the holding of meetings of the Scientific Council
shall be taken over by the Polish Academy of Science.

3. Participants in the work of the Centre shall be provided by the Polish
Academy of Science with living quarters and free medical service in accordance
with the legislation of the Polish People's Republic.

Rent and municipal services shall be paid for in accordance with the
regulations and rates in effect in the country in which the Centre is located.

4. If necessary, the conditions envisaged in paragraphs 1 and 2 of the
present article may be changed by the Academies of Science which are participants in the Agreement, taking into consideration the experience accumulated
and the work prospects of the Centre, by means of approval of a supplementary
protocol to the present Agreement.

Article 11

1. With the consent of all the Academies of Science which are participants
in the Agreement, other Academies of Science and respective scientific
institutions, which share its aims and take upon themselves the responsibilities
arising out of the present Agreement, may accede to the present Agreement.

2. The instruments of accession shall be deposited for safekeeping with
the Academy of Science that is depositary of the present Agreement.

Accession shall be considered to have taken place after the depositary
has received the consent to the accession of all the Academies of Science which
are participants in the Agreement.

Article 12

The languages of the countries whose Academies of Science participate in the present Agreement shall be the official languages of the Centre.

The working language shall be Russian. If necessary, other languages may also be used as a working language.

Article 13

1. The present Agreement shall be concluded for an indefinite period.

2. The Agreement may be amended with the consent of all the Academies of Science which are participants in the Agreement.

3. Each Academy of Science may withdraw from participation in the present Agreement, notifying the depositary of this not less than six months in advance.

Article 14

The present Agreement shall be subject to approval in accordance with the procedure established in the countries whose Academies of Science have signed the Agreement. The instruments of approval shall be deposited with the depositary within three months from the data on which the Agreement was signed.

The Agreement shall enter into force, for those Academies of Science which have notified the depositary of its approval, three months from the date on which it was signed.

Article 15

The present Agreement shall be deposited for safekeeping with the Polish Academy of Science, which shall perform the functions of depositary.

Signed on 13 January 1972 at Warsaw in one copy in the Russian language.

Certified true copies of the present Agreement shall be sent by the depositary to all the Academies of Science which participate in the Agreement.

SUBJECT INDEX

Agromash, 125
Albania, xviii, 4, 6–8, 14, 17, 40, 50–52, 91, 132–133, 141–142
Algeria, xxv, 40
Asian Development Bank, 104
Assofoto, 125
Australia, xv, xviii, 164
Austria, xxv, 5, 37, 54, 148

"Brezhnev doctrine"—see under Warsaw Treaty Organization
Bulgaria, xxv, 6, 9, 11, 17, 20, 26, 32–33, 48, 51, 68, 80, 84, 86, 106, 111, 113–114, 125–127, 135, 137–138, 143–144, 146, 152, 159
Bureau for the Coordination of Ship Freighting—see under Council for Mutual Economic Assistance

Cambodia, xi, 10
Central Commission for Navigation on the Rhine, xxi
Central Treaty Organization (CENTO), xix
Centre for Industrial Development of the Arab States, 98
Centre for Research on New Methods of the Use of Coal, xxv
Chile, 10, 42
China, 9, 10, 11, 17, 53, 60, 96–97, 132–133, 141–142, 148, 149, 157, 161
Communist Information Bureau (Cominform), xxvi–xxvii, 148
Communist International (Comintern), xxvi–xxvii, 152, 154, 163
Communist international governmental organizations:
Composition (individual bodies), xxiv–xxv

Future, xxiv, 45, 101–102, 159–160, 163
Hierarchy, xxviii–xxix
Semi-autonomous bodies, xxiv
Stages of development, xxii–xxiii, 147–153
Communist international non-governmental organizations, ix, xxvi–xxvii
Communist Party of the Soviet Union (CPSU), 4, 10, 26, 44, 74–75, 149
Conference on Security and Cooperation in Europe (CSCE)—see under Warsaw Treaty Organization
Coordination Centre for Sea and Ocean Research, xxv
Coordination Centre for Synthetic Leather, xxv
Council for Mutual Economic Assistance (Comecon)
Albania and Comecon, 50–52, 91
Amendments to the Charter, 50–51
Argentina and Comecon, 58–59
Austria and Comecon, 54
Basic Principles of International Socialist Division of Labour (1962), 59, 71–72, 93, 157
Budget
Amount, 67–68
Scale of assessments, 68
Bulgaria and Comecon, 48, 51, 68, 80, 84–86
Bureau for Integrated Problems of the Economic Plans (liquidated in 1971), 61
Bureau for the Coordination of Ship Freighting, xxv, xxix, 70
Charter, 49–51, 53–54, 60–65, 71, 103
China and Comecon, 53, 96–97
Columbia and Comecon, 58

Comecon in the future, 101–102, 159–160, 163
Comecon, stages of development, 93–94
Committee for Cooperation in the Field of Planning, 61, 63, 78–79, 83, 115
Committee for Scientific and Technical Cooperation, 61, 63, 79, 82–83, 85, 141
Committee for Cooperation in the Field of Material and Technical Supplies, 61, 63
Comprehensive Programme for the Further Deepening and Perfecting of Cooperation and Development of Socialist Economic Integration of Member Countries of Comecon (1971): xxiv, 54, 62, 71–78, 90–91, 94–96, 101, 104–105, 110–111, 122, 151, 159
    Basic provisions, 74–77
    Delays in realization, 90–91, 95–96, 101, 110–111, 159
    Provisions for the creation of new international organizations, xxiv, 104–105
    Provisions for participation of other countries, 54
Conference of the Chiefs of the Labour Authorities, 63
Conference of the Chiefs of the Patent Authorities, 63
Conference of the Chiefs of the Pricing Authorities, 63
Conference of the Chiefs of the Water Resources Authorities, 63
Conference of the member countries of Comecon for Legal Problems, 63, 91
Conference of Ministers of Internal Trade, 63, 151
Conference of Party and Government Leaders, 59–60
Conference of Representatives of the Freight and Shipping Organizations, 63, 70
Conference of the Representatives of the Countries in the Council (liquidated in 1962), 61

Coordination of national economic plans, 72, 76–79
Council for the Protection and Improvement of the Environment, xxiv, 83
Creation of Comecon, reasons for: official, 46–47
    real, 46–48, 93, 148
Cuba and Comecon, 52–53, 68, 77, 85–86, 95
Czechoslovakia and Comecon, 47–49, 51, 68, 73, 80, 84–85, 88–89, 94
Decisions (category of resolutions), 63–65
Difficulties, 88, 94–95, 109–111
Dumping practices, 46, 101–102
Duration of Charter, 59
East Germany and Comecon, 52, 60, 66, 68, 80, 83–89, 94
Environmental Protection, 82–83
European Community and Comecon, 98–99
Executive Board, 52–53, 60–61, 63, 67, 69–71, 78–79, 82–85, 90–92, 107, 111, 113, 123, 127
Far East and Comecon, 85
Finland and Comecon, 54–57
Five-year plan of multilateral integration measures, 79
Founding communiqué (1949), 48–49
Hungary and Comecon, 94, 99, 126–128, 134, 136, 140–141, 143
India and Comecon, 57
Institute for Standardization, xxv, xxix, 68–70
Integration, economic: long-range aims, 150–151, 159–160
International arbitration organ, proposed, 62
International Institute for the Economic Problems of the World Socialist System, xxvi, xxix, 70–71
International officials, 66–67
Iran and Comecon, 58
Iraq and Comecon, 57
Joint investments, 73, 83–86
Languages (official and working), 67, 70–71

Legal cooperation, 91–92
Manpower exchanges, 86–87, 160
Membership, 51–59
Mexico and Comecon, 57–58
Mongolia and Comecon, 52–53, 59, 68, 77, 85, 95
North Korea and Comecon, 50, 53, 60
North Vietnam and Comecon, 53, 60, 95
Notice of withdrawal, 59
Poland and Comecon, 48, 51, 66, 68, 73, 83–88, 90, 94, 97, 101
Polish-East German subregional integration, 86–88
"Politization" of Comecon, 95
Pricing problems, 88–91
Recommendations (category of resolutions), 63–66
Rumania and Comecon, 48, 51, 68, 74, 76, 79–80, 84–85, 101.
Scholarship fund, 93
Secretariat, 48, 64, 66–67, 69–71, 93
Secretary (and Assistant Secretaries), 64, 66–67, 69, 71
Session of the Council, 49–53, 55, 59–61, 63, 67–69, 71–73, 78–79, 81, 85, 93, 95, 97, 105, 129, 150, 152
Specialization and cooperation in production, 72–73, 76, 79–81
Specialization and cooperation in the field of scientific and technical research, 73, 76, 81–82
Stages of development, 93–94
Standing Commissions, 62–63, 69–70, 85, 93, 105, 127, 142
"Supranationalism", 75–76, 93–94, 157
United Nations and Comecon, 98
USSR and Comecon, 46–49, 51, 56–57, 59, 66, 68, 72, 73–74, 77, 79, 83–86, 88–89, 100–101
Voting, 64–65
World trade, Comecon's share, 94–95
WTO and Comecon, xii, 24–25, 74, 101, 148
Yemen (People's Democratic Republic of) and Comecon, 58

Yugoslavia and Comecon, 46–47, 52–53, 60, 79, 83
Council of Europe, xix
Cuba, xi, 32–34, 52–53, 68, 85–86, 95, 107, 120, 135, 137, 151
Czechoslovakia, xxv, 2–4, 6–8, 11, 15, 17, 20, 26, 31–33, 40–41, 47–49, 51, 68, 73, 80, 84–85, 88–89, 94, 101, 106, 111, 113–114, 121–122, 127–128, 135, 137–138, 144, 146–147, 150, 153, 157–159, 161

Danube Commission, xxi, xxv
Denmark, xxiii, 37

East Germany (German Democratic Republic), 3–4, 6, 11, 17, 26–27, 30–33, 38, 41, 43, 52, 60, 66, 68, 80, 83–89, 94, 106, 111, 113–114, 125–128, 135, 137–138, 143–144, 146, 158–159, 161
Estonia, xviii
European Community (EC), xvii–xviii, 53–56, 66–67, 96–99, 119, 123, 160–161
European Investment Bank, xxii
European Launcher Development Organization (ELDO), xxii, 136, 141
European Organization for Nuclear Research (CERN), xxii, 104, 134
European Railway Waggon Pool (Europ), 112
European Space Agency, 136
European Space Research Organization (ESRO), xxii, 136–137, 141
Eurovision, xxv

Finland, xxv, 54–57, 140, 147–148, 159
Food and Agricultural Organization (FAO), xxiii
France, xviii, 2, 40, 134–135, 146

General Agreement on Tariffs and Trade (GATT), xxiii
Greece, 6, 9, 31

Haldex, 125
Holland, 80

Hungary, xxv, 4, 6–7, 11, 17, 20, 31–32, 48, 51, 68, 80, 84–85, 90, 106, 111, 113–114, 121, 125, 127, 135, 137–138, 144, 146, 153, 156, 159

India, 18, 57

Indonesia, 18, 40

Institute for Standardization—see under Council for Mutual Economic Assistance

Inter-American Development Bank, xxii

Interatomenergo, xxvi, xxix, 127–128

Interatominstrument, xxvi, xxix
    First international economic association, 123–124
    Financing, 125
    Structure, 124–125
    Voting, 65, 124–125

Intercosmos, 135–137, 140–141

Interelectro, xxvi, xxix, 127

Interetalonpribor, xxv, xxix, 129

Intergasoochistka, xxvi, xxix, 129

Interkhim, xxvi, xxix, 117–120

Interkhimvolokno, xxvi, xxix, 129

Intermetall, xxv, xxix, 105, 114–115, 119

International Bank for Economic Cooperation, xxv, xxix
    Activities, 108–111, 125
    Agreements (on establishment and on cooperation with Comecon), 103, 105, 107–108
    Membership, 107
    Structure, 108, 120
    Voting, 108

International Bank for Reconstruction and Development, xxiii, 103–104

International Centre for Electron Microscopy, xxvi, xxix, 146

International Centre for Scientific and Technical Information, xxvi, xxix, 80–81, 105, 115–117

International Centre for Settlement of Investment Disputes, 104

International Centre for the Training of Civil Aviation Personnel, xxvi, xxix, 126–127

International Civil Aviation Organization, xxiii

International Court of Justice, xxiii

International Development Association, 104

International Finance Corporation, 104

International Institute for the Economic Problems of the World Socialist System—see under Council for Mutual Economic Assistance

International Investment Bank
    Activities, 85, 120–122, 125
    Agreements (on establishment and on cooperation with Comecon), 103, 105, 120–121
    Membership, 120
    Structure, 120–121
    Voting, 65, 120–121

International Laboratory for Strong Magnetic Fields and Low Temperatures, xxv, xxix, 143–144

International Labour Organization (ILO), 67

International Mathematical Centre, xxvi, xxix, 65, 138, 144–146

International Monetary Fund, xxiii

International Organization for Scientific and Technical Information in the Field of Black Metallurgy, xxv

International Radio and Television Organization, xxv

International Scientific Research Institute for Managerial Problems, xxvi, xxix

International Telecommunication Union (ITU), 137, 139

International Telecommunications Satellite Consortium (Intelsat), xxii, 136–137

Intersputnik
    Activities, 137–138
    Financing, 139
    Initial communiqué, 137
    Structure, 138–139
    Voting, 65, 138–139

Intertextilmash, xxvi, xxix, 128

Intervision, xxv

Intervodoochistka, xxiv, xxvi, xxix, 129

Iraq, xxv, 57

Israel, xi

Italy, xvii

Japan, xv, 18, 100, 148
Joint Institute for Nuclear Research, xxv, xxix
Activities, 134–135
Financing, 133–134
Membership, 132
Structure, 132–133

Korea, xi, xviii, 10, 147–148, 156

Laos, xi, 10
Latin American Solidarity Organization (LASO), xxvii
Latvia, xviii, 163–164
Lebanon, 40
Lithuania, xviii, 162

Mali, xxv
Marshall Plan, xxiii, 46–48
Middle East, xi-xii, 10
Mongolia, 9, 11, 19, 32, 52–53, 59, 68, 77, 85, 95, 132, 134–135, 137, 141–142, 149, 155

Nordic Council, 98
North Atlantic Treaty Organization (NATO), x-xiii, xix, xxii, 1–3, 5, 12–13, 18, 27–28, 33, 43–44
North Korea, 9, 11, 19, 32, 50, 53, 60, 132, 134, 141–142

Oman, 40
Organization for Cooperation of the Ball-bearing Industry, xxv, xxix, 105, 113–114, 119
Organization for Cooperation of Railways, xxv, xxix, 141–142, 148
Organization for Economic Cooperation and Development (OECD), former OEEC, x-xiii, xix, xxii-xxiii, 46, 53, 67, 93, 148
Organization of American States (OAS), former Pan-American Union, xix, xxi, xxvii
Organization of the Common Waggon Pool, xxv, xxix, 65, 105, 111–112, 119
Organization of the Joint Power Grid, xxv, xxix, 103, 105–107, 119

Poland, xv, 3–4, 6, 11, 14–15, 17, 20, 25–27, 31–33, 35, 37–38, 41, 43, 48, 51, 66, 68, 73, 84–88, 90, 94, 97, 101, 106, 111, 113–114, 121, 124–128, 134–135, 137–138, 140, 143–144, 146, 148, 153, 155–156, 158, 161–163

Rumania, xxiii, xxv, 5–6, 8–9, 11, 14, 17, 19–20, 31–32, 36, 40, 48, 51, 68, 74, 76, 80, 84, 101, 106, 111, 113–114, 117, 120–121, 127, 135, 137–138, 144, 157, 159, 161, 163
Russian language
as the working language in the Organizations, xvii, 67, 70–71, 106, 108, 112–113, 115, 117–118, 121, 134, 140, 143–144, 146
as lingua franca of the bloc, 158

South-East Asia Treaty Organization (SEATO), xxii
South Korea, xviii, 2
Soviet bloc
Disproportion between USSR and the remaining members, xviii
Help from the West, 100–101
Sudan, xxv
Sweden, xxiii
Syria, xxv

Tannu-Tuva, 155
Telecommunications and Postal Communications "Organization," xxv, xxix, 142–143, 145, 148
Transferable rouble, 109–111
Turkey, 6, 9, 148

United Kingdom, xvii, 1–2, 40, 48, 101, 146
United Nations (Organization and Charter), xxiii, 9, 12, 27, 40, 50, 98, 104, 136, 139, 145
United Nations Children (Emergency) Fund (UNICEF), xxiii
United Nations Conference for Trade and Development (UNCTAD), xxiv, 98, 121
United Nations Development Programme (UNDP), xxiii
United Nations Economic Commission for Europe, 98

United Nations Educational, Scientific and Cultural Organization (UNESCO), xxiii, 104, 152
United Nations Industrial Development Organization (UNIDO), xxiv
United States, xvii-xviii, 2, 7, 40, 48, 100, 134, 146, 149
USSR, ix-xii, xvii, xix, xxiii, xxv, 2–7, 11–12, 15, 17, 19–22, 29–33, 36, 41, 43, 45–49, 51, 56–57, 59, 66, 68, 72–74, 77, 84–86, 88–89, 100–101, 103, 106, 111, 113–114, 117, 122, 124–128, 132, 134–137, 140–141, 143–144, 146–150, 152–159, 161–163
Disproportion between her and the rest of the "partners," xvii
Housing situation, 149–150
"Overtaking of the United States," 149
Participation in the Organizations of the UN family, xxiii, 147
Political integration of smaller nations, 161–163
Russification, 95, 158, 163–164

Vietnam, xi, xvii-xviii, 10–11, 16, 30, 41, 53, 60, 95, 123, 132–133, 141–142, 158, 163–164
Viticultural Centre, xxv

Warsaw Treaty Organization (WTO)
Albania and the WTO, 4, 6–8, 14, 17, 40, 50–51, 91
"Brezhnev doctrine," 14, 159
Bulgaria and the WTO, 6, 9, 11, 17, 20, 26, 32–33
Casus foederis, 9–13
China and the WTO, 9, 11, 17
Comecon and the WTO, xii, 24–25, 101, 148
Committee of the Defence Ministers, 22–23
Committee on Internal Security, 25–26
Conference on Security and Cooperation in Europe, xviii, 27–29, 32, 41–42, 95, 99, 159
Conferences of Foreign Ministers (and Deputies), 18–19

Creation, reason for:
official, 1–3
real, 3–4
Cuba and the WTO, 32, 33–34
Czechoslovakia and the WTO, 2–4, 6–8, 11, 15, 17, 20, 26, 31–33, 40–41
Duration of Treaty, 14–15
East Germany and the WTO, 3–4, 6, 11, 17, 26–27, 30–33, 38, 41, 43
"Global ambitions" of the WTO, 42
Hungary and the WTO, 4, 6–7, 11, 17, 20, 31–32
Integration of national forces under the WTO, 32–36
Joint Command, 19
Joint military manoeuvres, 31–32
Joint Secretariat, 17–18
Membership, 6–9
Middle East and the WTO, 10–11, 40
"Militancy" of the WTO, 36–39
Military activities, 30–39
Military Council, 24
Military Structure, 19–26
Mongolia and the WTO, 9, 11, 19, 32
North Korea and the WTO, 19, 32
Notice of withdrawal, 14–15
Poland and the WTO, 3–4, 6, 11, 14–15, 17, 20, 25, 27, 31–33, 35, 37–38, 41, 43
Political activities, 26–30
Political Consultative Committee, 9–10, 15–18, 22, 26, 40, 42
Political structure, 17–19
Proposals of liquidation of NATO and the WTO, 27
Rumania and the WTO, 5–6, 8–9, 11, 14, 17, 19–20, 31–32, 36
Secretary-General of the Political Consultative Committee, 17–18
Staff of the Joint Armed Forces, 20–21, 33–34
Stages of development, 39–41
Standing Committee for the Elaboration of Recommendations in the Field of Foreign Policy Problems, 17

Technical Committee of the Joint Armed Forces, 24–25
USSR and the WTO, 2–7, 11–12, 15, 17, 19, 20–22, 29, 30, 31–33, 36, 41, 43, 45
Vietnam and the WTO, 10–11, 30
Voting, 16
WTO in the future, 159, 163
Yugoslavia and the WTO, xviii, 6. 14–15, 37

West Berlin, xvii, 2–3, 30, 33, 41, 147
West European Union (WEU), xxii, 1
West Germany (Federal Republic of Germany), xvii, 1–3, 41, 49, 80, 102, 146, 148
World Health Organization (WHO), xxiii, 67
World Marxist Review (Problems of Peace and Socialism), Prague, xxvi-xxvii

Yemen (Arab Republic and People's Democratic Republic), 40, 58
Yugoslavia, xviii, xxv, 6, 14–15, 37, 46–47, 52–53, 60, 79, 83, 113–114, 117, 120, 127, 129, 155–156

NAME INDEX

Acheson, Dean, 12
Afonin, N., 106
Agnelli, Umberto, 102
Agoston, Istvan, 47
Aleksandrov, W., 42
Alexandrowicz, Charles, 46
Amash, Salikh, Mahdi, 57
Amundsen, Gunnar, 68, 111
Antonov, General, 20
Apel, Erich, 89
Apel, Hans, 160
Aron, Raymond, xviii
Atherton, A. M., xix

Bagramian, Marshal, 36
Baker, Vice-Admiral, 100
Bakhov, A. S., 1–2, 13
Banach, Stefan, 144
Batov, General, 204
Bauman, L., 106
Beqir, Balluku, xviii
Beria, Lavrenty, 4
Bethge, Heinz, 146
Bilinsky, Andreas, 130
Blaisdell, Donald C., xix
Blochintsev, Professor, 134
Bogolubov, Professor, 134
Bogomolov, Oleg, 96
Bożyk, Paweł, 90, 97
Brezhnev, Leonid, xiii, xvii-xviii, 11, 14, 34, 58, 97, 137, 147, 150, 152
Broniarek, Zygmunt, 29
Brosio, Manlio, xiv, xix-xx
Brown, General, 100
Brzezinski, Zbigniew, 108, 143, 156–157

Candau, Marcolino, 67
Castro, Fidel, xxvii, 85
Ceaucescu, Nicolae, 19, 80, 159
Chandra, Ramesh, 28

Charnicki, J. F., 52
Chekharin, E., 14
Chirac, Jacques, 160
Ciamaga, Ludwik, 131

Davy, Richard, 125
De Fiumel, Henryk, 47
Degras, Jane, 154
Deniszczuk, Maciej, 79, 97
Dhar, D. P., 57
Dille, John, 20
Dimitrov, Georgij, 47
Djilas, Milovan, 46
Drabowski, Eugeniusz, 109
Dubček, Alexander, 6

Echeverria Alvarez, Luis, 57
Engels, Friedrich, 163
Etzioni, Amitai, 153

Faddeev, Nikolai, xxv, 47–49, 54–55, 57, 58, 66–67, 70–71, 85, 89, 94, 96, 98–99, 160
Faure, Edgar, xviii
Firyubin, N. P., 17–19
Florin, Peter, 38
Fock, Jeno, 74

Gebhardt, Hermann, P., xxvii
Gerö, Erno, 4
Gandhi, Indira 57
Giscard d'Estaing, Valéry, 161
Goodman, Elliot, R., 154
Góra, Stanisław, 79
Górnicki, Wiesław, 162
Gottwald, Klement, 88
Grechko, Marshal, 3, 19, 21, 33–34
Griffith, W. E., 17
Griniuk, B., 112
Gromyko, Andrey, 3, 14, 41, 148

Grzegorczyk, Mieczysław, 138
Grzybowski, Kazimierz, xvi
Gumpel, Werner, xvi

Hacker, Jens, xvi, 17, 51
Hammarskjöld, Dag, 6
Harriman, Averell, xviii
Herder, Wolfgang, 158
Hoffmann, General, 38
Honecker, Erich, 29, 86–87, 158

Ismail, Andul Fattah, 58

Jacob, P. E., xix
Jakubowski, Jerzy, 92
Jaroszewicz, Piotr, 72–73, 84, 89, 109–110
Jurek, Marian, 12

Kamiński, Z., 68–69
Kardelj, Edvard, 155–156
Kaser, Michael, 50–51
Kasprzycki, Jerzy, xx, 97
Kekkonen, Urho, 55
Kessler, General, 33
Khrushchev, Nikita, xiii, 33, 75–76, 93–94, 147–150, 157
Kiss, Tibor, 47
Klepacki, Zbigniew, 50
Knyziak, Zygmunt, 79
Koniev, Marshal, 16, 19, 33
Kormnov, Ju. F., 79, 80
Kosmin, Lt. General, 22
Kosygin, Alexei, 51
Koutikov, Vladimir, 130
Kovalev, S., 14
Kozakov, General, 20
Kozlov, Frol, 148
Kraszewski, Jerzy, 135
Krauze, Wiesław, 136–137
Kreisky, Bruno, 37, 54
Kruczkowski, Andrzej, 150–151

Latzo, Anton, 41, 43–44
Leber, Georg, 44–45
Lenin, Vladimir, 2, 38, 154, 160
Lesechko, Mikhail, 58, 72
Leznik, A. D., 80
Lie, Trygve, 88, 147
Lipski, Witold, 162

Luns, Joseph, xx
Lütgendorff, General, 37

MacIntosh, Malcolm, 17
Madej, Tadeusz, 79
Malfatti, Franco Maria, 53
Malinowski, Marshal, 19
Mandel, Ernest, 153
Manevich, J., 95
Mansholt, Sicco, 53
Marer, Paul, 90
Masaryk, Jan, 88
Mazurski, M., 72
Meissner, Boris, 14
Melcher, John, 29
Mendoza, E., 58
Metera, Jerzy, 73, 81, 117
Mikoyan, Anastasij, 148
Minič, Miloš, 53
Moch, Jules, 3
Molnár, Miklós, 4
Molotov, Vyacheslav, 47, 88, 128
Monat, Colonel, 20, 33
Morawiecki, Wojciech, 149
Morozov, V., 82, 93, 100, 113, 117
Morse, David, 67

Nagovitsin, A., 117
Nagy, Imre, 4, 6
Nazarkin, K., 108
Nieciusiński, Witold, 149
Novotny, Antonin, 6, 150

Orth, Robert, xxviii
Ortoli, François-Xavier, 53, 99

Pashuk, Lt. General, 21
Pavlov, Aleksandr, 66
Peaslee Xydis, Dorothy, xix
Petrov, Ivan, 137
Pietraś, Z. I., 39
Podgorny, Nikolai, 18, 55
Polaczek, Stanisław, 91
Pontecorvo, Bruno, 134
Poppe, Nikolaus, 155
Ptaszek, Jan, 78, 80, 110, 113, 118, 143
Putrament, Jerzy, 4, 156

Rakosi, Mátyás, 4
Redlich, Jerzy, 135

Remington, R. A., 36
Reutt, Bogusław, 52, 142
Rey, Jean, 98
Rotleider, A. Ja., 108, 121
Rudakov, Lt. General, 22
Ruszkowski, A., 68–69
Rutkowski, Józef, 96
Rüster, Lothar, 130
Rybkin, Colonel, 39
Ryżka, Stanisław, 137

Sawczuk, General, 25
Sawicki, General, 15
Schlogel, Maurice, 109
Schürer, Gerhard, 158
Sejna, General, 37
Shetu, Mehmet, 6
Shirjayev, Ju., S., 89–90
Shtemenko, General, 3, 20, 24, 34–35, 42–43
Sienin, Professor, 71
Skrzypkowski, Edward, 12
Skubiszewski, Krzysztof, 7–8
Soames, Christopher, 53
Solzhenitsyn, Alexandr, 41, 101
Sorokin, G., 76, 150
Spaak, Paul-Henri, 2
Spychalski, Marshal, 37–38
Staar, Richard, 102
Stalin, Joseph, xiii, xxiii, 2–3, 38, 46–47, 88, 93, 147, 156
Stelzl, Diethar, 122
Stepanenko, S. I., 69, 81–82
Stepaniuk, Lt. General, 19
Studziński, Vice-Admiral, 20
Sulzberger, C. L., 86
Suslov, Mikhail, 10
Sutton, Anthony, xviii, 100–101
Szawlowski, Richard, ix, xiv, xvi, 46, 51, 63–64, 67–68, 104, 118–119, 135
Szulc, Tad, 89

Światło, Lt. Colonel, 4

Tarski, Ignacy, 70, 112, 142
Tinbergen, Jan, xv-xvi
Tito, Joseph, xviii, 47, 147
Tokareva, P. A., 52, 131
Tolmachev, P., 44
Truman, Harry, 2, 12
Tsolov, Tano, 152
Twardoń, Engineer, 125–126
Tyranowski, Jerzy, 8, 13

Ulbricht, Walter, 3, 27, 118
Ulc, Otto, 4
Urbanowicz, General, 15, 33
Uschakow, Alexander, xvi, 17, 47, 51, 190
Usenko, E. T., 65–66, 160

Vorobev, V., 121

Wallenstein, A. M., xix
Wasilkowski, Andrzej, 65
Wasowski, S., 73
Weit, Erwin, 118
Wielowieyski, Andrzej, 162
Williams, D. L., 66, 108, 143
Wojciechowski, Bronisław, 90
Wujek, Tadeusz, 136–137

Yakubovsky, Marshal, 2–3, 9, 19–20, 22, 24, 30, 33, 35–36, 42–43
Ysheish, M. A., 58

Zarodov, Konstantin, xxvi
Zhivkov, Todor, 152
Zhukov, Marshal, 33
Ziller, Gerhart, 89
Ziółkowski, Zbigniew, 73, 81, 117
Zolotarev, W. I., 89, 91

T3